MW00355558

For my Friends,
Charles & Joan Platt

[signature]   28 Feb 08

FORGOTTEN BREAD

This publication was made possible by a generous grant from the Dolores Zohrab Liebmann Fund.

Forgotten BREAD

FIRST-GENERATION ARMENIAN AMERICAN WRITERS

EDITED BY DAVID KHERDIAN

With Contributing Essays by Nancy Agabian, Mark Arax, Christopher Atamian, David Stephen Calonne, Gregory Djanikian, Mona Ghuneim, Gary Goshgarian, Aris Janigian, Nancy Kricorian, Arthur Nersesian, Aram Saroyan, Alan Semerdjian, Hrag Varjabedian, Hrag Vartanian, and Patricia Sarrafian Ward

HEYDAY BOOKS, BERKELEY, CALIFORNIA

Copyright © 2007 by David Kherdian

All rights reserved. No portion of this work may be reproduced or transmitted in any form or by any means, electronic or mechanical, including photocopying and recording, or by any information storage or retrieval system, without permission in writing from Heyday Books.

Library of Congress Cataloging-in-Publication Data

Forgotten bread : first-generation Armenian American writers / edited by David Kherdian ; with contributing essays by Nancy Agabian ... [et al.].
    p. cm.
  An anthology of first-generation Armenian American writers introduced by second-generation Armenian American writers.
  Includes bibliographical references and index.
  ISBN 978-1-59714-069-0 (hardcover : alk. paper)
  1. American literature--Armenian American authors. 2. Armenian Americans--Literary collections. I. Kherdian, David. II. Agabian, Nancy, 1968-
  PS508.A7F67 2007
  810.9'891992073--dc22

2007013919

Cover Images: Pictorial tile, 1721, manufactured in Kütahya, Etchmiadzin
   chapel, St. James Cathedrale, Armenian Patriarchate, Jerusalem.
   Photo of immigrants at Ellis Island, courtesy of the Library of Congress,
   LC-USZ62-12595.
Book/Cover Design: Lorraine Rath
Printing and Binding: McNaughton & Gunn, Saline, MI

Orders, inquiries, and correspondence should be addressed to:
     Heyday Books
     P. O. Box 9145, Berkeley, CA 94709
     (510) 549-3564, Fax (510) 549-1889
     www.heydaybooks.com

Printed in the United States of America on 50% consumer waste recycled paper.

10 9 8 7 6 5 4 3 2 1

CONTENTS

ACKNOWLEDGMENTS

My research for this book began at the NAASR (National Association for Armenian Studies and Research) library and bookstore in Belmont, Massachusetts, where the director, Marc Mamigonian, and his assistants, Sandra Jurigian and Ruby Chorbajian, provided resources, knowledge, and support throughout the long year of my work on this anthology. They also assisted me in my application for the Liebmann Fund grant. I can't thank them enough. The Armenian General Benevolent Union also provided a grant. Also thanks to the William Saroyan Foundation and Stanford University for their exceptional generosity. Nancy Agabian put me in touch with the writers of her generation and helped me make the right matches for the critical essays on the writers in this anthology. Without her knowledge, understanding, and patience my work would have been stalled, if not defeated, before it began. My good friend Wayne Somers helped greatly with research and also with his extensive knowledge of bibliographic writing. Aris Janigian provided invaluable support, direction, and advice. Tatul Sonentz-Papazian of *Hairenik* was extremely helpful in sorting out dates and details on the publishing history of the *Haireniks*. I would also like to thank Jack Antreassian, Doris Cross, Aram Arkun, John A. C. Greppin, Gloria and Levon Boyajian, Harry Keyishian, Agop Hacikyan, Aram Saroyan, Dickran Kouymjian, and Lou Ann Matossian, for help, variously, with photos, bibliographic information, and work on the Glossary. My thanks also to Ruth Thomasian of Project SAVE Armenian Photograph Archives, Inc. My wife, Nonny Hogrogian, was a constant companion and collaborator. June Blake, our neighbor and friend, brought professional expertise to the proofreading of the manuscript. I would like to thank the staffs at Albany, Public Library of New York; the California History and Genealogy Room of the Fresno Public Library; the Armenian Research Center at the University of Michigan–Dearborn; the Armenian Museum of Fresno; Union College in Schenectady, New York; the Armenian Library and Museum of America in Watertown, Massachusetts; and also the Special Collections Department of the University of Wisconsin–Madison, which made available the papers and photograph of Leon Serabian Herald. Thanks also to my own Chatham Public Library for finding the books I needed when I needed them. I am further indebted to the second-generation writers, not only for their fine portraits, profiles, and essays on the writers of the first generation, but also for their overall support and general assistance, extending even to their capacity to instigate and influence grant support for the book. I cannot conclude this without honoring the support and wisdom of my editor, Gayle Wattawa, beginning with her enthusiastic reading and recommendation of the manuscript, and continuing through the long months of our joined labor in transforming the manuscript into a finished book.

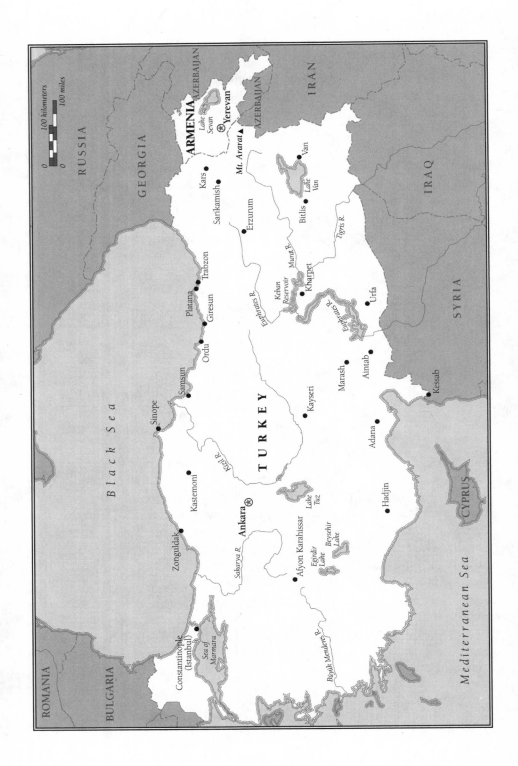

INTRODUCTION

> *"I have given orders to my Death Units to exterminate*
> *without mercy or pity men, women, and children belonging*
> *to the Polish-speaking race. It is only in this manner that we*
> *can acquire the vital territory which we need. After all, who*
> *remembers today the extermination of the Armenians?"*
> —Adolf Hitler, August 22, 1939

One and one-half million Armenians were exterminated by the Turkish government. The remaining number of those who survived the Armenian Genocide of 1915 tried to pick up the pieces of their lives once again: young orphans who married middle-aged men just to have a home; widows with children who tried to find a way to feed their children; young men and boys who hid in culverts and cellars before finding their way to America, hoping for a new life, a sane life; all suffered terribly, but they were survivors.

The parents pleaded with their children to tell their stories when they grew up. But the children, in turn, didn't want to listen, because the stories were too painful. They, the children, the first generation to be born in America, had a different set of problems; but unavoidably they absorbed the grief and concerns of their parents.

They needed to hold to their Armenian identity while becoming Americans, to the extent of fitting into the American landscape while making a promising life for themselves. Many talented young Armenian Americans found writing to be their salvation in their struggle for dignity, identity, and meaning, while creating a niche for themselves in this country that their parents called the Diaspora, but for them was home. Their story will be told in this anthology, but the ripples of their lives and the lives of their parents over the roiled waters of the great tragedy of a century past are still felt in the third and fourth generations of Armenian Americans today, and so this book is also for them.

Without our knowing it, our social, economic, and cultural history was being recorded in the pages of this new writing by these new writers, most of whom remained somewhat obscure even to their own people. It was a time of great uncertainty and unease, a time without perspective or understanding of what the living were experiencing, or even what their lives could mean or did mean within the context of history and time.

This anthology tells these stories in a way that volumes of history cannot. The human story of suffering and the building of a new life in America can best be told by the survivors and their offspring—who were also survivors, but with problems inherently different from those of their parents. In the act of reconstruction, these artists played a crucial role, and were alone in telling us how the Genocide impacted their lives and the lives of their parents. How they and their parents dealt with the suffering and the loss is an American story because these are American writers who had to simultaneously understand and come to terms with the Genocide while making a place for themselves in their own world. This could only be done by transforming their losses through the gains achieved in writing their lives. All of this is but a new variation on the age-old story of our country's founding and foundation, because from the beginning Europeans and others fled to America to escape religious and racial persecution.

This new freedom, discovered and created, is the heartbeat of this anthology. It tells us who we were, how we lived, and what we became, a process that is ever unfolding. It is essentially a two-generational story, double-pronged but held by a single vise. The new generation of writers and readers that have followed us, now with their own stories, need ours to build on and to help them understand their own. We are all of us still healing from our haunted past, but now our stories, created over the better part of the twentieth century, and preserved in this anthology, will stand as a record of our gift to ourselves and an offering to our two nations: America and Armenia (now recently independent).

Although the writing of the first generation of writers born in this country continues today, with nine of the seventeen writers in this anthology still alive and working, this is really a twentieth-century anthology that begins in 1912, when Leon Serabian Herald immigrated to America, as so many did then, to earn money to return to Armenia with. But when the Genocide struck in 1915, Herald was set adrift in America with no home or people to return to. Thus, writing his story became a life raft for him personally, as well as a missionary obligation to inform the world of his people's plight. His decision to write in English was pivotal in developing his material in a language the world could understand.

Two other Armenian writers came to America in their youth, but this time as refugees of the Genocide: Emmanuel P. Varandyan and Leon Surmelian, who also chose to write in the English language, both to record their past experiences and to make a new art in a new world. These émigrés, by writing in English, became Armenian American writers, and their inclusion here makes a bridge between them and the first generation and reveals that this distinctive Armenian sensibility, born in the old world, was carried into the new and can be seen and felt in all of the writers of this anthology. This as much as the subject matter is our contribution to American literature.

Following Herald, but in advance of Varandyan and Surmelian, William Saroyan, born in America in 1908 (unlike his three siblings who came to America with their parents the previous year), began publishing his stories in Armenian publications before turning to American journals and magazines. He became instantly famous with his first book, *The Daring Young Man on the Flying Trapeze*. His neighbor and Fresno playmate, A. I. Bezzerides, born the same year as Saroyan but in Turkey to a Greek father and an Armenian mother, published three novels of California's Central Valley before turning to screenwriting, when two of his novels were turned into motion pictures. Another Fresnan, Khatchik Minasian, first cousin of William Saroyan, was the first Armenian American poet of distinction.

Ten years after Saroyan burst onto the scene, Richard Hagopian began publishing stories and novels about the Armenians of Worcester, Massachusetts. In 1957 Marjorie Housepian and Peter Sourian published important novels with mainstream New York publishers, followed by Harry Barba, who published his first novel with Macmillan in 1960. Their successes inspired those who followed, and by the late sixties three poets emerged, each with a completely different style that uniquely reflected a common ancestral past while giving voice to their American presence: Diana Der-Hovanessian, David Kherdian, and Harold Bond. The poet Helene Pilibosian followed soon after. These and other writers of this era were published in *Ararat*, the first Armenian American literary journal, whereas the writers of Saroyan's generation were first published in *Hairenik*, a newspaper published in Boston that encouraged beginning writers. In 1971 Pantheon, a division of Random House, published Peter Najarian's *Voyages*, an autobiographical novel about his search for identity, a major theme that runs through the work of all Armenian American writers. Michael J. Arlen and Arlene Voski Avakian followed soon after, bringing new permutations to the themes of alienation, loss, and recovery.

In the late sixties Harry Barba founded The Harian Press, and David Kherdian The Giligia Press, publishing their own work and the work of other Armenian and Armenian American writers. The Armenian General Benevolent Union's Ararat Press soon followed, edited by Jack Antreassian, whose own

Ashod Press of this same period produced significant work by a number of important writers, notably Diana Der-Hovanessian and Harold Bond. Blue Crane Books in Cambridge, Massachusetts, published books by Armenian and Armenian American writers and continues to remain active, as does the Armenian Heritage Press in Belmont, Massachusetts.

In attempting to create a sense of tradition between the generations, I have enlisted second-generation Armenian American writers to introduce the seventeen writers in this collection. Their biographies can be seen in the Appendices, which also include checklists of the first-generation writers; a listing of other notable writers of the first generation; a list of relevant journals, magazines, and anthologies, as well as active and defunct small presses; and is followed by a bibliography of books concerned with the literature of first-generation Armenian American writers.

David Kherdian

LEON SERABIAN HERALD

> A bird sings on the crater of a volcano.
> Thirteen years ago Leon Serabian Herald left his native
> Armenian village. Today not a trace of his village remains,
> and he knows that where were his people, there is silence.

These are Zona Gale's opening lines for her introduction to *This Waking Hour*, the first (and only published) book of poems by Leon Serabian Herald, published in 1925. The bird is Herald himself, and the erupted volcano, the aftermath of the Armenian Catastrophe of 1915. The eruption has left nothing in its wake but silence. The bird on the crater is on the cusp of two worlds: the void created by the Catastrophe and the open horizon of a new world.

Throughout his life, Herald lived on this cusp, the crater of the volcano. Like the Roman god Janus, he simultaneously directed his gaze backward and forward without losing sight of one or the other. At no time, while embarking on a new beginning free of his past, did he lose sight of his village, his family, and his people that "have [all] been swept away." Neither did he disengage himself from his new environment in the States and dwell solely on his pains emanating from the silence. Zona Gale continues with her ever accurate description of his poems: "These songs have their own beauty, distinct from the other. It is beauty old yet ever new; it is old truth, new meaning; it is old impulse, new image; it is immemorial sadness, inextinguishable gaiety." His poems became the embodiment of these contradictory yet complementary aspects of experience and being, of memory and existence.

Levon Der Serabian was born in 1894 in Put-Aringe, a village of Erzinga (currently Erzincan) located within a landscape that was still called Armenia.

As an adolescent, he attended the Sanasarian Lycee in Erzroum, which he left in 1912 to immigrate to the United States, to join his brother Nicholas in Detroit, Michigan. Like many of his fellow Armenians who came to the States to escape the dire situation of the Ottoman Empire and earn money to send home, he found employment in auto assembly plants. First he went to work for the Ford Motor Company, soon realizing that these factories were out to gut the life of immigrants. This same feeling would resurface in his autobiographical short stories, like "Memories":

> What a morning! The living monsters curling their arms,
> waving them in sleeves, beckoning me. Their roaring and
> clanging is audible. They are calling for fresh wild blood. I
> am guided...in a fantastic land where youthful people are
> sacrificed to fiery gods....So I bowed to the raging, fuming,
> fire-spitting faces of gods in their temple of the foundry,
> gods more awesome than those in books.

Ironically, in a few years, the Armenian nation was to be sacrificed to gods that had become insatiable like nothing before, demanding the blood of an entire people.

Herald moved on to Pontiac, Michigan, where he taught himself English and worked in a foundry. Notwithstanding the living monsters ready to devour him, he eventually quit the foundry and attended the local high school, where he found intellectual sustenance and support for his writings. It was during this period that he changed his name and had his first English poems published in the school paper.

Although he had first started writing in Armenian, he soon switched to English because of the encouragement he received at school. It was only then that he was able to enter into America and find his true self, his calling. But learning English was instrumental not only in opening up America for him but also in conveying to the American public the unconveyable condition of his people and what had befallen them. As I was going through his archives in the special collections section of the University of Wisconsin Library, I came across two letters written by eyewitnesses describing the atrocities committed by various Turkish elements. One of them was a letter that Herald's elder brother Ohannes had written to him from Constantinople right after the war, describing in detail the horrors that they had gone through and how he had twice escaped the shadow of death. The other letter provided a description by an Armenian chauffeur of his witnessing a "show" put on by a Turkish bey, wherein two Armenian girls in his service were made to dance naked for the entertainment of his guests. Herald had translated these two letters into English with a note attached to his brother's letter. He wanted to convey to the world the heart-wrenching situation of the Armenians in the aftermath of the Massacres, something that was "beyond any man's power [to visualize]." He ended his note: "Perhaps one of the reasons why I struggled so hard to learn the English language is that I would be able to translate and read to you one letter—this letter. The needs of every group of people are different. Perhaps your need is to hear and feel these things over and over again. Perhaps what I need is to read this letter. Why are you there, why am I here, I do not know."

Herald made decisions that went against the norms of newly arrived, indigent immigrants: to forge a new life within mainstream America, to become a writer in the English language and bridge these two worlds and identities. As an Armenian immigrant writing in English, he became both an insider and an outsider to America-at-large, enriching American poetry by bringing his experiences from Put-Aringe. Leon Serabian Herald became the first famous Armenian American poet.

These were tumultuous years not only for Herald, who was trying to shape his future, but also all of humanity, and in particular the Armenian people. While he was still at the foundry, the "Great War" started. It wasn't much later that he got the news of the total decimation of his village and family. An inexplicable Event had taken place in his homeland, leaving behind nothing but a silent void. Through massacres and deportations, the Young Turk regime of the Ottoman Empire had embarked on a genocidal policy against the Armenians. When it was over, roughly half of the Ottoman Armenian population was dead, with the survivors scattering to nearby regions. A whole civilization had come to an abrupt end. The reverberations of the Armenian Catastrophe were to stay with Herald throughout his life, even though he tried to transcend it through the beauty he found in the world around and within him. But the pain would forever remain, embedded in his writings—in poetry, memoirs, fables, and short stories. The dedication for his book *This Waking Hour* is very telling. It reads:

TO THOSE DISINHERITED OF LIFE
IN 1915
THIS A HILL, A FLAG

As Herald's world—family, home, and people—were swept away by the convulsions of the Catastrophe, he was left with nothing but his "memories"—"his land had perished, taking with it every single soul." He had lost everything, yet his memories were more real than what he had physically lost. The only place where he could find solace was in his writings, where he tried to come to terms with the events of the Catastrophe and its aftermath. His writing embodies a constant search for all that was dear to him—his mother and father, and everything else that was lost. In his quest for answers he turned to books, and he wrote his "Memories," but the only reply he would get would be a firm "Don't ask questions!" He realized what man becomes when the world has cast him aside: "a piece of clay." The Event had created such a void, such a complete silence, that it was incomprehensible, impenetrable. His land and heritage pulled from under him, he was left afloat, with nowhere to go but into the essence of life. At times, his search would take him into severe depression and his behavior would come across as schizophrenia. In 1917 he had enlisted in the U.S. Army, but he was discharged after only three months, diagnosed as schizophrenic. It would be of interest to know how he was diagnosed with schizophrenia when there is no objective biological test for it. What role did the massacre of his family, the loss of his village and people play in the diagnosis? I wonder. How could one try to comprehend the Catastrophe without falling into some kind of inevitable depression? But apparently Herald was amused by the fact that he was discharged for being insane. His biography accompanying his inclusion in *The Best Short Stories of 1929* reads:

> In the fall of 1912 I arrived in Detroit from Armenia, to
> educate myself. But soon I found my feet lost on the way
> of job seeking and my head lost in factory smokes, and
> soon after I realized that I had insaned myself rather than
> educated; for that's what the officers of the United States
> Army told me.

But within Herald, next to the "immemorial sadness," there is an "inextinguishable gaiety," the two qualities fused together in a symbiotic relationship. No matter how heavy and insurmountable the pain within, there was always a gaiety that came from his "immeasurable love" of beauty, the power and mysticism of nature. This outlook is best expressed in "Power of Horizon," a short story first published in the literary journal *The Dial* and later included in *The Best Short Stories of 1929*. This story was chosen by the volume's editor, Edward J. O'Brien, and listed in the "Roll of Honor."

After the war, Herald joined the Wisconsin Players, a group in Madison that was attracting young writers, poets, and playwrights. He would attend readings, performances, and lectures by such writers as Carl Sandburg and Amy Lowell. It was here that he met Zona Gale, an eminent poet and novelist of her time, who became his mentor and wrote the introduction to his book.

His work began to appear in important literary magazines. He had his first breakthrough in *Poetry*, and then later in *The Dial*. This latter journal attracted the most avant-garde writers and critics of the time. The editor, Marianne Moore, serialized his "Memories" in seven consecutive issues, from late 1926 into 1927. In "Memories," Herald describes his village and family life in Put-Aringe, ending with his experiences in America.

In 1925 he followed many of his writer friends to Greenwich Village, the hub of avant-garde intellectuals. He participated in summer activities at popular artists' colonies, where he befriended the well-known poet Edward Arlington Robinson. By now Herald was at the forefront of modern American poetry. He had already published in such magazines as *The Nation, The New Republic, Back to Nature, American Poetry Magazine, American Review, Commonweal, The World Tomorrow, Pagany,* and others. He also had edited the pedagogical magazine *Learning*.

The period from the 1930s until the mid-1940s became his years of activism. But for some reason, after 1930 he didn't publish again until he was rediscovered by the Armenian press in 1967. He disappeared from the scene he had been so much a part of, and slowly lost touch with his poet friends. But as we will see, his energies were to be directed elsewhere. The drive within him against the injustices of the world eventually turned him into an activist. From the first, he took the side of the worker against the industrial machine and the capitalists, who were out to "take the life of immigrants." In the 1930s, he joined the John Reed Club (his Marxist period) and became a delegate to their 1932 convention in Chicago. As a member he attended meetings with writers such as Matthew Josephson, Alfred Kreymborg, and Malcolm Cowley, with whom he became good friends. He briefly worked as the editor of *The Armenian Youth,* a leftist newspaper for young Armenian Americans. He became a member of the Writers' Union and helped to initiate the Federal Writers' Project, which provided WPA-type jobs for authors during the Depression.

But suddenly, in the 1950s, he started writing philosophical articles—about man and the universe. He had returned to one of his favorite themes, the relationship between man and nature. He wrote treatises and essays such as "Man Is a Portable Universe" and "Life Is Based on the Laws of Physics," trying to find unifying principles that explain man's relation to the universe. He continued writing poems, but they lacked the creative energy of his earlier period. In 1957 he wrote the following: "Gave up the idea of amounting to anything or anybody on Earth." He had reached the nadir of his life and creativity.

Before his death in 1976, he donated all his papers to the University of Wisconsin–Madison, where he was a student for a few years in the 1920s before he dropped out. In 1976, soon after his death, Teresa Gloster put together an unbound manuscript of poems, spanning fifty years of his work: *A Late Harvest*. In her introduction she links his philosophical essays to experiences of his early years in Put-Aringe, Armenia, and his insights into the mysteries of life—"the first concrete poured deep, never know how deep."

Hrag Varjabedian

Memories from My Village
Put-Aringe, Armenia

The flowers in our orchards were of many kinds,
And their speech to us was as our speech is to God.
Above all my heart was bursting with its "Many Wonders,"
The meaning of your name, beloved Zarmanazan.

The trees in our orchard were as near the sunrise as yours,
And our fruits as plenty and ripe.
Still, you called my attention to yours,
Showing me the ones that were drunk with sunshine.

The creek running thru your orchard
Was just as clear and cool as ours,
And its banks as sunny and sandy;
But you came to bathe in ours every morning.

We filled our pitchers from the fountain
And laid them down—laid them down
To refill ourselves with the coolness of our words,
Not noticing the sun sipping our pitchers empty.

In what manner did you pass Makrouhi's door?
She often came to tell me
That she was sure, sure you had met me.

In what manner did you pass her door?

When at night your mother called you from me,
I went in the company of stars.
I conversed with the flowers of your orchard
When she kept you home for the day.

In daytime flowers are as bewildering as stars at night;
And like stars they vanished at your coming,
Leaving their perfumes with you.
I could not grieve for their disappearance, O my sun!

The name of our village was Put-Aringe,
The name of a once mighty god.
Put-Aringe has lost a lover,
And somewhere there is a dreamer.

God Aringe has lost his power,
And our village has been annihilated.
Some day I might be found, still dreaming somewhere;
But who will tell me, tell of your whereabouts?

With me your image is a flower
Fading for ten years and still unfaded;
Your name is a perfume vanishing—
But never, never vanished.

Homecoming

Each season I returned to the village
From school, with books and papers,
And laid them in the shelf

Of our natural stone wall;
Then each day I went to our orchard near yours
Lest you might be freeing the rose-bushes
From the impious mulberries and apricots.

But I often returned to my shelf
In the rustic wall
To file away my grief:
"The rose-bushes are prostrated
Beneath the storm of white and red fruit,
Fruits have taken freedom of your absence
And poured themselves upon the roses,
O savior of roses, my Zarmanazan!"

But often, often, upon my return,
O embodied Muse of mine,
I found you turning the leaves
Written of you, for you,
In my stone shelf.
I found you, you my future's plan;
And you asked me if they were my writings.
Then the light of your eyes
Gave answer to both of us.

Is our stone wall standing now? the roof?
Is Put-Aringe repeopled again?
(I wonder who the strangers are!)
And flower and fruit at their game?
And where are you, my "Many Wonders,"
Deathless hope of my mortal hopes,
Lost plan of my future?

I carry my books under my arms now always,
For I have no shelf to lay them in;

Nor are there inviting orchards
Where I can find you mediating
Between fruit and flower,
And no one is there asking
If the contents of the books I carry
Are mine.

The Parting of Day

I am glad that there are such clouds
That gather together at the station
When the sun is going to take leave of us
To say farewell, adieu, "We'll wait till you return."
I am glad that the parting sun has such staunch friends
To lean on their shoulders and shed his golden tears,
red and orange and purple tears
Till the station floor is red and orange and purple.

There is the sun, more lonely than alone,
Singing, singing in colors, throbbing, sobbing
Like me, at the 'farewell!' point at the end of my village,
Leaving behind my mother, never to see her again,
Brothers and sister, and father too,
And a host of relatives and friends, never again to see them.

Watching the parting sun I seem to hear my own voice again,
Sobbing in blue, purple and black, singing in red and orange
As the distance grew wider between us;
I, more lonely than alone on the horizon
Swallowing their waving handkerchiefs and hands,
Slowly but surely disappearing into myself
As those left behind disappeared from my sight one by one
But it seemed all at once, never again to be seen by me.

How I long to be just a bit of the sun
That would in another hour, and yet another, still another,
Return home, like the sun, to be met again
By horizonful of kinsmen and friends.
O fortunate sun! I envy you so,
For whichever way I turn, whichever way I proceed,
No one, no one anywhere to welcome me.
For me one, only, lonely sunset.

Dead Visitor
(My sister)

Helena, before our village goes to Heaven
To become a luminous city
(As lovely small things grow large in Heaven,
As unhappy little children
Rest in Jesus' arms in Heaven),
You have come to see me
At the meeting-place of Dream Hour.

Helena, call your followers,
And let us rest in this grove of stars
Before I arrive at Earth again and you at Heaven.
It is good that there is Heaven
To be reciprocated with,
Where you can go.
Tell God why you had to leave
Our village all together.
Helena,
You will be the spokesman of our village.

Helena, for your sake I will transplant
Our Armenian mountains in America,

In the state of Wisconsin,
In which to hear the echoes of your girlish voice
You seeded in our valleys;
For your sake I will pack our fields
And everything they hold—crops and animals—
On the back of my imagination;
My imagination, a fire-shod steed,
Will become a pack-animal
For your sake, for your sake.

Tornado

Its bed is the forest.

It wakes and leaps out,
Shaking and overturning its bed.

It rushes into the cornfield—
A city of destitute mothers,
Crying and running;
Each cornstalk a mother, hugging
Her child of a corn-ear, shivering.
The cornfield, a city of mothers,
Prays in vain for the bankrupt sun.
Mothers fall smothering their children
At the very gates of the city.

Its cutting hoofs—
A thousand-footed caravan in desert—
Prick and grind the elephant-hide
Of the waters into dust.
Waters groan like skinned-off animals.

It grabs the furry back of the road
Like a pitiless child a cat,
And hurls it up in the air—
Twists it before the nose of the hiding sun,
Bullying, "Do you know who I am?"

The Moon in 1915

Moon, I think your light is souls
That are torn,
Which you gather and mend
To your celestial robe.
Gather them fast,
And flash them faster,
And illumine the night, The Night!
Moon, lead me to where most men die now.
When my soul too is torn,
Patch it to your robe of patches—
Wedge it in some crevice,
Or throw it behind some walls,
Some darkening, tall Walls.

Biography of the Universe

Gods are waking up inside me, disguised as thoughts,
Seeking to inhabit the Pantheon of you.

Disguised as poems, gods are rotating in our orbit—
Rotating, they are out to form
A new planet for you to dwell upon.

Let the velocity of light

Be my yardstick to measure the dimensions
Of your grace, O harvest of my mind!

You, beloved environment of my life,
You, imagination's adorned warehouse!

Let us impress our footprints at heaven's gate.
Let us carve our initials on the floor of heaven,
With the pair of our voices as audible sunrise and sunset!

But first let us designate the green corridors
Of our movements on earth as Elysian Gardens
For lovers to perambulate and rediscover themselves

A woman, so loved, becomes the living
Biography of the universe.

My Book

My book is a wandering dog now.
Maybe a good fellow
Who can tell a well-bred dog
Will meet and make a friend of him
And give him a strong, yet tender name
And take him into his parlor
To surprise the grown-ups
And delight the children.

Or maybe broken, find himself
Where the city dumps its rubbish,
And howl at a star or two
And there leave his bones
Until, for a good turn, maybe,

To be discovered by an archeologist
A thousand years from now.

My book is a dog:
He may lick and heal a bad wound,
Or wound badly.

Death and Immortality

The Subconscious,
Wife of the mansion Body,
Implores of the Conscious mind:
"O husband, why do you not heed my warnings?
Why do you daily crowd me out
As if I were a burden to you?
If you insist on doing this,
I shall no longer tolerate you.
I tell you that I can step out of this place
Quicker than you realize,
And go to my Father.
But if you love me no less than you should,
I will tell my Father
Of your gentleness to me,
And live with you forever
Within this heavenly House.
If we live harmoniously,
I shall bear you children
That you never dreamed of.
And the scornful stars shall be as they are:
Our door-keepers, and not our masters."

Power of Horizon

Gavans which grew in the mountains were a most desirable kind of thistle for kindling. And in Put-Aringe where not everybody had the money to spend on everything, some could never buy the luxurious pine wood for the cold months. Those who were able to store a good supply of *gavan* were fortunate indeed. When dry this kindling burned like oil. There were no headaches from blowing on it in order to make it light. And the house was not filled with heavy smoke stretching from corner to corner, sinking almost instead of rising. Quick flames from the *gavans* shot the smoke straight up to the small windows and out.

Young Elisha was the only one whose work for the next day had not been decided upon. Mother, the Priest's Wife, suggested that he go with Simon, a relative, to bring home a load of *gavans* from the mountain. Overjoyed by this privilege, he jumped up at his mother's knees. How he loved her for this suggestion!

The village lay where the fields and the high steps leading to the mountain began. As Elisha watched people coming from or going to the mountain, his blood quickened and burned. He imitated their steps, going up, up, with their bodies bent forward as if they were going to lift the mountain, raise it still higher; and when he saw people coming down he became thoughtful, his blood heavy in him. He would feel at certain moments that he had been to the mountain, knew the mountain. He would walk up to the people as he saw them appear from above the village, mingle with them as if he too were coming from that mysterious height. How wonderful did the men and the beasts coming from the mountain smell! He could feel the shafts of fragrant air darting at him from the hides of the animals and from the hands and coats of the men. Then, realizing that he had never been to the mountain he would become dejected and miserable.

He had wanted to go to the mountain, for anything—to gather sweet rhubarbs, mushrooms, and vegetables, to eat or to preserve for the winter. Yet always he had been thought too young to carry a load from such a distance. There was too, danger from wolves and bears.

Although the hour was late, Elisha ran to tell his young friends of the trip; he would have no time in the morning. Had he but known of his going a day or two before, he might have talked about it to all, as much as he liked. Going to the mountain for the first time created as rich an enthusiasm

as going to the city for the first time. For the people of a village there is
magnetism in a strange city and not less in the awesome mountain towering
above the village. Each has an inspiring as well as an exciting quality.

The next morning when Elisha sprang from bed he felt as if he had been to
the mountain and back. But he did not see the bears and wolves he had killed,
nor the deer he had captured. They belonged to that part of him which had
slept. Well, if he had not been to the mountain he was on his way to it.

When Simon called, Elisha had had his breakfast of cheese and bread
and had tied his luncheon, consisting also of bread and cheese, around his
waist, and had strapped his sharp pick to his shoulder with a new rope.
Mother, the Priest's Wife, entreated Simon to take good care of her son.
"Don't let him carry a big load," she said, handing him a bagful of sun-dried
mulberries mixed with walnut meat, "or he will be so tired he will not want
to go to the mountain again. We have enough pine wood to last all winter.
And say—" but they had disappeared round the corner.

The road entwining the orchards and vineyards lifted the two youths to
the last plateau. Elisha began to feel as though the mountain were coming
toward him. After another half hour they were climbing the mountain
proper through a narrow streak which shot across and under the massive
rocks. Elisha felt as if he were something being built rapidly; he felt as if he
were a wall building itself, running fast to enclose the mountain within it, as
if the mountain were a strange large tree with rocks for fruit; he felt himself
going round the mountain to hide its leaves, fruit, trunk, and all, to protect
it from envious attack, but when he had made the mountain his own he
stood up straight and still. He turned and looked backward, down, away at
the distant mountains in the opposite direction. There was nothing to cut
off the view. A sea of colors—fields, hills, and mountains—were melted and
mixed together and above was the endless, curveless sky, as far as he could
see. The vortex of his vision had turned everything aside, a cry of joy broke
from his bosom, and the mountain answered him eagerly.

The path on which they were walking was the color of lightning. This
brought to Elisha's mind St. Nicholas who long ago had wandered alone on
this very path with beasts and snakes, and had died at the end of the path
where the palatial monastery now stood in memory of him. The lightning, it
was said, had glazed the path to pay the Saint homage and prove his holiness
to future believers. Indeed, so it seemed, for only the ground and rocks of
the path were the color of lightning, and none of the surrounding territory.
It showed that the Saint, instead of going around the rock, had preferred to
breast it and defy inaccessibility.

They now came to a creek and Elisha saw that even the water where the Saint had crossed was as indelibly the color of lightning as the rest of the road. Simon said this was the creek that sent floods to the village when the mountain so decreed and he told Elisha to wash his eyes and face before drinking of it, that he might have good luck and escape mountain fever. As Elisha held his face in the water he lifted his legs up from the knees and swung them sidewise, then jumped up, singing and shouting; then with suddenness came to a standstill. He gazed deep into the water and kept gazing, till a strange feeling ran through his spine. Elisha said, "The water is clear and crystal-like, whereas in the village it is not even clean. I could not have held my face in it in the village." This he said to the mountain rather than to his friend.

At last they arrived at the part of the mountain that was seen from the village. From this height Elisha looked into the horizon again—a horizon he had never before seen, incredible, almost fantastic. Then a thought came to him: might the mountain be a shepherd who, on seeing the horizon, forgot his flock and allowed it to become rills, brooks, fountains, creeks, and waterfalls—while he, waiting, became a mountain, unmovable, gazing into the eyes of the horizon forever?

Elisha had experienced beauty. His feet left the ground in the way that his lungs inhaled the mountain air. He had absorbed the intimacy of the mountain. He was mountain-drunk. The breeze coming from the horizon was the horizon's hair, touching his face and the mountain at the same time. The horizon lay close to him, making him wish he could plunge into her arms. Had he ever felt toward his father as he felt toward the mountain? Had he ever felt toward his mother as he felt toward the horizon?

A short walk brought them to an untouched patch of the fuel they sought. Gavans were umbrella-shaped thistle with long bristling needles, and like umbrellas the shapes varied. Some were like umbrellas little girls carried, some like men's umbrellas, and some like huge beach umbrellas. Their stems were short and close to the earth. In order to cut the gummy stems it was necessary to step on them from one side, press down with one foot, and aim with the pick.

Progress was slow, for Elisha would stand looking at the peak of the mountain as when questioning his father; then he would turn and look into the horizon, as when admiring his mother. He would say to Simon, "Do you feel the horizon the way you feel the mountain? The horizon, the horizon…" Then he would laugh so heartily that even Simon—intent though he was on the work—could not help laughing also. Simon knew

Elisha was not stricken with mountain fever, so was not alarmed, although he was aware that something had taken place in his young friend, for in reply to admonitions that he should work, Elisha would answer, "Did you hear the mountain sigh, did you hear the horizon sigh in answer? Did you?" Having understood the horizon and the mountain, Elisha applied his energy to the work, and soon enough *gavan* was gathered. Then they looked for mushrooms and rhubarbs. There were few rhubarbs because it was late in the season, but they found all the mushrooms they wanted—firm and large ones. These and the rhubarbs they put on top of their loads, Elisha's as large as, if not larger than Simon's, and arrived home an hour before sundown, an hour later than the customary time.

Elisha's mother embraced the wind in embracing her son. All day she had felt as if she were in a place of very little air. She felt that the mountain had given her son not only a load but something else, as real as it was indefinable. His eyes seemed larger and more beautiful, more understanding. Many neighbors and friends came to congratulate him on his return from the mountain. They said that his load was as big as any man had carried, his rhubarbs as sweet as any in spring, and what large thick mushrooms he had brought!

After the visitors had left, Elisha asked his mother, "Have you ever gone to the mountain?" She had indeed, when a girl, but had never climbed as high as her son had. Then he asked his father, "Surely you have gone to the mountain?" "Surely, many times, but not when I was as young as you are. You are only eighteen, and lucky. I was twenty-five when I went there first, and I had gone to many other places. I have never gone since I became a priest." Elisha said to them, "The mountain is my father, and the horizon is my mother." His parents did not hear, or did not pay attention to what he said, but they praised the rhubarbs and mushrooms on a table before them.

Elisha was different after his return from the mountain yet no one knew why. He was like the wind, lonesome—like a narrow house, his eyes and feet handicapped. The village seemed too small for him. He would stand in the door, on the streets, or on the housetop, and forlornly look at the mountain. Although it seemed so virile, and smooth as a wall, it existed so realistically that actuality around him seemed thin, and robbed of its individuality. Then he would look in the other direction, at the horizon. But it was now close to his eyes, as if it were brushing against his eyelashes. It was an artificial horizon compared with what he had seen from the mountain. He wrung his hands and said to himself, "How appreciate the mountain from this distance? It looks like a plaster wall. How fathom the depth of the horizon at such close range? It looks scared."

The people who saw him turning from the mountain to face in the other direction said to one another, "Why does he turn around like that, gaze at the mountain, and then the other way?"

"Maybe he is mountain-possessed," some said. "Yes, he's mountain-possessed!"

"And what is it to be mountain-possessed? What is it?"

"It's like being in love. Only in a way it's more terrible because it is impossible to explain or know what one wants. Instead of being sad, in this case he becomes possessed with too much laughter, laughing constantly even when one realized that he is in pain."

"Let us bring him the mountain then, or take him and lock him up in the mountain," someone said humorously.

"See, see!" they said again. "When he looks away from the mountain he holds his eyes as if they pain him." Then they asked, "What is it you are looking for, Elisha?"

He answered laughing, "I am looking for the horizon, but I cannot see it. You don't either. What you see is not the horizon."

On Sundays the youths of the village were bound by almost no duties. They went out to play and whether they returned on time or not at all for their meals, no one cared. They would go up to the vineyards, running and playing, or become absorbed in bringing down an apple or pear that still hung on its leafless tree. Elisha had forgotten the vision of the horizon in his play and his senses had been shrinking to their usual scope. The narrow horizon had become almost natural to him again. But as soon as he came to the top of a hill and looked around, memory rang in his body like a church-bell wakening him. He stood there till his friends, unaware, left him. Stillness increased him to the self that was his when he had returned from the mountain.

That afternoon he found himself at the same place where he had cut *gavans* and had gathered rhubarbs and mushrooms. He had never been to the crest of the mountain; no doubt from it the horizon would be still vaster and more beautiful. The mountain now yielding to the power of his stride, the horizon came closer and closer to him. He felt as if he were standing in the horizon. He rose to the crest of the mountain and saw other crests and other mountains. It was like a city of many churches, hundreds of spires rising into the air. He seemed to hear bells sounding from the tops of these spires, every sound different from the other. Then he heard the silence of the horizon break and words coming to him. He was in the arms of the horizon.

There came a time when the people of the village went to the monastery to celebrate a feast-day. It was Saturday evening and they were to stay until the next day. Sacrifices were cooking in the courtyard in a large cauldron. Twilight fell and the smoke was no longer visible in the air.

Someone made Elisha the subject of conversation and soon everybody was talking about him, wondering where he was now, why he had left home. An entire week his parents and friends had looked for him in the mountains, thinking he might be lost there. They had taken Simon with them, asking carefully what Elisha had said to him. He could only remember the words, "I can stand here like the mountain and look into the horizon forever."

Others recalled that Elisha had spoken to them of the lightning-colored path through which he had walked, through which St. Nicholas had walked. His parents remembered his saying that the mountain and the horizon were his parents. "Who could think he was serious?" they repeated.

When the shepherd of the monastery was bringing in his flock for the night, everybody asked him as they had asked many who came from the direction of the mountain, "Any news by any chance?" The shepherd was tempted to say yes, that he had seen Elisha and that Elisha had promised to come home that night. But such an answer would dishonor the mountain, which in a way was his friend, as much as it would hurt the people. He sighed and shook his head.

While conversation began afresh, the crowd in the courtyard became excited, and exclaimed at a vision—a human shape, of light, rising toward the sky from the monastery. All hastened out. Gradually it took the shape of a cross and dissolved in the air. The people became hysterical, weeping, chanting, crossing themselves. They said it was the spirit of Elisha bringing them a message. He had become a saint, he was still living in the mountains, and some day would come to them in person.

A shred of smoke, as often happens, had rolled light into itself. But why it had taken human form and then the form of a cross, none could explain.

The Ass and the Sunbeam

The ass, tied to the manger all winter, was getting lazier and lazier—contented and accustomed to the darkness of the stable. One day he was startled by a sunbeam which fell across his back from a crack in the barn, and supposing it something with which a mischievous fellow was trying to goad him, looked at it wildly, kicked and moved about to avoid it, and then forgot it. But again he moved in such a way that the sunbeam could not but fall on him. He was positive this time that a devil was about to torture him.

Having felt the point of the stick in his skin, he made a quick move forward as if to run to the open fields but he only bumped his head against the manger, nearly fracturing his jaw. As soon as the pain subsided, he looked back again. Again the instrument of torture was pressing against him. This time he decided to back away, and as he retreated, the halter, which he had forgotten, nearly pulled his neck off his shoulders. Now completely frustrated, the ass kicked and kicked indiscriminately till he had broken the planks which served him as a bed, and shattered the shoes on his hind feet. His legs were now lame and bleeding and the goad still pointed at him.

Finally, he was so lame he could kick no more. His sharp ears drooping and his eyes contracted till they were lost under his eyelashes, he groaned, swooned, and fell down in his stall. When he recovered consciousness, he was aware that a certain part of his back was warm and more eased than the rest of his body, and looking behind him saw the sunbeam resting on him like the hand of a loving master. He perceived that it was not a goad but a sunbeam and getting up, though his legs could hardly support him, he cursed his asininity in having afforded humanity an epithet so opprobrious to himself.

The Watermelon and the Saint

I never saw my father with a spade or a hoe trifling with other crops for so much as an hour, but have seen him come out of the watermelon patch with soiled greenish hands. Boastfully he would show us the weeds he had extracted and would watch his sons weeding the patch as if he could see the death of every tare being added to each vine as life.

He would explain to us that most great things have humble lineages. The good melon vines were an example, and akin to the human race. Human beings bearing the standards of Time have been nurtured by humble parents as had these luscious watermelons.

To the son that was fired by such analogies to work hardest, the father made a promise: "This summer on the Feast Day of Saint Ouleanus you shall take a load of watermelons to distribute to the worshippers." This pledge meant little to any but the one who received it. For Saint Ouleanus was only a poor saint, the patron of the neighborhood. He was so poor that he owned not even a small monastery. Nor was he known to the people, either through books or on the wings of folklore. The Armenians—essentially a water-worshipping people—had given the name to a sweet little spring which bubbled out of the rock. Why should children be jealous of their brother? Almost every spring coming out of a rock was christened, or sanctified by a name—was called a saint. Indeed, aside from the cognomen nobody knew anything about him. His shrine was close by our land. The only offerings denoting a saintly presence were the native shrubs decorated with innumerable rags or ribbons which people had torn from their clothes or brought with them in homage to the unknown martyr.

My father's love for his watermelon patch was greater than for all the rest of the crops. The watermelons—kings of the realm of the fruits—were to him as gold to a miser. It was not his wish to keep them to rot but to be with them, to give them away with his own hands, and to boast of his new crop, or hear others praise it. How often I have contracted the joy that was his as I watched him artfully manipulating a watermelon and opening the heart of the fruit—as if it were his own heart—to serve to an appreciating friend.

To be able to convince him that it was necessary he should be in such and such a place, even for one day, rather than abiding by his patch was difficult. During the entire summer not more than half a dozen matters could challenge him to leave his hallowed post. If the people saw him in the village during the summer months they would attach a mysterious meaning to his visit. How could he prefer them to his watermelons? And they would devise a cause with dimensions.

To guess his grief in detaching himself from his watermelons was easy. But his joy on returning to them was inconceivable. On his return then, how befitting a miracle in relation to them! He would fall among the vines as a parent after a long absence embraces his children. Crisscross, the breadth and length of the field he went several times, arranging each vine that had been disturbed by the wind, apportioning the ground equally among the vines which were tender, pulling a large weed here or there, straightening himself, with a victorious snort—a sign also that he was in good humor. Then simultaneously he would make a pompous show of the tares as if they were thieves or destructive animals he had captured, and would cast them on top of a promising young melon to protect it from the sun, and as warning to the uninitiated.

He would then take slow and courteous leave of plant, blossom, and fruit, and begin his tour of inspection. First he noticed a freshly excavated rat hole on the rim of the field. The cursed rats always know the rim from the field! Well, that could be settled; he would have someone flood the hole. A little farther on hoofmarks arrested him—as irritating as rat holes. That son of his should not graze the oxen so close to the vines! Inspecting every dale, hill, and tree, he would make his circle wider and wider, as an eagle in search of something gyrates until he reaches his apex.

I recall a time when he left his field for a day and a night. A cousin had been appointed in his place to guard the watermelons with me, and in Put-Aringe a cousin was more sociable with a cousin than a father ever could be with a son. When I was with my father sleep always came early to sharpen the dullness. But a cousin's quips were more powerful than sleep. We stayed up until the late moon was out. That was the first time I had seen the big watermelons in the moonlight—animals more mysterious than minotaurs—drinking the moonlight, slowly expanding. It was only after much joy that fun and sleep were reconciled.

Cousin left early in the morning and I went to irrigate the turnips and cabbages. While I was guiding the water, oblivious of everything, the previous night's vision of the watermelons was recreated in me—of the watermelons like giant elephants drinking moonlight. I hastened to open one of the fruits with my long knife. I had never before given a thought to what the real watermelon was. But no sooner had the fruit revealed its remarkable red pattern than I remembered the untrustworthy stream, and looking, I could see it tear the side of the field as when a live wire comes in contact with a human body. I left the watermelon and hastened to the accident, forgetting to observe the almost animate designs of the fruit, forgetting to drink the moonlight, forgetting my celestial breakfast.

My father's impatient form burst from the opposite horizon as the sun all at once, standing on its rays, illuminated the field. Man and the sun embraced the watermelon patch at the same instant. One could not tell whose was the glory. My father's hands, which were clasped on his back, fell pendulous to his sides. He had seen the divided watermelon. He looked all around. Could someone have played a trick? The only human outline was his son's a field away. The fruit was freshly cut; his son would have had no reason to abandon it. He sat on his haunches and let himself think. Finally he arrived at a startling conclusion and pined that one worthy of a miracle should hear it.

The thought was sent out; the answer came in the person of the venerable miller. All millers are venerable. As in winter a priest is being sought, so in summer is a miller expected—either to come, or to go. The village mills were near because the stream of water was close by our land. The miller had brought for my father a cake made by his own hands, which was a proof that he had not come simply to be treated to a watermelon.

Having finished my morning's duties, I went to my father who was sitting

under the tall poplar trees with his friend, to answer what questions he
considered necessary to ask. But he did not seem to be interested in asking
questions. He was in a reverent mood. I thought: Is this mood in honor of
the miller?—this miller whose grey beard reached down as the branches of
the trees reached up, and was sensitive to the wind as the poplar leaves. This
miller, it was said, was never known to have buttoned the breast of his clothes
even in the bitter cold of winter. He looked reverently toward the melon field,
then at my father. "May God wither evil eyes ere their greedy looks wither a
single leaf of your bountiful patch!"

"Aye, aye, friend," assented my father, "God has already established your
wish." The miller stroked his beard with both hands for having expressed
God's wish so appropriately.

"It is a miracle, no less," continued my father, and the miller was awed as if
he had already been told of the miracle. "I have been looking around the field
and have found no trace of robbers, no foreign foot tracks, no plant disturbed.
Yet, friend, on yonder hill is a freshly cut melon, as sweet as it looks. It seems
not to have been touched by human hands. Had this been the work of human
hands, the man would have tasted it, would have taken it along with him,
would have done something....It would be false for me to have any belief but
that Saint Ouleanus has visited this humble patch, has selected a small fruit,
yet undoubtedly one of the finest, and has opened it for the birds that they
might help themselves...."

I sat clasping my wet legs with my bare arms, watching rainbows in the
waterdrops that were rolling down my legs—embryos of rainbows implanted
in the drops by the morning sun. The prisms rolled down and disappeared—
were shattered about my feet.

"Aye, aye, friend," sighed my father, "so it must have been!"

"Aye, aye," said the vibrant beard of the miller, "so it must!" The intonations
of their voices sounding sweeter and sweeter. My father gave me a side glance
to see if I were moved, weeping. But at this moment I detached myself from
them. A gigantic egoistic feeling was beginning to arise in me and I was forced
to slip away from the spellbound narrator and his audience—to laugh.

The story so faithfully sown took root in the miller and grew and spread till
it became one of the most famous and accepted of miracles. The miller stated
that he had seen the very Saint with his earthly eyes, had observed the martyr
in the patch and the manner in which he had cut the melon, how he had
prayed with outstretched arms, and finally drifting away, had disappeared in
the air.

As a result the miller was given the privilege of taking unto himself as many
watermelons in a year as he could use.

EMMANUEL P. VARANDYAN

Emmanuel P. Varandyan was born in 1902 near Urumia, in present-day Iran. When the war started, he lied about his age and joined the army to fight the Turks, later settling with his family in Tabriz, where he finished secondary school at the American Memorial School. In 1926 he won a scholarship to the Ford School of Technology and moved to the United States. He eventually became an author and teacher of comparative literature, interrupting his graduate work to serve in the Middle East during World War II as a cultural advisor to the U.S. forces. Over the course of his career, he wrote two novels, several novellas, and stories, poems, translations, and reviews, and was writing his memoirs at the time of his death in 1988.

I was particularly curious to read Emmanuel P. Varandyan's 1938 novel, *The Well of Ararat,* because of our shared experience of laboring over a first novel at the University of Michigan; I enjoyed this strange coincidence, that he had walked the same streets and campus all those years before, and now his novel lay in my hands. *The Well of Ararat* opens with a long, dreamlike passage in which the twelve-year-old narrator, Sassoon, meets Mullah Baba in a field, and the old mullah expounds on life, love, and faith. The effusive language gave me pause: "Mullah Baba smiled knowingly, his face aglow with a joy which came from an insight into the mysteries of life....My heart danced within me, my cheeks grew warm. I was bewildered, excited and mystified..."

Aglow with joy? Heart danced within me? In my time at the University of Michigan, this whole novel would have been cause for horror, calamitous breakage of the Less Is More law. Mr. Varandyan would be exhorted to tighten and sharpen, to Show Not Tell, above all to excise the clichéd dancing hearts and girls dashing like gazelles! Still, the book was engaging; I have always secretly enjoyed excessive verbiage, even if a cliché pops up here and there, and most of *The Well of Ararat* is a word feast all but forbidden in today's market. The modern practice of paring language down to its barest elements is like sweeping up the sweet mystery of a junk shop into a bleached, neon-lit room. There is something so deliciously chocolaty in an ecstatic profusion of words, and Varandyan, as one review said when the book was published, has "descriptive powers quite equal to the most complex scene before him." Yes, the action in this love drama unfolds with often agonizing slowness through the lengthy wedding rituals, which are criticized as much as memorialized— the author himself referred to *The Well of Ararat* as an "anthropological novel" in his CV. But he has an ingenious ability to characterize his young hero's mishmash of longing, anger, resentment, and hope, as well as to evoke with intimacy and immediacy the complex, subtle changes in relationships that carry the novel to its violent and very melodramatic end.

This tendency to melodrama is bewildering, incongruous with the many scenes that render so well the most subtle emotions, and, more distressingly, capture the essential beast of physical violence. The reader, at least this one, feels more for the sacrificed heifers than the heroine's death. This odd inconsistency of effectiveness exists in all the writings I was able to get a hold of. Everywhere are scenes of terrible agony and grief written with a precision that leaves you gagging, whether over the German soldiers crushed to death in their cabin in *The Moon Sails* or the boy in the story "Death Is an Empty Coffin," who gets fingers jammed down his throat, his swollen, infected glands pressed until they explode. This is an author who knows his subject intimately, and is capable of expressing himself with utmost effect. And yet on the whole, plots verge on the miraculous, his characters swoon and sway and expire in scenes that elicit more eye-rolling than tears, and the action is rendered in such majestic language that the reader becomes detached.

Perhaps Varandyan simply wasn't as accomplished a storyteller as he was a writer. But as I read, I couldn't help feeling there was more than that going on; that this flaw of contradictory styles reflected deeper contradictions gripping the author's creative imagination. In *The Well of Ararat,* Sassoon remarks, "She said all this with the simple naturalness of those rare souls whose inner beauty refuses to believe that the dominant aspect of things in life is dark and perpetually ugly." This remark is jarring in a novel that strives, no matter the social criticisms and clashing anguish in the young hero's heart, to look upon the world through Mullah Baba's gentle gaze. This cannot be Sassoon speaking—he, unlike Salim, the old, old boy in "Death Is an Empty Coffin," has not yet died many times. No, this is the author letting slip a truth, and this note of bitterness, once its strain has been caught, echoes throughout his writings.

I confess, I was haunted by the story of Varandyan's youth as I read his apparently autobiographical works:

> At the age of 14, pretending to be 16, Prof. Varandyan
> joined the army defending his people from an invading
> Turkish force and, after an eight-month siege, he was part
> of the cavalry force that launched a counterattack and
> broke through the encircling enemy forces, leading a march
> for several days and nights that, with tremendous losses,
> brought the surviving population to safety in Hamadan,
> then controlled by the British.*

It is tiresome of a reader to poke about in an author's life and make hypotheses, yet I could not help but note that Sassoon is an accomplished horseman, and that the novel is set "in the ominous years preceding the Great War," as the flyleaf states. I pondered Varandyan's decision to pour his anguish into the well of adolescent desires rather than the "tragic history" mentioned so obliquely here and there, and of course his own history, which in the timeline of the novel lies just on Sassoon's horizon. For as much as ideas for novels surface unexpectedly, so do we writers also make choices—consciously, deliberately, ruthlessly, to tell or not tell. What is striking is that even when Varandyan makes war his subject, as in his 1971 World War II novel, *The Moon Sails,* he seems unable to fully render the experience, despite the many exceptional scenes that thrust the reader, if only briefly, into the reality of war. Instead, the novel describes war as from a distance, couched in high verbiage and philosophical ruminations, and built around improbable, metaphorical scenarios. The narrator, Armen, does not have Sassoon's life as a character, and the cast of multinational seamen reads like a panoply of archetypes. "We fly and fly—where to, O Lord?" begs Armen.

I wondered myself, until I read the earlier "Death Is an Empty Coffin."

> *Certain things have to be killed and buried, like in war,*
> *otherwise one would rot in his soul and die ignominiously....*
> [He] did not want to unearth the buried relics of the past,
> for himself or for the boy; and yet, with the passing of time,
> they had become, in spite of his will, more acutely alive,
> more poignantly real, than the pains of his flesh and bones.

---

* National Association for Armenian Studies and Research press release on Varandyan Memorial Service, September 1988.

These tormented words awakened understanding, and Varandyan's uneven writing style in some way began to make sense. I heard my parents in those lines, determinedly putting behind them the tragic loss of home and self, and I heard my Tante Marie Sarrafian and other relatives begging me to stop asking questions about the past because they caused so much pain. I had wondered why Varandyan did not write about war in his first novel; quite simply, he probably didn't want to. After all, I myself had to be pushed and pushed by my professor to write about the war in Lebanon, and I went through far less than what Varandyan must have endured. I suppose, also, that in his generation, it wasn't considered proper to dig into one's grief. And when he finally did, thirty, forty years later, he fell short of fully realizing war for the reader—yet *The Moon Sails,* like "Death Is an Empty Coffin," is not so much about war as the desperate quest to make sense of life *despite* war.

Where to, O Lord? The dramatic language is off-putting because we, in the world of modern fiction, are more polite in our own quest. We prefer subtlety, questions evoked by gesture or muted action, rather than open, heartfelt inquiry into the meaning of things. We Show, we do not Tell! But if you forgive the unabashed questioning and longing soliloquies of Varandyan's characters, you find their truth, that they are soldiers in battle against the viciousness of life—whether the enchanting tyranny of rituals or war itself. *The Well of Ararat,* perceived through this lens, is far less a romantic "picture book," as one review put it, than about the constant, incomprehensible juxtaposition of violence and joy. Similarly, Armen's lofty, inward searches are an all-out effort to combat the bloody mess of war, to wrench some kind of meaning out of a dreadful reality. Varandyan himself is waging battle in his writings—against tradition, against war, against despair.

This battle rings harshest in "Death Is an Empty Coffin." Varandyan was in his early sixties when he published this story. If the young author's 1938 novel is a heroic effort to hang on to Mullah Baba's benevolent wisdom, to keep alive all that has been lost, then this dark tale of succumbing to death is its opposite. Here, the Mullah is a cruel bigot and the child Salim is "an old, old boy," an "empty little coffin" who wants only to die, and the narrator, Paul Victor (the name rings with sad irony), no matter his effort to keep hope, finally yields to the truth: *"I am a black coffin with a bleached empty skull, with hollow gun barrel legs, wandering in the starlit gloom of deserts, and deathfields. I am Salim and Salim is I."* For all its melodrama (Fatima mourning the dead dove, etc.), one cannot withstand the harrowing despair of this story, some passages as evocative of war's wreckage as anything I have ever read, and chillingly apropos, given the setting and our current unfolding history. Varandyan's obsession with opposites—peace and war, joy and misery, beauty and ugliness—is laid out in this soldier's desperate quest to put the war behind him and get home. War has driven Victor to the outside of life, and he lurks behind bushes, longing to fit back in. He tries and tries: he flies on a fantasy of fixing up the boy, cleaning up the mess, making a little family out of the broken lot of them. But the only family he has left is his own destroyed youth. He himself is the old, old boy in the end, and there is no going home.

Where to, O Lord? It is tempting to read Paul Victor's more skillfully rendered despair as truer than the metaphorical, fanciful novel of resilient seamen whose blind Captain says grandly, of his near-destroyed ship and crew, "We can still sail under our own power." But given Varandyan's real life history, it would be obtuse and selfish to dismiss that bulldog optimism just because it arrives somewhat clumsily packaged. The mix of romanticism and brutality that marks his style, for all its flaws, serves in the end as heartfelt testament to the paradox of experience, that alongside horror live beauty and hope, always.

Patricia Sarrafian Ward

Death Is an Empty Coffin

The spring was in full bloom in the valley of the Tigris River. For Paul Victor it was different from any other spring. He watched the desert of the Bedouin and the fellahin sway in a sea of blood-red poppies and white daisies. His eyes wandered pensively from the fields to the black Bedouin tents huddled against the horizon. The sun was up, above the crests of palm groves; and he imagined that the sky suspended over the celebrated city of Baghdad was the immense dome of a temple. The sky-line of blue mosques and towering minarets, crowned with crescents, gleamed in the stream of the rising sun. The crescent was, of course, supreme in this Islamic land; but here and there he also saw the cross of Christ and the star of David catching their share of Allah's vernal glory.

He was sitting in the garden of a café on the east bank of the Biblical River. *This is a very ancient River*, he thought, *a River of many stories and legends.* He recalled his white-haired, austere-faced Sunday school teacher, a wiry woman of fifty, describing the Garden of Eden in burning colors. *Thank God the War is over!* he said to himself with a sigh. Though its scars were still

raw and rankling, he was happy that he was having his breakfast in peace—
getting ready to return home. Sipping black Arabian coffee, he listened to
the chorus of the birds in the apricot orchards and watched the great River
flow by with turbulent power and timeless memory. *How often before*, he
thought, *had it seen empires and religions rise and fall, conquerors wield their
bloody swords and vanish like desert dust!*

He rose and said good-bye to Kemal, the handsome proprietor of the café,
a young man of Levantine finesse and poetic tongue, and started walking up
along the River toward the center of the city. Despite the peace and prospect
of home, he was still thinking of war and death. He tried to drive the twin
tormentors out of his mind, but the struggle was not merely a matter of
willpower.

He turned to the right and, bowing to the River in silent farewell, entered
the King Faisal Boulevard, a throbbing thoroughfare cutting through the
heart of the metropolis. For Muslims it was a great religious holiday; for
the Christians of Assyrian, Chaldean, and Armenian origin, it was a solemn
Sunday. The *muezzins* from high minarets chanted glory to Allah; the church
bells chimed summons to morning worship. All the streets and government
buildings were decorated with banners and garlands of flowers. The city was
a sea of polyglot peoples, of costumes and colors, as festive as a city of holy
pilgrimage. *But under this surface glitter,* thought Paul Victor, *there is a seething
morass of poverty and misery.*

Drifting with the flow of the people, he reached the east arch (a
temporary, triumphal arch of wreaths) of the city park, just off the main
thoroughfare. As he was a free man now, free from the hectic, corrosive
duties of an intelligence officer, he had a wanton desire to float, to kill time
with a vengeance, before catching a plane to his native city of Chicago. More
than anything else in the world he longed for peace; he wanted to merge
with the spring, become part of its very breath and spirit.

He passed through the arch of garlands and entered the park. Sauntering
down the lanes of evergreens and flowers, he watched dark-eyed children
playing with flocks of white pigeons. He envied the birds and the children:
he wished he were one of them. He, too, imitating the boys and girls,
offered the pigeons dried dates—the wormy staple of the fellahin—and
the insatiable birds in a swarm made a perch out of him. And the children
watched and laughed with delight. When the bag of dates was exhausted the
pigeons flew away, seeking lonely strollers with *full* bags.

He continued his walk: something vague and deep-rooted kept on
gnawing him. In the center of the park sparkled the tall fountain of a pond

with a Byzantine mosaic bottom. He sat on a stone bench of Babylonian lions and watched tropical mallards, gifted with passionate colors, perform their immortal game. They were chasing their mates in a gambol, diving and ducking, splashing and quacking with heat. The mother duck, indulging in the game with equal zest, did not seem to be worried about their broods. *Courting*, he thought, *can at times be more compelling than mothering.* The sprightly ducklings whirling around in a spray, like a cloud of colors, seemed to enjoy the exuberant ritual more than their parents. Unmindful of the carnival, two magnificent white swans glided on, neck to neck, elegant and serene, like white nuns.

The mallards exhausted themselves but the swans continued their placid sailing with an air of timeless unconcern. Paul Victor's brown, examining eyes turned from the aftermath of the earthy game to a sky game. Like twin spirits, two white doves were displaying their dazzling art of aerial acrobatics. A gray hawk dived out of the blue and struck. One of the birds staggered and, spinning in a spiral, fell on the open veranda of a limestone building at the edge of the park. A young woman in red silk ran out of a room and picked up the limp body of the bird and pressed it to her cheek, to her bosom, as if trying to breathe life into it. Her sensuous lips were open: she was breathing hard, stroking the throat and the crest of the bird. Paul Victor felt as if one of his many scars had burst open: he reproached himself because he couldn't understand the reason for his response. Despite her apparent compassion, he thought her dark intense eyes could be cruel and dangerous. Shielded by a yellow rosebush near the veranda, he watched her with intense absorption. He heard her saying, almost chanting, in melodic Arabic:

"Poor little bird! What struck you? You have no wounds. I have many, many...."

Paul Victor grew breathless; he listened fascinated.

She rolled the bird over in her palms and examined it under its wings and feathers, searching for the cause of its end. Suddenly she winced and cried out: "Poor bird, one of your eyes is bleeding—a tiny trickle of blood and maybe tears. It's pierced—you're blind!"

The mystery baffled her, and she didn't know what to do with the dead body of the bird. An emaciated beggar boy in tatters was watching her from behind a eucalyptus tree. He ran to her and said:

"Give it to me, lady."

"Did you kill it?"

"No, lady. I don't like to kill."

"What will you do with it?"

"Eat it."

"How?"

"Just pluck the feathers off and eat it."

"Raw?"

"Yes."

"You have no place to cook?"

"No."

"No mother?"

"No."

"What happened to her?"

"She was killed by her father." Paul Victor pressed his ear closer to the prickly bush.

"Why?" she asked.

The boy hesitated...mumbled...but didn't answer.

"What happened to your father?"

"Never had one."

One of the many bastards of the blessed Baghdad, thought Paul Victor.

The young woman started, then froze. The dove hung from her motionless hand. "Oh, dear!" she cried out, as if waking from a haunting dream. "You are fatherless like...like...my—"

The beggar boy was silent, his big haggard eyes fixed on the bird.

"Where are you from?" she asked.

"I was born in Baghdad but my mother came from the desert," he said in clear Arabic. "She was a Bedouin; she used to tell me stories about her tribe."

"What tribe?"

"Shamsullah tribe." Paul Victor jumped: as an intelligence agent, he had had dealings with the tribe. In fact, he knew the chief of the tribe, Sheikh Hassan, personally.

The dove dropped from her hand on the marble slabs of the veranda. She picked up the bird with a trembling hand and offered it to the beggar boy.

Suddenly a little girl ran out to the portico and cried:

"Mother, mother, give the bird to me!"

An angelic spoiled brat, Paul Victor thought.

"No, my dear," she said in a quivering voice. "It belongs to this boy."

"Why?" asked the girl glumly.

"Because he needs it."

"What's he going to do with it?"

"Eat it."

The little girl with a yellow butterfly knot in her hair began to cry: "No, no," she begged, "don't eat the poor bird." Then her pity suddenly turned into fierce anger: "You mean, dirty boy, don't eat the poor bird!"

The mother lifted her hand to slap her, but seeing terror in her eyes she stopped. For a moment ignoring the fear and concern of her daughter, she turned to the boy and said:

"I wish I could cook it for you, but I can't now. I'm expecting a 'visitor.'" *There seems to be bitterness in the last word,* Paul Victor thought. "Wash it in the River before you eat it," she added.

She wiped her daughter's tears and kissing her eyes said:

"Don't be mean to a brother Shamsullah. He is of our blood; his mother came from our tribe. He is like you—he has no father." She put a silver coin in the girl's hand and said: "Give it to him, dear, and shake hands with him." The girl offered him the money, but refused to shake his hand. "He's too dirty," she said. "Why doesn't his mother keep him clean?" The boy's adam's apple moved up and down like a hard knot, but he didn't cry.

"He has no mother, dear."

"Why? Where's she gone?"

The young mother hesitated a moment, looked up and said:

"She is in heaven—way up in that blue sky."

The little girl's dark sad eyes turned toward the sky, and suddenly she shouted with joy:

"Look, look, mother!"

All of them, including Paul Victor, looked up and saw two doves, soaring, looping and somersaulting in ecstasy.

"You come here tomorrow morning," said the young woman to the boy, "I'll give you food and a nice bath. I'll buy clothes for you, too. Can you take care of this little girl when I'm out?"

"Yes, lady," he said, "but she doesn't like me."

"She will after you have been cleaned up. With a nice suit on you, she'll be your admirer."

The beggar boy took a deep breath and suddenly blurted out: "What's your business, lady? Like my mother's? But they will kill you."

I sure would like to know her business, thought Paul Victor.

The sharp, penetrating question seemed to have shocked the lady—for a moment she was speechless. Then she asked:

"How old are you, my boy?"

"I don't know—maybe ten, maybe twelve."

"What's your name?"

"Salim. The beggar boys call me Jinnee."

"You are a good, smart boy, not a Jinnee," she said. "From now on,
we'll always call you Salim. Your mother must have given it to you—it's
a nickname for our tribe. My brother's given name, too, is Salim, but he
changed it. You look very much like my brother. Would you like to be my
brother, my son?"

"Yes, lady."

"Salim, when you come here tomorrow morning, don't tell the other
beggar boys, don't tell anybody. Promise?"

"I promise."

"If you whisper a word to anyone, I can't help you and take care of you.
Will you remember that—always?"

"Always, lady. I swear by the honor of our tribe!"

She shuddered at the ominous words.

"Where did you learn that oath? Who taught you?"

"My mother used to mutter it in her dream over and over again. Then
she'd scream and spit. I'd run for cold water—she'd drink it and be all
right."

"Did she ever tell you why she muttered it?"

"No. But she said when a boy was initiated into the mysteries of the tribe,
he'd be asked to take that oath. After that he'd be ready to die for his word
and the honor of his tribe. You and I are Shamsullah. I'd die for you, lady."

The blood-sealed code of the tribe is sacred and inviolable, recalled Paul
Victor. *Whoever breaches it must die. Once I almost did die by getting tangled up
with a Bedouin girl.*

"I don't want you to die or kill," she said to the boy, as if trying to give
him a new code.

He put the dove down—the pierced eye up, by accident—and kneeling
on the stone kissed both her hands.

"Good-bye, Salim!"

"Good-bye! When I return whom shall I ask for? I don't know your
name."

"My name is Fatima. Don't ask for anybody, I'll be waiting for you by the
pond. You can come after sunrise—about this time."

As she pointed her finger toward the pond, she saw Paul Victor, standing up
above the yellow-clustered bush, looking at her point-blank, with an unabashed
interest. She was startled, probably suspecting that he had been eavesdropping.
After a brief hypnotic pause, her eyes shifted abruptly: she stared after the boy
who was slowly walking with bowed head toward the River.

A mottled mongrel dog was prowling in the bushes, around the pond, watching the ducklings pantingly, with lolling tongue and flowing mouth. Paul Victor whistled at him, but actually the signal was aimed at Fatima rather than at the dog: he hoped she could look again with her electric eyes. The mongrel came, smelled the cuffs of his trousers, wagged his tail—but the lady of the beggar boy did not look.

Suddenly the animal saw the boy with the dove. He leaped after him and tried to snatch the bird from his hand. The boy fought doggedly, but the mongrel was relentless, more anxious than vicious. For some reason or other the young woman did not go to his aid: she just clenched her fists and waited; and the boy did not kick the dog because he was barefooted. The little girl, biting her nails, began to cry. Paul Victor ran up, grabbed the mongrel by the neck and patted his haunches. He grew docile and began to fawn and lick his hands. The boy grinned and his even teeth, white as milk, looked sharper than those of the dog. The lady waved at Paul Victor and, lifting her daughter into her arms, ran inside; the boy thanked his rescuer and went away. Paul Victor was left with the dog: he didn't know what to do with it.

He waited until the boy had disappeared; then he released the mongrel, hoping he would find a stray mate rather than pursue the boy with the dove. The dog heard the laughter of children and the barking of dogs: he pricked up his ears, and ran to join the merrymakers. Paul Victor stood up, tall and erect; two currents of emotion, evoked despite himself, pulled in opposite directions—toward the boy and toward the strange Bedouin woman whose child had no father. He thought he was being sucked, involuntarily, unnecessarily, into the eddy of a mystery. On the one hand he had a desire, perhaps a profound need, to see the Bedouin woman again, to talk to her, to find out who she was—he thought he had seen her before; on the other hand, he had an urge to follow the boy and watch him devour the dove with his lovely teeth. He gazed at the stone building searchingly; it looked like a formidable, mysterious fortress, inaccessible to a foreign intruder. *Perhaps through the boy I can reach her*, he said to himself hopefully. He picked a half-open forbidden narcissus, stuck it in the lapel of his camel's hair jacket and left in search of the boy. At the gate a policeman caught him, pointing at the flower. He greased the palm of the officer with an American dollar. The swarthy guard beamed, grinned and winked—Paul Victor strode on.

His destination was the River. He found Salim alone, sitting on a flat stone, his feet in the water, plucking the dove and humming a melancholy Bedouin tune. *His mother must have taught him. The Bedouins love their songs* *as passionately as they love and hate their women. They are a curious combination of nobility and brutality. They fascinate me. Maybe I should marry a Bedouin girl and become one of them. After all, people are basically the same everywhere....*He smiled, but suddenly he became very serious as his thoughts turned on the boy. He hid himself behind a huge palm shrub and watched him.

Salim cast the white, fluttering feathers on the muddy waters; he paused and watched, with intense fascination, the angry swirls catching and swallowing them. He seemed to be lost in a strange reverie. Suddenly he woke up, started plucking again, nervously, savagely, fast, like a desert buzzard carving his prey. He neither hummed nor studied the feathers' struggle in the fierce eddies. When the frail body of the dove emerged naked in his hands, he dug his thin fingers into its belly and tore its guts out and threw them into the river. No sooner had the entrails touched the water than a school of dogfish jumped on them in a churning tussle. He heard the voracious riot and, looking up, laughed in neighing, weak ripples. He was both excited and frightened; he withdrew his feet from the water and didn't dare to wash the bird in the River.

He looked around to see whether anybody was watching him. Feeling secure in his solitude, he clutched the head and the legs of the bird in his wiry fingers and dug his teeth into the breast of the dove. He pressed his jaws, like a miniature vise, around the wishbone and crushed it; he pulled and champed and crunched. Finally he succeeded in ripping off a bite and chewing it with famished gusto. He wrenched its legs out of their sockets; he clawed and gnawed at them like a cub. Then he yanked off its wings and chewed them, skin, cartilage, and all. The little bird could not yield much meat, only slivers and tough gristle. In his hunger he looked fierce and desperate; he laid the dove on the slab on which he had been sitting and, using a round rock as a mallet, he pounded the bird into a pulp and tried to swallow it all. But the rough ragout would not go down; he gagged and coughed and retched. His face grew purple, his eyes swam in tears—he was choking. Paul Victor rushed up and grabbed his shoulders, held his head down, and thumped him on the back. The boy disgorged the bloody mess, but something had stuck in his throat and wouldn't come out. Paul victor stuck his finger down into the boy's throat and pulled out a piece of wishbone. He plied scoops of water into his mouth to assuage his pain and calm his panic. When the boy felt relieved, he looked at the stranger with his sad, aged eyes and suddenly burst into tears, sobbing pitifully.

"You are all right now, Salim," he said, "don't cry, cheer up, be brave." Suddenly he felt embarrassed, his words sounded empty to him. *Cheer up, be brave! How? For what? There are hundreds and thousands of derelicts like him in the war cities of the world. Baghdad is full of them. They roam in the streets day and night—skeletal ghosts, whining, weeping, begging; when they can't beg and steal enough to eat they die. Every morning the street cleaners sweep them into their garbage trucks and dump them into the River.*

He thought as if he were talking to somebody else—to a friend, to an enemy, to another man within himself, or perhaps to God.

Salim was a delicate boy; if Allah did not intervene soon he would be on his way to the River. He tried to stop crying, but he couldn't control himself. As he strained his will to choke his sobs, he began to hiccup, mildly, then violently. Paul Victor rubbed his back, massaged his neck and diaphragm to no avail.

"Heaven has been good to you, Salim," he said, resorting to mystic powers, without conviction, to divert his attention from himself. "There are many boys and girls like you, but you are one of the fortunate ones. Soon the beautiful lady will take care of you like a sister, like a mother. Lucky Salim!"

When Paul Victor mentioned the lady, the boy's face lighted up a little; he started to say something—he mumbled and stammered, but no words came out of his throat. The hiccup jolted him spasmodically and stifled his voice. His breath issued in gasps, his face grew livid, then ashen. His teeth shone with hideous beauty in his gaping mouth. He began to sweat; his brow, framed within a shock of dark hair, shone like a film of frost. His knees shook and he started trembling, as if struck by icy palsy. His mouth foamed and his eyeballs quivered in their sockets. A strange haze descended on his eyes; there seemed to be no light in the pupils. His head doddered and dropped on his chest—suddenly he collapsed by the edge of the River. Every limb of his body jerked, kicked and quivered like a decapitated chicken. A Moslem Mullah, in a gray cassock, with an austere countenance and steel-gray beard, his turban perched on his head like a little white dome, came out of a handsome brick house overlooking the River. He had been watching the scene from his balcony. His head up, his hands behind him, he approached Paul Victor and the boy slowly, with heavy dignity and stern mien. He looked at the fallen boy and said:

"An evil spirit has entered into him. He is in the clutches of the devil. Don't touch him—leave him alone for a while. The cursed Jinnee is trying to choke him, extinguish the spark of life in him. Poor bastard! The sins of whoring mothers are visited upon their issue. His fit is a punishment from on high. The reason he is kicking and spitting is because he is in mortal combat with the demon."

The Mullah looked at the stranger with angry eyes, reproachfully, as if he had been responsible for his fate. Paul Victor started to say something, but the Mullah interrupted him:

"Poor Jinnee! He's a bastard, but a gentle one. He has changed though. When his mother was alive he was one person, but now he has become another. His soul and heart seem to have been torn apart, at war with each other. Now he is as gentle as a dove, now as fierce and keen as a viper. Before he was well-fed and well-dressed—no evil fits and no tears. His mother used to take care of him like the apple of her eye. She'd whore and steal and spy, do anything for him. Now he is all alone; every day he comes to the River, sits on that rock, chants, weeps and talks to himself. I watch him from my window. There are many like him, flocks of them. The police drive them out into the desert, across the River, but they swarm back like locusts. Allah's curse has descended upon our land, upon this city of whores, drunkards and infidels. Foreign soldiers everywhere, brothels everywhere."

"So you know him?" said Paul Victor with a bit of surprise.

"Yes, of course," he retorted, "I knew his mother, too. That sloe-eyed bitch with the guiles of a serpent! May her soul rot in hell! She corrupted my son. Now he has joined a newfangled foreign cult called *Fedayin-il-Hoobb.*"

"Out in the West," said Paul Victor hastily, "we would call it 'The Society of Free Lovers.'"

"You invent all kinds of things!" said the Mullah with a loathing grimace and shot a lump of phlegm into the River.

"Why, don't you like free love?" asked Paul Victor.

"Poof!" snorted the Mullah contemptuously. "You Westerners are too free in too many things. You are such experts in free living and free-grabbing that you have become the tutors of the world, of our youth. These so-called liberated young men and women meet in a den of vice called *Baith-il-Hoobb* (House of Love). It's a stone house near the park." Paul Victor felt as if somebody had suddenly jabbed a thin wire up his spine. "But we are determined to wipe it out, every den of free love and prostitution. *Ikhwan-il-Muslimin* (the Brotherhood of Moslems) have taken a solemn oath of blood to fight *Fedayin-il-Hoobb*, eliminate them completely. The sacred bloodletting will be undertaken first by fathers and brothers against their daughters and sisters. That's the way Jinnee's mother was eliminated. I shadowed my son and found where she lived, sent word to her father. He came, cut her locks, shaved her head, smeared it with cow's dung and, dragging her into the streets, publicly sacrificed her to Allah. He took her locks home and buried them under the threshold of his tent. Every time a member of the family steps over the threshold, he or she will spit on her remains as a perpetual curse and reminder."

He looked at Salim, still in the throes of epilepsy, and said to Paul Victor, with a sweep of the hand:

"Stand aside, you foreigners are responsible for our misery. In the past it was the bloody Turks; now it is you."

Paul Victor was mesmerized by the Mullah's complex of anger, pity, and hate. He stepped aside and watched him, with fascination and misgivings. The Mullah got hold of the boy's arms and dragged him away from the brink of the River. He lifted his eyes to heaven and began chanting melodic incantations, Koranic verses, and magic formulas. Then he drew a circle around him, bowed his head, locked his hands on his heart, and tramped around him, clockwise, counterclockwise. He unlocked his hands and went through strange motions and contortions; he pantomimed in a trance, in a pattern of gesticulations intricate as an arabesque talisman. His gestures were now directed toward the sky, pleading with angel Gabriel for succor; now toward the bowels of the earth, challenging Iblis, the Prince of hell—he was fighting, praying, and cursing.

Then he bowed over the boy and blew on his face, into his nostrils; he took pinches of dust and sprinkled it on him, around him in curves of crescents and scimitars. He stood silent, solemn, in a deep trance. Slowly, as if waking from a dream, he shook his head; then in words of exorcism, with chasing gestures he tried to expel the evil spirit from the boy. He declared that he was the loyal slave, the soldier of Allah. He dared the devil to come out and fight with him, not with a little, helpless boy. "I am the sword of God," he cried. "By Allah I'll fight with the honor and valor of my tribal ancestors!" *The amazing thing is that his mouth is foaming and sputtering like that of the boy.* When he saw the fit subsiding, he became exultant, jubilant. He started chanting and dancing around the boy with graceful steps and sinuous motions; it was a strange snake dance, hypnotic and awesome. Then he rushed to the River, washed his face, winnowed water in the sky, a kind of offering; then forming a scoop with his hands, he fetched water and poured it on the boy's face, on his feet, and on his head. He brought water again and washed his brow, his eyes. Then he called and exhorted the boy: "Jinnee, Jinnee, wake up! You are all right now, you are cured! The evil spirit has left you. Allah has been merciful to you!"

The boy grew calm and slowly opened his eyes. "What did I tell you?" cried the Mullah triumphantly. "By God I have defeated the devil! By the sword of Allah I have laid him low. I have done my duty—now you take care of him. Do whatever you want with him. After all his mother used to sleep mostly with foreigners because they could pay more. For all I know, he may be part British, or French, or Anzac, or American. May Allah curse you all for sucking the lifeblood of our land dry and turning our wives and daughters into free lovers and whores."

He spat, braced his hands on his hips and walked away with fierce dignity. Paul Victor seemed to be stunned; he couldn't say a word. Slowly his eyes turned from the receding broad back of the Mullah to the boy.

Salim lay still prostrate on his back, his face gray as dust, his lips dry with the remains of the dove. His motionless eyes, as if drained of light, stared at the sky. He seemed to be in a trance; there was a strange play of light on his pale face. The sun shone warmly on the River, in the sky: Paul Victor hesitated to disturb his peace. Instead, he thought of the Muslim hell and heaven—of the Christian hell and heaven.

He reasoned that he was no better, no worse than the Mullah; he felt no responsibility for the fate of the boy—and yet there was something in the little fellow that would not let him go. Aside from the lure of the girl, he felt he was caught in a tangle of emotions and compulsions stronger than reason, love or hate. He was not thinking of ethical issues either: he recoiled from what they called the moral ruse of proving to one's self that one is a good man. Putting a coin, even a gold coin, in the palm of the boy would be a soothing salve, an easy way out. He hated self-flattering charity. Hardened by war and death, he felt pity was a self-destructive luxury. *I am no better, no worse, than a native; no more human than a brutalized lonely soldier.* He had come to the conclusion that in his profession there was no morality, no pity, no conscience, no soul. And yet, he felt that if he left Salim, he would be *lost forever. Lost forever....*Suddenly he grew hot with shame—he hadn't felt shame for a long time—that he was really more solicitous of his own loss than that of the boy. This was a kind of discovery, a paradox that made him very uncomfortable. He squatted on his heels and bending over the boy asked:

"How do you feel, Salim?"

"I feel like an empty coffin."

Paul Victor was puzzled—*empty coffin!*

"What do you mean?"

"I saw death, Sahib. It was like a black empty coffin, walking behind the Mullah. I hate that Mullah—he squealed on my mother—his son hates him, too. I feel empty, like death. Death is an empty, black coffin. My mother was buried without a coffin, all alone, in the desert. That black Mullah wouldn't let her be buried in the cemetery. He said she was unclean. Every night I dream big coffins and little coffins. They all walk one after another, Sahib, like soldiers, like mullahs and monks. Why do they do that, Sahib?"

"Because all coffins are alike," said Paul Victor, without thinking of the reason or accuracy of his answer.

"There are poppies and thistles on my mother's grave, but no stones," continued Salim in a strange vein. "Jackals with blood-red eyes, like poppies, tried to dig out my mother, but I made a torch and burned their tails, and they all ran away, like crying beggar boys chased by the police."

For a moment Paul Victor felt as if his head were sinking in a dark, empty grave—then it bobbed up, fluttering, with incongruous images—white upright coffins, black coffins, yellow coffins with embossed brass nails, with wooden legs, steel legs, files after files, stretching for miles, marching in funereal silence through the forests of the night; then the sky was rent with a million jagged flashes of lightning, and he saw myriads of carrion birds with fierce beaks and colors, milling, hovering over desolate cities and battlefields. He saw countless dazzling medals sparkling on wooden crosses stretching from horizon to horizon; an owl hooted, a loon cried, then the barren fields of the crosses were showered with laughing flowers—crimson poppies, virgin daisies, sunflowers, tiger lilies, larkspur, purple morning glories, lotuses with giant petals, all mocking and wailing and chanting a dirge of curses.

Suddenly an immense spiral rocket descended from the sky and exploded with a blinding, thundering flash. Then a stygian darkness shrouded everything, except a waning, trembling moon on the horizon. Just below the deathly light of the moon, in the midst of the boundless field of ashes, he decried a solitary grave, without a stone, without poppies and thistles, unmarked and unknown. Around the grave squatted a pack of jackals, new species, with iridescent striations, long curved claws, horns and tusks. They had assumed prayerful postures, circle within circle, bowing and bobbing, as if in worship of a great Deity; but being seared with thirst, they dug their claws and tusks into the burnt earth feverishly, groaning, howling, and weeping like babies.

Is this boy driving me crazy, or merely evoking in me what is already latent in me? He forgot to lift the boy to his feet.

"Don't think about death, Salim," he said in a spurious attempt at solace, emoting rather than thinking, perhaps trying to hearten himself as much as comfort the boy.

"But I want to die," said the boy with a frightening finality. "I've seen death, Sahib, I know his face…I'm not afraid. Death is an empty coffin."

"But death is not an empty coffin," said Paul Victor—then he realized that his logic, under the circumstances, was fatuous.

"Oh, yes," insisted the boy. "A young New Zealand soldier with blue eyes used to come and see mother. When he drank wine, he became sad. He looked out of the window and sang: *Death is an empty coffin. Yes, death is an empty coffin. Oh, glory, oh heroes.*...Then he'd sigh and say, *Ladies, sweethearts, all dead soldiers are buried without coffins.* He had shining buttons and a red beard, soft as my mother's hair—but he never smiled. Mother said he was a good man. 'I love him, son, as much as I love you. He is your—' I got angry, I hated him. He had a bullet hole in his ear. I stuck my finger through it and watched it wiggle on the other side, like a baby snake trying to go through a key hole. Then something happened inside me and I laughed and laughed. *He* never laughed. Mother pulled my finger out and hit it with a fork and bit its end. It hurt and I cried. The soldier looked at me—his blue eyes were sad—never smiled—and gave me fresh figs. Every time he came to see mother, he brought sugar, and tea, and perfume.

"Sahib, can you find fresh figs for me? I couldn't find any, the stores were closed. I'll pay for them. The little girl gave me money."

He searched for the coin in the pockets of his rags. "Oh, it's gone, I've lost it—there's a hole in my pocket." He bit his lips and turned his face away.

"Don't cry," said Paul Victor, "I can find figs for you, fresh or dry.

"Tell me more about the soldier and your mother."

"The soldier had a deep cut under his beard, near the hole of his ear. Mother put her fingers on it and kissed it. She wanted to know where he got it. 'In the battle of El Alamein,' he said, 'where I buried my brother in the sand, *without a coffin.*'

"Mother wanted to know everything about war and death. He said he didn't like to talk about death, but he liked to sing about it. He drank wine and sang—he was sad, he never smiled.

"Mother kissed his scar and his hands, and cried. But I didn't cry, I wanted to hit her. She said she was going to get killed like a soldier, with deep wounds in her belly. She said she loved soldiers, she wanted to give herself to them and die for them.

"I didn't want to die for anybody. But I want to die now, *for myself*. Please finish me, not with a bayonet, but with a thin little sword. My grandfather used a big one on my mother. Put deep wounds in my belly, in my heart, but please don't hurt me, do it gently—not like my terrible grandfather."

Paul Victor, who had thought of himself as a "tough operator," immune to blood and shock, suddenly shuddered. He was baffled and deeply

disturbed. In all his complicated and devious career, he never had had
such an experience. For a moment the beggar boy appeared to be a little
monster holding him in his tentacles. As he stared into the big dark eyes
of the boy, he saw himself, as if in a deep black mirror, in the role of a mild
executioner, slowly and gently pushing a thin scimitar into the belly of the
boy. Fully conscious of the strange ambivalent operations of his nature, he
was flabbergasted. He cried out, *Salim!* like a man waking up from the shock
of a dream of horror and unholy delight.

"Yes, Sahib," responded the boy quietly.

"SSSalim," he stammered a bit, struggling to shift the focus of his mind,
"what kind of a man was your grandfather?" Then, unable to resist his more
compelling motive, he added, "How did he kill your mother? Why?"

The boy, too, stammered a bit: "I, I had never seen my grandfather," he
said, "until he came to kill my mother. He was a tall dark man; his beard
was black and white and his little eyes were like daggers. He grabbed my
mother by the hair and dragged her out into the street. I ran after him and
bit his hands and legs. He kicked me in the belly and called me the son of
a whore—a foreign cur. He cut my mother's locks and put cow's dung on
her head. He thrust a big sword into her belly. She didn't cry, she spat on his
beard and called him a mad dog. When she fell, my eyes went black. I, too,
fell—I didn't see my mother any more."

He stopped, blanched—his face became a white death mask. His eyes,
though wide open, appeared frozen, lifeless. Paul Victor touched him,
involuntarily—he didn't want him to die. *No, no, it would be a pity!* The word
pity had an anomalous ring: it stung him like a wound under pierced armor.
He bent over the boy and asked anxiously:

"Salim, are you all right?"

The boy's eyes came to life; they turned on him vaguely, and he said:

"No, Sahib—I'm not all right."

"What happened?"

"I saw my mother. A lady in a black veil took me out into the desert and
showed me my mother. She had no hair on her head and her clothes burned
like flames of blood. But the moon shone on her face coldly, and she waved
at me and went down into a black pit, all alone, without a coffin. I wanted
to follow her, but her grave was covered with thorns and poppies. I want to
die, I have no place to sleep. At night I go and sleep by my mother's grave.
I'm an empty little coffin, Sahib. Death is an empty coffin, ringing like a
hollow drum, calling me, calling me.

Paul Victor could not reason any more with himself or with the boy:

that death was the concrete reality of a *full* coffin. Little Salim had drawn him into himself and made him part of himself. Though fully conscious of his identity, he had the curious feeling that Salim and he were the same person. *I too, am a child of war, an orphan born of a despised woman: I have never known a father. I am the soldier with the pierced ear; I am my unknown father. I am a black coffin with a bleached empty skull, with hollow gun barrel legs, wandering in the starlit gloom of deserts, and deathfields. I am Salim and Salim is I.*

Now he realized why he could not tear himself away from Salim, buy his freedom and conscience by putting a few coins in his palm. In his silence, in the frenzy of his trance, he must have appeared frightful, for he noticed the boy crawling away from him with terror in his eyes. He grasped his thin wrist and said:

"Salim, don't be afraid of me, I won't kill you (*I'll never kill again, never, never, no matter—*) Salim, the war is over—cheer up!"

"I want to die," said Salim fatalistically. Please kill me, but don't hurt me, don't scare me. Your eyes look terrible, like my grandfather's. Please put me to a happy sleep. Once a dervish gave me opium—I was in heaven; I want to go there. Bury me in my mother's grave. It's on the other side of the flood dam, near a big black rock, in the Fatima Pit."

"No, Salim, you shouldn't die yet," said Paul Victor, "you and I are going to see Fatima. The war is over—everything is going to be all right. There isn't going to be any more killing." He sensed, despite his ardent hope, that his affirmation did not really have the firmness of conviction. Nevertheless, he continued in the same vein: "I know you have died many times, but you needn't die again."

"Why shouldn't I die?"

"Because you should grow up and be a good soldier of peace, a true brother to all, so that little boys like you and women like your mother won't die again."

Suddenly he felt hot and furious. *I don't know why,* he castigated himself, *I lapsed into a cheap glory of preachment, knowing damn well that such pious pronouncements and prayers have been trumpeted from thousands of temples, churches, mosques and synagogues for centuries in these blighted lands of great religions, everywhere, without giving to suffering humanity even a blessed glimpse of the blissful millennium. They have all vanished like hollow reverberations, mere dismal echoes in the blood-soaked fields of holocausts.*

He was just beginning to feel the startling delight of self-laceration and denunciation, waxing to a new dimension, when Salim jolted him with his serious, enigmatic voice:

"But I don't want to be a soldier of peace. If you don't put me to sleep, I want to be a soldier of war—a real soldier. Soldiers were good to my mother, better than my grandfather and the Mullah. No war—no chocolates, no figs, no bread, no mother. I want to be a real soldier, find my grandfather and the Mullah, cut their beards, put cow's dung on their faces and heads, and stab their big bellies with a sharp sword."

The boy's ashen face beamed for a moment as if with the ecstasy of a triumphant vision.

"I thought you didn't like killing," said Paul Victor. "That's what you told Fatima."

"That's true. But this is different. I want to cut my grandfather's head and the Mullah's tongue—throw them to the dogs. Then I'll feel good, like being in heaven. I'll tell my mother what I have done. She, too, will feel good—proud like the mother of a real soldier."

Paul Victor recalled, with a sense of futility, the age-old desert code: tooth for tooth, eye for eye, blood for blood. Then, he thought, with a cold nihilistic disgust, of the so-called civilized code: gun for gun, ship for ship, plane for plane, bomb for bomb, death for death—tenfold, hundredfold—all vicious and repetitious like an eternal curse, returning to damn the very Curser.

"But, Salim," he said in a matter-of-fact tone, "if you kill you'll be killed. You can't die and be a soldier, too." He tried to reason with the boy, no less with himself, but he knew that reason was neither the key nor the issue.

"I want to do both," asserted the boy. "You said I have died many times. Why can't I die and live many times?"

"Maybe you can," said Paul Victor diffidently, as if forced to concede the hopelessness of logic and reason in matters of ultimate paradoxes. *Death is an empty coffin*, he muttered in refrain, and added distinctly, *blood is strong red wine.*

"Sure it is," confirmed Salim confidently. "Soldiers drank red wine and fought for my mother. There was blood on their faces and it was like red wine. Mother was happy when they fought for her. She licked their faces, kissed them and laughed. But I cried. The soldiers were drunk, happy. They mixed their blood in the red wine and drank toasts to each other, to my mother. Some cried out, 'Down with the bloody war.' Others shouted, 'No, no—down with peace.' Then they hugged each other, hugged mother and kissed her hair, her eyes, and lips. They undressed her and made her dance. Then they all laughed and threw silver money, paper money, on her head, on mine. Mother's eyes were full of fire, she laughed and cried and danced. But I couldn't laugh, I just cried and wanted to run away. But the soldiers wouldn't let me. They were good to me—every one said he was my father and patted my head."

The more Salim revealed his past, in a fevered outpour, the more Paul Victor became involved in him, in himself. He saw himself as never before: Salim was the mirror of his memories, his conscience, more turbulent and varied than that of the boy. What Salim described, with the fire-sharp perceptions of an epileptic, was not alien to him, not fantastic. For the maximum efficacy of his missions, he had had to abandon his former religious scruples; his profession demanded that he operate, unflinchingly, unswervingly, on one cardinal principle: *The end justifies the means.* In order to attain his goal, he had had to be more chameleonic than a Jinnee, more versatile than a serpent. In ingenious disguises, he had taken extraordinary risks, entered enemy territory, employed every technique and ruse in the trade—cunning, deception, bribery, wine, women, even "liquidation." When Salim said he wanted to die, he, too, often wished he were dead.

"Poor little boy," he muttered to himself audibly, in English, "he was born in the hot passion of blood and violence, like myself. There is too much death and sex on his mind: he doesn't comprehend their maddening depth and power."

"I'm not a little boy, Sahib," he said with a knowing, faint smile.

"You understand English?" asked Paul Victor, in a surprised tone.

"Yes, Sahib—quite a bit," he answered gravely, in English.

"Then why haven't you said a word in English all this time?"

"I used to be," he shifted to Arabic again, "a spy for soldiers and officers— for anybody who would pay mother—tell them where they could find pretty women. Some of these women were foreign spies. I was told to look and listen carefully, remember everything, but keep my mouth shut. You see, Sahib—I understand many things, I remember a lot. I'm not a little boy, I'm an old, old boy. As a spy and beggar, I have been to many places, sneaked into all kinds of holes and dens in this big city. I have seen a lot and know a lot. I understand plenty about men and women and sex, too. Sometimes I used to hide myself and watch, all night, naked women sing and do harem dances, then undress men and dance with them, drink and do all kinds of things. Sometimes I dream of their strange faces and eyes. I think you are a spy, too, but I bet I have seen more than you have. You see, Sahib—I'm not a little boy, I am a very old boy."

"You certainly are!" said Paul Victor. He was astounded—nearly jolted out of his wits, not because he had seen and done less, but because of the incredible, almost demonic, acumen of the boy. And yet, he suddenly felt a strange emotion welling up in his bowels—not hate, not love, but a toxic blending of both, a kind of plasmic essence which by torturing him made him drunk with a peculiar sense of elation. The boy seemed to be a protean creature, like his own shifting emotions and imagination, now real, now unreal. In his bewilderment of delight and fear, groping for a new bearing, he asked:

"What should I do with you, Salim?"

"Nothing—just finish me," he said with absolute seriousness. "I'm tired, very tired—I want to sleep and sleep, get far, far away from this earth. Every night I dream of ugly faces and eyes, blood, knives, naked men and women biting at each other. I dream of wolves, snakes, barking fish, and fire-tongued monsters. I don't want to wait and kill my grandfather and the Mullah. You kill them for me and for my mother—you can do it. I want to go to another world. The lady in the black veil told me when I die I'll go to the happy land of *jannat* where my mother is. I don't want to see Fatima—I want to see my mother. Maybe I can find my father, too. But who is my father? Are you my father, Sahib?"

Paul Victor didn't know what to answer; he was in quandary in more than one way. He didn't really know what to do with the boy, for in truth he didn't know what to do with himself. The boy both fascinated and repelled him: when he thought of conscious love, he reverted to unconscious hate. One time he had thought that all such emotions were dead in him. His mind recoiled from himself and concentrated on the boy: *He must be sick, suffering from traumatic experiences and hallucinations, not only epileptic but schizophrenic,* he thought. *Ah, nonsense—mere labels! He is saner than I am, more intelligent than many a killing hero.*

He looked up and saw the Mullah watching them from his balcony of white columns with a beady cold stare, probably wondering why they were tarrying so long by the River, under the shadow of his home. In order not to arouse any more suspicion in a suspicious man, he turned to the boy and said:

"Salim, can you get up on your feet? Let's go, the Mullah is watching us."

"Where to?"

"Where there are figs and chocolates," he said with an ironic, bitter smile. "For you and me war is not over yet."

"I don't want figs and chocolates any more—I don't want anything. You go away, I want to sleep here. Once I saw a white puppy sleeping in the River, floating on and on like a little boat."

Paul Victor couldn't go away; he coaxed Salim to stand up. The boy got up, but he reeled and his bony legs buckled under him. Paul Victor lifted him in his arms and started walking toward the Shamiram Hotel where he had a lodging which he occasionally used as a base of operation. He didn't want to go by the Royal Boulevard. In the stream of the gala holiday crowds, with the grimy, tattered boy in his arms, he would have looked a strange sight. He also knew that the liveried eunuch with an oxlike stature, beardless and stolid, standing guard at the gate of the hotel, would not let him in with his uncouth load. So he worked his way through back alleys and by-streets and sneaked into the hotel by a back door. He tiptoed up the stairs of the fire exit, and as he reached the second floor, he halted with a start. He heard the owner of the hotel, a handsome, sensual man of fifty, standing at the door of his private suite and whispering in seductive tones to a young woman who looked very much like Fatima. He felt a sharp jabbing pulsation in his stomach. "Salim," he whispered in his ear, "is that Fatima?"

"No, Sahib, she is the daughter of the Mullah."

"Don't be a fool," she said, "you are as old as my father."

"What difference does it make?"

"The difference is that I loathe you." Then she added with a snarl, "Don't forget, my father wants to see you."

"Why?"

"You know why! I just came from your den, the so-called *Baith-il-Hoobb*. He wants to know abut your new catch, a singing and dancing wench by the name of Fatima, who has become the idol of the *Fedayin-il-Hoobb*. She is nothing but a high-priced whore. She has taken my fiancé away from me."

"Jealousy!" he taunted.

"Damn right!" she snapped. "But it's more than jealousy. You are corrupting our youth. Look at my brother—nothing but a drunken debauchee, like you."

"Poor, unliberated virgin, you don't know what you are missing!"

She spat on his threshold and walked away. He laughed and withdrew into his suite—a key clicked and his door was locked. Inside a woman started singing a spicy ditty in Arabic; there was a dulcet strumming of a guitar: a rich male voice responded in a salacious Turkish song.

Paul Victor, in an incongruous flash, recalled his body floating down in the dark behind the enemy lines in the Balkan mountains on a demolition mission. He remembered how he had ignited munition dumps, mined tunnels and bridges with the cool impersonality of death. But now the tremor in his knees irritated him like gangrene, and the violent palpitation of this heart reminded him, tauntingly, ironically, of the pigeons which he used to release after each mission. Thinking of them as trusted intelligence agents, he had more regard for his pigeons than for some of his fellow spies. When the hawk in the sky of the park, over *Beth-El-Khoob*, had blinded the pigeon and brought her down, like his own floating body in a parachute, he had felt a genuine pang, though the circumstances of his life had taught him the paradox that in war hawks were more apt, even more admirable, symbols. Hence, he had no hate for the hawk as he had not hate for the enemy.

Suddenly conscious of his situation, he pulled himself together—his trained will instantly choking his tremors—and, throwing a glance down the corridor, he made his key ready. "All clear, Sahib," signalled Salim like an expert spy. Paul Victor rushed into his room noiselessly and locked his door. The arabesque bedspread was too clean, too beautiful, for Salim's caked feet and rags: he laid him on the carpet. Then he filled the bathtub with hot and cold water. As he undressed the boy, he found his body crisscrossed, like a talismanic tattoo, with weals and scars. Though he surmised their cause, he asked:

"What are these, Salim?"

When I get caught stealing or spying, they tattoo souvenirs on me," he said casually.

Paul Victor passed his fingers over them, like a blind man trying to read Braille: "Are they sore?"

"A little—in spots."

He lifted him into the bathtub, soaped his body carefully and, as he gently rubbed his back, his limbs and parts, the boy squirmed and writhed with delight and pain. Although Paul Victor was conscious of the polarized sensations through touch and memory, recalling his mother scrubbing him briskly, pantingly, he asked:

"How does it feel?"

"Like being drunk in a bathtub."

Paul Victor started laughing: it was a peculiar laugh, as though coming from a dark shaft of untouched regions. "Is there anything you don't know, you little devil?"

"I'm an old, old boy, Sahib. Sometimes soldiers used to make me and my mother drunk. Then we'd do all kinds of things together. The soldiers would laugh and clap. One time the New Zealand soldier put his arms around me and said, 'Son, this is no good for you—you'll be like me, a drunken bastard.' A big soldier pushed him aside and poured whiskey into my throat and laughed and kissed me. I cried, but felt warm inside, like being in a bathtub. Then I fell asleep. I had a dream: I was a little bird with

one red wing and one blue, and my tail was silver. I had white feet and a
black beak. From my neck hung a red snake. He tried to strangle me, but I
pecked out his eyes, and he cried like a little baby hanging from a palm tree.
I was hungry, I wanted to eat him, but he turned into one of my mother's
locks—I couldn't chew it. I began to cry like the snake—then I saw one of
my mother's breasts, flowing with milk, but I couldn't reach it. The milk
flowed into the spring of an oasis, and the trees around the spring began
to laugh like drunken soldiers. I flew around and around over the oasis,
trying to dive into the spring, but I couldn't. Somebody was pulling me up,
up, calling me. I turned my eyes toward the sky and saw a flag with black
borders, my mother's locks hanging from its four corners like tassels. A little
girl, like Fatima's daughter, was sitting on the flag. She sang and waved and
smiled at me. I forgot my mother's breast. I flew up, up toward the flying
flag. I wanted to reach her and ride with her. Now it seemed I was both a
boy and a bird. As I grabbed one of the locks, suddenly the sky opened up
like a great garden of trees and fruits. The little girl picked grapes and pears
and offered them to me, but as I reached for them, she disappeared. I heard
a crash, then I saw the feathers of my broken wings fluttering in the empty
sky—I fell and woke up. I opened my eyes and found the room dark and
empty. All the soldiers were gone, but I saw my mother standing by the
window, naked, all alone, weeping. The moon shone on her breasts and
hair—she was beautiful.

"Sahib, if I drink whisky you think I can see my mother again?"

"I'm not sure, but I wish I had a miraculous drink that could make you
see her and be with her. I wouldn't mind taking a glass of it myself."

*Maybe heaven is nothing but an aching, deathless desire, a fond hope, an
eternal dream-vision.*

"Sahib, you have a mother?"

"No, Salim."

"No father?"

"No."

"No brothers or sisters?"

"No."

"No wife?"

"No."

"Poor Sahib, you're all alone, like me."

"Yes, Salim."

"Was your mother like my mother?"

"Yes."

"Did they kill her?"

"Yes, but not with a sword."

"With a bullet?"

"No."

"Strangled her?" the boy pressed.

"No!" He felt anger and resentment rising in him.

"But how did they do it?" The boy sat up in the fluffy suds of the tub and waited for an answer with an intense, anxious look.

Paul Victor grew morose; he was straining his will to keep calm. Though the War was over, he was at war, in a curious concurrent manner, with himself, with the boy, with his past. He had reasoned out: *Certain things have to be killed and buried, like in war, otherwise one would rot in his soul and die ignominiously. Ashes and the dust of moldering bones are good only as fertilizers for new seeds.* Though on occasion death had the fascination of a mistress, he did not want to unearth the buried relics of the past, for himself or for the boy; and yet, with the passing of time, they had become, in spite of his will, more acutely alive, more poignantly real, then the pains of his flesh and bones. Sometimes they sprang up unexpectedly, in strange situations and relations, and haunted him like ghosts.

He was determined to ignore the boy's question, because he was afraid it would unlock a floodgate of too many memories. But when he looked into the boy's eyes, he was surprised: what he saw in them was not merely a morbid, boyish curiosity for sex, blood, and death, rather a poignant sorrowful realization of a common fate. He sensed that the boy, moved by something more than conscious intention, was, as it were, standing at the locked gate of his life, knocking forlornly, begging for admittance.

Paul Victor washed the boy's face, his ears, his throat, his hands pensively: suddenly he felt like crying. He took his clean, sensitive face between his palms and kissed his eyes.

"Salim, my son, when you grow up, capable of understanding not just what happens but why it happens, I promise to tell you all."

"But Sahib," said the boy tearfully, deeply touched by the stranger's affection, "I feel I won't live very long. Can't you tell me now, just in a few words, how your mother died? I understand death, Sahib—I have seen him, many times. Was she buried in a desert, without a coffin, like my mother?"

"No, Salim. She was buried in a lake—she drowned herself."

"But why?"

"Because she didn't want to be like your mother any more." He suddenly realized the brutal implications of his remark. In the turmoil of his mind, he had unwittingly twisted his meaning. He felt pangs of remorse, in a manner which in itself was shocking and new to him. "I mean she didn't love men any more," he hastened to correct his blunder without revealing everything starkly. "She was tired of them, she was tired of herself and of life."

The boy remained silent: slowly a cloud of pain and melancholia descended upon his little face like a death mask. Turning his head gravely, he stared into Paul Victor's eyes penetratingly, as if searching deep in his soul for the secret truth of his answer. Then he said, somberly:

"You, too, are tired, Sahib—very tired, like your mother, like me. I wish we had a miraculous drink, like the paradise of Allah. My mother and the lady in black told me it was a wine of many colors, made from a thousand flowers. It was more powerful than the magic of Harun-al-Rashid. One glass of it would make all your wishes come true. It would turn you into anything you wanted: you could be a rich Sultan or a green snake; you could be an angel or a devil—all you had to do was to make a wish and take a sip. You could be a flying horse or a shooting star, a cloud, a bird. It made you so happy that once in a while you would cry for the poor people of the earth.

"Oh, I wish we had a bottle of Allah's wine! We would invite Fatima and her daughter; we would go to the banks of Mother Tigris. Sitting under the blossoms of pomegranate trees, we would first drink a toast to Allah and thank him for his good wine. Then we would drink a toast to ourselves and become rainbow flames. We would hold hands, sing and dance and pray until our bodies and hearts and tired bones all turned to sacred ashes.

"The Mullah watching us from his balcony would be terribly frightened. He'd think Allah had come down to earth, working miracles. The black priest would come down and kneel over our ashes and pray and sprinkle them on the holy waters of Mother Tigris. The muezzins would chant prayers from the minarets of the city and sacred doves would fly and circle around the blue domes of the mosques. Maybe the Christian bells would ring, too.

"But our ashes, hearing the evening *azzan* of the muezzins, would turn into swans—four of them, two big ones and two small ones—and swim on peacefully in the arms of our sacred River, and sail on and on until we reached the shores of *jannat*. There under the wings of angels your mother and my mother, young and beautiful again, will be waiting for us. They will have music, and they'll receive us with song and dance and heavenly wine. Allah's chief angel will sprinkle and anoint us with the miraculous wine straight from Allah's springs. Then, our spirits will rise out of the white swans and become blessed sons and daughters of paradise. We will hug

and kiss our mothers and live happily ever after in the wonderful Garden
of Allah, where springs and rivers of wine and honey and milk flow for all
the soldiers who were killed in the War, for all good people, but not for my
grandfather and the Mullah."

Paul Victor was for a moment spellbound; he felt as if he were a child
again, listening to an enchanting Oriental tale, floating in the rosy glow of a
dream world. He smiled and, laying his hand on the boy's head, said:

"Yes, Salim, I wish we had a whole barrel of Allah's wine!"

Then he lifted him out of the bathtub and, after carefully drying his body
with a Turkish towel, put him to bed between clean sheets. "Now have a
nice rest," he said, "be a good boy, don't run away. I'll go and get you red
wine and something to eat." He patted his cheek and tucked him in under
the beautiful bedspread. The boy grabbed his hand and kissing it tearfully
asked:

"Sahib, why you do this for me?"

"I don't know," said the stranger.

He rolled Salim's tatters in a newspaper and, after locking the door,
carried them down to an incinerator behind the hotel. No sooner had he
turned his back when several beggars descended upon the incinerator and
began fighting for the package, thinking it contained the remnants of a
holiday feast. He shook his head and quickly reentered the hotel. He walked
into the dining room and ordered, with a sting of compunction, a bottle
of red wine, beefsteak for two, chocolate ice cream, a dish of fig preserves
(the season of fresh figs had not arrived yet) and tea. He told the maitre
d'hotel to be double quick, he was in a hurry. "I'll take the lunch up to my
room myself." The maitre d'hotel smiled, his eyes flashing. While waiting
for the order, he took a chair by the window facing the flowers of the front
garden and King Faisal Boulevard. Though staring at the flowing pageant of
humanity he thought of the beggars, of Fatima, of Salim and of himself.

Despite the pains and paradoxes of his mood, he was filled with a sense
of expectancy. Suddenly he felt warm inside, as if a secret spring of new
life was born in him. The welling sensation started at his solar plexus and
flowed into his veins and arteries like warm wine. He couldn't exactly
explain the nature and origin of his strange experience. True, he was aware
that Fatima played a tantalizing role—he wanted to surprise her, he was
anxious to present Salim to her in a form she would not recognize—but the
mystery was deeper than beauty, or passion. *Though the stores are closed,* he
said to himself, *I'll go to my friend Hasso, the Chaldean, and urge him to go to his
department store with me and sell me a suit of clothes for a boy of ten or twelve.*

He is not an ordinary boy—he is a wise old man who has become a boy again. I'll also buy a pair of shoes, a straw hat, and a handsome necktie for him. Then I'll get the barber in the hotel to give him a haircut. After he has been all decked out, like a little bridegroom, we'll have dinner together; then I'll take him to the holiday fireworks. Tomorrow morning, soon after the sun has touched the crescents of the minarets and the crosses of the belfries and the star of David, Salim and I will go to the park and meet Fatima and her daughter by the pond.

The maitre d'hotel appeared with a brass tray. "The Sahib must have a very special guest," he said with a glint in his eye. "Our guests never carry their own trays."

"Special, indeed!" Paul Victor replied boldly.

"No objection, Sahib, no objection—our aim is to please. We have adopted, among many other things, your famous American motto—'The customer is always right.'"

"The more he pays, of course, the righter he is!" retorted Paul Victor.

"Sure, sure!" the maitre d'hotel coughed, beamed obsequiously, and departed.

Paul Victor went up and unlocked the door of his room quietly. Salim appeared sound asleep; his eyes, fringed with long eyelashes, were partly open, like those of a sleeping hare. All tension in him had disappeared; his face was in deep repose. Paul Victor noticed that his fine, symmetrical features had attained, in their serene quiescence, new harmony and beauty. His face, set within the dark frame of his curly hair, was like a magnificently molded sculpture. Paul Victor was fascinated by his profound peace; he stood and gazed at him, the shining tray still in his hand, as if he were in a trance. He did not want to awaken him and disturb the spell; he put the tray away and sat down by his head.

After a long pause, his eyes slowly descended from his face to his chest, then to his legs. His tranquility was uncanny. Paul Victor felt his throat tightening; he coughed, involuntarily; the boy did not stir. He shifted his weight in the chair uneasily. He looked around and it seemed to him that every article in the room had suddenly become alive, watching him intently, watching the boy; they seemed to wait with bated breath for the taut wire of the big clock on the wall to snap. To his motionless eyes the arabesque bedcover spread out like a desert field of red poppies and white daisies at sundown. Salim's lovely head was there, before his eyes, and yet he had the eerie feeling that the bed was vacant, like an empty coffin.

Suddenly he winced and felt chilly; he touched the boy and felt a sharp, cold pang as if a long lance-like icicle had lunged into a pool of blood. He watched his breast, thinking, rather imagining, that the spearing shock might wake him up—but there was no motion, no heaving and panting. He held his hand over his nostrils for signs of breath—no stir; he passed his fingertips on his cheeks and lips—they were cold as ice; he touched his legs, his calloused bare feet—they too were cold. He hesitated to feel his pulse.

"Salim, Salim!" he called. There was no answer. He shook him gently, then rocked him, as though he were in a cradle. "Salim, Salim, I have brought you chocolate ice cream and figs!" He wanted to say fresh figs, but stopped. He didn't want to believe; hesitantly he reached for his left hand, felt its pulse. *Maybe I'm not sensitive enough to low pitch throbs.* He pulled the bedcover and the sheet back; his bruised and bony body was if ready for shrouding, for an empty coffin. He put his hand on his heart—it was as mute as a broken flute.

"*Death is an empty coffin,*" he muttered and pulled the sheet and the floral bedspread over his body, and covered his face.

LEON SURMELIAN

Leon Surmelian was born in Trebizond in 1907. Trebizond (Turkish "Trabzon," ancient "Trapezus") is described with tender nostalgia in his essay "Armenia" as well as in his best-selling *I Ask You, Ladies and Gentlemen*, an account of his boyhood and escape during the Genocide. Following the Genocide, Surmelian was sheltered at the Essayan orphanage in Constantinople and studied at the Armenian Central Lycee. The Armenian poet Vahan Tekeyan became the dean of the Lycee and encouraged the sixteen-year-old Surmelian's literary efforts, and the precocious teenager published a volume of Armenian poetry entitled *Louys Zvart (Joyful Light)* in 1924.

Surmelian came to America at the age of seventeen to study agriculture and graduated from Kansas State University. In addition to *I Ask You, Ladies and Gentlemen* (1945), he wrote several short stories, the novel *98.6* (1950), and translated both *The Daredevils of Sassoun: The Armenian National Epic* (1964) and *Apples of Immortality: Folktales of Armenia* (1968). *Techniques of Fiction Writing: Measure and Madness* appeared in 1968. Surmelian taught at California State University at Los Angeles and taught advanced workshops in the novel and short story in the University of California Extension Division from 1958 to 1964.

Although in many ways a "traditionalist" and a romantic in his literary sensibilities and style, Surmelian was fully aware of the complexity of the Armenian writer's relationship to contemporary American life. In an essay entitled "A Note on the American Writer of Armenian Birth," published in 1964 in *Ararat*, he declared:

> The alienated and the ambivalent, the beatnik and the
> hipster, recognize a fellow-American in the Armenian
> writer, and the Armenian knows his way around in the
> American underground, he is a subterranean by a long
> historical conditioning of his race.

Surmelian perceived that Allen Ginsberg, Jack Kerouac, and William S. Burroughs were fellow Armenians—they were also subterraneans. (*The Subterraneans* is the title of one of Kerouac's novels.) The Armenians were "beat" long before the Beats and knew profoundly the Beat writers' sense of meaningless time, of losing connection, of homelessness, of dispersion, of profound spiritual loss and exile. Surmelian's work chronicles the *agon* to achieve inner wholeness and to assert poetic values in an America without soul.

William Saroyan, for example, had a deep influence on Jack Kerouac, who spoke of his love for Saroyan's work in his *Paris Review* interview with Aram Saroyan (who himself became deeply involved in the California literary counterculture during the Sixties). The onrushing, lyrical, hip, Benzedrine-fueled prose of *On the Road* would have been impossible without Saroyan's Whitmanian, lyrical, syncopated, jazzy prose-poetry. For example, Saroyan wrote in his 1936 story "Baby":

> Sang baby. O maybe. Sang motors and wheels till saturday
> night in America, and a hundred thousand jazz orchestras
> sang *So come sit by my side if you love me*, and the sad-eyed,
> weary-lipped Mexican girl silenced Manhattan uproar with
> soft, velvet-petaled singing of darkness and death, O heart
> there is no end to the river's flowing.

Charles Bukowski, an "underground writer who was not a member of the Beat group but who shared many of their obsessions, also frequently acknowledged Saroyan's example. David Kherdian—who published *Beat Voices: An Anthology of Beat Poetry,* and *Six San Francisco Poets*—has also continued the Armenian/Beat spiritual quest in his prose and poetry as well as in his work on the esoteric philosopher G. I. Gurdjieff. Finally, Peter Najarian, in his novels *Voyages* and *Daughters of Memory* and a collection of short narratives, *The Great American Loneliness,* explores the intersection of the Armenian tragic sensibility and the consciousness-expanding, flower-power, transcendence-seeking Sixties. Surmelian observed and commented on the relationship between the Beat and Armenian sensibilities, but his work is shaped more powerfully by his childhood in the "old country" than by any contemporary American literary trends. He was, after all, born in Turkey.

I Ask You, Ladies and Gentlemen recounts Surmelian's boyhood during the Genocide and is distinguished by its sensitive and lapidary prose style. In the first chapter, Surmelian describes the death of his uncle Harutiun with great delicacy:

> My grandmother, talking to her dead son, before the
> portrait of his father, now covered with a black gauze
> so that he would not see him, was the image of Mother
> Armenia with all her ancient sorrows; the tears she shed
> were also the tears of countless Armenian mothers sobbing
> over the dead bodies of their stalwart sons. And it seemed
> to me Uncle Harutiun heard and saw it all, but did not say
> anything.

Surmelian's mastery of the lovely phrase is evident in this passage: he is a natural, fluent artist who shapes each sentence with great skill and musicality. He writes directly in a pure, warm, finely modulated manner and is a "born storyteller." He tells us in the introduction to *Apples of Immortality* that it was his paternal grandmother Nene (nanny)—she could not read or write—who told him the folktales of Armenia during his boyhood in Trebizond and it may be that Surmelian's storytelling gifts have one source in her archaic powers.

It is appropriate that the book begins with Uncle Harutiun's death scene—whose name in Armenian means "resurrection"—for in a sense Surmelian himself miraculously survived the Genocide, rose from the dead, and managed the epic journey to the United States. He describes the book in his *Techniques of Fiction Writing* as "an autobiographical non-fiction novel" and we observe the narrator as he makes the transition from Turkey to America. As is true for all Armenian American writers, the mythic past—or what the great historian of religions Mircea Eliade called "sacred time"—becomes now a problem, for Armenian glory can be retrieved only in fragments. In Chapter Sixteen, "Dream's End," Surmelian includes the myth of Satenik and Ardashes as well as the terrific epic lines from Khorenatsi on Vahagn—"Heaven and earth were in travail / Was in travail the purple sea. / The sea gave birth to a red reed / And from that reed came forth smoke / And from that reed came forth flame / And out of the flame ran a lad. / His hair was of fire / His beard was of flame / And his eyes were like suns"—which are reported as weird, jeweled bits of archaic splendor within Surmelian's narrative of his escape during the Genocide.

The narrator is poised right at the point of the breaking of time into pre-/post-Genocide, so even when he conceives of the present it is in terms of Armenia's glorious mythic sacred past time: "This terrific scene of the Armenian dawn impressed me like the mighty stage of God on which the drama of the world's creation and man's early history was still being enacted with Biblical lightning and thunder." Past/present are continually counterpointed within Surmelian's imagination because this is the only means by which he can save the memory of sacred time.

Indeed, whenever the narrator describes ancient Armenia, his style invariably becomes intensely lyrical, as if in the effort to recapture the past. He describes Father Leo Alishan's poem "The Moon of Armenian Cemeteries":

> [The poem] revealed the grandeur of ancient Armenia. In a
> sacred mystic land lambent in the moon, I could see mighty
> saints, Christian warriors with abundant locks and giant
> limbs, lying dead but deathless amid a vast litter of shields,
> lances and arrows.

Lake Sevan is also intensely perceived in Zoroastrian terms: "Lake Sevan glowed like blue sacrificial fire in an immense marble basin." Similes and metaphors abound, and reading it aloud, one can hear the alliteration and assonance of the poet resonate as the narrator strives to bring lost time to life.

One might call Surmelian a "neo-Romantic" somewhat in the style of the American composers Samuel Barber or Howard Hanson, who although composing in twentieth-century America chose the idiom of late-nineteenth-century classical music. Sometimes, however, Surmelian is just on the edge of what the Germans call *schmaltz*: a bit *too much* feeling.

Yet in a way this *excessiveness,* this *soulfulness,* is highly intentional, for Surmelian is nothing if not earnest. There is an innocent, sincere, direct quality to his voice, and it stands in stark contrast to the falsity of much of American culture. Like the Armenian American novelist Emmanuel P. Varandyan, who in *The Well of Ararat* describes Americans as people who "do things in a scientific way, as steady as a machine. The most steady companion in their lives is a watch…I wager they are machines themselves"—so too Surmelian also sees American life as spiritually empty.

At the close of *I Ask You, Ladies and Gentlemen,* Surmelian contrasts Armenian and American life: "There was a certain large, spacious quality about the American character. But culturally and spiritually they were far behind my companions in the old world." Indeed, he remarks, "American civilization is very powerful….It will swallow you up, as it has swallowed up millions of others. You would cease being an Armenian there. You would be lost to our literature and nature." Yet Surmelian, unlike the characters in Varandyan's *The Well of Ararat*, actually makes the trip to America and although he wants to begin a new life, the book ends with the narrator uncharacteristically drunk on New Year's Eve, attempting to deal with his mixed emotions and his struggle "to be, and not to have."

This theme of American versus Armenian sensibility recurs in the story "The Sombrero." Here too the Armenian narrator (his ethnicity is not mentioned, but we may assume the story is autobiographical) is aware of America as representing "logic" and Armenia "emotion" and of his own self-division:

> Poetry might well heal the inner split and bring my two
> disparate selves together and make me whole again. This
> was my basic problem: how to be whole again. A poem
> necessarily expressed an emotion—and I was trying to
> abolish my emotions in America and be all utilitarian logic
> and iron will. The commissar of common sense. Emotions
> were messy affairs, explosions of irrational dark forces
> within us, sheer anarchy, but the point was that the heart
> took over when I wrote a poem, and try as I would I could
> not abolish my heart.

In addition to his struggle with his "inner split," the narrator is also refused service in a Nebraska barbershop because he is wearing a sombrero and taken for a Mexican. The struggle to find a place in an America torn by racism and prejudice is thoughtfully portrayed. He is divided within but finds solace in poetry and in the Midwestern American earth. (We remember that Surmelian came to America to study agriculture.)

The story "M. Farid" also deals with racism and recounts the relationship between the Christian university–student narrator and an Islamic fellow student from Egypt. In post-9/11 America, the tale has a poignant relevance as the narrator struggles with his own prejudices against Islamic culture (largely due to the killing of his family by the Turks) and his self-professed Christian philosophy of love. The story has a surprising ending in which the narrator's hopes for universal brotherhood seem to be fulfilled.

Surmelian's career as a teacher is illustrated in his *Techniques of Fiction Writing: Measure and Madness* (with an admiring introduction by Mark Schorer). This is a superb, original, and informative book which deserves to be brought back into print. It is a virtuoso performance containing an astonishing number of illuminating references to writers from Homer, Plato, Aristotle, and Euripides to Joyce, D. H. Lawrence, Proust, Flaubert, James, Woolf, Faulkner, and William S. Burroughs, and it is full of thoughtful comments on the psychology and mysteries of artistic creation. Surmelian must have been an excellent teacher, for he deftly illuminates the intricacies of fiction writing. The book also contains many revelatory comments on Surmelian's own writing and intentions.

The novel *98.6* describes the dying of a young university student, Daniel Moore, from tuberculosis. When I sought a copy at the University of Michigan, I discovered that it is kept at the Taubman Medical Library—a testament to the precision and verisimilitude of Surmelian's treatment of disease and its relevance to today's medical students. However, later in his career Surmelian found fault with his novel and in his *Techniques of Fiction Writing* remarked that:

> As I see it now, the story was not properly distanced; it was
> too vivid in spots. A more relaxed, ironic tone would have
> been better, and irony requires distance. One can be too
> grimly realistic and hell-bent on mimesis.

Leon Surmelian was a gifted and multifaceted author. His work was not flashy, avant-garde, or *au courant*, and he eschewed the fashionable preoccupations of contemporary writers. He was a modern Romantic in many ways, holding up the ancient Armenian high-mountain values of heart, soul, feeling, and compassion in a modern, lonely, "existential," absurd, and fragmented world where, in the words of Shelley's "Ozymandias," the lone and level sands stretch far away. For as Friedrich Hölderlin sang, it is poets we most need in destitute times. Surmelian celebrated what he called, in his introduction to *The Daredevils of Sassoun*, the quixotic "knightly code" of the search for innocence, beauty, and honor. His work merits a new readership and his ideas are newly relevant in an America struggling with new questions about assimilation, multiculturalism, and the relation of the West to the "Arab/Islamic" world. What Surmelian memorably wrote of one of his characters might justly be said of himself: "he could not abolish his heart."

David Stephen Calonne

The Sombrero

All that summer—my first American summer—I gloried in my suntan as I worked on the experimental farms, stripped down to my waist. I soaked up the sun, being a sun worshipper, but in July the sun got unbearably hot and I thought I'd better buy a straw hat to protect my head. Cutting and bailing alfalfa hay was an operation of epic proportions, and I drove a tractor, and hoed the weeds, and had a real love affair with the American earth. At the same time I worked as a milker in the University's dairy barns, and took a couple of courses in summer school. I was in charge of a special group of high producers, all conforming to the ideal dairy type, and I could almost see the corn silage and beet pulp and grain mixture and alfalfa hay I fed them at each milking churned into milk in their mighty barrels. I slept in the barn, and the cows slept in the pasture. I was roughing it, and felt more American by doing so.

One of my beautiful Ayrshires reacted positively to the tuberculin test and had to be removed from the herd. I loved my cows and the Ayrshires made me feel like the King of Scotland. My friend Scotty and I drove His Majesty's Favorite Pet to Grand Island in a truck. My first trip to another town. Combines drawn by tractors were harvesting the wheat. I liked these powerful earth smells mixed with the smells of food processing plants and of dehydrated alfalfa in the Platte River Valley. I felt once a man breathes the pure prairie air he would always want to come back as to a fountain of youth. On both sides of the highway spread out, in huge geometric patterns, and in perfect squares and rectangles, fields planted to wheat and corn and oats and alfalfa and sugar beets and sorghum and potatoes and soybean, and there was no end to the steady march of the sunflowers by the roadside.

The earth of Nebraska had a sensuous, physical appeal for me. I remembered that as a young boy of seven or eight I used to dig a hole in the earth, insert my penis in it, and lie as though in the arms of a loving woman.

A freight train almost a mile long steadily pounded away with a tremendous rattle and rumble of wheels, and red beef cattle with white faces, Herefords, Scotty said, were being taken to the stockyards of Chicago, Omaha, or Grand Island to be slaughtered. There were also refrigerator cars. Union Pacific. Missouri Pacific. Chicago Burlington & Quincy. Chicago and Northwestern. Rock Island. Chicago Great Western. Santa Fe. Illinois Central. Denver & Rio Grande. A second locomotive pushed from behind with short rhythmic blasts of its funnel. Buses went in both directions at 70 miles an hour, and I watched the license plates of automobiles: Idaho, Potato State; Kansas, Wheat State; New Mexico, Land of Enchantment. New Jersey, the Garden State. All boosting their states. In this country people drove two or three thousand miles to go fishing.

Grand Island had a busy metropolitan air about it. The atmosphere was different here, in a more thickly populated and greener part of the state. The largest city after Omaha and Lincoln, but it had only 25,000 people. Looked bigger. The world's greatest inland livestock market.

Scotty signed some papers, and we turned our cow over to a man who appraised it. I patted her on the back and said goodbye. I hated to think jello would be made from her skin, tendons and ligaments; her bones would be powdered into cleaning agents for scouring sinks and kitchen utensils. Nothing was wasted in packing plants. We drove next to a feed store and loaded our truck with sacks of beet pulp from a local sugar factory.

Scotty wanted to visit a friend before we went back to the University, and I said I'd just walk around and see the town, buy a straw hat, and get a haircut. "You need it," he said. I had not had a haircut for two months. We agreed to meet again before the county courthouse, which had a handsome nineteenth-century European look about it and was not of the strictly utilitarian type. Grand Island had European touches in its architecture. There was a large Roman Catholic cathedral here.

I strolled along the streets, with a cowboy gait, proud of the overalls I wore: my American uniform. Instead of buying an ordinary straw hat I bought a sombrero, a high-crowned hat with a very wide brim rolled at the edges and with a string that went under the chin. And wearing my sombrero I paused to watch a group of Mexican laborers repaving a street in the center of the town. The Spanish they spoke had a sweet European sound in Nebraska. Their foreman, the sheriff type, big, ruddy, kept a sharp eye on them and gave orders. Machines laid out the liquid asphalt, which had a pleasant bituminous smell, and the Mexicans spread it out to the proper thickness before heavy rollers tamped it down. These machines were like flame-throwers in the broiling heat, with the temperature 105° in the shade, and probably only Mexicans could do this kind of work in summer. I noticed the sign on a hamburger and cold drink stand: "For whites only. We do not cater to Mexicans." These earth-colored men, looking so docile and glad to have their jobs, could not even have a coke or a hamburger where they worked. I shook my head and walked away, thinking I'd rather have equality before this hamburger stand than equality before the law.

These Mexicans were probably paid ten times the wages they could

expect to earn in Mexico, yet I wondered, is it worth it? No immigration
quotas for them, they were needed in Nebraska and did much of the back-
breaking field work for the sugar and grain barons. Were they allowed to
enter the Grand Island cathedral these barons built and say a Hail Mary
in Spanish? Mexico: Europe's bastard spawned by a squaw. A Latin failure
beside Anglo-Saxon success. Men in sombreros, uprooted from their own
land and rootless in Nebraska.

No use being so sentimental about the pioneers, I thought, as I walked
on. They had their merits and were, yes, a heroic breed, but most of them
were businessmen after all. Trade opened up the West. The trader came first.
Others followed. No wonder the businessman occupied such an exalted
position in Nebraska. The Spanish were here long before the real traders got
in with their Bibles and rifles—and their violence. Coronado was a damn
fool, Don Quixote in the Missouri Valley. He sought a mythical kingdom
where even the poor ate from gold plates, and overlooked the real gold that
lay in the land.

I strode jauntily into a barbershop and before I could say "Howdy folks"
the barber, a short fat man with sagging jowls, wearing rimless glasses,
frowned at me while giving a haircut.

"What you want?"

"I want a haircut."

He shook his jowls.

I looked at him, puzzled. Wasn't this a barbershop?

"Haircut," I said, gesturing with my fingers, as though holding a pair of
scissors myself.

"We don't cut Mexicans' hair in this shop. You came to the wrong place,
señor."

And maybe to the wrong country. I wanted to tell him I was not a
Mexican, but I was too shocked to say a word. There were two other men in
the shop who glanced at me and said nothing. The customers looked more
civilized than the barber, and had the appearance of successful business or
professional men. Couldn't they see I wasn't a Mexican? I felt betrayed by my
own class.

"You heard me, get out. This shop's only for whites."

I wanted to shout at him, "Don't you talk to me like that! I am not a
Mexican." I stood glaring at him, which a Mexican wasn't likely to do. But
again, I could not say a word. I did not want to tell him—and these other
men—my nationality. I did not want this barber to touch me, I recoiled from
him, just as he found me untouchable himself. He had a phony professional

look with his glasses, in his white coat, as if he were a surgeon, and was so very proud of being a white man in Grand Island, and a hundred per cent American. He had my blood boiling, and I did not care what happened to me if I struck him. I could have killed this barber. But I realized I could *never strike an American.* It would be like striking at America, slapping Uncle Sam in the face, smashing a dream, a vision, I knew I would never give up.

I turned on my heel and walked out of the shop, pondering on a discovery I just made about myself, that it was impossible for me to strike an American.

I stopped and watched the Mexicans again. The machines belched their hell-fire in the blaze of noon and the Mexicans toiled for their American masters, their faces and bodies smeared and blackened with asphalt. God pity them. I glanced at that sign again on the hamburger stand and thought these dark earthmen might prevail in the end, the USA and the USSR might burn each other out in nuclear war and the Mexican pop up from behind a cactus grinning under his sombrero and throwing his serape over his shoulder, Olé!

I put my sombrero away in the truck and entered another barbershop with a panicky feeling inside me. What would I do if this barber also took me for a Mexican and refused to cut my hair? By God, I'd go to Mexico and start a revolution of my own. But I was not untouchable here, thank Heaven. I did not speak a word for fear my accent would give me away, and I had turned so pale that I was a few shades lighter when I looked in the mirror.

"Medium?" asked the barber, tying the white hair cloth around my neck, over a strip of gauze, as sanitary laws required. I nodded, pretending to be absorbed in the magazine I was reading, an old copy of *Life* I had already read. "Clippers all around?" I nodded. "Trim the eyebrows?" I nodded. I did not let him stick his scissors into my nose, though. There was no sanitary law against this abominable practice, a good way of spreading colds. I said "Thank you" when he finished, got off the high chair, took out my wallet and handed him a $5 bill. He rang up the cash register and returned the change. I tipped him 25 cents; he was worth it. I was a gentleman and I hoped a white man once more. A close shave, though.

When we were driving back to the University, Scotty asked me, "Why so quiet?"

"Just thinking," I said.

I could not tell him there are moments that destroy a world.

I wrote a new poem, in Sycamore Creek, which was my retreat, my private
sanctuary in Nebraska, and comforted me even more than the library.
Here I felt rested, unburdened, renewed. Nature had this soothing, healing
power over me, and its harmonies seemed to straighten out my own twisted
thinking. I sat under the same apple tree, now bearing apples, turning red,
like my girl's cheeks, and the brook gleamed through the thick willow-
green. I heard a woodpecker drilling, and listened to the flute-like notes of
the blackbirds. The place was alive with birds, butterflies and ladybugs. My
cows grazed in the pasture behind the barns or rested in the shade, chewing
the cud.

> I see wheatfields that are in heat
> Soak up the Platte, and in their need
> Swollen so big with the sun's seed
> Kiss the rough hands, dancing bare feet
> And tomahawks of bronze-skinned gods
> For it's their joy to have all men
> Feed upon them, to be just wheat.

I became aware of the fact that my anxiety, which never left me despite
my euphoria on this campus, lessened, and I felt better and freer when I
wrote a poem—and at the same time, I felt more American too. Poetry might
well heal the inner split and bring my two disparate selves together and
make me whole again. This was my basic problem: how to be whole again.
A poem necessarily expressed an emotion—and I was trying to abolish
my emotions in America and to be all utilitarian logic and iron will. The
commissar of common sense. Emotions were messy affairs, explosions of
irrational dark forces within us, sheer anarchy, but the point was that the
heart took over when I wrote a poem, and try as I would I could not abolish
my heart.

Suddenly clouds gathered out of nowhere and the sun disappeared as
in an eclipse. A flash of lightning, then a cracking roll of thunder, the first I
heard in Nebraska, and sounding like the chariot God rode in the skies of
my childhood. Or was this a thunderbolt of the Indian gods crashing over
Nebraska? I watched a dark sheet of slanting rain move toward the campus,
and the first drops struck the ground like bullets and splashed against my
eager face. The rain scared away a swarm of sparrows. I ran to a giant oak
for cover as the rain came down in cataracts. I could see in the pasture the
cows huddled under the trees and against the fences in that awkward way
of theirs. The rain beat down the blackberry and raspberry bushes and the

flaming purple crowns of bull-thistles. It shook a loquat tree, which by some miracle grew in this soil. It was exactly like the summer showers of my childhood in Greece.

I leaped with joy and ran from tree to tree and jumped over to the other side of the muddied creek that boiled over and swirled along with willow leaves. With wild goat cries I danced into the wood, entering a kingdom I knew of old and where the earliest memories of man, and of my own, came back. The rain swept into the wood, too, driving leaves, twigs, bits of moss before it. I let the wet branches brush against my face and licked the sky-sweet drops with the tip of my tongue. Every opening through the trees was like a magic casement through which I saw green castles where goblins dwelled and my own face as a child flattened out against a window pane, watching the wonders of the rain.

I sat down under a canopy of branches in a dry spot and rubbed my hands gleefully. The wood was small, just a bower of oak and sycamore and hickory and basswood and cottonwood, but I had the sensation of being in the boundless aboriginal forests of America and at the same time—that was the wonderful thing about this summer shower—in the woods of my childhood. I could hear the drumming and thrashing of the rain in a cottage in a summer camp for homeless children, where I built houses with playing cards and staged cavalry battles with horses I modeled in a village clay pit and which had matchsticks for their legs and tails.

A dreamy lassitude gradually overcame me, and closing my eyes I leaned my head on the spicy moss of a rock. I could smell the tobacco leaves strung on the frames before each house in a village close by the Turkish border in Thrace. I breathed in the fragrance of basil and dill and verbena, of mountain mint and thyme, pungent with the aromatic foliage of Byzantine chapels. I sniffed at the heavy tantalizing odors of walnut trees and citrons soaked in the rain; the sharp delicate fragrance of little lemons we called limonakia; of stolen apples and pears gleaming with raindrops and sweeter because of them.

Sheep bells that rang in Macedonian meadows tinkle-tinkled on the tympanum of my memory. Shepherd pipes bubbled through the morning blue. The sound of the ax was bandied back and forth by the rocks. I listened to the drip-drip of water trickling down the walls of rock-hewn monasteries and heard a mountain torrent dashing against the walls of a narrow gorge passable only for the devil, and the roaring surf of Greek shores rang in my ears.

I thought the rain makes children of all of us.

This shower ended as abruptly as it began. The sun came out and lighted the lattice-work of the underbrush. The birds and rabbits came out of their hidings and pecked at the ground or nibbled at the grass and leaves. I crawled out of the wood, holding my verses under my T-shirt, and looking up, I saw a rainbow, somehow my first in America, and looking like Christ spreading his arms over Nebraska.

I was wet, but it did not matter. Maybe this summer shower was my baptism as an American, and it washed out the barbershop in Grand Island. Standing under the rainbow I no longer felt like a stranger in a strange land, no longer an alien. If there are moments that destroy a world, there are also moments that remake it.

Armenia

Armenian folk tales invariably begin in this delightful manner: "There was, there was not, there was"—a king or beggar, merchant or peasant, wise man or fool—and the story that follows is told as something that did and did not happen. In the same way, Armenia itself exists and does not exist.

To begin with, there are several Armenias: an ancient kingdom; Roman, Byzantine, Persian, Turkish, Russian Armenia; Versailles Treaty or Wilsonian Armenia, created on paper when America considered taking Armenia under her protective wing, and declined; the Armenian SSR; the Armenian Diaspora, with colonies all over the world; Armenia as a dream, a vision. There is no other country like her. She has played a unique and perhaps indispensable role as a buffer between Asia and Europe, a mediator between two seemingly irreconcilable civilizations. And her dark beauty is eternal.

If you ask a group of average Americans precisely where Armenia is, I doubt that you'll get a correct answer. It's a tricky question. Geographically Armenia lies on the Soviet-Turkish and Soviet-Iranian frontier, a formidable natural fortress thrust into the sky between the Caucasus and the Taurus. To the Greek and the Roman, to the Arab and the Persian, it was a remote, inaccessible land, awesome and silent. Much of it remains so to this day.

If you can get a Soviet visa, you can visit Russian Armenia comfortably enough by plane or train. Yerevan, the capital, is at the base of 17,000-foot Mt. Ararat, about twelve hours' flying time from Moscow. By train the route runs either along the Black Sea or the Caspian, through Georgia or

Azerbaijan; Moscow-Sukhumi-Tblisi-Yerevan, or Moscow-Baku-Yerevan (Tblisi being the official Georgian name for Tiflis). The Turkish portion of Armenia can be reached by plane from Ankara, or, if you happen to be in no hurry and want to see more, by the boat which follows the old Argonautic route to Trebizond, where I was born.

As your ship sails up the Bosporus, leaving Istanbul astern, the waters become perceptibly darker and the shadows lengthen in the wooded bays. You feel something distinctly northern, of the mountains, in the cooling air: prelude to Pontus and Armenia. Your ship stops at or passes by Zonguldak, Sinope, Samsun, Ordu, Giresun, and you'd call all of them "picturesque." This is the classic coast of the Black Sea, the most sea-like of all seas, which the Greeks called *Pontos Euxeinos*, the "hospitable" sea, or simply, *Pontos*, the sea. Turkish boys row out in medieval high-prowed rowboats to sell you the fruits of the season. You eat delicious grapes, plums, pears, apples, figs, melons, cherries. The word cherry, by the way, comes from Cerasus, the ancient name of Giresun. And Sinope was the birthplace of Diogenes.

At last you reach Trebizond (Trabzon in Turkish) in Versailles or Wilsonian Armenia, the Queen of the Euxine and a jewel of a city when I was a boy. Here Xenophon's Ten Thousand cried, *"Thalassa! Thalassa!"* "The sea! The sea!" as they came down from the Armenian mountains, groggy from the intoxicating honey they had eaten on the way. The city excited the Greeks, and it is still an exciting place though shorn of its former importance as an emporium of world commerce with a cosmopolitan population.

What you see from the deck is a radiant white town with red-roofed houses clustered at the foot and climbing up the slopes of a huge solitary rock 900 feet high. The bright green of its walled gardens, filled with oranges, pomegranates and figs, is interspersed with the dark green of cypresses, clumps of which indicate cemeteries. The top of the rock is table-flat, a trapezoid—whence, probably, the original name of the city, Trapezus. We boys liked to romp and somersault on it, intoxicated by the invigorating air and the smell of the springy turf with its little golden flowers we called "Tears of the Holy Virgin." This venerable rock snuggles the city to its breast like some Cyclopean divinity, and at night it looks like a cowled monk.

The convent near its summit fascinated me as a boy; it ascended like a white aerial stairway to the throne of God. The frescoes on the damp walls of this rock-hewn cloister glowed with a dark luminosity—saints, emperors and empresses in Byzantine vestments, lamenting forever the crucifixion of Christ. There was an everlasting sadness in their almond-shaped eyes, they looked tortured by the world's evils and very much alone in these sacred caves. What moved me even more was the bewilderment I read in their flat, pious faces—the dread of the rude archers from the East, the mounted hordes of Alp-Arslan and the terrible Turkish infantry that followed under Mohammed II.

A few miles west of Trebizond's ancient walls, where the Greco-Roman world stopped the barbarian manswarm of Goths, and waves of Turcomans, lies the neat little town of Platana with its olive groves, facing a bay so well sheltered from the winds that sweep down from the Russian steppes and the Caucasus that ships take refuge there in stormy weather. To the east of the city you can see the sharp crest of Lazisran, the old Colchis, in the wooded magic of which the Argonauts sought the Golden Fleece. The magic is still there. You are on the Turkish edge of the Black Sea Riviera that runs all the way to the Crimea. No doubt many will differ, but to me no other region on the five continents can match this south-east corner on the Black Sea—not even the European Riviera, or Southern California, or any other stretch of coast you care to name.

Here you can see lateen-rigged Turkish coasters scudding along like great white-winged birds kicking back showers of spray, or floating at anchor like painted swans in deep-blue bays. The mountains with their pine forests rise tier upon tier from the very edge of the water. The cargo boats in the harbor of Trebizond have high, incurving bows and sterns, like Roman or Egyptian galleys, and they are rowed by stalwart Turks of the Laz tribe, who stand up and drop to their seats together. The Lazes form the substratum of Trebizond's population. Georgian by race, Moslem by faith, they man Turkey's ships and make the best foot soldiers in her armies. Mustafa Kemal's personal bodyguard was composed of Lazes, and as pirates and cutthroats they have a history scarcely equaled anywhere.

Ashore in Trebizond, you find yourself in a town with narrow, breakneck streets and the battlemented grandeur of antiquity. There are rows of silent houses with their upper stories jutting out; public fountains with a wild tangle of Arabic inscriptions from the Koran, or with a modest Christian cross on a marble facade. Swallows build their nests under eaves and balconies. Wisterias and climbing roses cascade over doors and garden walls. There are fan-shaped lights over the doors, and brass knockers in the form of lyres or doves.

"*Varda!*" "Look out!" (from the Italian *guarda*) shout the *hamals*, those human vans of the East, as they make their way through the traffic under heavy loads, competing with motorcars and horsedrawn vehicles. You are likely to see a few GI's riding in jeeps, for the Soviet border is only a hundred miles away and this is a closely guarded military zone. The harbor and the roads are being improved with American aid, and there are other evidences of progress, but barefoot men still tin copper utensils here, and goldsmiths turn out bracelets, broaches, rings and earrings in exquisite filigree. There are also combmakers, basket weavers, potters, artisans making clogs or printing flower patterns on cloth. The old marketplace is a labyrinth of medieval lanes.

My father's pharmacy was in the center of Trebizond, on the main business street. Its name, *Central Pharmacy*, was written in gold letters on its broad panes in French, Turkish, Armenian and Greek. It was exclusively a prescription pharmacy; my father would have been puzzled, not to say horrified, by the modern American drugstore. In the back room a Greek physician, Dr. Andreas Metaxas, examined his patients, some who came on mules and donkeys from distant villages.

We lived in a little residential street that was walled at one end to bar traffic. Its flagstone pavement was so clean you could spread your bed on it and sleep, as we said. But it was not closed to peddlers. First to come by in the morning was the baker, with his donkey loaded with two panniers of bread fresh from the oven, and he kept his accounts with us by cutting notches on a tally stick kept in our dining room. He was followed by one or two *simitjis*, young Turks who sold crisp sesame rings in round wooden trays suspended from their necks. Then came the vegetable men in their hobnailed shoes, one carrying a basket on his back and the other holding a primitive weighing instrument with pebbles of various sizes for weights. My mother always bargained with them, bringing the prices down a penny or two, before she bought the day's supply. Village women in the costumes of Byzantine frescoes cried in shy voices *"Xino ghala!"* as they sold milk and yoghurt in clay jugs of classic form. The fishmongers shouted in hearty voices, *"Barbunya! Mezit! Khalkhan!"* (I don't know their English names, but these are the best fish in the world) or *"Hamsi! Hamsi!"* "Anchovies! Anchovies!"—which were so abundant and cheap at the height of the run that peasants used them as fertilizer. At night we heard the cries of popcorn vendors, and at intervals our watchman struck the flagstones with his iron-tipped staff to report that all was well.

When my father came home in the evening we all gathered in the living room, which was furnished *a la Turca*, with a map of Italy and a blackboard on the wall. Father loved wall maps. After slipping off his black shoes with the elastic at the sides, he would sit cross-legged on a little mattress by the stove. Victoria, our maid, a very beautiful girl born in a village and taken into our home when she was nine, would bring him the silver tray with his aperitif, a daily family rite. Father would pour himself a spot of *raki* (mastic brandy) from a decanter in a silver holder, add a little water, which turned the drink milky white, and toss if off as we all said, *"Anush ella,"* "May it be sweet." Then he would wipe his mouth with a cloth napkin, exhale with a sound of noisy enjoyment, and help himself to a bit of caviar, or Roquefort cheese, or a pickle, or squeeze a few drops of lemon juice on a raw oyster and swallow it.

"I am a lord, a lord!" he would shout, meaning an English lord, the epitome of good living and worldly comforts. "Here are my four children, here is my woman. What more can a man ask?" And my mother would blush, for he said "woman" as if he meant "wench." Mother was thirteen years younger than my father, and taller. She was the "Circassian princess" type, with ivory-white skin and long light brown hair tied in a knot at the back of her head, while father was swarthy. According to family legend, she was so beautiful in her youth, before she married at nineteen, that a handsome Austrian prince, exiled to Trebizond for some mischief in Vienna or Istanbul, had fallen in love with her and wanted to marry her. She was the daughter of a rich merchant who played backgammon with the Turkish governor-general and headed the Armenian community in Trebizond before he was shot down in the central square by order of Sultan Abdul Hamid—to suppress an Armenian "rebellion."

Our dining room was strictly European, except for a copper brazier on which we toasted bread. A map of Greece hung on the wall. We called supper tea. It lasted an hour, and we children had to mind our table manners. When we returned to the living room my father would resume his cross-legged position by the stove and read *Byzantion*, a conservative Armenian daily published in Istanbul and opposed to our revolutionary hotheads. A frustrated teacher, my father believed that mathematics is mother of all knowledge. The two other requirements for a good education were Greek and music. He sent my sister Nevart to a Greek school—an insult to the Armenian community, which was proud of its schools—and my brother Onnik took private lessons in Greek. Nevart studied piano, Onnik violin. I was too young.

At night my father would entertain us by playing his violin and singing church hymns. Or he would stand up, stamping his foot and waving his arms, and lead us in singing his favorite songs. When we had guests, which was often, there would be a musical program in our drawing room, which was furnished *a la Franca,* with some of the furniture imported from Paris. Onnik had to play his violin, accompanied by Nevart at the piano, and I would stand on a chair and recite a poem at the top of my voice. Later the women and children would retire to the living room and let the men play baccarat and *chemin de fer.* My father was a noisy player, always clowned, and always lost, which he thought the proper thing for a host to do. Midnight snacks were served. On special holidays my father engaged a European orchestra, the guests danced waltzes and quadrilles in our home, and several cases of champagne were consumed.

Easter was our greatest holiday. School closed for two weeks. Holy Week began with a vigorous house cleaning. Mother was busy preparing our Easter Sunday feast (a whole lamb stuffed with rice and roasted in our neighborhood bakery), baking paschal cakes, dyeing eggs, sewing new outfits and buying new shoes for us children. On Maundy Thursday she took us to the public bathhouse, a onetime Byzantine church renamed the Bathhouse of Infidels— *Giaour Hamami.* We took along a few bundles containing Turkish towels, clogs inlaid with mother-of-pearl, silver bowls (heirlooms) for pouring water, and a basket of food with a bottle or two of lemonade, for this was an all-day ceremonial affair. The manager was a handsome, white-faced Turkish woman who smoked cigarettes and sat on a dais by the door. She and mother exchanged compliments as we entered. We undressed in the cool outer hall, which had a fountain and a fish pond in the center, and bathed in the inner hall, a torrid steam-laden rotunda filled with an infernal din.

Rubens should have painted that bathhouse. The women of Trebizond are famous for their beauty, and during the Middle Ages they were the city's most valuable export. They were sought in marriage by Western and Eastern rulers alike—by the Duke of Burgundy and the emperors in Constantinople, no less than by the Turcoman chief of the White Sheep, and the kings of Georgia—all of whom sent ambassadors to Trebizond to find wives for them. Genoese and Venetian merchants, who had colonies in the city and controlled the commerce of the Black Sea, spread the fame of Trebizond women as the loveliest in the world, and their charms supplied the troubadours of France with an inexhaustible theme.

On the evening of Maundy Thursday, flushed from our long bath, we went to church, where the bishop washed the feet of twelve choir boys, myself among them. This was a dramatic ceremony, an imitation of Christ's humble gesture toward His Disciples, and when it was over we were supposed to kiss the jeweled episcopal cross which lay on the velvet-bound silver-mounted Bible beside the bishop. One time, when I was eight, I disgraced myself by attempting to kiss my foot instead. As I struggled with it, trying to bring the spot that had been touched with holy ointment to my lips, the congregation roared.

On Easter Day everyone wore his best. Even the poorest children had at least a pair of new shoes. Sophisticated women came out in the latest Paris styles, even though the bishop had denounced them as sinful. And for two days afterward, people made and received calls, greeting each other with the Easter salutation "Christ is risen from the dead"—and answering with the traditional response—"Blessed is the Resurrection of Christ."

The next greatest holiday, excepting New Year's, was Ascension Week, when we used to spend a few days at the Armenian monastery overlooking the site of Xenophon's camp. Built on a hill just off the highway to Erzurum, it had thick walls and a tower like a fort. Mother rented an apartment for us in the pilgrims' house, which had a gallery running along its entire length. From here we could look out over the walled-in quadrangle, where latecomers and poorer people stayed in tents. Soon the villagers came, and musicians with their bagpipes and drums—*davoul zourna*—and their *kemanchas,* native fiddles played upside down. The men wore the Laz garb: tight black jackets with long sleeves and two decorative cartridge pockets across the breast; black breeches very roomy at the seat and glove-tight at the legs; a black cloth hood knotted smartly around the head with its two ends flapping on the shoulders; cowhide moccasins or heelless shoes with toes ending in a leather thong turned backward.

The village women sported gorgeous costumes. Their skirts rustled as they moved, and their red or blue velvet jackets, embroidered with gold or silver thread, fitted tightly around their sumptuous bosoms. Gold coins were strung around their disk-like red velvet caps (part of their dowry), and silver buckles shone on their red velvet shoes.

As our peasants danced, the village virgins stood coyly on display and the young men picked and wooed their future wives. Men and women danced in a circle, hand in hand, round and round, backward and forward, the basic circular dance of the Near East and the Balkans. The village men had martial dances of their own. They formed a closed circle, interlocking little fingers and raising their hands above their heads. With a warlike cry, *"Alashaghah!"* they dropped or crouched together on one knee; then jumped up and came down again on the other, every muscle in their lithe strong bodies quivering with tension.

The sacrificial rams, lighted tapers fastened to their spiral horns, were led around the church three times in a religious procession, then butchered under the chestnut and walnut trees just outside the gate and roasted. The meat was served in free communal meals for the salvation of the souls of our dead, while a couple of blind minstrels played their fiddles and sang of heroic deeds or metaphoric rhapsodies of love, either improvising or performing works by Sayat Nova, Ashugh Jivani and other celebrated troubadours.

> Your voice is sweet, your speech full of flavor;
> May he whom you serve protect you, my love.
> Your waist is the gazelle's and rose your color,
> Brocade from Frankistan you are, my love.
>
> If I compare you to brocade, it will fray;
> If to a plane tree, it will be felled one day;
> All girls are likened, to gazelles, you'll say;
> How shall I describe your miracle, my love?

From Trebizond you can go to Erzurum by bus, heading into the interior of Armenia by a highway that was once the golden road to Samarkand. Erzurum "Roman fortress"—is headquarters of the Turkish Third Army, deployed along the rugged 350-mile Armenian-Georgian frontier from the Black Sea to Mt. Ararat. A cold, grim city, with miles of army barracks and crooked, narrow, undrained streets, Erzurum hardly excels in the arts of peace and the more pleasant aspects of modern living, but it does produce fine *basterma*, slabs of highly seasoned dried beef eaten in very thin slices—excellent after a shot of *raki*.

You are now on a treeless plateau, 6250 feet above sea level, under the grand dominions of the eagle and the hawk. But wheat is grown even at this altitude, and flocks of sheep graze on mountain slopes, their little bells tinkling in the frosty air. The sheep dogs are big hairy beasts with spiked steel rings around their necks to protect them from the jaws of wolves. Each flock is led by a vanguard of male goats, bearded warriors of the range, whose bells are larger and make deeper, clanging tones. The sheep have fat tails and belong to the hardy karakul breed.

From Erzurum you can go to Kars by rail or bus. Take the bus. You will pass more army barracks at Sarikamish, 7500 feet above sea level, but the pine woods hereabouts will make you think you are in Switzerland, except that the winters are colder, with temperatures down to 30° below zero. Kars, which has changed hands many times, is another famous fortress city of great strategic importance—the key to the Caucasus. With its straight broad streets, built by Russians, it looks much more European than Erzurum.

East of Kars, you travel by rail for thirty-five miles to the closely guarded Turkish-Soviet frontier. Then you are in Soviet Armenia and change to a Russian train to go to Yerevan. This city, once Persian, has grown fast in the last two decades and is a modern town today with a population of 400,000. You have descended to the comparatively low plain of Ararat, only 3000 feet high, and the sun is warmer here. In the surrounding irrigated vineyards and orchards grow grapes that melt in your mouth and apricots—*Prunus armeniaca*—that make you wonder if they dropped from heaven, such is their aroma.

Remember that Noah planted his own vineyard when he climbed out of the Ark. Armenian vintners have Noah's original recipe for making wine, and Yerevan will not bow even in the direction of France. I hope someday you taste Armenian cognac and champagne. You are now close enough to Iran to feel the presence of the nightingale and the rose, and many of the city's new buildings are roseate, being constructed of a light volcanic rock called tuff, which is quarried in all the colors of the rainbow, with pinks predominant.

Twin-peaked Ararat towers over Yerevan, and surely no other city in Europe or elsewhere has such a majestic setting. There are no other mountains in Ararat's immediate vicinity, as though the Armenian Giant would tolerate none. That's what makes it appear so high. I have compared Kazbek with Ararat; they are about the same in height, but the Georgian Giant seems half as big. Great Ararat, with its cloudlike summit, looks like a mighty Biblical lord, with Little Ararat, a perfect cone, beside him as his gracious consort. They look like a royal couple reigning truly by the grace of God, with a kingdom of amber, amethysts and rubies spread at their feet. Though they seem very close to Yerevan, these peaks lie twenty-two miles away in Turkish territory. The Turkish name for Ararat is Aghri Dagh, which I admit has the right rocky sound. Nevertheless, the picture of Ararat is on Armenia's state seal, for this mountain is the eternal symbol of our people, regardless of international treaties.

Said a Turk to an Armenian: "By what right do you use the picture of Aghri Dagh on your state seal when you don't own it?"

The Armenian shot back: "You show a crescent on yours. Do you own the moon?"

Northeast of Yerevan flashes the vast blue flame of Lake Sevan. This lovely alpine sea is the highest lake in Europe; its water is fresh, its fish delectable. It supplies hydro-electric power for Armenia's industries. (Articles in the European and American press have placed the Russian *atomgrad* here; can't vouch for it.) Sevan is ringed with icy peaks in winter. I'll never forget a blizzard near its shores. I groped blindly after an oxcart, my breath turning to ice and locking my lips. I was mercilessly whipped by "dragon-voiced" winds loosed from the crags of Mt. Ararat. The storm ceased at last (I prayed, believe me), and I saw wolves and foxes skulking in the white night, their eyes blazing like live coals. This is a rich land in furred animals; we get "ermine" from "Armenian."

The population of the Armenian republic is nearing two million; a million more Armenians live in neighboring Georgia and Azerbaijan. It is the smallest of the sixteen republics in the Soviet Union, and all that is left of Armenia as a political entity. Another million or so of our people live in Iran, Turkey, Syria, Lebanon, Egypt, Greece, France, Bulgaria, Rumania, South America and the United States.

A few miles from Yerevan, in Armenia's oldest monastery at Etchmiadzin, lives the Catholicos and Supreme Patriarch of All Armenians. The Armenian Apostolic Church, founded by the Apostles Bartholomew and Thaddeus according to our tradition, is independent of both the Greek Orthodox and the Roman Catholic Churches.

My cousin Karekin fell in love with a Greek girl named Soteria, a proud slender beauty living in an old ramshackle house with her mother, a hunchbacked widow. This woman would cross herself with three fingers and cry to heaven that if her daughter married an Armenian, who crossed himself with five fingers, they would be damned forever. Late one night Karekin got together a few tough-looking fellows, who didn't mind a bit of shooting in defense of our church, and entered Soteria's house brandishing his revolver. "Soteria is leaving with me right now," he announced. "An Armenian priest will marry us." The mother cowered in a corner as a few shots were fired around the house, and crossed herself (with three fingers), saying, "Holy Mother of God!" Karekin seized Soteria by the waist and carried her off. She was only too happy to marry him at the point of a gun. Her mother was ultimately reconciled—but only after she was convinced that Armenians also crossed themselves with three fingers, only a careless minority using five—and in the end they all lived peacefully together.

It seems we were Phrygians once, of the tribe of King Midas and his gold. Greek historians, from Herodotus on, place our original habitat in Thrace, as early neighbors of the Macedonians. Unlike the Turk, the Arab, the Georgian, we speak an Indo-European language related to Greek and English. As the Armeno-Phrygians migrated to Asia Minor, they picked up the Hittite nose on their way. We are a nose-conscious nation, and nothing is so persistent as a nose. But the aquilines are not the majority everywhere.

Of Western origin, living in the East, the Armenian combines the two within himself, and this duality in the unity of our people is the key to a complex, confusing phenomenon. East and West have fought it out in Armenia for at least two thousand years. And Europe and Asia have merged in Armenia. Hence our unique place in world culture.

In the development of architecture, for instance, Armenia played an extremely important part—witness the clean-cut geometric beauty of the Armenian church, with its stone dome over a square. Armenians took certain architectural laws from the East, notably from Persia, perfected them and passed them on to Byzantium and the West.

Every other Armenian is a poet. ("And a rug dealer," I can hear some saying, but there is poetry in Oriental rugs.) Lyric poetry is an expression of a people's innermost feelings, and ours shows the fusion of East and West. It is at once European and Oriental, or perhaps I should say neither, but rather an art that is peculiarly and profoundly Armenian. I have in mind especially our medieval and early lyrics. They have the brilliance and color of Persian poetry, but are more restrained. Passion is held in check. You don't find the Armenian poet indulging in the gaudy abandon of the Persian and the Arab; his is not the song of the seraglio. The nightingale sings in these poems and the gazelle exhibits her graces, which are those of the poet's beloved, but the girl doesn't live in a harem and is never a mere object of lust. She is extremely modest. Before marriage she is expected to be a chaste virgin, and as a wife absolutely faithful. Until recent years infidelity and divorce were unknown among us. We are a hot-blooded but moral race, with something puritanic in our national character. And our poetry is full of sorrow, the sadness of mortality and time, the grief of lost glory, of Armenia's subjection to this or that foreign foe.

Similarly, our music is Western-Eastern, a harmonious blending of opposing forces. You have probably heard the compositions of Aram Khatchaturian. His Sabre Dance has made the juke box. The fire and color

of the East are in his concertos Gayne ballet, cantatas and toccata. There is
other music like it in Europe or Asia. It is Armenian—vigorous, dramatic,
dreamy, melancholy. Khatchaturian speaks to the Armenian soul, and
at the same time interprets the modern temper. He derives much of his
inspiration from our folk songs. They are sunny songs about bubbling
waters and the snow peaks that shine like drawn swords on the blue
Armenian sky, with words set to vibrant melodies that spurt from the
heart. The trees and the flowers of the fields are in these songs, the cry of
the exile pining for his native land, the somber joy of the plowman as he
drives the oxen.

Our merchant also has brought East and West closer together. He has
been the middleman between Europe and Asia. He led the caravans of the
world from India and China to Persia, from Persia to Turkey and Russia,
he bought and sold in Calcutta and Tabriz, in Aleppo and Trebizond, in
Moscow and Venice, in Hamburg and Amsterdam. He spoke the languages
of East and West with equal fluency, as no other merchant could, not even
the Greek and the Jew, both of whom to this day have a healthy respect for
his shrewdness.

There was, there was not, there was a merchant who went to Baghdad—
or Istanbul, or Ispahan on business and saved his neck from the executioner's
ax by outsmarting evil men, finding the right answer to a riddle or to a
question put to him: this is a recurring theme in our folk tales. We admire
verbal ingenuity. At the last moment the harassed hero quips his way to
freedom or turns the tables on his enemies.

I remember a story my father told. He was in Istanbul taking his final oral
examinations for his degree. Pharmacy came under the medical school in
those days, and he had to know a good deal of medicine.

"Name all the drugs you know that produce heavy perspiration in a
patient," asked a doctor with the title of pasha, who acted as the personal
representative of Sultan Abdul Hamid. The room was full of government
dignitaries.

My father mentioned several drugs, but the pasha wasn't satisfied. "You
have missed an important one, Karapet effendi."

My father named one or two more. The pasha shook his head and
told my father he would fail if he could not remember this particular
drug. Grave heads nodded. My father thought hard. "Your Excellency,"
he said at last, taking out his handkerchief and wiping the perspiration
off his face, "to make the patient sweat I would have him take this
examination."

The laughter was loud. The sultan's representative laughed, too, and my father was graduated—with a gold medal.

When I was editing an Armenian paper I used to get articles trying to prove that the Anglo-Saxons originated in Armenia—that Columbus and Napoleon were Armenians—that God speaks in Armenian. We sing in one of our popular songs: *Armenia, land of the Garden of Eden, Thou the cradle of the human race.*

To us Armenia is mother of the world, and on that basis you can trace everything and everybody to Armenia. I used to smile at Napoleon's supposed Armenian origin; actually, there is some evidence that his forebears came from Trebizond, but if so it was a Greek family that settled in Corsica, translating its name literally from Kalo-meroi to Buonaparte. But I find in a history of Armenia, by Dr. Artasches Abeghian, a recognized authority, that Murat, Napoleon's general and brother-in-law, was an Armenian. Napoleon's personal bodyguard was an Armenian, and when he abolished all the monastic orders in Italy he made one exception—the Armenian Monastery in Venice, where Byron studied our language. You will never know who will turn out to be an Armenian next.

We dote on such information. We want you to know that Michael Arlen, who looks Irish, is our Dikran Kouyoumdjian. Our pulse quickens when we see Rouben Mamoulian's name on the screen, and we enjoy *Oklahoma!* better because an Armenian directed it. We see William Saroyan's plays and read his books with the proud feeling that he is one of us and that he proclaims it loudly.

My friend Archie is a grocer, a prosperous one. When you enter his home you see a large portrait of Tigranes the Great (another spelling of Dikran) hanging in the hallway. When Tigranes, king of Armenia, saw the Roman legions under Lucullus he said contemptuously, "If they come as ambassadors they are too many. If they come as soldiers, they are too few." Archie's heart glows every time he looks at this picture. Tigranes lived two thousand years ago, but it doesn't matter. Past and present are mixed in the consciousness of the Armenian.

But much as the Armenian loves his homeland, he has always felt a little out of place in his native environment. He doesn't quite fit there. The Turk, the Georgian, the Iranian doesn't emigrate as a rule—the Armenian has always headed West. He is for Europe heart and soul—and has paid dearly for it.

We have been a small nation, squeezed in between colossal neighbors
and often trampled under their feet. We have been in close contact with the
great civilizations of the world from the very beginning of our history, and
in the path of marching empires. We did some marching ourselves. We were
the first nation in the world to accept Christianity—and have battled for it
constantly, either with our own armies or through the Armenian emperors
and generals of Byzantium, and there were many of them. We have been put
to the sword, wiped out time and again, yet by some miracle have survived
to defy our foes. Our history is an unending series of wars and bloodshed, of
insurrections and resurrections.

But now we are haunted by our old fears of national extinction as never
before. Armenians have been completely uprooted from four fifths of their
homeland. No more Armenians live in Trebizond, in Erzurum, in Van, in Kars.
In the past, large Armenian colonies have melted away in Poland, Hungary,
and Rumania, becoming part of the general population. So we wonder how
long we can last this time, afraid our nearly three million kinsmen in the
USSR will be Russianized eventually—though not in Armenia, I am sure—and
knowing we cannot survive in our foreign colonies.

"After we die no more Armenians will be left." You hear this complaint in
all Armenian gatherings.

We get together to hear our music and poetry, and to enjoy tribal dinners.
Choice bits of lamb marinated overnight in wine and spices and barbecued
on skewers, and served with pilaf, made either with rice or cracked wheat.
And before we get to them we eat a rich flaky pastry filled with ground
meat or with cheese, and sample a variety of cold and hot dishes elaborately
prepared with eggplant, tomatoes, green peppers, green beans, sugar peas,
artichokes, vine leaves. Our bread is baked in flat sheets and is delicious.
Our etiquette requires that there should be at least twice as much food on
the table as can be eaten.

"Don't refuse, I beg you. Try another bite of this."

"What kind of Armenian Christian are you? You haven't eaten anything."

And more food is piled on your plate. The best food in the world. We get
up and dance hand in hand, round and round, the leader waving a twisted
handkerchief, while native musical instruments play the old familiar songs.
And constantly we argue over how to save Armenia.

Uprooted, divided, scattered, Armenians cling to their identity with all their
might, unwilling to give up their dream, while the dissolving torrents of time

flow past the remaining ramparts and the walls crumble under our feet.

The Armenian is mad, of course. A fool in the cruel court of time, singing his undying song. Babylonia, Assyria, the Hittite Empire, Parthia, Medea, Rome, Byzantium—all have vanished from the stage of history, but Armenia, their contemporary, lives to this day.

Our poets still write, architects build, musicians compose, merchants contribute to national causes. There is no letup. Classes are held in dilapidated old buildings in the slums of Beirut and Aleppo, in Arab villages along the Euphrates (which flows down, as does the Tigris, from our mountains). Ragged, barefoot, bright-eyed children, whose parents have been DP's for forty years, learn the Armenian alphabet, sing our folk songs, recite the cherished words of our national poets. You may see the ravages of hunger on their faces—but Tigranes the Great still enters Antioch at the head of 500,000 troops and routs the Parthian cavalry, the battle under St. Vardan the Brave is fought again for Church and Nation, and Armenia continues to guard the eastern marches of Christendom, vanguard of Western civilization in the East.

And while East and West clash in the immemorial fight, they remain one in the soul of the Armenian. For an example of what a peaceful and united world could be like, I give you my Armenia.

M. Farid

He was a fat swarthy man wearing conservative English clothes and a black bowler hat, a gold chain hanging on his ample vest, and with so foreign an appearance that I walked up to him and introduced myself when the weekly student assembly was over and we were coming out of the auditorium. I had not seen him at the meetings of the International Club. He turned out to be an Egyptian, and his name was Mohammed Farid. *"Turkje biliorsun?"* I said.

"No, I can't speak Turkish," he said, "Just a few words. How long have you been here?"

"This is my third year. I am a junior. You are new?"

"Yes, I am still feeling my way about, getting oriented."

"You'll like this university," I said. "You've come to a good school."

"It has a good reputation. I heard about it in England."

That pleased me. Its fame had reached England. He said he attended an English engineering college before coming to America. He took a card from his wallet, jotted down his address on it with a gold pencil, and asked me to have dinner with him. "It's nice to meet someone from my part of the world," he said.

I did not know how friendly I wanted to get with a man called Mohammed, even though on the card his name was simply "M. Farid."

La ilah ill'Allak, Mohammed rassoul Allah, "There is no God but Allah and Mohammed is his prophet," were to me terrible words, and my father had refused to recite them as a boy, preferring death to the renunciation of his Christian faith, and had miraculously survived the massacre of the Armenians in his town.

But this Mohammed with his bowler hat and English accent looked harmless enough and I thought I'd risk a dinner with him. I tried to be diplomatic. I thought a man like him might be useful in saving Armenian and Greek lives in Egypt if there was an outbreak of Mussulman fanaticism and armed mobs attacked foreigners and infidels, as had happened in the past. The Arab world was aflame, and I knew how strong was the Pan-Islamic movement among certain intellectuals and the rank and file of the Turkish people in a country that had abolished the Sultanate and Caliphate but was reintroducing the teaching of Islam in the schools, and where violent Islamic sentiments, linked with Pan-Turkism, were by no means dead. They had the tacit support of some government leaders.

Farid lived in the home of a professor of engineering, who opened the door when I rang the bell and took me to a room upstairs. A Moslem living in a Christian home—that in itself was something unusual for me. To the American professor Farid was just another foreign student and renting him a room made for "international goodwill and understanding." This professor would probably call a mosque a Moslem church, but I was still fighting the Crusades, and to me Farid was somebody who had wandered to America from the enemy camp.

The Egyptian had been reading his Arabic newspapers. I saw daggers and snakes in that familiar script, so strange in Nebraska, so out of place. This was the real thing and not the Shrine version of it.

"Make yourself comfortable," he said, offering me a chair. "I've asked a friend to join us—an Arab from Palestine. I think you'll enjoy meeting him."

I wondered. What was this, a Moslem invasion? There were already two students from Pakistan who passed around propaganda pamphlets written by Indian apologists of Islam. One of these authors, a Dr. Sir Mohammed something, writing in an impressive scholarly style, and even with a certain poetic grace, went so far as to say that there is no fundamental difference between Christianity and Islam, but I knew better. The Pakistanis talked about the essential principles of Islam being democracy, freedom, tolerance, social justice and progress, and were engaged in a missionary activity in Brighton, holding out the ideal of Pan-Islamism as the cure for all the ills of the modern world, which made me smile. Meanwhile there were bloody riots in India and the Moslems there massacred the Hindus. The Hindus, I was glad to read in the papers, struck back. Non-violence might work against the British, but not against the sword of Mohammed.

A family portrait on Farid's dresser attracted my attention. As I was looking at it, he said, "That's my brother in London with his English wife and children."

How could an English woman marry a Moslem? She looked happy too. As a family picture it was charming, but its implications disturbed me. She had probably adopted her husband's faith, as Islamic law required. I wanted to tell him an Armenian woman would never marry a Moslem voluntarily; we had lived with the Turks more than a thousand years but there was never any inter-marriage between Turks and Armenians, except by force, and if such a tragedy happened the woman ceased being Armenian. That's how we managed to preserve our Christian faith.

On his bedside table Farid had two large Arabic volumes. "They are dream books," he said, when I glanced through them. "Rather valuable. They belonged to my father, and before him to his father. Books like this aren't printed any more."

"You believe in dreams?" I said.

"Don't you? This is a very wise old book. You tell me your dreams and we'll look them up in this book and find out what they mean," he added smiling.

"I'm afraid my dreams are a little too dirty," I said, smiling myself.

He did not smile again. Something about his manner indicated that for a Moslem he was strict in morals, if not a prude, and I liked this quality in him. Of course I myself was above such oriental superstitions. I was reading Freud and Jung.

Presently his friend came in. He was younger, about my age, light-skinned, with short curly black hair, and spoke perfect English through his Bedouin nose. His name was Jelal Ahmed. And Ahmed is another variation of Mohammed.

"My father's name was Jelal for a while, when he was made a Turk after his parents were massacred and he pretended to have become a Moslem until he escaped," I told them.

"The Armenians have suffered much," said Farid. "We like them in Egypt. Perhaps you know that at one time we had an Armenian prime minister in Egypt, Nubar Pasha. There is a monument to him in Alexandria."

I was glad to hear him mention Nubar Pasha, who reformed and modernized Egypt and presided at the opening of the Suez Canal.

"Nubar Pasha introduced many improvements in your country," I said.

"He was an excellent administrator," said Farid.

Ahmed also spoke a few words of sympathy, and praised the Armenians in Palestine for not siding with the Zionists during the Arab-Jewish war, and for not taking up arms against the Arabs in Syria and Lebanon when the French tried to "bribe" them and provoke them against the Arabs, he said, when the Arabs demanded independence. He mentioned the names of some Armenian students in the American University of Beirut he had attended for two years.

Farid took us to a good restaurant, and it struck me as strange that I should be dining with two Moslems. In Turkey my family had no social relations with Moslems, the barrier of religion was too great even after the republican reforms, and I went to an Armenian and not a Turkish school. Armenian history was a forbidden subject, but it was taught secretly when none of our Turkish teachers appointed by the government were present and if one or two suspected something was going on in their absence they closed their eyes to it when they pocketed their *backshish*. Ironically, it was here in Nebraska that I met Arabs for the first time, and was dining with Moslems for the first time. I broke bread with them, as it were, to forget our past differences and the Arab-Armenian wars. But it was impossible for me to say "Mohammed," and I called the Egyptian by his last name, and the Palestinian by his first name, to avoid calling him Ahmed, although Jelal brought back my father's ghastly memories of Shabin Karahisar. They called me Valadian.

After dinner we went to a movie. Farid was an ardent movie fan. By the time I returned to my room I was their friend. They ate, walked, smiled or laughed like me. We had so many thoughts and sentiments in common that I almost forgot they were Moslem Arabs.

From that day on I was their constant companion. Jelal was Americanized in Beirut and I didn't mind it too much when I saw a Koran in his room. He probably brought it with him for sentimental reasons and, if he ever read it, he read it secretly. I never saw him doing his *namaz*, the chief prayer of Moslems, recited five times daily. He wore a hat. He was studying agricultural engineering to teach Palestine Arabs American methods of farming. He wanted the Arabs to catch up with the Zionists, as he always called the Israelis. Zionists had bombed his family out of Ramleh, and he was waiting for the second round with Jews.

Jelal's father, once a rich landowner, was a refugee in Jordan. Evidently the father made great sacrifices to have his son study in America. I took him to be an Arab gentleman of the old school. He had refused to sell any of his land to the Zionists, though they had offered him large sums for it. Jelal's grandfather had been a school teacher and an official of the Turkish ministry of education when Palestine was part of Turkey. Sometimes the check Jelal expected from his father did not come, which put him in a difficult position, but Farid was glad to loan him the money he needed. I understood father and son were very close, and Jelal was his family's hope, and perhaps of many other displaced Arabs, for a better life, through the American technical and scientific skills he was acquiring in Brighton. It touched me. Moslem-wise, Jelal never mentioned his mother and sisters and the womenfolk, but it was my impression they were all very dear to him and he was dear to them, and they were bound together by affectionate family ties. Just like us, I thought.

Jelal was a good student, and made himself so likeable that he became president of the International Club, while the only office I managed to get elected to in this organization was that of marshal, to which I gave its more military meaning when, standing erect like a soldier, I swore the new members in. I voted for Jelal as president.

Farid was so shy that I could not drag him to any meeting or lecture or party with me, and he would not even join the International Club. He was too self-conscious. He thought everybody would be looking at him and see how ungainly he was in appearance. He exercised regularly with a couple of dumbbells he kept in his closet and claimed to be all muscle, but he was built somewhat on the proportions of King Farouk, though with his short wiry hair and thick lips, he looked much more Egyptian than the king, who is, if I am not mistaken, largely of Albanian descent.

Farid was no scholar. I tried to help him with his lessons, and he studied hard enough, but it was tough going. He wanted to specialize in geology. He lived on the income of his cotton plantation in Egypt and was probably the richest student on the campus. In a pinch, foreign students could borrow from him. He was generous with his money and always picked up the check.

I took Farid and Jelal to Dean Miller's home for a Christmas dinner, and I was always glad to introduce them to my friends. Jelal got around, made speeches in Brighton churches, presenting the Arab side of the complicated Palestine question, and soon he had his own circle of American friends.

Everybody liked Jelal, and I thought he and the Egyptian were inseparable friends, but he fell out with Farid, and they stopped seeing each other. Neither would tell me what happened. I tried to bring them together, without success.

"For the love of Allah tell me what happened," I said to Farid. "Why don't you want to see him any more?"

"Very well, I'll tell you. He has been using black magic on me."

"Black magic!" I exclaimed. "You aren't serious. Jelal wouldn't harm anyone, and least of all a fellow-Arab."

"I was never more serious in my life. I know him better than you do. He is perfectly capable of it."

"So you believe in black magic? Don't be funny."

"I'm not being funny, I caught him just in time." He snapped his fingers. "Don't mention him to me any more. You can be friends with him if you like. I'm through. Valadian, sometimes you're so innocent. Jelal is a snake in the grass."

I would not even repeat to Jelal what Farid told me. It was the most absurd thing I had heard, and I could not convince the Egyptian with his ancient dream books that his fears were imaginary, there is no scientific basis whatever for such superstitions. The old East still lingered in Farid, despite his English clothes and college textbooks, and I tried to root the dark Sudan out of his mind. I figured that if an Armenian could reform and modernize the whole of Egypt there was no reason why I couldn't reform one Egyptian and make him forget his jinn and the Evil Eye.

He decided to move from his room, and asked me to help him find another room. He was too timid to look for a room by himself, and I went around with him and noticed how he suffered under the gaze of landladies who had rooms to let and glanced, doubtfully, at his hair and swarthy features, and said the room was already rented, or they wanted to rent it to a woman, or found some other excuse for not renting it to him.

Nothing was said between us, but I realized it would not be easy for him to rent a desirable room or apartment, and he was very particular. In the end he had to be satisfied with a two-room apartment in an old rooming house near the campus where by a sort of gentlemen's agreement only Indian, Filipino and other oriental students lived. It was a depressing place. He did not have to share, really, this voluntary segregation, and I was sure to find a better apartment for him, but he felt freer and more comfortable in this rooming house. He furnished his new quarters with oriental rugs and silks.

"This looks like a pasha's penthouse," I said.

"I am a pasha," he said with his shy smile.

I did not know he belonged to one of the most influential families in Egypt. I urged him to pass himself off as a prince, and on occasion, much to his discomfort, I introduced him as "Prince Farid" and pretended to be his secretary. On Sundays we cooked pilaf, green beans or okra, with lamb, and other Near Eastern dishes in his kitchenette and played backgammon. He wanted me to go to Egypt with him and manage his properties there. He talked of forming a company and prospecting for oil in the Sinai peninsula and other areas of Egypt. My economic future would be assured, he said. And I could marry a pretty Armenian girl in Egypt.

I was already doing some managing. I helped him make his purchases in local stores and acted as his guide and companion—and meanwhile I enlightened him on America and the West.

"But I don't trust Western women," he said. "My brother was lucky, his wife is an exception. My experiences with Western women have been rather unfortunate, and they took me, as Americans say, for a ride. They care for nothing but money and good times."

However, he was quite taken up with his chemistry teacher, an unmarried woman about his age, I supposed, getting to be an old maid, but not unattractive, and it tickled my funny bone when I saw them dining together in the town's best restaurant. On her birthday he gave her an expensive present, and I suggested she would make a good wife for him. She was quiet, plump, and did not have a Ph.D.

Farid would not tell me his age, but I took him to be about thirty—so much older than I that he was a mature portly man in my eyes. My own youth was passing; I was twenty-one, going on twenty-two, and I hadn't started to live yet. I was missing so much for lack of money, perhaps the most important part of my American education. I could not afford to take a girl to dinner, to travel a bit and see America, to enjoy life as Farid was doing. He took weekend trips to Omaha or Kansas City and came back with a box of his favorite candy, chocolate cherries. These were mysterious trips, but I had my suspicions, and sometimes I did not know he had been away until I saw a new box of chocolate cherries in his apartment. He had a sweet tooth. When I questioned him, discreetly, about these weekend trips the color deepened in his face and he changed the subject.

Indian and Filipino students living in the same building with Farid often gathered in his apartment. Their rooms were quite bare in comparison, although one or two Indians were reputed to be rich. I liked the Filipinos, always dapper, always well barbered, and decidedly Western in their thinking: the Spanish Catholic and American influence, I thought. They danced with bamboo sticks during our International Club programs, and they were equally adept at what seemed to be the courtly dances of old Spain, and the Filipino records they played on Farid's phonograph had nothing Malayan or oriental in them. It was rich Western music, that aroused visions of balls in the palaces of Spanish governors, and I wanted to visit Manila, which seemed to be a modern Western metropolis in the Far East. These dignified little men worked their way through college as houseboys, and I enjoyed their company. In Europe I had never seen Filipinos.

But the Indians were always arguing with me about America and the West. In general I loathed Asia with its ignorance, its miseries, its cruelties, its mysticism, and the Taj Mahal was not enough to make me change my opinion about India. The leader of these Indian students—ten of them—was Dr. Chandra, a brilliant chocolate-brown biochemist doing graduate work. He had a string of degrees from Indian and American universities, all of which were printed on his card, and he spoke in a soft velvety voice which changed to a snarl when the subject of Western civilization vs. Eastern came up, and more specifically the civilization of India, which he considered superior to that of the West. Dr. Chandra spoke not only as an Indian, but as an Asian patriot, and saw nothing good in the West. He said he would take nothing from America except the knowledge he needed in his specialty, "and how to use the machine guns and our own atomic bombs," as he put it.

"Look at America," said Dr. Chandra. "Here is the perfection of your Western civilization. Twenty-five million Americans have been classified as borderline mental cases by the United States Army. In India, we put the emphasis on what is permanent, and we don't work ourselves to death or a mental breakdown. Americans are such hypocrites. I thought I came to the land of the Declaration of Independence, but do you know, my dear, that I was beaten up and thrown out of a train in this wonderful America of yours when I refused to ride a Jim Crow car in the great state of Georgia? That I couldn't get a haircut in Chicago; that there are restaurants in this town that will not serve me? You can travel from one end of India to the other and no one will hold you up and rob you or kill you, and I can assure you, my dear, that you'd be safer there than in the streets of any American city."

"How about your caste system?" I countered. "Aren't there millions of untouchables in India? Don't you treat them worse than negroes are treated in this country? Don't tell me about the glories of Indian civilization. You were ruled by a few thousand British soldiers, all four hundred million of you."

"If we spat on them we could drown them all. We bided our time, and our day has come. In five years India will be the third greatest power on earth and will hold the balance between America and Russia. And if we have to choose between America and Russia, it will not be America."

"Russia is part of Western civilization," I said. "Russia is Europe. You're contradicting yourself. You're not against the industrialization of India, are you? You don't want millions of Indians to continue starving and living in filth. Who will save India? Yogis and snake-charmers? Or the machines created by the West? You've to choose between Karma and production."

I spoke as the commissar of common sense. Farid took no part in these arguments, and let me slug it out with his Indian guests, and particularly with this America-hater, though I could not blame him for feeling about America the way he did, after the indignities he had suffered because of his dark skin. I never mentioned my own experience in a small-town barbershop, when I was mistaken for a Mexican. Thank God I did not have to live in this building and I could eat in any restaurant in Brighton.

One day my Egyptian friend said to me, "You are going to churches all the time. Why don't you take me with you? Why are you so surprised? I'd like it very much."

"Okay," I said. "Next Sunday we'll go to the Congregational church, and I'll introduce you as His Royal Highness, Prince Farid of Egypt."

On our way to church I told him about the Christian religion and answered his questions as best I could.

"We recognize Christ as a prophet," he said, "and honor him for it."

"Christ wasn't just a prophet," I said.

"He was the Son of God, and He was God. He was divine, in human form. We believe like you that there is only one God, but our God is a trinity—the Father, the Son and the Holy Spirit. Sounds complicated, doesn't it? I can't say I understand it very well myself. We Christians accept these things with faith rather than reason."

"Christ was the son of Mary and Joseph?"

"Of Mary, but not of Joseph. He was born by what we call the Immaculate Conception. Joseph had nothing to do with it. Joseph was a good man, a carpenter by trade. Christ always said, 'My father in heaven.'"

Farid listened carefully to what I said, though I didn't think it made much sense to him. I tried to explain the doctrine of free will, or as much as I knew about it, and told him according to our religion man is free to choose between good and evil and is responsible for his acts. His fate is not written on his forehead.

"That's why Christian nations have made so much progress compared to Mohammedans. When you have free will, and your fate is not determined in advance by some supernatural force, you can do much to improve your lot. Take Turkey. As long as Islam was a powerful force in Turkey and the only way of life for Turks—and your religion more than ours is a way of life—the Turks were lethargic and fell behind their Christian subjects. The Turks realized they had to have science or perish as a nation. The only science that was acceptable to them at first was medical science, besides military science. Doctors were as necessary for their armies as generals. So you might say the new republican Turkey began in the medical school of Istanbul, where my father also studied. We believe man is master of his own destiny, and not a slave to his kismet, or to dark supernatural forces."

I did not directly refer to black magic, but I was working on him. I granted that Islam is a more simple and perhaps logical religion than Christianity—designed, originally, for the primitive people of the desert, as my instructor of medieval history used to say in Cyprus. He used to dramatize the rise and military conquests of Islam—how it spread like wildfire among rude backward peoples, but could make no headway among Christians and superior pagans, and maintained its solidarity among the peoples it conquered by the sword by making apostasy from Islam punishable by death.

And much for the same reason, I thought on our way to church, Islam is spreading today among the blacks of Africa, to whom it does give a certain pride and dignity as human beings, and admits them into the family of Mohammedan nations. And then of course Islam does not deny these new converts a man's right to have four wives and an unlimited number of concubines. That's a talking point with the *mullahs* preaching among the bookless blacks—the *"kita-bsiz"*—in Africa, south of the Sahara.

"I'll tell you what Christianity is in one word: love. Forget the Trinity, the Immaculate Conception, free will and all that stuff. Christians are still quarreling over what Christ meant, or the apostles meant, or the Fathers of the Church meant. There has been and still is a lot of interpretation in our religion. But all of our theologians and interpreters agree on one thing: love.

"To us, Farid, God is love. Ours is not a religion to be spread or maintained by the sword. It champions the weak against the strong, the poor against the rich. We don't have *Dar-ul-Islam* and *Dar-el-Harb*. For us the world isn't divided into two, the country of peace on one side, for the believers, and the country of war on the other side, for the infidels—for *Giaours* like myself. It's peace and love for all. Christ said, Love your enemies. If they strike you on one cheek, turn them the other. Resist not evil, by evil means, that is. That's the whole thing in a nutshell. Of course we Christians don't live up to it. It's not the fault of our religion that Christians kill, hate, have prejudices. If everybody practiced Christ's teachings there would be no wars, and Chandra wouldn't be thrown out of a train or refused service in a restaurant, and Egyptians wouldn't be robbed by Western companies controlling the traffic on Suez Canal."

It was a long speech. As we entered the Congregational church I remembered that Sunday when, wearing my diplomatic trousers, I was afraid to step inside this white limestone building and wondered now if my Egyptian friend was holding his breath as I did then. We sat in the last pew, for I knew he would attract attention if we walked down the aisle and I wanted to save him the pain of being stared at. I was relaxed, I felt at home in this Protestant church, and the old fears and prejudices were gone. Did I really find the soul of America in this small-town church, with its atmosphere of Old America I was so partial to? I hesitated to answer this question, fond as I was of the Congregational church and recognizing the part it played in my Americanization, the sense of belonging it gave me. The "soullessness" of America used to bother me in those days and now I had to admit I was less concerned with it; this "soullessness" was not peculiar to America but a sign of the modern industrial age spreading to other parts of the world, although here the contact between soul and soil was not fully established yet. The Armenian words were alike too: *"hoq"* for soul, *"hogh"* for soil. As always, I found myself drawn to the Puritans, those tough theocrats, and I thought maybe some atavistic connection in me with the Paulicians, the Armenian sect that originated in the region of Shabin Karahisar and which may be said to be the first Puritan movement in Christendom and the forerunner of modern Protestantism, has something to do with my affinity for American Puritans. But another side of me resisted the Protestant Ethic, and I knew I was still enamored with the vow of holy poverty, still a monk at heart. I could not rid myself of the conviction that the real purity lies in purposeful poverty. What my mind approved my heart rejected. I was disappointed in the Puritans for not measuring up to their own moral code. I wished they were as indifferent to the world's goods, and as bird and flower loving as St. Francis of Assisi.

Farid wanted to show himself as being broad-minded, and with all his superstitions I knew he was a man of good will. I saw him following the simple service of the church with respectful attention, sitting or standing with me in the last row. I tried to appear a better Christian than I was, singing the hymns and bowing my head in silent prayer with the rest of the congregation. When the service was over he begged me not to introduce him to anyone and we slipped out of the church before Dr. Smith took his position by the door and began shaking hands.

"Well, how did you like it?" I asked him.

"It was very interesting…different from what I thought it would be," Farid said thoughtfully.

I was absorbed in my own thoughts, and we walked under the wide-branching elms that lined the main street, Holtz Avenue, without speaking for some moments. A wild idea occurred to me—Christians and Moslems uniting and becoming as friendly as Farid and I were, now. I thought it would open a new chapter in the history of the world and bring East and West closer together. If Islam is in need of reform, so is Christianity, I said to myself. There are some good things in the Koran also, not so different from our Christian ethics, and no Christian can quarrel with what Mohammed said about charity and benevolence, for instance. I thought we should forget the past and find a common ground of cooperation with the three or four hundred million Moslems of the world. I saw myself at the head of a movement to unite Moslems and Christians—Christians speaking in mosques, Moslems in churches, during an annual brotherhood week set aside for that purpose, and myself addressing the biggest crowds of all from Cairo to Karachi.

Maybe that Indian apologist of Islam wasn't so far off the mark. A man could be a Moslem and still be a good man, like Farid, and like Jelal.

My Egyptian friend dropped out of college before graduating and I lost track of him after a brief correspondence. Years later I met Jelal in California. He was buying seeds and machinery for an agricultural project in the Gaza strip, where he worked as a representative of the United Nations refugee commission, and was a young man of some consequence among Arabs. We spent a few days together driving up and down the Coast and remembering our college days in Nebraska.

"Have you heard from Farid?" I asked him. "I wonder what happened to him?"

"Don't you know?" said Jelal. "Farid became a Christian and married an Armenian girl."

WILLIAM SAROYAN

He was born in Fresno in the late summer of 1908, just as the grape farmers were setting down their bunches to make raisins. His father, a minister and frustrated poet, moved the family to the San Francisco Bay Area in search of better work, only to die three years later when his appendix burst. His mother was forced to take a job as a domestic and place her four children, Willie the youngest, in an orphanage in Oakland. It would be five years before the family would reunite and make the return journey to Fresno. Death, or rather the need to squeeze everything out of ever-dwindling life, would become one of the central obsessions of his work.

"Try as much as possible to be wholly alive with all your might," he once wrote in a code for aspiring writers. "When you laugh, laugh like hell. And when you get angry, get good and angry. Try to be alive. You will be dead soon enough."

He dropped out of high school at fifteen, picking up his education at the public library, bedazzled by Edgar Lee Masters's *Spoon River Anthology*. When he wasn't reading or stealing pears from the next-door neighbor's tree, young Saroyan was walking the ditch banks and fields, discovering the eternal struggle between the horned toad, who was trying to hold onto his world, and the farmer, who was trying to engineer a new one. "Fresno had a great early appeal for me," he wrote. "It had a fine smell of dust, of the desert, of rocks baking in the sun…of leaf and blossom and fruit."

By eighteen, he wanted nothing more than to leave Fresno's small-town "rot and decay and ferment." He moved to San Francisco and then bought a one-way train ticket to New York City.

He may have put three thousand miles between him and Fresno, but all the stories he began to write, in a bursting, spontaneous style, were about his family and the childhood he had left behind. Just as swiftly came the rejection letters from magazine editors. Who was this cocky Armenian who dared to riff a whole page on the miracle of breathing?

He was holed up in the Mills Hotel, thinking of calling it quits but possessing too little money for the train fare home. On New Year's Day, 1929, he wrote his best pal in Fresno about his desire to return to a simple life of pruning vines. "Xmas brought me the flu; fever 104; burning hot in sweat; no friends; too homesick to want to die; had dreams for four days and nights of home and the old scenes and meals. I am positive now that I am a God damn fool."

His fever broke, and he turned it into a story about a poverty-stricken young writer with only tap water and Proust to fill his belly. The publication of "The Daring Young Man on the Flying Trapeze" in 1934 was all the break Saroyan needed. Over the next decade, he would become one of the most celebrated writers in America, his work appearing in short story collections (*My Name Is Aram*) and novels (*The Human Comedy*), on Broadway (*My Heart's in the Highlands*) and on records (*"Come On-a My House"*). He bragged he could write an entire play in three days and then wrote the Pulitzer Prize–winner *The Time of Your Life* in six days. He ended up rejecting the prize because the play was "no more great than anything else I have ever written." So unmistakable was his style that he became an adjective: Saroyanesque.

What he never quite mastered was family life. Willie Saroyan and Carol Marcus were quite a pair. She was barely seventeen years old, a New York City debutante who wiped off her lipstick with fifty-dollar lace hankies, when they met. He tried to fit into her glittering world, surrounded by her best friends Gloria Vanderbilt and Oona O'Neill, Eugene's daughter and later the wife of Charlie Chaplin. Saroyan and Marcus married, had two children, divorced, remarried, and divorced again, before she wound up with actor Walter Matthau.

Saroyan had lost so much money at the roulette table and race track—at one point in the 1940s his debts topped $100,000—that he became a kind of literary panhandler, hawking third-rate stories to stave off the taxman. By the time he turned fifty and wrote *Not Dying*, he was considered washed up by all the big literary critics.

In the spring of 1981, estranged from his son, Aram, and daughter, Lucy, alone and almost forgotten, Saroyan lay dying in his tract house in Fresno. Prostate cancer riddled his body, and he kept toying with the idea of suicide. Yet each day, he dragged himself out of bed and trudged to the old Royal typewriter that sat on a draftsman's table in the middle of his cluttered living room. There he stood, as was his writing practice, and began to fill blank paper with words—some lousy, some mediocre, and some as funny and sad and razor-sharp as anything he had ever written.

In those last months, he wrote more than 337,000 words, a memoir he variously titled "Adios, Muchacho" and "Etc. Etc. Etc." After his death, literary executors searching through the boxes in the little house on Griffith Way couldn't believe the output of his final years. Long after the New York publishing world had finished with him, long after the college professors had stopped teaching him, Saroyan and his typewriter kept clattering, millions and millions of words.

When it came time to catalog his short stories, plays, memoirs, journals, novels, and essays, published and unpublished, the Saroyan collection—two hundred and fifty linear feet of shelf space—dwarfed those of Mark Twain and John Steinbeck, a mere forty feet combined. Saroyan didn't stop at words. He made hundreds of free-form drawings in pen and documented the smallest facets of his existence. When he finished eating a can of green beans, for instance, he would peel off the label and sign the backside with the year, month, day, and hour. He clipped and saved his mustache hairs and collected rocks and twine on his bicycle rides through town.

What fueled these compulsions isn't clear. Was Saroyan building a great wall against mortality? Was he performing the last act of a writer convinced that the flotsam of his life would someday be of value to biographers? Or had his gaze turned so inward that it grew into a sort of fetish or maybe even madness?

None of these questions, sadly, have been posed, much less answered, by a handful of Saroyan biographers. In the most definitive of the lot, *A Daring Young Man*, author John Leggett obsesses on a single theme: Saroyan, forever the ragged dropout, envied every polished person he encountered in his life. And this envy masqueraded as hubris and ultimately doomed Saroyan to the fate of a B-list writer.

Is this a fair summing up? It is true that Saroyan never produced a heavyweight novel. The longer form seemed to run contrary to his extraordinary gifts: the short bursts of perfect energy, the impatience with formal structure, the need to finish one story so he could move on to the next. And yet this criticism seems trifling. His best short stories—"The Pomegranate Trees," "The Hummingbird That Lived through Winter," and "70,000 Assyrians"—each bring to mind a rock that a kid finds in the dust and keeps in his pocket: polished, simple, perfect, forever.

Mark Arax

The Daring Young Man on the Flying Trapeze

Chapter 1, Sleep

Horizontally wakeful amid universal widths, practicing laughter and mirth, satire, the end of all, Rome and yes of Babylon, clenched teeth, remembrance, much warmth volcanic, the streets of Paris, the plains of Jericho, much gliding as of reptile in abstraction, a gallery of watercolors, the sea and the fish with eyes, symphony, a table in the corner of the Eiffel tower, jazz at the opera house, alarm clock and the tapdancing of doom, conversation with a tree, the river Nile, the roar of Dostoyevsky, and the dark sun.

This earth, the face of one who lived, the form without the weight, weeping upon snow, white music, the magnified flower twice the size of the universe, black clouds, the caged panther staring, deathless space, Mr. Eliot with rolled sleeves baking bread, Flaubert and Guy de Maupassant, a wordless rhyme of early meaning, Finlandia, mathematics highly polished and slick as a green onion to the teeth, Jerusalem, the path to paradox.

The deep song of man, the sly whisper of someone unseen but vaguely known, hurricane in the cornfield, a game of chess, hush the queen, the king, Karl Franz, black Titanic, Mr. Chaplin weeping, Stalin, Hitler, a multitude of Jews, tomorrow is Monday, no dancing in the streets.

O swift moment of life: it is ended, again the earth is now.

Chapter 2, Wakefulness

He (the living) dressed and shaved, grinning at himself in the mirror. Very unhandsome, he said; where is my tie? (He had but one.) Coffee and a grey sky, Pacific Ocean fog, the drone of a passing street car, people going to the city, time again, the day, prose and poetry. He moved swiftly down the stairs to the street and began to walk, thinking suddenly. *It is only in sleep that we may know we live. There only, in that living death, do we meet ourselves and the far earth, God and the saints, the names of our fathers, the substance of remote moments: it is there that the centuries merge in the moment, that the vast becomes the tiny, tangible atom of eternity.*

He walked into the day as alertly as might be, making a definite noise with his heels, perceiving with his eyes the superficial truth of streets and structures, the trivial truth of reality. Helplessly his mind sang, *He flies through the air with the greatest of ease, the daring young man on the flying trapeze,* then laughed with all the might of his being. It was really a splendid morning: grey, cold, and cheerless, a morning for inward vigor; ah, Edgar Guest, he said, how I long for your music.

In the gutter he saw a coin which proved to be a penny dated 1923, and placing it in the palm of his hand he examined it closely, remembering that year and thinking of Lincoln, whose profile was stamped upon the coin. There was almost nothing a man could do with a penny. I will purchase a motor-car, he thought. I will dress myself in the fashion of a fop, visit the hotel strumpets, drink and dine, and then return to the quiet. Or I will drop the coin into a slot and weigh myself.

It was good to be poor, and the Communists—but it was dreadful to be hungry. What appetites they had, how fond they were of food! Empty stomachs. He remembered how greatly he needed food. Every meal was bread and coffee and cigarettes, and now he had no more bread. Coffee without bread could never honestly serve as supper, and there were no weeds in the park that could be cooked as spinach is cooked.

If the truth were known he was half starved, and there was still no end of books he ought to read before he died. He remembered the young Italian in a Brooklyn hospital, a small sick clerk named Mollica, who had said desperately, I would like to see California once before I die. And he thought earnestly, I ought at least to read *Hamlet* once again; or perhaps *Huckleberry Finn.*

It was then that he became thoroughly awake: at the thought of dying. Now wakefulness was a state in the nature of a sustained shock. A young man could perish rather unostentatiously, he thought; and already he was very nearly starved. Water and prose were fine, they filled much inorganic space, but they were inadequate. If there were only some work he might do for money, some trivial labor in the name of commerce. If they would only allow him to sit at a desk all day and add trade figures, subtract and multiply and divide, then perhaps he would not die. He would buy food, all sorts of it: untasted delicacies from Norway, Italy, and France; all manner of beef, lamb, fish, cheese, grapes, figs, pears, apples, melons, which he would worship when he had satisfied his hunger. He would place a bunch of red grapes on a dish beside two black figs, a large yellow pear, and a green apple. He would hold a cut melon to his nostrils for hours. He would buy great brown loaves of French bread, vegetables of all sorts, meat, life.

From a hill he saw the city standing majestically in the east, great towers, dense with his kind, and there he was suddenly outside of it all, almost definitely certain that he should never gain admittance, almost positive that somehow he had ventured upon the wrong earth, or perhaps into the wrong age, and now a young man of twenty-two was to be permanently ejected from it. This thought was not saddening. He said to himself, sometime soon I must write *An Application for Permission to Live*. He accepted the thought of dying without pity for himself or for man, believing that he would at least sleep another night. His rent for another day was paid; there was yet another tomorrow. And after that he might go where other homeless men went. He might even visit the Salvation Army—sing to God and Jesus (unlover of my soul), be saved, eat and sleep. But he knew that he would not. His life was a private life. He did not wish to destroy this fact. Any other alternative would be better.

Through the air on the flying trapeze, his mind hummed. Amusing it was, astoundingly funny. A trapeze to God, or to nothing, a flying trapeze to some sort of eternity; he prayed objectively for strength to make the flight with grace.

I have one cent, he said. It is an American coin. In the evening I shall polish it until it glows like a sun and I shall study the words.

He was now walking in the city itself, among living men. There were one or two places to go. He saw his reflection in plate-glass windows of stores and was disappointed with his appearance. He seemed not at all as strong as he felt; he seemed, in fact, a trifle infirm in every part of his body, in his neck, his shoulders, arms, trunk, and knees. This will never do, he said, and with an effort he assembled all his disjointed parts and became tensely, artificially erect and solid.

He passed numerous restaurants with magnificent discipline, refusing even to glance into them, and at last reached a building which he entered. He rose in an elevator to the seventh floor, moved down a hall, and, opening a door, walked into the office of an employment agency. Already there were two dozen young men in the place; he found a corner where he stood waiting his turn to be interviewed. At length he was granted this great privilege and was questioned by a thin, scatter-brained miss of fifty.

Now tell me, she said; what can you do?

He was embarrassed. I can write, he said pathetically.

You mean your penmanship is good? Is that it? said the elderly maiden.

Well, yes, he replied. But I mean that I can write.

Write what? said the miss, almost with anger.

Prose, he said simply.

There was a pause. At last the lady said:

Can you use a typewriter?

Of course, said the young man.

All right, went on the miss, we have your address; we will get in touch with you. There is nothing this morning, nothing at all.

It was much the same at the other agency, except that he was questioned by a conceited young man who closely resembled a pig. From the agencies he went to the large department stores: there was a good deal of pomposity, some humiliation on his part, and finally the report that work was not available. He did not feel displeased, and strangely did not even feel that he was personally involved in all the foolishness. He was a living young man who was in need of money with which to go on being one, and there was no way of getting it except by working for it; and there was no work. It was purely an abstract problem which he wished for the last time to attempt to solve. Now he was pleased that the matter was closed.

He began to perceive the definiteness of the course of his life. Except for moments, it had been largely artless, but now at the last minute he was determined that there should be as little imprecision as possible.

He passed countless stores and restaurants on his way to the Y.M.C.A., where he helped himself to paper and ink and began to compose his *Application*. For an hour he worked on this document, then suddenly, owing to the bad air in the place and to hunger, he became faint. He seemed to be swimming away from himself with great strokes, and hurriedly left the building. In the Civic Center Park, across from the Public Library Building, he drank almost a quart of water and felt himself refreshed. An old man was standing in the center of the brick boulevard surrounded by sea-gulls, pigeons, and robins. He was taking handfuls of bread crumbs from a large paper sack and tossing them to the birds with a gallant gesture.

Dimly he felt impelled to ask the old man for a portion of the crumbs, but would not allow the thought even nearly to reach consciousness; he entered the Public Library and for an hour read Proust, then, feeling himself to be swimming away again, he rushed outdoors. He drank more water at the fountain in the park and began the long walk to his room.

I'll go and sleep some more, he said; there is nothing else to do. He knew now that he was much too tired and weak to deceive himself about being all right, and yet his mind seemed somehow still lithe and alert. It, as if it were a separate entity, persisted in articulating impertinent pleasantries about his very real physical suffering. He reached his room early in the afternoon and immediately prepared coffee on the small gas range. There was no milk in the can, and the half pound of sugar he had purchased a week before was all gone; he drank a cup of the hot black fluid, sitting on his bed and smiling.

From the Y.M.C.A. he had stolen a dozen sheets of letter paper upon which he hoped to complete his document, but now the very notion of writing was unpleasant to him. There was nothing to say. He began to polish the penny he had found in the morning, and this absurd act somehow afforded him great enjoyment. No American coin can be made to shine so brilliantly as a penny. How many pennies would he need to go on living? Wasn't there something more he might sell? He looked about the bare room. No. His watch was gone; also his books. All those fine books; nine of them for eighty-five cents. He felt ill and ashamed for having parted with his books. His best suit he had sold for two dollars, but that was all right. He didn't mind at all about clothes. But the books. That was different. It made him very angry to think that there was no respect for men who wrote.

He placed the shining penny on the table, looking upon it with the delight of a miser. How prettily it smiles, he said. Without reading them he looked at the words, *E Pluribus Unum Once Cent United States of America*, and turning the penny over, he saw Lincoln and the words *In God We Trust Liberty 1923*. How beautiful it is, he said.

He became drowsy and felt a ghastly illness coming over his blood, a feeling of nausea and disintegration. Bewildered, he stood beside his bed, thinking *there is nothing to do but sleep*. Already he felt himself making great strides through the fluid of the earth, swimming away to the beginning. He fell face down upon the bed, saying, I ought first at least to give the coin to some child. A child could buy any number of things with a penny.

Then swiftly, neatly, with the grace of the young man on the trapeze, he was gone from his body. For an eternal moment he was all things at once: the bird, the fish, the rodent, the reptile, and man. An ocean of print undulated endlessly and darkly before him. The city burned. The herded crowd rioted. The earth circled away, and knowing that he did so, he turned his lost face to the empty sky and became dreamless, unalive, perfect.

Seventy Thousand Assyrians

I hadn't had a haircut in forty days and forty nights, and I was beginning to look like several violinists out of work. You know the look: genius gone to pot, and ready to join the Communist Party. We barbarians from Asia Minor are hairy people: when we need a haircut, we *need* a haircut. It was so bad, I had outgrown my only hat. (I am writing a serious story, perhaps one of the most serious I shall ever write. That is why I am being flippant. Readers of Sherwood Anderson will begin to understand what I am saying after a while; they will know that my laughter is rather sad.) I was a young man in need of a haircut, so I went down to Third Street (San Francisco), to the Barber College, for a fifteen-cent haircut.

Third Street, below Howard, is a district; think of the Bowery in New York, Main Street in Los Angeles: think of old men and boys, out of work, hanging around, smoking Bull Durham, talking about the government, waiting for something to turn up, simply waiting. It was a Monday morning in August and a lot of the tramps had come to the shop to brighten up a bit. The Japanese boy who was working over the free chair had a waiting list of eleven; all the other chairs were occupied. I sat down and began to wait. Outside, as Hemingway (*The Sun Also Rises, A Farewell to Arms, Death in the Afternoon, Winner Take Nothing*) would say, haircuts were four bits. I had twenty cents and a half pack of Bull Durham. I rolled a cigarette, handed the pack to one of my contemporaries who looked in need of nicotine, and inhaled the dry smoke, thinking of America, what was going on politically, economically, spiritually. My contemporary was a boy of sixteen. He looked Iowa; splendid potentially, a solid American, but down, greatly down in the mouth. Little sleep, no change of clothes for several days, a little fear, etc. I wanted very much to know his name. A writer is always wanting to get the reality of faces and figures. Iowa said, 'I just got in from Salinas. No work in the lettuce fields. Going north now, to Portland; try to ship out.' I wanted to tell him how it was with me: rejected story from *Scribner's*, rejected essay from *The Yale Review*, no money for decent cigarettes, worn shoes, old shirts, but I was afraid to make something of my own troubles. A writer's troubles are always boring, a bit unreal. People are apt to feel, *Well, who asked you to write in the first place?* A man must pretend not to be a writer. I said, 'Good luck, north.' Iowa shook his head. 'I know better. Give it a try, anyway. Nothing to lose.' Fine boy, hope he isn't dead, hope he hasn't frozen, mighty cold these days (December, 1933), hope he hasn't gone down; he deserved to live. Iowa, I hope you got work in Portland; I hope you are earning money; I hope you have rented a clean room with a warm bed in it; I hope you are sleeping nights, eating regularly, walking along like a human being, being happy. Iowa, my good wishes are with you. I have said a number of prayers for you. (All the same, I think he is dead by this time. It was in him the day I saw him, the low malicious face of the beast, and at the same time all the theaters in America were showing, over and over again, an animated film-cartoon in which there was a song called 'Who's Afraid of the Big Bad Wolf?' and that's what it amounts to: people with money laughing at the death that is crawling slyly into boys like young Iowa, pretending that it isn't there, laughing in warm theaters. I have prayed for Iowa, and I consider myself a coward. By this time he must be dead, and I am sitting in a small room, talking about him, only talking.)

I began to watch the Japanese boy who was learning to become a barber. He was shaving an old tramp who had a horrible face, one of those faces that emerge from years and years of evasive living, years of being unsettled, of not belonging anywhere, of owning nothing, and the Japanese boy was holding his nose back (his own nose), so that he would not smell the old tramp. A trivial point in a story, a bit of data with no place in a work of art, nevertheless, I put it down. A young writer is always afraid some significant fact may escape him. He is always wanting to put in everything he sees. I wanted to know the name of the Japanese boy. I am profoundly interested in names. I have found that those that are unknown are the most genuine. Take a big name like Andrew Mellon. I was watching the Japanese boy very closely. I wanted to understand from the way he was keeping his sense of smell away from the mouth and nostrils of the old man what he was thinking, how he was feeling. Years ago, when I was seventeen, I pruned vines in my uncle's vineyard, north of Sanger, in the San Joaquin Valley, and there were several Japanese working with me, Yoshio Enomoto, Hideo Suzuki, Katsumi Sujimoto, and one or two others. These Japanese taught me a few simple phrases, *hello, how are you, fine day, isn't it, good-bye,* and so on. I said in Japanese to the barber student, "How are you?" He said in Japanese, "Very well, thank you." Then, in impeccable English, "Do you speak Japanese? Have you lived in Japan?" I said, "Unfortunately, no. I am able to speak only one or two words. I used to work with Yoshio Enomoto, Hideo Suzuki, Katsumi Sujimoto; do you know them?" He went on with his work, thinking of the names. He seemed to be whispering, "Enomoto, Suzuki, Sujimoto." He said, "Suzuki. Small man?" I said, "Yes." He said, "I know him. He lives in San Jose now. He is married now."

I want you to know that I am deeply interested in what people remember. A young writer goes out to places and talks to people. He tries to find out what they remember. I am not using great material for a short story. Nothing is going to happen in this work. I am not fabricating a fancy plot. I am not creating memorable characters. I am not using a slick style of writing. I am not building up a fine atmosphere. I have no desire to sell this story or any story to *The Saturday Evening Post* or to *Cosmopolitan* or to *Harper's*. I am not

trying to compete with the great writers of short stories, men like Sinclair
Lewis and Joseph Hergesheimer and Zane Grey, men who really know
how to write, how to make up stories that will sell. Rich men, men who
understand all the rules about plot and character and style and atmosphere
and all that stuff. I have no desire for fame. I am not out to win the Pulitzer
Prize or the Nobel Prize or any other prize. I am out here in the far West, in
San Francisco, in a small room on Carl Street, writing a letter to common
people, telling them in simple language things they already know. I am
merely making a record, so if I wander around a little, it is because I am in
no hurry and because I do not know the rules. If I have any desire at all, it
is to show the brotherhood of man. This is a big statement and it sounds a
little precious. Generally a man is ashamed to make such a statement. He is
afraid sophisticated people will laugh at him. But I don't mind. I'm asking
sophisticated people to laugh. That is what sophistication is for. I do not
believe in races. I do not believe in governments. I see life as one life at one
time, so many millions simultaneously all over the earth. Babies who have
not yet been taught to speak any language are the only race of the earth, the
race of man; all the rest is pretense, what we call civilization, hatred, fear,
desire for strength....But a baby is a baby. And the way they cry, there you
have the brotherhood of man, babies crying. We grow up and we learn the
words of a language and we see the universe through the language we know,
we do not see it through all languages or through no language at all, through
silence, for example, and we isolate ourselves in the language we know. Over
here we isolate ourselves in English, or American as Mencken calls it. All the
eternal things, in our words. If I want to do anything, I want to speak a more
universal language. The heart of man, the unwritten part of man, that which
is eternal and common to all races.

Now I am beginning to feel guilty and incompetent. I have used all this
language and I am beginning to feel that I have said nothing. This is what
drives a young writer out of his head, this feeling that nothing is being said.
Any ordinary journalist would have been able to put the whole business into
a three-word caption. Man is man, he would have said. Something clever,
with any number of implications. But I want to use language that will create
a single implication. I want the meaning to be precise, and perhaps that
is why the language is so imprecise. I am walking around my subject, the
impression I want to make, and I am trying to see it from all angles, so that I
will have a whole picture, a picture of wholeness. It is the heart of man that I
am trying to imply in this work.

Let me try again: I hadn't had a haircut in a long time and I was beginning to look seedy, so I went down to the Barber College on Third Street, and I sat in a chair. I said, "Leave it full in the back. I have a narrow head and if you do not leave it full in the back, I will go out of this place looking like a horse. Take as much as you like off the top. No lotion, no water, comb it dry." Reading makes a full man, writing a precise one, as you see. This is what happened. It doesn't make much of a story, and the reason is that I have left out the barber, the young man who gave me the haircut.

He was tall, he had a dark serious face, thick lips, on the verge of smiling but melancholy, thick lashes, sad eyes, a large nose. I saw his name on the card that was pasted on the mirror, Theodore Badal. A good name, genuine, a good young man, genuine. Theodore Badal began to work on my head. A good barber never speaks until he has been spoken to, no matter how full his heart may be.

"That name." I said, "Badal. Are you an Armenian?" I am an Armenian. I have mentioned this before. People look at me and begin to wonder, so I come right out and tell them. "I am an Armenian," I say. Or they read something I have written and begin to wonder, so I let them know. "I am an Armenian," I say. It is a meaningless remark, but they expect me to say it, so I do. I have no idea what it is like to be an Armenian or what it is like to be an Englishman or a Japanese or anything else. I have a faint idea what it is like to be alive. This is the only thing that interests me greatly. This and tennis. I hope some day to write a great philosophical work on tennis, something of the order of *Death in the Afternoon,* but I am aware that I am not yet ready to undertake such a work. I feel that the cultivation of tennis on a large scale among the peoples of the earth will do much to annihilate racial differences, prejudices, hatred, etc. Just as soon as I have perfected my drive and my lob, I hope to begin my outline of this great work. (It may seem to some sophisticated people that I am trying to make fun of Hemingway. I am not. *Death in the Afternoon* is a pretty sound piece of prose. I could never object to it as prose. I cannot even object to it as philosophy. I think it is finer philosophy than that of Will Durant and Walter Pitkin. Even when Hemingway is a fool, he is at least an accurate fool. He tells you what actually takes place and he doesn't allow the speed of an occurrence to make his exposition of it hasty. This is a lot. It is some sort of advancement for literature. To relate leisurely the nature and meaning of that which is very brief in duration.)

"Are you an Armenian?" I asked.

We are a small people and whenever one of us meets another, it is an event. We are always looking around for someone to talk to in our language.

Our most ambitious political party estimates that there are nearly two million of us living on the earth, but most of us don't think so. Most of us sit down and take a pencil and a piece of paper and we take one section of the world at a time and imagine how many Armenians at the most are likely to be living in that section and we put the highest number on the paper, and then we go on to another section, India, Russia, Soviet Armenia, Egypt, Italy, Germany, France, America, South America, Australia, and so on, and after we add up our most hopeful figures the total comes to something a little less than a million. Then we start to think how big our families are, how high our birthrate and how low our deathrate (except in times of war when massacres increase the deathrate), and we begin to imagine how rapidly we will increase if we are left alone a quarter of a century, and we feel pretty happy. We always leave out earthquakes, wars, massacres, famines, etc., and it is a mistake. I remember the Near East Relief drives in my home town. My uncle used to be our orator and he used to make a whole auditorium full of Armenians weep. He was an attorney and he was a great orator. Well, at first the trouble was war. Our people were being destroyed by the enemy. Those who hadn't been killed were homeless and they were starving, *our own flesh and blood,* my uncle said, and we all wept. And we gathered money and sent it to our people in the old country. Then after the war, when I was a bigger boy, we had another Near East Relief drive and my uncle stood on the stage of the Civic Auditorium of my home town and he said, "Thank God this time it is not the enemy, but an earthquake. God has made us suffer. We have worshiped Him through trial and tribulation, through suffering and disease and torture and horror and (my uncle began to weep, began to sob) through the madness of despair, and now He has done this thing, and still we praise Him, still we worship Him. We do not understand the ways of God!" And after the drive I went to my uncle and I said, "Did you mean what you said about God?" And he said, "That was oratory. We've got to raise money. What God? It is nonsense." "And when you cried?" I asked, and my uncle said, "That was real. I could not help it. I had to cry. Why, for God's sake, why must we go through all this God damn hell? What have we done to deserve all this torture? Man won't let us alone. God won't let us alone. Have we done something? Aren't we supposed to be pious people? What is our sin? I am disgusted with God. I am sick of man. The only reason I am willing to get up and talk is that I don't dare keep my mouth shut. I can't bear the thought of more of our people dying. Jesus Christ, have we done something?"

I asked Theodore Badal if he was an Armenian.

He said, "I am an Assyrian."

Well, it was something. They, the Assyrians, came from our part of the world, they had noses like our noses, eyes like our eyes, hearts like our hearts. They had a different language. When they spoke we couldn't understand them, but they were a lot like us. It wasn't quite as pleasing as it would have been if Badal had been an Armenian, but it was something.

"I am an Armenian," I said, "I used to know some Assyrian boys in my home town, Joseph Sargis, Nito Elia, Tony Saleh. Do you know any of them?"

"Joseph Sargis, I know him," said Badal. "The others I do not know. We lived in New York until five years ago, then we came out west to Turlock. Then we moved up to San Francisco."

"Nito Elia," I said, "is a Captain in the Salvation Army." (I don't want anyone to imagine that I am making anything up, or that I am trying to be funny.) "Tony Saleh," I said, "was killed eight years ago. He was riding a horse and he was thrown and the horse began to run. Tony couldn't get himself free, he was caught by a leg, and the horse ran around and around for a half-hour and then stopped, and when they went up to Tony he was dead. He was fourteen at the time. I used to go to school with him. Tony was a very clever boy, very good at arithmetic."

We began to talk about the Assyrian language and the Armenian language, about the old world, conditions over there, and so on. I was getting a fifteen-cent haircut and I was doing my best to learn something at the same time, to acquire some new truth, some new appreciation of the wonder of life, the dignity of man. (Man has great dignity, do not imagine that he has not.)

Badal said, "I cannot read Assyrian. I was born in the old country, but I want to get over it."

He sounded tired, not physically but spiritually.

"Why?" I said. "Why do you want to get over it?"

"Well," he laughed, "simply because everything is washed up over there." I am repeating his words precisely, putting in nothing of my own. "We were a great people once," he went on. "But that was yesterday, the day before yesterday. Now we are a topic in ancient history. We had a great civilization. They're still admiring it. Now I am in America learning to cut hair. We're washed up as a race, we're through, it's all over, why should I learn to read the language? We have no writers, we have no news—well, there is a little news: once in a while the English encourage the Arabs to massacre us, that is all. It's an old story, we know all about it. The news comes over to us through the Associated Press, anyway."

These remarks were painful to me, an Armenian. I had always felt badly about my own people being destroyed. I had never heard an Assyrian speaking in English about such things. I felt great love for this young fellow. Don't get me wrong. There is a tendency these days to think in terms of pansies whenever a man says that he has affection for man. I think now that I have affection for all people, even for the enemies of Armenia, whom I have so tactfully not named. Everyone knows who they are. I have nothing against any of them because I think of them as one man living one life at a time, and I know, I am positive, that one man at a time is incapable of the monstrosities performed by mobs. My objection is to mobs only.

"Well," I said, "it is much the same with us. We, too, are old. We still have our church. We still have a few writers, Aharonian, Isahakian, a few others, but it is much the same."

"Yes," said the barber, "I know. We went in for the wrong things. We went in for the simple things, peace and quiet and families. We didn't go in for machinery and conquest and militarism. We didn't go in for diplomacy and deceit and the invention of machine-guns and poison gases. Well, there is no use being disappointed. We had our day, I suppose."

"We are hopeful," I said. "There is no Armenian living who does not still dream of an independent Armenia."

"Dream?" said Badal. "Well, that is something. Assyrians cannot even dream any more. Why, do you know how many of us are left on earth?"

"Two or three million," I suggested.

"Seventy thousand," said Badal. "That is all. Seventy thousand Assyrians in the world, and the Arabs are still killing us. They killed seventy of us in a little uprising last month. There was a small paragraph in the paper. Seventy more of us destroyed. We'll be wiped out before long. My brother is married to an American girl and he has a son. There is no more hope. We are trying to forget Assyria. My father still reads a paper that comes from New York, but he is an old man. He will be dead soon."

Then his voice changed, he ceased speaking as an Assyrian and began to speak as a barber. "Have I taken enough off the top?" he asked.

The rest of the story is pointless. I said *so long* to the young Assyrian and left the shop. I walked across town, four miles, to my room on Carl Street. I thought about the whole business: Assyria and this Assyrian, Theodore Badal, learning to be a barber, the sadness of his voice, the hopelessness of his attitude. This was months ago, in August, but ever since I have been thinking about Assyria, and I have been wanting to say something about Theodore Badal, a son of an ancient race, himself youthful and alert, yet hopeless. Seventy thousand Assyrians, a mere seventy thousand of that great people, and all the others quiet in death and all the greatness crumbled and ignored, and a young man in America learning to be a barber, and a young man lamenting bitterly the course of history.

Why don't I make up plots and write beautiful love stories that can be made into motion pictures? Why don't I let these unimportant and boring matters go hang? Why don't I try to please the American reading public?

Well, I am an Armenian. Michael Arlen is an Armenian, too. He is pleasing the public. I have great admiration for him, and I think he has perfected a very fine style of writing and all that, but I don't want to write about the people he likes to write about. Those people were dead to begin with. You take Iowa and the Japanese boy and Theodore Badal, the Assyrian; well, they may go down physically, like Iowa, to death, or spiritually, like Badal, to death, but they are of the stuff that is eternal in man and it is this stuff that interests me. You don't find them in bright places, making witty remarks about sex and trivial remarks about art. You find them where I found them, and they will be there forever, the race of man, the part of man, of Assyria as much as of England, that cannot be destroyed, the part that earthquake and war and famine and madness and everything else cannot destroy.

This work is in tribute to Iowa, to Japan, to Assyria, to Armenia, to the race of man everywhere, to the dignity of that race, the brotherhood of things alive. I am not expecting Paramount Pictures to film this work. I am thinking of seventy thousand Assyrians, one at a time, alive, a great race. I am thinking of Theodore Badal, himself seventy thousand Assyrians and seventy million Assyrians, himself Assyria, and man, standing in a barber's shop, in San Francisco, in 1933, and being, still, himself, the whole race.

Credo: The Time of Your Life

In the time of our life, live—so that in that good time there shall be no ugliness or death for yourself or for any life your life touches. Seek goodness everywhere, and when it is found, bring it out of its hiding-place and let it be free and unashamed. Place in matter and in flesh the least of the values, for these are the things that hold death and must pass away. Discover in all things that which shines and is beyond corruption. Encourage virtue in whatever heart it may have been driven into secrecy and sorrow by the shame and terror of the world. Ignore the obvious, for it is unworthy of the clear eye and the kindly heart. Be the inferior of no man, nor of any man be the superior. Remember that every man is a variation of yourself. No man's guilt is not yours, nor is any man's innocence a thing apart. Despise evil and ungodliness, but not men of ungodliness or evil. These, understand. Have no shame in being kindly and gentle, but if the time comes in the time of your life to kill, kill and have no regret. In the time of your life, live—so that in that wondrous time you shall not add to the misery and sorrow of the world, but shall smile to the infinite delight and mystery of it.

The Hummingbird That Lived through Winter

Sometimes even instinct is overpowered by individuality—in creatures other than men, I mean. In men instinct is supposed to be controlled, but whether or not it ever actually is I leave to others. At any rate, the fundamental instinct of most—or all—creatures is to live. Each form of life has an instinctive technique of defense against other forms of life, as well as against the elements. What happens to hummingbirds is something I have never found out—from actual observation or from reading. They die, that's true. And they're born somehow or other, although I have never seen a hummingbird's egg, or a young hummingbird.

The mature hummingbird itself is so small that the egg must be magnificent, probably one of the most smiling little things in the world. Now, if hummingbirds come into the world through some other means than eggs, I ask the reader to forgive me. The only thing I know about Agass Agasig Agassig Agazig (well, the great American naturalist) is that he once studied turtle eggs, and in order to get the information he was seeking, had to find fresh ones. This caused an exciting adventure in Boston to a young fellow who wrote about it six or seven years before I read it, when I was fourteen. I was fourteen in 1922, which goes to show you how unimportant the years are when you're dealing with eggs of any kind. I envy the people who study birds, and some day I hope to find out everything that's known about hummingbirds.

I've gathered from rumor that the hummingbird travels incredible distances on incredibly little energy—what carries him, then? Spirit? But the best things I know about hummingbirds are the things I've noticed about them myself: that they are on hand when the sun is out in earnest, when the blossoms are with us, and the smell of them everywhere. You can hardly go through the best kind of day without seeing a hummingbird suspended like a little miracle in a shaft of light over a big flower or a cluster of little ones. Or turning like gay insanity and shooting straight as an arrow toward practically nothing, for no reason, or for the reason that it's alive. Now, how can creatures such as that—so delicately magnificent and mad—possibly find time for the routine business of begetting young? Or for the exercise of instinct in self-defense? Well, however it may be, let a good day come by the grace of God, and with will come the hummingbirds.

As I started to say, however, it appears that sometimes even instinct fails to operate in a specie. Or species. Or whatever it is. Anyhow, when all of a kind of living thing turn and go somewhere, in order to stay alive, in order to escape cold or whatever it might be, sometimes, it appears, one of them does not go. Why he does not go I cannot say. He may be eccentric, or there may be exalted reasons—specific instead of abstract passion for another of its kind—perhaps dead—or for a place. Or it may be stupidity, or stubbornness. Who can ever know?

There was a hummingbird once which in the wintertime did not leave our neighborhood in Fresno, California.

I'll tell you about it.

Across the street lived old Dikran, who was almost blind. He was past eighty and his wife was only a few years younger. They had a little house that was as neat inside as it was ordinary outside—except for old Dikran's garden, which was the best thing of its kind in the world. Plants, bushes, trees—all strong, in sweet black moist earth whose guardian was old Dikran. All things from the sky loved this spot in our poor neighborhood, and old Dikran loved *them*.

One freezing Sunday, in the dead of winter, as I came home from Sunday School I saw old Dikran standing in the middle of the street trying to distinguish what was in his hand. Instead of going into our house to the fire, as I had wanted to do, I stood on the steps of the front porch and watched the old man. He would turn around and look upward at his trees and the back to the palm of his hand. He stood in the street at least two minutes and then at last he came to me. He held his hand out, and in Armenian he said, "What is this in my hand?"

I looked.

"It is a hummingbird," I said half in English and half in Armenian. Hummingbird I said in English because I didn't know its name in Armenian.

"What is that?" old Dikran asked.

"The little bird," I said. "You know. The one that comes in the summer and stands in the air and then shoots away. The one with the wings that beat so fast you can't see them. It's in your hand. It's dying."

"Come with me," the old man said. "I can't see, and the old lady's at church. I can feel its heart beating. Is it in a bad way? Look again, once."

I looked again. It was a sad thing to behold. This wonderful little creature of summertime in the big rough hand of the old peasant. Here it was in the cold of winter, absolutely helpless and pathetic, not suspended in a shaft of summer light, not the most alive thing in the world, but the most helpless and heartbreaking.

"It's dying," I said.

The old man lifted his hand to his mouth and blew warm breath on the little thing in his hand which he could not even see. "Stay now," he said in Armenian. "It is not long till summer. Stay, swift and lovely."

We went into the kitchen of his little house, and while he blew warm breath on the bird he told me what to do.

"Put a tablespoonful of honey over the gas fire and pour it into my hand, but be sure it's not too hot."

This was done.

After a moment the hummingbird began to show signs of fresh life. The warmth of the room, the vapor of the warm honey—and, well, the will and love of the old man. Soon the old man could feel the change in his hand, and after a moment or two the hummingbird began to take little dabs of the honey.

"It will live," the old man announced. "Stay and watch."

The transformation was incredible. The old man kept his hand generously open, and I expected the helpless bird to shoot upward out of his hand, suspend itself in space, and scare the life out of me—which is exactly what happened. The new life of the little bird was magnificent. It spun about in the little kitchen, going to the window, coming back to the heat, suspending, circling as if it were summertime and it had never felt better in its whole life.

The old man sat on the plain chair, blind but attentive. He listened carefully and tried to see, but of course he couldn't. He kept asking about the bird, how it seemed to be, whether it showed signs of weakening again, what its spirit was, and whether or not it appeared to be restless; and I kept describing the bird to him.

When the bird was restless and wanted to go, the old man said, "Open the window and let it go."

"Will it live?" I asked.

"It is alive now and wants to go," he said. "Open the window."

I opened the window, the hummingbird stirred about here and there, feeling the cold from the outside, suspended itself in the arc of the open window, stirring this way and that, and then it was gone.

"Close the window," the old man said.

We talked a minute or two and then I went home.

The old man claimed the hummingbird lived through that winter, but I never knew for sure. I saw hummingbirds again when summer came, but I couldn't tell one from the other.

One day in the summer I asked the old man, "Did it live?"

"The little bird?" he said.

"Yes," I said. "That we gave the honey to. You remember. The little bird that was dying in the winter. Did it live?"

"Look about you," the old man said. "Do you see the bird?"

"I see hummingbirds," I said.

"Each of them is our bird," the old man said. "Each of them, each of them," he said swiftly and gently.

Gaston

They were to eat peaches, as planned, after her nap, and now she sat across from the man who would have been a total stranger except that he was in fact her father. They had been together again (although she couldn't quite remember when they had been together before) for almost a hundred years now, or was it only since the day before yesterday? Anyhow, they were together again, and he was kind of funny. First, he had the biggest mustache she had ever seen on anybody, although to her it was not a mustache at all; it was a lot of red and brown hair under his nose and around the ends of his mouth. Second, he wore a blue-and-white striped jersey instead of a shirt and tie, and no coat. His arms were covered with the same hair, only it was a little lighter and thinner. He wore blue slacks, but no shoes and socks. He was barefoot, and so was she, of course.

He was at home. She was with him in his home in Paris, if you call it a home. He was very old, especially for a young man—thirty-six, he had told her; and she was just six, just up from sleep on a very hot afternoon in August.

That morning, on a little walk in the neighborhood, she had seen peaches in a box outside a small store and she had stopped to look at them, so he had bought a kilo.

Now, the peaches were on a large plate on the card table at which they sat.

There were seven of them, but one of them was flawed. It *looked* as good as the others, almost the size of a tennis ball, nice red fading to light green, but where the stem had been there was now a break that went straight down into the heart of the seed.

He placed the biggest and best-looking peach on the small plate in front of the girl, and then took the flawed peach and began to remove the skin. When he had half the skin off the peach he ate that side, neither of them talking, both of them just being there, and not being excited or anything— no plans, that is.

The man held the half-eaten peach in his fingers and looked down into the cavity, into the open seed. The girl looked, too.

While they were looking, two feelers poked out from the cavity. They were attached to a kind of brown knob-head, which followed the feelers, and then two large legs took a strong grip on the edge of the cavity and hoisted some of the rest of whatever it was out of the seed, and stopped there a moment, as if to look around.

The man studied the seed dweller, and so, of course, did the girl.

The creature paused only a fraction of a second, and then continued to come out of the seed, to walk down the eaten side of the peach to wherever it was going.

The girl had never seen anything like it—a whole big thing made out of brown color, a knob-head, feelers, and a great many legs. It was very active, too. Almost businesslike, you might say. The man placed the peach back on the plate. The creature moved off the peach onto the surface of the white plate. There it came to a thoughtful stop.

"Who is it?" the girl said.

"Gaston."

"Where does he live?"

"Well, he *used* to live in this peach seed, but now that the peach has been harvested and sold and I have eaten half of it, it looks as if he's out of house and home."

"Aren't you gong to squash him?"

"No, of course not, why should I?"

"He's a bug. He's *ugh*."

"Not at all. He's Gaston the grand boulevardier."

"Everybody hollers when a bug comes out of an apple, but you don't holler or *anything*."

"Of course not. How would we like it if somebody hollered every time we came out of our house?"

"Why *would* they?"

"Precisely. So why should we holler at Gaston?"

"He's not the same as us."

"Well, not exactly, but he's the same as a lot of other occupants of peach seeds. Now, the poor fellow hasn't got a home, and there he is with all that pure design and handsome form, and nowhere to go."

"Handsome?"

"Gaston is just about the handsomest of his kind I've ever seen."

"What's he saying?"

"Well, he's a little confused. Now, inside that house of his he had everything in order. Bed here, porch there, and so forth."

"Show me."

The man picked up the peach, leaving Gaston entirely alone on the white plate. He removed the peeling and ate the rest of the peach.

"Nobody else I know would do that," the girl said. "They'd throw it away."

"I can't imagine why. It's a perfectly good peach."

He opened the seed and placed the two sides not far from Gaston. The girl studied the open halves.

"Is *that* where he lives?"

"It's where he used to live. Gaston is out in the world and on his own now. You can see for yourself how comfortable he was in there. He had everything."

"Now what has he got?"

"Not very much, I'm afraid."

"What's he going to do?"

"What are *we* going to do?"

"Well, we're *not* going to squash him, that's one thing we're not going to do," the girl said.

"What *are* we going to do, then?"

"Put him back?"

"Oh, *that* house is finished."

"Well, he can't live in our house, can he?"

"Not happily."

"Can he live in our house *at all*?"

"Well, he could *try*, I suppose. Don't you want to eat a peach?"

"Only if it's peach with somebody in the seed."

"Well, see if you can find a peach that has an opening at the top, because if you can, that'll be a peach in which you're likeliest to find somebody."

The girl examined each of the peaches on the big plate.

"They're all shut," she said.

"Well, eat one, then."

"No. I want the same kind that you ate, with somebody in the seed."

"Well, to tell you the truth, the peach I ate would be considered a bad peach, so of course stores don't like to sell them. I was sold that one by mistake, most likely. And so now Gaston is without a home, and we've got six perfect peaches to eat."

"I don't want a perfect peach. I want a peach with people."

"Well, I'll go out and see if I can find one."

"Where will I go?"

"You'll go with me, unless you'd rather stay. I'll only be five minutes."

"If the phone rings, what shall I say?"

"I don't think it'll ring, but if it does, say hello and see who it is."

"If it's my mother, what shall I say?"

"Tell her I've gone to get you a bad peach, and anything else you want to tell her."

"If she wants me t･) go back, what shall I say?"

"Say yes if you want to go back."

"Do you want me to?"

"Of course not, but the important thing is what you want, not what I want."

"Why is *that* the important thing?"

"Because I want you to be where you want to be."

"I want to be here."

"I'll be right back."

He put on socks and shoes, and a jacket, and went out.

She watched Gaston trying to find out what to do next. Gaston wandered around the plate, but everything seemed wrong and he didn't know what to do or where to go.

The telephone rang and her mother said she was sending the chauffeur to pick her up because there was a little party for somebody's daughter who was also six, and then tomorrow they would fly back to New York.

"Let me speak to your father," she said.

"He's gone to get a peach."

"*One* peach?"

"One with people."

"You haven't been with your father two days and already you *sound* like him."

"There *are* peaches with people in them. I know. I saw one of them come out."

"A *bug*?"

"Not a bug. Gaston."

"*Who*?"

"Gaston the grand something."

"Somebody else gets a peach with a bug in it, and throws it away, but not him. He makes up a lot of foolishness about it."

"It's not foolishness."

"All right, all right, don't get angry at me about a horrible peach bug of some kind."

"Gaston is right here, just outside his broken house, and I'm not angry at you."

"You'll have a lot of fun at the party."

"OK."

"We'll have fun flying back to New York, too."

"OK."

"Are you glad you saw your father?"

"Of course I am."

"Is he funny?"

"Yes."

"Is he crazy?"

"Yes. I mean, no. He just doesn't holler when he sees a bug crawling out of a peach seed or anything. He just looks at it carefully. But it *is* just a bug, isn't it, *really*?"

"That's all it is."

"And we'll *have* to squash it?"

"That's right. I can't wait to see you, darling. These two days have been like two years to me. Good-bye."

The girl watched Gaston on the plate, and she actually didn't like him. He was all *ugh*, as he had been in the first place. He didn't have a home anymore and he was wandering around on the white plate and he was silly and wrong and ridiculous and useless and all sorts of other things. She cried a little, but only inside, because long ago she had decided she didn't like crying because if you ever started to cry it seemed as if there was so much to cry about you almost couldn't stop, and she didn't like that at all. The open halves of the peach seed were wrong, too. They were ugly or something. They weren't clean.

The man bought a kilo of peaches but found no flawed peaches among them, so he bought another kilo at another store, and this time his luck was better, and there were two that were flawed. He hurried back to his flat and let himself in.

His daughter was in her room, in her best dress.

"My mother phoned," she said, "and she's sending the chauffeur for me because there's another birthday party."

"Another?"

"I mean, there's *always* a lot of them in New York."

"Will the chauffeur bring you back?"

"No. We're flying back to New York tomorrow."

"Oh."

"I liked being in your house."

"I liked having you here."

"Why do you live here?"

"This is my home."

"It's nice, but it's a lot different from our home."

"Yes, I suppose it is."

"It's kind of like Gaston's house."

"Where *is* Gaston?"

"I squashed him."

"Really? Why?"

"Everybody squashes bugs and worms."

"Oh. Well. I found you a peach."

"I don't want a peach anymore."

"OK."

He got her dressed, and he was packing her stuff when the chauffeur arrived. He went down the three flights of stairs with his daughter and the chauffeur, and in the street he was about to hug the girl when he decided he had better not. They shook hands instead, as if they were strangers.

He watched the huge car drive off, and then he went around the corner where he took his coffee every morning, feeling a little, he thought, like Gaston on the white plate.

Najari Levon's Old Country Advice to the Young Americans on How to Live with a Snake

Najari Levon went to Aram's house on Van Ness Avenue for some legal advice about a private matter, but Aram hadn't come yet, so the old man with the gargoyle face was asked to make himself at home somewhere.

He saw Aram's two small sons and two small daughters on the linoleum floor of a glassed-in porch, playing a board game and keeping score on a small pad with a small pencil, and so he went there and sat down to watch.

A metal arrow at the center of the large board was spun, and if it stopped in the space where there was a picture of a bright star, for instance, the player was given ten points, but just beside the picture of the star, there was a space in which there was a picture of a small green snake, and if the needle stopped there, ten points were taken away from the player's score.

The scorekeeper was Aram's firstborn, a boy of ten or eleven.

"Star," Aram's secondborn, a daughter, said, but the scorekeeper told his sister the needle was on the *line*, and *nearer* to the snake than to the star.

"Snake," he said, picking up the small pencil to put the score on the pad. His sister knocked the pad and pencil out of his hand, saying, "Star." And they began to fight.

Najari Levon said in Armenian, "In our house in Bitlis lived a very large black snake, which was our family snake."

The fighters stopped to listen, and he said, "No proper family was without its proper snake. A house was not complete without a snake, because the long snake crawling back of the walls held the house together."

The fighters relaxed, and he said, "Our snake had great wisdom. It was the oldest house snake in Bitlis."

The scorekeeper sprawled belly down on the floor, not far from the corner of the room where the small pencil had fallen during the fight.

"Did you see the snake?" he said.

The storyteller glanced at the small green pencil and then at the boy, and he said, "Yes, I saw the snake. His door into the house was at the top of the stone wall in the room where I slept, a door just big enough for the snake to pass through, about the size of a saucer. In the evening as soon as I got into my bed, I looked up at the snake's door, and there I would see him looking down at me."

"*How much* of him would you see?"

"Only the head, because it was nighttime now, and he would soon go to sleep, too."

"Did you ever see *all* of him?"

"Oh, yes."

"How big was he?"

"As big around as a saucer, with a very sensitive face, very large eyes—not the little eyes of English people, but the large eyes of Armenian people. And Kurdish people. And a very thoughtful mouth, like the mouth of John D. Rockefeller, but of course with a different kind of tongue, although I can't be sure of this, because I have seen in a newspaper only a picture of John D. Rockefeller, but not a picture of his tongue."

"Did you see the snake's tongue?"

"Many times, in and out, like words, but of course in his own language, not ours."

"How long was he?"

"Ten times the length of a walking stick. He was not small."

"What would he do back there?"

He lived there. His house was on that side of the stone wall, our house was on our side. But of course there was no such thing as his and ours. The whole house was ours and the whole house was his, but he *lived* back of the wall. In the wintertime I would not see him, and I would almost forget he was there. And then one evening in the springtime I would look up at his door, and there he would be again. He would speak, but I would say, 'Not now, because it's night and time to sleep, but in the morning come down and I will bring you something to eat.' So in the morning..."

"What did he eat?"

"Milk. In the morning I filled a bowl with milk—not one of those little bowls soup is served in for a small man, but one of those large bowls for a large man. My mother asked where I was taking the bowl of milk, and I said, 'Mama, I am taking the bowl of milk to the snake.' Everybody in our family, every man, every woman, and every child comes to my room to see the snake, because to have a snake in a house is baracat.* Everybody stands in the room and waits to see the snake. Thirty-three men, women, and children, instead of thirty-four, because during the winter my grandfather Setrak died."

"Did the snake come out?" the boy sprawled on the floor said.

"I took the bowl of milk, and put it in the corner straight across from the snake's door so that all of the snake would be able to come out of the door, down the wall, and across the floor. And then the thirty-three of us would be able to see *all* of the snake, from the head with the mouth like John D. Rockefeller's mouth, and with the eyes that are not the little eyes of English

* "Baracat" is "good fortune" in Arabic.

people, but the large eyes of Armenian people, and Kurdish people. I put the bowl down and looked up at the snake's door, but the snake is not there, so I speak to the snake, I say to him, 'Sevavor, I have put the bowl of milk on the floor in the corner of the room, so come out of your door and down the wall and across the floor and have something to eat; it is no longer wintertime, it is springtime.'"

"Did he come down?"

"The snake came to the door to see who it was who was speaking to him, he came to see, he came to see who it was, was it me or was it somebody else, so when he came to see, I said, 'Don't worry, Sevavor, it is me, Levon, your friend. I am the one who is speaking, Najari Levon.' The snake looked at me, and then he looked at each of the others in the room, but he did not come down, the snake did not come down because we had been thirty-four and now were thirty-three, so the snake did not come down. I said, 'Sevavor, in the wintertime my grandfather Setrak died—that is why we are no longer thirty-four, we are now only thirty-three, but two of the wives are pregnant and in August we will be more than thirty-four, we will be thirty-five, and if one of the wives has twins, we will be thirty-six, and if both of the wives have twins, we will be thirty-seven, the Najari people will be thirty-seven, Sevavor, so come out of the door, and down the wall, and across the floor to the bowl of milk in the corner.'"

"Did he?"

"Very slowly, like this, like my arm, the snake came out of the door, slowly, down the wall, like this, one walking-stick length of the black body like this, slowly, down the wall, two walking-stick lengths, very hungry, very old, very wise, three walking-stick lengths, very black, four lengths, five lengths, six lengths, and now the snake's head is on the floor like this, but his tail is still behind the wall, and all of the Najari people are watching and waiting, and slowly the snake pushes himself forward on the floor a little nearer to the bowl of milk in the corner, seven lengths out of the door, seven lengths down the wall, eight lengths, nine lengths, and now all thirty-three of the Najari people are almost not breathing, to see better the Najari snake, the snake of the Najari people, from the head to the tail, and now there is only one more length. As soon as the snake moves one more length toward the bowl of milk in the corner, every man, woman, and child in the room will see *all* of the snake of our house, of our family, of the Najari people. But the snake stops. With only one more length to go the black snake moving to the white bowl of milk in the corner stops."

"Why?" the boy said, and the storyteller said, "An old snake who does not see an old man in the springtime because the old man is dead, an old snake who does not see an old man he saw in the summertime, because in the wintertime the old man died, an old snake stops to think about a thing like that. I said, 'Sevavor, do not be unhappy about my grandfather Setrak who died in the cold of wintertime; it is good for an old man to go to sleep in the snow, it is good for him to go home; if nobody went to sleep, if nobody went home, the house would soon be crowded and there would not be food enough for everybody. Do not be sorry for the old man, he is asleep, he has gone home, go and have the milk I have put in the bowl for you."

"Did he go?"

"The snake did not move, the black snake with his head and two walking-stick lengths on the floor, and seven lengths up the wall, and one length behind the wall, did not move, because when my grandfather Setrak was born the snake saw him, and every year of Setrak's life the snake saw him, but now the old man was dead, and the snake was on his way to the bowl of milk in the corner, but the snake did not want to move any more and all of the Najari people did not want to breathe. I said, 'Sevavor, do not worry about the old man, he is home, he is asleep, he is a small boy again running the meadows, go and have your milk.' And then the snake, slowly, like a big black snake with eyes not like the little eyes of English people…"

"Yes, yes," the boy said. "Don't stop."

The old storyteller glanced at the small stub of green pencil on the floor, and then back at the boy, directly this time, scaring him a little, and then in English he said, "Dat your pancil?"

At that moment Aram came in and said, "What is it, Levon?"

The old man got up and chuckled deeply in the manner for which he was famous all over Fresno, and he said, "Aram Sevavor, I came for advice about a private matter. I came all the way from my house on L Street to your house on Van Ness Avenue, past the place where they have those red fire engines, all the way up Eye Street, where the police have their building, all the way up Forthcamp Avenue, I came, Aram Sevavor, one foot after the other, from my house to your house, I came, and now I go, I go all the way back, Aram Sevavor, because I can't remember the question I came to ask."

He went out the back, and down the alley, and the boy with the green pencil stood in the alley and watched him go, taking with him forever the end of the story about the snake.

A. I. Bezzerides

He was closing in on a hundred years now, still writing, still living in that strange house on a hill in the suburbs of Los Angeles. Each morning, Albert Isaac Bezzerides woke up, took a sip or two from the bottle of Shiraz beside his bed, and returned to the novel he had been writing for the past fifty years. As he saw it, the story would contain every swindle and hard time he had ever witnessed, and the list was as stretched out as the century he had lived.

It began even before he was born in Ottoman Turkey, when his Armenian mother was swindled into marriage by a Greek man twenty-four years her senior who peddled goods from the backs of donkeys. When she learned she was pregnant, she tried five different ways to abort him. He was one year old in 1909 when his father, a dollar bill in his pocket, settled the family in Fresno and tried to make his way hawking fruits and vegetables in the neighborhoods of Armenians, Italians, and Volga Germans. "From as far back as I can remember, the endless wranglings of my mother screeching for money-money-money and the endless efforts of my father to 'mehk-de-mohney.'" His story follows father and son to the produce markets of San Francisco, where the "puny-primitive swindles" become less puny, less primitive, and then on to college at Berkeley, where the son washes dishes to cover room and board and then drops out just shy of a degree in electrical engineering because all that learning has only taught him that his real love is writing. The son moves to Los Angeles to repair motion picture sound equipment and begins writing short stories on the side, trying to make his literary mark even though another Armenian from Fresno—born the same year he was born—has already achieved fame by writing about the same neighborhoods, the same faces, the same privations. To feed his new wife and child and still send money home to his parents, the son must choose between writing novels and screenplays. Given all the poverty he has seen, the choice is simple. The son picks Hollywood, where the moguls at Warner Brothers Studio make the produce brokers on Embarcadero Street look like piddlers when it comes to swindle. The son then makes a last visit to the San Joaquin Valley, to the tiny house where his mother is dying and his father, burying a wife he never thought he would live to bury, comes face-to-face with the failure of his life.

> She was dying on the sofa when I got there, and he was
> looking terribly, terribly unhappy. I said, "What's a matter,
> Pa?" And he said, "You know what's a matter. I work and
> I work, and I make no money." And I said, "Money is not
> important." He said, "I'm a failure," and I said, "You're not
> a failure. What you did made me do what I did." He said,
> "I no got money. I no got anything." I said, "You had nerve,
> Pa. You kept going and going. And that was the greatest
> lesson you could give a son, especially a son who is a
> writer." He said, "You don't think I fail?" And I said, "No
> you didn't fail. You kept trying and tying and trying." Pretty
> soon, he was crying like hell, and I took him in my arms,
> and he said, "Why you no think I fail?" And I said, "Well,
> because I couldn't fail watching what you did. You made
> me brave, Pa." He said, "I make you brave?" And I said,
> "Yes, very much." He was in my arms crying and he died
> like that, right in my arms.

How much of the story was real life, how much was fiction no longer mattered. It was on the page, and the ninety-eight-year-old man with a beanie slung low over his face, a sweet toothless face now all white except for Armenian eyes more black than brown, vowed to finish it before he died. The manuscript, nine hundred pages long, sat in a dusty box on the shelf in his bedroom. He said he added and subtracted words each day, but the pages next to the IBM typewriter looked as if they hadn't been touched in months, maybe years. Like everything else in the house, they smelled of smoke from the junk wood his son Peter, sixty-five years old himself, burned in the fireplace.

"It's a big fat story, and I need to finish it," he said. "I'll make it better. I'll cut it down." He dunked an Armenian *choreg* filled with apricot into his coffee and gazed out the second-floor kitchen window at the falling rain. His visitors had plenty of questions, but his thoughts had gone dead again. For several minutes, he said nothing. Then he began whistling a long-ago tune and repeating, in a singsong voice, "Oh well...what the hell."

"Do you regret that you spent all those years writing scripts for movies instead of novels?"

The question was just offensive enough that it snapped him back. "No, I wrote those scripts to please me, and they apparently worked, because I sure had a reputation, huh?"

"But you had the talent to do so much more."

"Maybe I would have written a book like nobody's ever written," he said, eyes twinkling. "But I'm writing that book now."

That I had found him alive and putting the finishing touches on his masterwork, writing in his mind if not on the page, was one of those gifts of perfect timing. It was the spring of 2006, and I had agreed to write this biographical sketch fully expecting that Buzz Bezzerides had died a peaceful death at a ripe old age. Instead, he was leaning on a cane in the doorway of his house in Woodland Hills, where everything—the air included—seemed to have stopped moving in 1959.

Before the visit, I had read several of his short stories and novels and determined right off that his storytelling skills were more artful than advertised. "Hard-boiled, full of violence, gritty, taut, fast-paced, crackling," went the reviews from the 1940s. Yes, he had vividly portrayed the bitter struggles of first- and second-generation immigrants trying to climb the ladder. The critics, though, had overlooked the beautiful way he wrote about his place, the San Joaquin Valley, and his people, the Armenians and Greeks. Consider his portrait of the dying father in *Thieves' Market,* his best-known novel (published in 1949 and republished in 1996), which depicted the grim world of farmers, truckers, and wholesalers in the California produce industry:

> He had been a big man once, walking loud, talking loud,
> trying to make his scratch upon the world, but he grew
> older and older, shrank smaller and smaller until one day
> the stride that had been hard and vigorous faltered and
> tripped into the cot in the living room where the wood
> stove burned all night to keep his thinning blood warm.
> His head shrank until it became a death's head, but his eyes
> grew bigger and bigger until all that seemed left of him
> were his shining eyes looking feverishly about the room. He
> could not sleep. He would toss for hours on the cot, sighing
> endlessly, and call out softly in the middle of the night.

It was tempting, given all they shared, to compare Buzz and Saroyan. As kids, they gravitated to the same books, one trying to beat the other to the checkout counter at the Fresno County Library. They even got their literary launches the same way, selling short stories to Whit Burnett's *Story* magazine in the 1930s. Yet Buzz let everyone know that he went out of his way not to read Saroyan. He never would have been able to write his own stories, he said, if he knew that another author had plowed the same ground first. To write about the Valley, he had to forget about Saroyan, no matter how looming his presence. "It makes me feel as if it were no use to write any longer because [Saroyan] has already beat me to the things which I feel and want to say," he wrote to Burnett upon acceptance of his first published story, "Passage into Eternity." "I want you to know that this stuff I send to you, good or bad, comes out of me and is not passed through me from someone else."

It was Faulkner, not Saroyan, whose influence Buzz felt most deeply. They became friends in 1944 when the Southern novelist joined Buzz as part of a stable of writers at Warner Brothers. By this time, Bezzerides had published two novels, *This Is a Happy Land* (1942) and *Long Haul* (1938), which was adapted into the movie *They Drive by Night,* starring George Raft, Humphrey Bogart, and Ida Lupino. He had written the screenplay for *Juke Girl,* a film about the Dust Bowl Okies who had migrated to the middle of California to harvest the crops. The leading role, a liberal-minded trucker, was played by none other than Ronald Reagan. If Buzz had well learned the Hollywood game, Faulkner proved less willing to bend. They drove to work together every day and paired up on several scripts. Buzz came to see that the long and winding voices that distinguished Faulkner's fiction could stop a movie script cold. He watched Faulkner win the Nobel Prize and then return home.

All these years later, he recalled their goodbye. "As he was leaving, he told me, 'Buzz, keep writing. You're a good writer.'"

Bezzerides went to work adapting Mickey Spillane's *Kiss Me Deadly,* a book he so thoroughly despised that he tossed aside the tough-guy genre and fashioned his own thriller with humanity finding itself on the brink of nuclear annihilation. He then created the television series *The Big Valley,* as homage to the San Joaquin Valley and its rich immigrant tradition. Starring Barbara Stanwyck, it became one of the most popular syndicated shows in history, though Bezzerides never forgave the producers for removing all the ethnic flavor. By the time he retired from Hollywood in the late 1970s, his name had been etched as one of the pioneers of the film noir genre.

Still, it didn't seem enough, and he retreated to that decaying house on the hill to write the great novel that Faulkner saw in him. "Every day, still, I write like hell," he said. "I think it's going to be fantastic."

Mark Arax

The Vines

It was winter. We had moved to the city and the failure of the season's crops was forgotten. My mother had finished her sweeping and the house was in order.

We lived our quiet lives, not hurrying nor trying to hasten the time, the tedium of the year not boring us. We enjoyed the dragging days and the long nights. There was always the quiet and the darkness of winter. November. The holidays. Christmas only a month away and already the spirit of it stalking through the house. New Year. We sat around the red belly of the stove and waited. Everything like this, quiet and restful, life pausing, gathering strength so that it could grow with a rush during summer.

But my father was restless in the house. The pruning was finished. The cuttings were burned. There was nothing more to be done, but a fit of impatience seized him and he could not stay in the house. The eyes of his mind were continually turned to the farm. "I wonder how the vines are doing," he said. "Do you think the river flooded the land? Maybe this year will be an early summer." He got up at six every morning and fussed in the garden.

He missed the summer. When the rain came at midnight, he awoke with the patter of it on the roof and standing in his long underwear he looked out the window and even went to the porch to take a look at the sky. "Look at the clouds," he said. "It looks like a storm. This rain will do the vines good."

He did not like the frost. It laid in bed with him and stiffened him with cold. He arose, shuddering, and laid on his clothes. Outside the roofs were white and pools of water were plated with ice. He lighted the stove and as he warmed his hands he said, "Damn this cold. The frost will hurt the cuttings."

But there was nothing to fear. The vines had no leaves and were naked in the fields, but they were safe from the cold, the soul of them withdrawn and hiding deep in the ground. My father only wanted to go to the farm.

One night he said to me, "Will you go to the *Aiky* with me?" I did not want to go. "What's there at the farm?" I said. It was the same as when we had left. "Nothing," he said; "we'll go and then we will come back. Will you come?"

The imminence of Christmas made me cautious and I could not say no. Early the next morning we hitched the horse to the wagon and drove eighteen miles into the country.

The earth was hibernating and was tucked away beneath a profound sleep. Silence lay everywhere heavy on the land. The sky was gray and far away hung the dark veils of winter. This picture of the earth resting was depressing and sad. We sat on the wagon seat, huddled together in the cold, swaying a little from the roughness of the road, each of us having his thoughts.

When we got to the farm, we did not get down at once, but continued to sit, simply looking at the vines. Then my father said, "Let us go look at the Zinfandels."

"What is there to see?" I asked.

"Nothing," he said, "just the vines. We'll look at them." We walked up and down the rows. The earth was brick-hard and our feet left no prints, making only the clumsy sounds of walking. Now and then my father bent down to clear the weeds and pebbles which crowded the rough stump of some vine. When we got to the railroad track that ran on a high mound along the back of the farm, he climbed up and looked at the land which he owned. He simply stood and looked, but, somehow, he radiated the impatience which we felt, his longing that it were summer again and the vines green and bearing grapes.

When it grew dark we climbed into the wagon and returned to the city. It was late when we got in and my mother met us at the door. "Well, did you speak to your vines?" she said.

"All we did was walk," I said. It was a mystery to me how all this, the walking in the fields, the fondling of the vines, could do any good. They were inanimate, unemotional things that could not reflect the love which my father gave them.

Now and then we went to the ranch again. The same fields, the same vines, the same air of sadness over everything. We went and later we came back. Just that. He liked to be with the vines.

At home my father was quiet, not saying much nor doing much, but his unrest could be felt. He hoed the plants in the garden or he came into the house and sat on the *sadir*, smoking and looking out the window. Calm he was, even motionless with the cigarette on his lips, yet expressing his impatience, suggesting somehow the fury of his unrest.

Christmas passed and rains came. Rains passed and early spring came. My father, filled with not doing, suddenly burst into a riot of doing. He plowed, he irrigated, he worked day and night. He came home muddy and tired. As he ate his late supper, he paused to say, "Today I watered the Thompsons. How the greedy soil did drink it up." He spoke eagerly, trying to convey to my mother the excitement of the crop, the delight in watching the growth of it. "You should see the earth," he said, "everything is changed."

My mother was not easily aroused. She had seen too many crops fail, too many hopes become unrealized. "One crazy person is enough in this house," she said.

School closed for the summer and my brother and I stayed home and played in the yard. My father could not stand this unproductiveness. And he must have thought, If two of us get impatient, the season will hurry and the crop will come sooner. *"Oghloom,"* he said to me, "I want to start you young. Learn early and don't make the mistakes of your father." He even wanted to hurry me along, to pass me through childhood to maturity. "If he stays with the old folk," he said to my mother, "he will grow up sooner and get big ideas."

We drove down the roads to the country, but now the sadness had left the earth. Dawn streaked the sky and presently the red eye of the sun winked at us from the edge of the earth. The veils of winter had risen and the air was clear to a great distance.

Orchards covered with blossoms pinked the morning air. No one was to be seen in the farm yards or on the road. The young sun sifted down its mild light upon the fields and wherever one looked were pictures, delicately colored prints well hung.

We drove and drove and the kind sun, holding back its light to accustom the plants to the coming heat of the day, grew warmer. Soon there were no trees and the fields on both sides of the road were covered with the naked shapes of vines.

The sun was high when we came to our place. Now I could see that the vines were covered with buds. I tore one apart: nothing but curled leaves. "Don't do that," said my father, slapping my hands. "You are ruining grapes."

"Will they be grapes?" I said.

"Yes, they will grow into leaves and the grapes will come." He swept his arm to the whole vineyard. "Everywhere are leaves growing," he said. I felt that he could sense the growth of the vines, feel each uncurling of the leaf from the bud and the bursting of the pregnant twigs into blossom. Even I felt this, the infinitesimal change of the earth in the heat of the sun, the moment by moment growth of the vines.

"Tell mama," said my father. "Tell her how the fields are changing."

That night I said to her, "You should see the blossoms. They are like snow on the trees. The leaves are growing on the vines and the ground is soft." My father touched my shoulder, as if to say, Well done, Oghloom.

Later when we were in bed, I heard him say, "Don't you think it's time we moved to the farm?"

"So soon," said my mother. "Do we have to go so soon?"

The next day we began to pack our belongings. My mother complained, saying, "What is there in the country? Nothing but dry grass and dirt. Dear God, why did you give me a farmer?" We loaded the wagon, locked the house and drove to the farm.

My father unloaded the goods and carried them in. He helped my mother and grandmother clean the house and arrange our belongings in the three rooms.

In the evening we ate wood-cooked food that tasted of the country and later my father sat on the front porch and admired the growth of the vines. "See the leaves," he said, "they have grown." The vines beckoned in the dusky air, as if to say, Here we are, all your hopes, we have come.

It was pleasant living in the country. We clung more closely to one another because it was lonesome. My father came home less tired and more happy. My grandmother dug in the garden.

Across the road loomed the high hum of Mount Campbell. My grandmother pointed at it and said to my father, "Ahk man, your hopes are as big as that mountain." My father looked and nodded his head. "That is the way they are," he said.

The fields began to reward my father's labor. The grape flowers came, fell away and were replaced with little clusters of hard green berries. The vines joyously waved green arms in the air and the sun, proud of all that it had created, beamed down with a bright smile upon the lush fields.

And even my mother, cautious of hope, seeing the green of the leaves and the abundance of the crop, gave herself to the excitement of the season. "Let us be careful," she pleaded to my father, "let us make a little money."

My brother and I followed my father down the vine rows. The earth was powder to our feet and we left tracks, two heavy shoes and four small ones, in the dust. My father raised the skirt of the vines and showed us the crop. "This is the way grapes grow," he said.

Storms came, leaving the face of the earth pocked with the marks of the rain. The sun shone and dust laden with heat swirled over the growing fields.

July yellowed the Thompsons. The Zinfandels grew into tight purple bunches. Men came to the house and offered to buy the crop, but my father shook his head, trusting his hunch and biding his time. "The price will go up two cents," he said.

The season ran like a warm river. Heat reeled off the earth in dizzy waves. The grapes had come, had grown and were now held to pause. Tired in the haste of their growth, the vines seemed to hold their breath. Suspense held the air tight.

One day a big-wheeled wagon drawn by four nodding horses brought clean yellow boxes and scattered them about the fields. August brought the Japanese grape pickers behatted in miniatures of Fujiyama in straw. They waddled about the yard on thick crooked legs and grunted strange words. Tents were raised and smoke from fires rose in thin blue whiskers to the sky. They invaded the fields with their hooked knives, tore at the leaves and ravished the vines. Dust clouded the sky as if announcing, Here someone is working.

Trucks hauled the boxes away. In two weeks the vines were cleaned with only a dry bunch hanging here and there. The Japs struck their tents and departed, leaving the vine rows filled with the prints of their heavy shoes and the yard, where their tents had been, beaten as hard as concrete.

The pruning season was here and my father busied himself among the vines. But his mind was with his grapes in the boxcars far away. My mother worried and could not sleep at night. "What do you think," she said, "will the grapes bring money?"

"Of course," said my father, "what do you think?"

In the meantime the sun, angry at the rape of the fields, began to sear the leaves, browning them and dropping them to earth. The vines grew bare and the wind drove the leaves up and down the rows.

August passed and in September the returns came. Nothing was said to us, the children, but I could hear my father saying, "This can't be. Surely there must be some mistake."

The next morning he looked tense and tired. He walked among the spent vines, my brother and I following. "Papa, is there any more work?" we asked. "Yes," said my father, "we must prune, we must put the vines to rest."

The vines were bare and the restless trailers waving in the air gave them an appearance of children waiting to be undressed. My father, walking among them, seemed resigned. There was no more impatience and no more restlessness. He was hopeless, and even the weary sun was hopeless. It stood wanly in the sky and cast down its cold sad light.

The tribe of Japanese returned and prowled down the rows dipping the sharp-beaked shears into the vines, snipping the naked tentacles and leaving the vines shorn and the ground littered with trailers. The iron-sided wagon wove down the rows and the cuttings were burned. Fire licked over the sides, peeping shyly and hiding, seeming to want to free itself from the confines of the wagon. The iron sides glowed red from the anger of the flames and ashes sifted through the grating to the ground. My brother and I stepped into the cold ashes of the dead fire which had so recently leapt in the wagon and was now dust to the feet.

When the pruning was finished, the farm looked trim and neat as if tucked in for the winter. Already the land was gray and cold. The greyhounds were always chasing. We could see them running across the bare fields, their bodies doubling and extending in furious chase. They would vanish beyond the line of fig trees and presently come trotting back, their tongues dripping and the object of the chase hanging limply from the mouth.

At night the mosquitoes awakened us and we could hear the croaking of frogs and the mild tenor barking of the greyhounds.

The melancholia of autumn settled on the land and we began to long for the city. "When are we going home?" we cried. "When are we going back to town?"

"When your father finishes his work," said my mother. We began to bundle our belongings. The Japs were paid and sent away.

We sat in the wagon and wound through the vineyard to the road. The vines were tired, the night was tired, even we were tired, not with the weight of day but with the burden of summer. Far away against the ends of the earth the day's last fires burned. My father slapped his shoulders and said in a shivery voice, "*Vush*, it's cold."

The floor of the wagon trembled. The night was endless, eternal. Wheels creaked and crickets chirred; yet all about us was the silence, vague and pressureless. The horse trotted tediously, patiently drawing us into it.

My mother began to weep, the shy tears unafraid in the darkness. Simply, child-like she wept for promise broken and hope unrealized. "What is this?" she said. "Year after year fate tortures us."

My father said nothing. All about us were the vine shapes, stumpy and shorn, slumbering in the darkness. His whole being was filled with thoughts of the vines. He slapped the reins and drew his coat more tightly about him. Already the past was forgotten. He sat quietly on the seat, hunched in the cold but not feeling the cold; his body here but his mind past and beyond itself.

On and on we went, drawn imperceptibly into the future, the winter before us, the wind and the rain. And my father sat there, restless and impatient, yearning beyond this into the summer.

Dreamers

One quiet, sleepy Sunday afternoon, my father walked down the porch steps to the path. The tall, brick chimney of the brewery sent a lazy wisp of gray smoke twisting into the sky and the subdued sounds of kids shouting came from the playground across the tracks.

"Where you going, Pop?" I said.

"To Hajji's house," my father said. "I'll be back pretty soon."

"Can I go too?"

"Well, why not?" my father said. "Come on then."

I jumped to the lawn and my father took my hand as we went down the street and cut across the empty lot to the Santa Fe tracks.

Hajji was an old Armenian who lived near California Field. He was such a vicious, unfriendly man that I wanted to see what he looked like at close range.

"Now when we get there, sit still and don't open your mouth," my father said. "You know how Hajji is?"

I nodded.

We walked along the embankment on which the tracks ran, to M Street, and there turned left to a small white-washed house surrounded with Chinaberry trees. I could hear chickens in the high-fenced yard and a rooster chukking to his hens.

"All right, here we are," my father said.

We went up the steps to the porch and he knocked. There was a stretch of silence, then a soft sound of slippers and the door swung open. Ahna, Hajji's wife, stood in the opening. She was a skinny, dark woman with black, friendly eyes and she wore a woolen shawl over her wrinkled, ape's head. "Eh," she said in Turkish, "is it you?" and she smiled at me with her puckered mouth. "Come in, come in," and she stooped forward and led us into the house.

Hajji, a solid chunk of a man in his late nineties, sat on the *mindaar* with his legs folded under him and his tassled fez on his head. A *narghileh* nipple was in his mouth and a quiet smile was on his face. He looked at my father and said, "Did you come?" Then he looked at me, puffed twice on the tube, received a bubbling answer from the jar, patted my head with a heavy hand and said, "You came too."

I was surprised that he did not remember me as one of the boys who annoyed him and I was relieved when my father hoisted me up to the top of the high *mindaar* and sat down between me and the patriarch. Hajji puffed again and said, "Good, I'm glad you came."

I had expected some great conversation when we got into the room, in the manner of people from the old country, such as:

"Eh, how are you, Bahrone Boghos?"

"I am well, and how are you, Hajji-Agha?"

"*Ahk*, thanks to God, I too am well. It is a good day today."

"Yes, it is a good day today."

"Yesterday was a good day too."

"Yes, yesterday was a good day too."

"Tomorrow will also be a good day."

I had visited a number of men with my father and this is how the conversation usually ran, eventually getting to a discussion of crops, last year's, this year's and next year's. But this time I sat on the *mindaar* and waited and waited and nothing happened.

Time gradually stood still. A bee buzzed against the window pane, Ahna's slippers shuffled from room to room, and these sounds were remote, as if coming from another world. Sunlight glinted on the Chinaberry leaves and in the yard a rooster crowed. Occasionally Hajji sucked on the narghileh, gurgling the water in the jar, and exhaled, filling the room with smoke.

A tin of tobacco covered with the crooks and elbows of Turkish words stood on the low coffee table and beside it lay a tiny book of cigarette paper, the leaves flirted open. My father leaned forward, gathered tin and booklet into his hands, sat back and rolled a cigarette, placed it between his lips and lighted it. Soon he too was inhaling, holding his breath, then exhaling, ahhhh, in a full, vaporous sigh.

We sat quietly, not saying a word. I wondered how long this silence was going to last. A cold, tingly sensation crept up my legs and I grew restless on my bottom and shifted from side to side. I tried to sit still, but my whole body itched to move. I turned my head and rolled my eyes.

On the floor, on the sofa where we sat, even on the walls were Turkish rugs in a profusion of color and design. Brass pots and tarnished vases stood on the tables and shelves. A photograph of a girl, her face barely discernible, gazed quietly at us from the wall.

Gradually I noticed a strange odor in the room, not the choking smell of tobacco nor of anything nameable, but simply an odor of the old country.

Such an odor my Grand Aunt had brought with her when she had come from Turkey. It was in her clothes, in her bundles, even in her face when she bent down to kiss me. The odor made me think of all the old country people that I had ever known, boys and girls, men and women, and I tried to remember what had happened to them.

Outside the Summer sky glowed and the Summer sun flashed and here we were, in the United States, in Fresno, and this was a new time, a new place, but in this room, my father and Hajji were far away, thinking of the old country, trying to remember old happenings, living again an old life. Even I felt myself drifting away to a strange land.

They were dreamers lost in their thoughts, wrapped in the veil of their past. They blinked their eyes, stroked their mustaches and sighed. And they sat. They did not exchange one word, though Hajji looked at my father and my father looked at Hajji, each without being conscious of the glance.

But dreams must come to an end. A long time had passed, when my father shook his head and said, "*Akh*, those days." And Hajji said, "They are gone, all dead, and one day we will be dead too."

This thought held them for another moment; then Hajji called out in a voice sharp as a whip, 'Ahna!—O'Sahna!" The spell was broken and I moved around on the seat.

Ahna came and Hajji said, "*Gaiffa*," and she shuffled away to return soon with two tiny cups of coffee not much larger than thimbles. The odor of the thick, black Turkish coffee dispelled the other odor. And she brought a big, red apple for me.

I listened to the ritualistic drinking of the coffee. Siiiip, my father said, Siiiip, Hajji said, then alternately they said Ahhhhh, cooling their scalded mouths, for the coffee was very hot. Even now they did not send a word back and forth in the shape of conversation.

Though the cups were small, it seemed to me that an eternity had passed before they were done with sipping and ahhing and the cups were turned over in order to tell their fortunes. A moment upside down and the cups were righted again, inspected, exchanged and carefully inspected once more.

Outside the sky was growing dark. My father arose and I slipped down from the sofa. "We must go," my father said.

"Don't go, don't go," Hajji said. "You just came, what is your hurry, it's still early, sit down. Sit down and let us talk some more."

"It's getting late," my father said, and he pointed outside where the shapes of houses were blocked in shadow and red was gathering in the sky. We walked to the door where Ahna was waiting.

"Eh, come again," Hajji said.

And though my father knew that Hajji never visited anyone, my father said, "*Hai-yah*, and you come too."

We walked down the steps and behind us Ahna quietly shut the door, sealing in the past, preserving it for another time. We walked in the cool evening down the tracks. A mile away the lights of the city glowed in the sky.

At home my mother said, "Where have you two been all this time?"

"At Hajji's house," my father said.

"What do you find to do at Hajji's house?"

My father stroked his mustache, the way he always did when he was thinking. Then he looked at my mother with brooding eyes. "We talk," he said.

The White Mule

When my father had a farm (the bank now owns it and the vines are run down; weeds grow in the rows and the ground is hard like concrete from lack of care) he had a desire to own a mule. Horses, he heard, ate much and tired easily, while mules ate little and could be worked harder. "By golly," he said, "I'm going to trade Charlie in for a mule." The next day he tied a rope around Charlie's neck and led him to Eddy Longworth's farm where, for ten dollars and the horse, he purchased the mule.

We hated to see Charlie go for he was a friend of the family. He was gentle and allowed my brother and I to hang on his neck while he tossed his head high. When he curled back his lips to take the apples we gave him, he was careful not to bite our fingers. But he was old. He had clumsy hairy legs and large splayed hooves. He had the loose lips and large yellow teeth characteristic of old horses.

But in the evening when my father led the white mule to the house, we quickly forgot all our regrets that Charlie was gone. The mule was a beautiful animal. He had small trim hooves and a fine shapely head. His ears were alert, turning this way and that to catch every sound, and his firm tail switched from side to side.

"He's young and strong," said my father. "Look how he flips his ears and swings his tail. Only a young mule would do that."

He led the mule to the barn. "Here is your new home," we could hear him saying. He forked hay down from the loft and returned to the house.

The mule had found the door and was wandering in the corral. With a grunt he kneed himself to the ground and began to roll in the dust. He rolled one way, rested a moment and rolled back, groaning with pleasure. "Look, Papa," we shouted, "He's taking a bath."

"He's enjoying himself so much," said my grandmother, "he makes me want to roll on the ground."

The mule had risen and we could hear him voicing himself, half bray, half whinny. Then he returned to the stall and buried his nose in the hay.

"A fine animal," said my father with satisfaction. "Now we will be able to do twice the work in half the time."

The next morning my father arose early, laid the harness on the mule's back and hitched it to the plow. "Gluck-gluck-gluck," he said with his tongue, and the mule pricked up his ears. "Giddap," urged my father and the mule gathered its strength and heaved at the plow. Off he went in a burst of energy that left us amazed. The plow bit deeply into the ground and the earth flew. "My, how he pulls," said my father over his shoulder. "I can hardly keep up with him. Giddap Jake, gluck-gluck-gluck, show us how strong you are."

They went three rows and my father stopped him for rest. The mule's sides were frothy with sweat and he was panting for breath. He turned once to look at my father and flicked his ears and switched his tail.

"Off we go again," said my father. "Giddap, Sweetheart, *hah dey.* Tonight I will feed you oats, barley, anything you wish." And he slapped the reins on Jake's tight rumps and again he gathered himself and lunged against the traces. The plow threw up the earth.

My brother and I tried to follow them along the furrows, but they were going too fast. We stood in the wet soil and watched them dwindle away down the rows. A cloud of dust followed them.

All that day we watched the mule and my father and how they sped up and down the rows. The poor mule had probably never been worked so hard in all his life. At night, when my father unhooked him from the single tree and drove him home, my mother imagined she could detect a trace of puzzlement in the mule's face. "My, how surprised he looks," she exclaimed.

"Surprised at what?" said my father.

"At you. He wonders if you are the mule or he. How you made the poor animal work."

Jake took a long drink at the trough. Then my father filled the small bin in the manger with oats and stuffed the trough to bristling with hay.

We stood at the fence, waiting for the mule to take his bath, but he was so tired, he did not come out. He did not even eat. "He fell right to the floor," said my father, "without once poking his nose into the oats. Even I am tired. How my bones ache."

Late at night we heard the peculiar sound of the mule, half donkey, half horse, coming from the barn. "He's braying," said my father. "He is rested now. See how quickly they recover."

The following morning the hay was gone from the manger and the oats had vanished from the small bin.

"Another morning, my beauty," said my father. "Off to work we go again," and he reached for the halter, but Jake raised his head, the whites of his eyes showing. "Whoa," shouted my father, "Whoa now," and he jumped up and caught the halter, laid on the harness and hitched him to the plow.

"Gluck-gluck," he said. The mule bunched his muscles and heaved forward and once more the day's work began. Back and forth, back and forth, the whole day long under the hot dusty sky.

"He is better than a tractor," said my father. "If the crop is good, I'll buy another one. We can work for the neighbors and just think of the profit we'll make."

Thus it went for a whole week. The mule worked like two mules from morning to night. If my father grew tired, then Sinan took the plow and steered a straight course down the vine rows.

"That mule is a bird," said Sinan. "He flies down the field."

"Tomorrow we will be finished," said my father. "It would have taken two weeks with the horse."

We went to bed and that night there was a faint sound of thunder in the direction of the barn, then the sharp clatter of hooves. The next morning when we awoke, the whole back of the barn was smashed out and the mule was gone.

"Somebody stole my mule," cried my father.

"Stole?" said my grandmother, "He escaped, you mean. He grew tired of your tyranny and kicked out the side of the barn and ran away."

My father spent the whole day looking for Jake, the white mule. "I can't understand it," he said. "Why did he do this? I gave him the best of everything and he runs away. Imagine knocking down the barn!"

Toward evening the mule was found near the river, on the bank, sporting among the trees. When he saw my father, he flung his tail and galloped down the fields. It was late at night before he would allow anyone to come near.

Jake was led to the repaired barn and tied to his stall. "Whoa," said my father, "quiet now. What got into you? Weren't you happy? Did we hurt you?"

For a time he and the mule worked easily, but after a few days, my father began to get unreasonable again. "The irrigation ditch will go dry and the watering will not be finished. We must dig furrows." From early morning until late at night, off they went once more.

Three days and one night again there was the sound of thunder, the sputter of hooves, and the following morning the mule was gone. This time he was found in the swamps beyond Sanger.

"The devil is in him," said my father. "Why can't he work like a decent beast and stop all this nonsense!" The barn was repaired and the mule was tied. But now the spirit of rebellion had been aroused in him. Twice he had been betrayed. He had learned his lesson. No sooner did my father leave the barn than up went his rumps and bang went his heels, like machine gun shots, striking anything within reach. My father ran in. "Hoy, there, whoa, Izmir *Ashak*, brainless *sabig*, stop your kicking. Are you trying to wreck the barn?"

Jake reared his head and laid back his ears, blasting air through his dilated nostrils. His eyes, glaring white, were charged with a violent anger. He struck out with his front hooves and my father backed away.

"Lazy good-for-nothing beast," he exclaimed. "Work one day and go on a strike the next."

"He would not be having such funny notions if you had not abused him," said my grandmother.

Jake would not work any longer. He became a regular rebel. My father had to tie him in the middle of a bare field in order to save the barn.

"He'll quiet down," he thought. "He'll come to his senses."

But the mule never recovered. If anyone approached, up went the rumps and out struck the hard round heels, whistling with speed.

Eventually my father had to return Jake to Longworth's farm, and for ten dollars and the mule, took back Charlie.

He began to plow with the horse, going tediously down the rows, Charlie's head nodding slowly with each step, his large loose lips rattling every twenty feet or so. He would have worked day and night, plodding tirelessly along the vines, never complaining.

"No more mules for me," swore my father. "Horses are good enough. Let them work slowly, let them eat a little more. They have no revolution, no funny ideas in their heads. They stick to their work and mind their business and never give any trouble."

"Horses have no brains," said my grandmother.

RICHARD HAGOPIAN

The twentieth century was a period of enormous migration to America by people in search of hope and freedom from social and economic repression. Common to all immigrants' experience, whatever their ethnic origins, was the struggle to maintain a sense of selves and values in a new land. Out of that struggle rose a category of literature—of first- and second-generation narratives capturing the hardships of adapting to an alien, often hostile, country, of children trying to grow up while torn between old-world family values and their adoptive brave new world, of identities lost and new ones found.

One of the seminal voices of the Armenian immigration was Richard Hagopian. Born in Revere, Massachusetts, in 1914, Hagopian was endowed with a rich tenor singing voice, and considered a career in singing while attending the New England Conservatory of Music in Boston. However, after two years he withdrew and attended Pomona College, in Oregon, graduating with a degree in English in 1941. Following his service in the armed forces, he began his career as a professional writer, specializing in short stories.

After a short teaching stint he returned to college, receiving his M.F.A. from the University of Iowa in 1948. He was appointed a lecturer in the Department of Speech at the University of California, Berkeley, becoming a full professor in 1962. Richard Hagopian would spend the rest of his life dividing his time between teaching and writing.

Although his canon consists of only two novels and a collection of short stories, Hagopian was considered a promising talent. His works appeared in various magazines, including *The Atlantic Monthly, Harper's Bazaar,* and *Mademoiselle,* as well as in *The Best American Short Stories: 1945.* According to *New York Times Book Review* editor Nona Balakian, Hagopian's stature as a writer had grown steadily since the end of World War II, and deserved to be more widely read. Unfortunately, his untimely death in 1969 curtailed that promise.

Hagopian's first book, *The Dove Brings Peace*, published in 1944, is a collection of seventeen short stories linked by continuing characters, drawn from Hagopian's own family members. Told from the point of view of a child, these tales reflect the bitterness of a people in cultural transition as well as the optimism and warmth of a humble Armenian home, held together by a desire to be happy in spite of the strangling grip of poverty and the innate melancholy of an ill-fated people.

Written with lyrical grace and an eye for exacting detail, these narratives follow the young Levon as he observes poignant moments: his mother trying to make of their cramped tenement home an ordered and happy place, his siblings coming to terms with Armenian family life in an American world, and his father playing *tavloo*, entertaining friends, eating *sarma*, and drinking *raki* while recounting tales of the old world. The collection projects a broad spectrum of expression, from humorous trifles to ironic parables to dramatic conflicts of universal insight. And while several of the tales evoke an Armenian melancholy, the stories ultimately celebrate the redemptive power of love. The title story, "The Dove Brings Peace," introduces one of the common themes in the collection and in his two novels—that we are the authors of our own joys and, through ignorance and foolish pride, our own sorrows. The story centers around two old *tavloo*-playing companions whose friendship is shattered over Dai's remark about Dikran's reputation for cheating. When poverty forces Dai to leave, he sends to the latter a dead dove, which Dikran construes as an insult. For weeks Dikran's mood turns from anger to abject misery, casting a pall over family life until word of Dai's death open's Dikran's eyes—that the gesture was one of friendship: "A dove brought to me...Like Noah you sent it to a place of safety—your Ararat—your refuge. Akh, Dai, I dreamed the truth, but I dreamed too, too late." In his guilt he tells his young son to cherish the friends he will make in life—"to be wise and faithful to them." In that realization, joyful warmth is restored to their home. And the story closes on father and son playing *tavloo*, Dikran slyly vowing to play fairly.

As in the short stories, family is the celebrated heart of Hagopian's first novel, *Faraway the Spring* (1952). The main character, Setrak Dinjyan, is the hapless but loving father of four, a fancy shoe-stitcher, and a champion backgammon player. More than anything else, Setrak wants his family to be whole and happy. But they are poor, and the resultant grief and humiliation force them into desperate choices. Something of a quitter, Setrak hates his job and keeps moving from one dehumanizing shoe factory to another. To his chagrin, his wife, Maryam, has done the "American thing"—she has taken a job to supplement his paltry income. Their oldest son, Leo, is a cripple in mortal need of medical attention that only specialists on the West Coast can provide. The daughter, Sarah, so much wants a new hat for Easter that Setrak turns to gambling. Alas, he takes his weekly pay (twenty-four dollars) to the home of a woman of dubious reputation where he challenges a young Armenian noted for his formidable talent at backgammon. Of course, Setrak loses his wad, his reputation, and his self-respect, and shoplifts a hat for his daughter—an act that mortifies his wife.

But it is springtime, a time of rebirth and redemption. Rather than some spiritual epiphany to reverse bad choices, the redemption comes by way of a bequest from the man who beat him at *tavloo* and who suddenly died soon afterward. While money is power and a chance to live a better life in the new world, Hagopian reminds us at the end that while celebrating "the slow dissolution of the evil" of the poverty that had ruled their lives, the Dinjyans know that "all was not won, and that suffering and pain were still nearby."

This ending is emblematic of the difference between the writing of Richard Hagopian and that of the more celebrated William Saroyan, whose stories are characterized by a lightness of mood and high exuberance. By contrast, Hagopian projects a "heavy Armenian spirit," an endemic Armenian sadness. As he says in the preface to *The Dove Brings Peace*, he had tried to capture the "little people about me"—Armenian families "groping in the transplanted ruins of a lacerated past."

Hagopian's second novel, *Wine for the Living*, published in 1956, is a superior work. More ambitious and sophisticated than its predecessor, the novel demonstrates his considerable talent and unfulfilled promise. The story has more action, more characters, more breadth, and a very contemporary feel with its multiple, shifting points of view. It also has more to say, and not just to Armenians.

Set in his hometown of Revere, Massachusetts, the story vividly captures the experience of tenement living, of bustling streets and Italian grocers, and still-open cow pastures and apple orchards yet to be crammed with condos and strip malls. The novel centers on the Aroian family and, in particular, the uneasy quest of eleven-year-old son Paul. The core conflict is not the evil of poverty but a bad mix of family egos. Ara, Paul's "once valorous" father, has been reduced to a "confused coward" in his loveless marriage. Paul's mother, Lucy, is a self-pitying woman of toxic bitterness. Raised in Armenia as the favorite daughter, she resents the loss of her youth and promise and how marriage in America has strapped her with children—two of whom she has renounced in disgrace for marrying *odars,* the third, Paul, the child she never wanted. Adding to the depressive atmosphere is her pompous, freeloading brother Atanas from Constantinople who constantly reminds Lucy that Ara is a mere waiter in an Italian restaurant—another family disgrace.

Much of the action centers on Paul's search for belonging inside and outside the home. But given the poisonous atmosphere in the Aroian household, it is no wonder he looks elsewhere, namely to his friend Mario Cataldo, with whom he shares fantasies of knightly heroics and whose home is more tightly knit and full of laughter and music. Paul also befriends a kindly old Italian barber who teaches him about opera and who becomes a surrogate father figure. Of course, the bigoted Lucy and Atanas forbid Paul to fraternize with the Italian "savages" and successfully turn him against his friends as well as his own father.

Feeling the sting of his son's displaced attention, Ara vows to make of his family a friendly, more unified entity. Toward that end he asks his friend Garo to observe the Aroian family dynamics in a social visit in order to make suggestions for improvement. What turns out to be a mercy mission backfires when womanizing Atanas puts the make on Garo's pretty but vacuous wife, Mabel. The ensuing affair, humorously dramatized, ends when Atanas rejects the stupid woman, who, broken-hearted, runs away from home. Unfortunately, Garo discovers fatuous love notes from Mabel and denounces his old friend.

As in Hagopian's first novel, *Wine for the Living* ends with a conditioned victory and redemption. Paul wins a medal for his artistic achievement in school; his friendship with childhood pal Mario is reestablished; the old barber dies, but Ara reasserts his place in the home and bodily throws Atanas out of the house, thus allowing himself to reconnect with his son. But as is characteristic in Hagopian's work, celebration is tempered; the mother, momentarily warmed by Paul's award, says that he can have dinner with the Cataldos, then mysteriously walks out of the house, leaving readers to wonder if she'll return a changed person or not at all.

Because we observe the story through these various characters, Hagopian's layered tableau successfully explores the gaps between husbands and wives, parents and children, Armenians and non-Armenians, the old world and the new—gaps that are eventually bridged by communication and love. This shifting perspective strategy also demonstrates Hagopian's ability to create rich characterizations with realistic sounding dialogue (and dialects) and a variety of moods, ranging from lyrical ruminations to humorous satire. And, as in his shorter works, the writing is masterful, the language carefully worked at.

At his death Richard Hagopian was working on a third novel, *A Day for Sparrows*. We can only speculate as to what heights that and subsequent works might have taken this very gifted man.

Gary Goshgarian

Saint in the Snow

Fat Garabed Agha told good stories. Unlike my father, who bored his children over and over again by telling every visitor who came to our house the same story of his experiences while traveling from Alexandria to Constantinople and back, Garabed Agha had a fund of different ones. And they were all true. He swore to that. If I behaved well when he came over to our house for an afternoon of coffee and cards, that is, if I kept silent and listened to the old men talk and brought him a glass of water the polite way, with a saucer under it, every time his throat got dry—and that seemed to happen all the time—he took time off to tell me a story. Just for me. The kind he thought young ears would enjoy. This was his way of repaying me for the little services I offered on those long afternoons when it was snowing or raining outside and I was forced to stay inside and put up with their everlasting talk, cardplaying and coffee drinking.

On this particular afternoon it was snowing hard, and whether his selection of the story and his constant comments on the snowstorm were to be taken as hints by my father to invite his fat friend to stay to dinner, I do not know. Garabed Agha was a good hinter: the kind that makes it a joy to take a hint and a pleasure to pay for it. After having finished his cigarette he placed another one in the holder and looked out the window for a long time. Then lighting the fresh cigarette, he said, "Whew, what a snowstorm. It makes me freeze to look at it. How much it reminds one of our own *kugh* in January. Yes, and it reminds me of a story too. A true story. Your son has been a good boy today," he commented to my father. "I can see he is waiting for a story." He smiled at me and said, "This cold weather and the snow remind me of a good one. Be a good boy and bring me another glass of water. This will be the last, then I will tell you the story."

I brought him the glass of water the polite way and waited for the story. Garabed Agha drank the water and started:

"You will not appreciate this story as much as one who was raised in the old country. In this country even the poorest soul prepares for his death by taking out a few dollars' insurance. But in the old country people have a hard enough time to take care of themselves and their families while they are alive, let alone after they are dead.

"Well, once upon a time there lived a poor old man and his wife in our kugh—that is our word for village. They were very poor people, like so many others of our kugh, and one winter night, very much like this one," he looked out the window and meditated for a moment, "the old man took sick and died. Now, in our country when someone dies we go to the village priest at once and arrange for the burial. So the old woman put on her rags and went to the priest's house. But the priest of our kugh was a miserly, cruel man, and when the old woman came to him weeping and told him her story and said she wanted her husband to have a good Christian burial, the priest asked, 'Are you able to pay for such a good Christian burial? You know a good burial takes money. Any burial takes money for that matter.'"

"Why did he ask?" my father interjected. "Didn't he know the woman was penniless?"

"Didn't he know? Of course!" answered Garabed Agha. "My own mother used to send me over to their house with pilaf or cheese when we could spare it. Didn't he know?" went on Garabed Agha angrily. "Didn't he see the old woman in rags? Wasn't she part of his flock? The whole kugh knew. But better to ask what new room the good priest was planning to add to his house or what old barrel of wine he wanted to add to his cellar. Better to ask questions like those, then you will know why the old scoundrel tried to squeeze money out of stones. Oh, he knew," went on Garabed Agha slyly. "He knew, but widow's gold pieces are as good as any."

I grew impatient with all these side remarks the old men made. How these people loved to ruin a good story with their interruptions of pity and anger! Garabed Agha lighted another cigarette and went on:

"Well, in any case, the woman cried and said, "No, I am penniless, my husband never saved. But please, good father, bury him and my prayers shall forever be for your health and the prosperity of the church of God." But the good priest knew that the church would live without her prayers and he knew how cold and uncomfortable the snowy journey would be in the procession from the church to the cemetery. So he told the old woman to do the best she could with her dead husband. As for him he had other burials to attend to—and his time was limited."

"Liar!" exclaimed my father. "Who was he trying to fool—a child? Was there a plague in the kugh that year? No." Then to me, "Mind you, there was only a handful in our community. He had other burials!"

"So the woman went home and wailed and wept over her poor husband's body. She cried so loud that all the neighbors were touched. Her wails broke their hearts and brought tears of pity to their eyes. Finally, some of the good people appealed to the elders of the city to do something for the old lady. The elders listened to their pleas and decided to visit the old woman. When they go to her house they found the old lady sitting by the body of her husband, crying and melting herself with suffering. 'I am penniless. I have no friends. My poor husband will decay before my very eyes, and I am helpless to do anything. The priest would not listen to me. My poor man will go unburied,' she mourned to the elders.

"And what could the elders do? They, too, were poor—shoemakers and farmers. They scratched their heads and felt ashamed before the old woman, for they had brought no food, no money and no advice…

"Then they went to a far corner of the room and talked. They talked and talked while the woman waited patiently. But they found no answer to the problem. Obviously the old man was dead and had to be buried. But how?

"Finally, in desperation, Girkor Govgas, one of the old men, discovered that he had an idea. He said it wasn't a very good one, but that it was a possible answer to the old woman's problem.

"'If the old lady will consent to my plan we can go ahead with it tonight.'

"'What is your plan?' asked his friends anxiously.

"'It is a simple one,' said Girkor Govgas. 'Since the priest is obstinate, and more a servant of the devil than of God, and since it is unhealthy for a dead man to live with a live woman, and since we have no money to dispose of the corpse, we must find a way of getting rid of it without money, perhaps in the hills, where we shall not have to pay for a lot. But it is out of the question for three old men like ourselves to undertake this job. A journey to these hills in this snow needs young limbs. And a dead man, when you are old, is no light weight. It must be carried by strong, young arms.'

"The old men were of one mind. It was a job for strong young men. But what of the pay for their services? No one would brave this storm for nothing. And, after all, a dead man is a disagreeable thing even for young men.

"But Girkor Govgas had the answer. 'Wine is cheap. I will donate a bottle if the rest of you will. We were young once ourselves, and we must admit that a little wine made the hardest job seem easy, the most disagreeable one an adventure.'

"His friends were amazed at the idea. Why hadn't they thought of it before? The old men nodded their heads and solemnly pledged a bottle of wine apiece. When they told the widow of their plan she took comfort and prayed the blessing of God on their heads, their wives' heads, their children's heads, and their children's children's heads.

"In a short time the news of the three bottles of wine spread through the kugh and that evening three young stalwarts braved the storm and knocked on Girkor's door. With a bottle of wine each they marched to the widow's house to get her husband. There they made a stretcher, and after the old lady had cried some more and kissed her husband good-bye, the young men placed him upon the stretcher and started off toward the hills."

"Ahk, that is the young men for you!" exclaimed my father.

"Young men is right," went on Garabed Agha as he looked out the window. "Winters were made for youth. As for old men (he was thinking of himself), the inside is the place for them. The inside." He settled back in his chair and sipped his coffee. "So the young men went off, drinking and singing, and jouncing the old man round on the stretcher. Behind them the old woman's cries and prayers for their children's children were drowned in the storm. Into the night they went, singing and drinking and making jokes. Now and then they stopped to rest, drinking more wine, wrestling, and having all sorts of fun. Then they grew drunker and became very careless. They bounced the old man around more freely, playing all sorts of games with him, seeing how high they could bounce him from the stretcher without dropping him.

"But a bad thing happened. Once when they threw the stretcher down to rest and play, the old man slipped off into the snow and was lost. But the young men didn't realize this until they had traveled about a quarter of a mile farther. All they were carrying was snow. Finally one of the young men said:

"'Durtad, do you feel as strong as I feel? The wine has made a powerful man out of me. I don't feel as though I was carrying anything.'

"And of course he wasn't. They all looked at the stretcher more closely and realized what had happened."

"'Where is he?' asked Durtad.

"'What happened to the old man?' asked Atanas.

"'What trick are you trying to play?' each one asked the other.

"The cold air and the missing man sobered them up. They realized that there was nothing else to do but to find the corpse. But where?"

"'We must find him!' they cried.

"So the poor young men looked around in the snow all night long. But they had no luck. A lot of snow had fallen and in some places the drifts were up to their shoulders. How could they find him? It was impossible. Tired and frightened they returned to the kugh that morning and told the old woman what had happened, how the old man had disappeared from the stretcher.

"'Disappeared!' she cried. 'You have lost him, you drunken fools. Oh, my husband,' she cried, 'where are you, where are you? Bring him back, bring him back,' she wailed. 'Oh, find him. I want to see his tired face and hands again. Find him for me.' She went on and on.

"But the young men knew this was impossible. They had searched all night without any luck. Meanwhile the old woman kept crying and telling them to bring the old man back. The young men, fearing that she might go mad in her grief, went to Girkor Govgas and told him what had happened. They begged him to do something for the old woman before her mind became damaged with suffering. Girkor cursed them.

"'Drunken fools, you have disgraced us all. Now, what will all the people say?' Then he worried about his friends, the other two men, and wondered what he would tell them."

"That is youth," said my father. "Drink and play games. They have no respect for death and old age."

"That is right," agreed Garabed Agha. "As I say, if you want something done right, don't depend on youth, do it yourself, old and tired as you are."

My father nodded and Garabed Agha went on.

"Girkor saw his friends the next morning and told them what had happened. The old men bit their fingers and cursed the day they had been born.

"'This disgrace will follow us until we die,' they said. 'What will the people of the kugh, the priest, think? Drunken youth!' they cried.

"While they were calling the young men names the old woman knocked on the door.

"'Don't say anything,' said Girkor Govgas.

"So the old men sat in a corner and listened to the woman's curses for a long time. Then she said she was going to report the whole thing to the police and the priest. She cursed them again and was about to leave when Girkor Govgas stopped her. His two friends watched to see what he was going to do.

"'We can turn your grief into happiness,' said Girkor. He crossed himself. The elders followed suit.

"'What do you mean?' asked the old woman. 'Have you found my husband?'

"'Better than that,' answered the dignified Govgas.

"'A Christian burial?' asked the old woman.

"'Even better,' answered Girkor Govgas.

"The old woman waited with tears in her eyes. 'You are joking with a poor old widow,' she cried.

"'No,' said Girkor. Then he made the sign of the cross again and said, 'Woman, your husband has ascended. Bless his soul.' And the other men repeated, 'Bless his soul.' 'He is not lost,' went on Girkor. 'Armenian young men reverence their elders. They don't lose our aged dead in the snow. Your husband ascended to heaven like an innocent dove. He left his sorrows, his stretcher, and the cruel world behind.'

"The poor woman wept with happiness. In her heart she believed what the wise Girkor said. Her husband would be called a saint.

"'Now go and tell everybody,' Girkor said.

"And the woman told everybody. And everybody in the kugh was amazed. All day long people went around saying a miracle had happened. Everybody made the sign of the cross and repeated, 'Our own Sukias Nalbantian has ascended—a saint. Who would have thought it?'"

"A clever man, Girkor," said my father.

"A clever man," said Garabed Agha.

"Is that all?" I asked.

"Be patient," answered Garabed Agha. He then sipped the rest of his coffee and finished the rest of the tale.

"It is getting late," he said, looking at his watch. "I shall make the rest of the story short. There isn't much more. When the spring came there was another miracle. For when the snows melted, there was the old man's body, stretched out right in front of the priest's house."

"Oho," exclaimed my father, "in front of the priest's house, ha?"

"Yes," said Garabed Agha, "the same priest who had refused to bury him. 'A miracle!' cried the people of the kugh. 'St. Sukias has descended to give the old scoundrel a lesson. Ignore the poor, build new houses for yourself, eat and grow fat while others starve,' they cried. 'God bless St. Sukias. He will protect the poor.'

"The wicked priest was wise. He was afraid. From his own pocket he bought a beautiful coffin for the dead saint. From his own pocket he paid for a lot in the cemetery. From his own pocket he paid for the singers. And with his own voice I heard him chant the mass for the dead."

"Good," said my father.

"From that day on the people of our kugh were happy to die. They knew they would get a good Christian burial, money or no money. A miracle had happened. The priest had learned his lesson.

"Well, that is the end of the tale," said Garabed Agha. He looked out the window for a long time. "The snow is very deep," he commented sadly. "Well, I should be going. My wife is at my daughter's and I'll have to cook my own supper. By the time I get home it will be eight o'clock."

He got up and stretched. "Please get my coat," he said.

My father was looking out the window. He was thinking. When I gave Garabed Agha his coat he hesitated before putting it on. He was glancing at my father. "And a glass of water too?" he asked.

But this time when I returned the coat was on a chair and the two men were smoking again.

"Are you going?" I asked.

"How can he go?" my father said. "Winter is for young men. It is better for old men to stay inside in weather like this." He winked at me. "Go and tell your mother that Garabed Agha is eating supper with us tonight."

Reuben Finds Love

My brother's first and greatest love affair fell upon our family with an ominous silence, that is, until the family could collect its wits and commence action. He did not break the news in so many words. He did not come home one fine evening and say, "Well, folks, I'm going to bring the little woman around to see you one of these evenings. And I want all of you to like her—you might as well—because she's going to be the little missus." This was not his style of approach to the family; it was too American. No, the consequences of such an outbreak before the assembled family might have done great harm. I mean great harm. It might have turned father against son, mother against father, sister against brother, child against parent, relative against relative, and so forth and so on. It might have caused years of silence between two or more members of the family, who had taken sides for and against him, so that in the future all sorts of inconveniences might have arisen.

As it was, the problem of his love life did not come to any sudden head, so that the members of the family didn't have occasion to take sides either for or against him. Whether my brother was too sick to talk, or whether he was just sick contemplating how a jobless man could live a normal married life under the same roof with his family, was a question. He said nothing.

In time his silence at table began to affect the rest of the family, so that after awhile we found ourselves eating without the usual scoldings, chattering and gossip, which had been the regular accompaniments to our meals since I was old enough to sit up and break bread with the rest. But this was taken care of easily enough by my father. Really, in one short lecture. As he put it:

"What good large family if not going to be happy at table? Look at rich family with one kids. How that kids is skinny! No appetite when only one kids at table. Everybody be happy. Eat. I am sick and tired when everybody look like funeral."

After that we forgot my brother's lack of appetite and his unhappy expression and just ate and thanked God that we were a big family and didn't have to share the fate of the one skinny kids of the rich family who had to eat alone.

But this kind of eating didn't last long. Soon we became uneasy again when we noticed how quiet my brother was and how little he was eating. Things became so serious after a while that my mother had to warn my father not to get too much food when he went shopping.

If our appetites had been affected by my brother's predicament, what had happened to my poor mother's soul! She was the first to see into my brother's plight, to sense danger, to grieve night and day, until, as she put it, "only undertaker can give rest." She didn't mention her suspicions before the children, and when she tried to preserve her home, by urging my brother to stay home just this one evening, Reuben would always make the same reply, "For the love of Mike, can't a guy even go out to see a guy?" This was always the reply he made to her. "*Vakh*, Reuben no stay late outside. Where, you don't tell me. Sleep late all day. What is going to happen? No good, this kind of life. How I know where you are, what you do? Stay home, read book. See you father? He work hard all life long. Now he has nothing. Study some book, Reuben. Make man of yourself. Stay home, Reuben."

Sometimes my mother would plead with my father to be firm, to demand that the children be good family children and stay home. But my father could do nothing. What should he do, tie their hands and feet?

"No, Yeksapert, this is a different world. Here, like they say at the Armenian Club, the home is like a gasoline station, where the parents must stay while the children come in and out."

Sometimes my mother spoke to him in Turkish, the language the children had never been taught, and then, and then only did my father make an attempt to assert his strength as the head of the family. When Turkish was spoken we always felt embarrassed and angry. In the first place, we knew that they knew we didn't know what they were talking about. In the second place, we knew something interesting was being said, but something quite unmentionable before the children.

Despite my mother's lectures, sly Turkish, and my father's strained protests, my brother continued to stay out late at night and sleep late in the mornings, never reading a book or trying to be more than "zero" as my father put it. Most of us knew the cause of my brother's condition. He wasn't fooling us when he said, "Can't a guy go out to see a guy, for the love of Mike?" From time to time we saw him in different places, and always with the same girl. That is, all of us saw him except my mother. She never went out. But my mother had a way of getting news, and it was always a little more interesting than the kind we got firsthand. We knew what we saw. She knew what Mother Pyloon had heard, seen, and conjured up in visions; and all this made the kind of news my mother could impart to my father only in ununderstandable Turkish.

One day Mother Pyloon came to drink coffee with us, saying she was tired of the world and needed rest. After drinking four or five cups, she began to question me, asking: "Are you saved?" Then, "There is no use being like your brother. That is what comes of hanging around poolrooms when you should be in church or working in the shoe factory, making money to bring home to your old parents. But there is still hope for you if you will give up sin and be good to your mother and father."

My mother interrupted. "He is a good boy; he is still young and innocent. He does my errands, and someday he will marry a good Armenian girl like his people want him to."

"Akh, Armenian girl," exclaimed Mother Pyloon, "they are the best in the world. They will live under the same roof with the people from the old country and never say a word. They will be quiet like mice and do all the work. They will take care of the sick when no one else will look after them. Akh, Levon, marry a good Armenian girl."

"That is what I tell him," said my mother sadly. "Our race is too thin as it is. We need to talk Armenian more; we need to have our children marry Armenians so that their children will be pure like their mothers and fathers. What is going to happen if they marry Americans? After a few months it is good-bye, divorce court."

Then Mother Pyloon touched a sore spot in my mother's soul. "He will find out soon enough, that Reuben. He will find out what it is to be married to an outsider."

"He isn't married yet," interjected my mother quickly. "Nobody has said anything about marriage."

"What is going to stop him? Marriages in this country can happen in five minutes. It is not like the old country where we take months to arrange everything according to God and our customs." Then leaning over and touching my mother on the knee, "My daughter, think it over. I speak the truth. Look at Levon Pesa's son. See what happened to him when he married the Irish girl?"

My mother nodded and silenced the old woman with a look of tragic knowledge.

"I know, I know, but what can I do, where can I go?"

"That is in the hands of God," Mother Pyloon replied. "Maybe it is too late, maybe it isn't. You should have thought of these things before."

But this gave my mother little consolation and for a long time she sat and looked sadly at her fortune in her coffee cup. And when Mother Pyloon asked her what she saw, she replied in a lost voice, "Strife, confusion, and fight." Then she sighed and said no more.

My mother's temperament wasn't of the kind that could leave such important things like the marriage of her son to an outsider in the hands of God. She trusted God more than any other person I knew, but sometimes when things didn't move along fast enough, she tried her own hand, and this was usually most of the time, and it was always her tongue and not her hand.

She had read the coffee cup right, for within a few days strife, confusion, and occasional fight characterized the atmosphere around our house. She did not allow one occasion to pass at which time she could admonish my brother about the folly of marrying an outsider. Long before he awakened in the morning her voice could be heard cursing the outsider who had alienated her son, putting a mother's curse on her own son's head for having traded evil paths, for not having read a book, for the inevitable disgrace which he was going to bring down on the honorable name of his family.

When he awoke and came down to breakfast, sleepy-eyed and heavy-headed, she started again, first sweetly and with gentle coaxings, then, when her words were disregarded in favor of his breakfast, with more vehement arguments, threats of disowning him, and finally, great curses on his and her head.

My brother stood for this just so long, then he commenced to do some cursing and yelling of his own.

"What's eatin' you? This ain't the old country where the old man and the old lady make matches with little kids before they can even walk. I'll be all right. It's that old lady." (He was referring to Mother Pyloon.) "She's always filling your head with a lot of bunk. And you believe her."

"Never mind bunk." My mother was protecting Mother Pyloon. "She worry for you."

"Well, tell her to forget me and start worrying about herself. If she keeps up that damned gossip about everybody she'll find herself not saved one of these days."

"Ahk, Reuben, why can't you go with nice Armenian girl?"

The poor woman was near tears.

"Who the hell wants an Armenian girl! We're different, Ma. For the love of Mike. We've been brought up in a different country. It ain't that they're no good; it's just that they're not my type. That's all."

But my mother did not see. "Type, no type! What you mean? When time come for wife to have kids they are all same. Only Armenian girl good. She is good *type*!" She emphasized the newly discovered word. "My mother was type!" Her mother. That made her cry.

At this point Reuben rose, tossed the outer crust of his toast into the tea dregs and left, muttering under his breath that one of these days he would leave the God-damned house.

Thus the tension within our house began to grow, until after a while no one could do anything without being reminded of the miserable fate which lay in store for us if my brother didn't mend his ways in a hurry. Every time anything went wrong, if any of the children misbehaved, the moral, after we had been reprimanded, was always connected with my brother's sins. The air was always filled with words, cries, and tears about the American girl and the disobedient son, until one day my older sister threatened to leave the house and take an apartment in the city. She said she was going crazy; that it was enough to type all day long, without having to come to a hell!

This stopped my mother temporarily. For what could be worse than losing a son would be for her daughter to run off and live by herself in the big city—and of all places, in an *apartment*. The very word breathed disgrace. What would people say?

But the poor woman was weak. There was too much to tear down her strength of mind—Mother Pyloon's persistent pleas for her to save her son, the growing warnings of the coffee cup, and her unleashable tongue that was bursting for action.

In a few days she was at my brother again, calling the American girl all sorts of names, and so forth and so on, until the air became so oppressive with her words that there was little left for my sister to do but scream and cry in bad Armenian that she had gone over the brink to a nervous breakdown.

How could my mother stop now? This was the climax of all the suffering her son had brought upon her house. This was the living example of what she had been forewarning us. See, his sister was sick, and all over him and that unmentionable American girl. And this was just the beginning. Just wait a few months; the mother, the father, one by one would be led to their graves.

Now, there was no respite from my mother's ire, her great passion to see my brother freed from the clutches of the outsider. When physical and spiritual exhaustion slowed down her crusade, Mother Pyloon was always on hand to prod her on to renewed efforts.

"Fight on, daughter, before she is under your roof. Pray that this does not happen. Remember, there are young ones here." Then in a holy whisper, "Remember what I have said, daughter; remember that in the end you must leave all in the hands of God, for I see from your fruitless struggles that things have already gone too far. Remember this, and in the future you will be able to spare yourself and your young children the curse which that wicked Reuben has brought upon this house."

The poor woman listened, but was little consoled by the words of Mother Pyloon. She had tried everything, everything within her power, until, in her despair, I had heard her more than once sigh and utter, "What shall I do? Where shall I go?" No, my mother could no longer continue in her present course. There was no place she could go—a massacre had long ago left not a trace of home or relative. There was nothing she could do. The lashings of her tongue had failed to cut through the armor of my brother's great love for the American girl.

Her appeals to my father? What could he do? He left the house occasionally; he went to the Armenian Club and listened to his friends talk. He had a little understanding of this great country. He knew the power it had over young minds—and young hearts.

One day, early in the morning, Mother Pyloon came over, and from the conversation which followed I knew that things would come to a head pretty soon: that either my mother would have to deal a decisive blow against the

American girl, or forever hold her tongue and harbor her under her roof as
she would her own daughter.

"Make known to him," warned Mother Pyloon, "that he has made of this
home a house of the devil. Tell him," she continued more hotly than ever,
"that such things cannot go on any longer, that it is the street for him; that
the door is locked, locked to him forever, unless he comes to his senses and
removes himself from that *orospi*."

She made the motion of locking the door and cleaning her hands of the
dirty business. Then admonishingly: "And, daughter, if you relent, if you
weaken in the least, it will be the end for us. Never again will I cross this
threshold, or talk to you on the street, or remember you and your mother in
my prayers. That is all."

In the corners of her eyes and at the edge of her wasted mouth she waited
for an answer.

My mother became very excited and wrung her hands. Then she arose to
the occasion, and, holding me close to her, she said:

"See these little ones. What can I do, Reuben is my own flesh? How can
I throw him into the streets, he has no job and he is always hungry? But see
these little ones. For them if I do anything, for them!" Then with a burst of
resolution, "For them, the door shall be closed to him until he drops that
orospi forever."

Then Mother Pyloon patted my mother's hands comfortingly, told me to
remember this occasion, and settled down to tell my mother about the new
and glorious fortune she saw in her coffee cup.

Before my mother's new resolve could be carried to the conclusion
Mother Pyloon desired, something most unpredictable happened, call it fate,
accident, or just the suddenness with which the New World moves. Mother
Pyloon had left, and my mother and I had gone into the garden. Perhaps
my mother wanted to pray, but I didn't give her much chance. I brought her
a knife and picked wind-blown russet apples from the ground. These she
peeled mechanically and cut into small pieces so that I could eat them. For
some time she peeled, and I ate with the relish of a rabbit.

We hadn't been there more than a half hour when we heard the front door
slam.

"Who can it be?" my mother asked. "Reuben?" she questioned. "But he is
in bed. Front door. It must be a visitor."

The front door; yes, that would be a visitor. The front door was the
company door. So we went around the back way. As we came around the
garden to the back steps we heard voices. This puzzled us, these voices, so

we hurried up the steps and opened the door. Yes, there were voices, angry voices. My mother's first impulse was to rush into the room from which the voices were coming, but she hesitated and drew me close to her. Then, as the voices mounted, she motioned for me to follow her to the dining room. I followed. From there, through a crack in the portieres, we could see what was going on. My mother took one look and became petrified.

"Oh," she gasped, "is my house falling around my head?"

Then I edged around her and took a peek too.

All the time the voices were rising, getting angrier and angrier. I peeked a long time. It was a woman. I knew her. It was Reuben's woman—the American girl! I felt ashamed. My brother was in his nightgown. She had got him out of bed. But this didn't seem to bother her. She just stood against the wall, her arms folded, tapping her foot nervously. She was mad about something.

My brother was trying hard to pull himself together. His granulated eyes were popping over with excitement.

"What the hell, are you crazy coming here? What if the old lady sees you? For the love of Mike, couldn't you make it some other place to see a guy?"

She opened her red mouth halfway. "I'll see you where and when I damn please."

"Never mind that talk…" My brother was getting angry.

"You had a helluva nerve not showing up last night, and telling Jim Weeder what you did about me. What do you mean I'm the wrong type? Type or no type, we've played around too long for you to be spreading around stuff like that. I'm a good girl, and I don't want to hear any talk about my *type*!" She emphasized the word.

"What do you mean, what do you mean?" my brother came back menacingly. "Come on, come on, get out. I'll see you later. If the old man or the old lady was to catch us like this—me just out of bed—there'd be hell to pay. No saying what they'd do. Come on, May, get out."

I could see my brother wasn't handling her right.

"Why, you rat, if you think I'm afraid of the likes of your old man and old lady…"

"Lay off them," my brother warned.

"Those old-country foreigners. That black…"

My brother did a surprising thing. He went up to her and put his hand over her mouth and started to push her out of the house.

"Lay off them," he breathed. Then he yelled an awful word at her and began to nurse the hand which had been over her mouth. It was bleeding.

"All right," she cried in her throat, "I'll go, but you'll never see me again. So remember this…" She let him have a good punch in the face, some scratches and slaps, and some kicks which hurt me to watch. All the time my brother was hopping around because she was stepping all over his bare feet.

Then he got mad and began to cry. "You dirty…"

At this point my mother steered me out of the house, into the garden and the apples. While the excitement was going on, and even when the door slammed again, she just peeled apples and gave me the nice white insides to eat. Everything she did was calm, automatic, and serene. I couldn't eat.

When Mother Pyloon came over the following day to see if her advice had been carried out, she found my mother puzzlingly calm and unperturbed. For a while she didn't come to the point of her visit; she just drank coffee.

My mother ventured nothing, and when Mother Pyloon finally uttered the first syllable of her retarded question, my mother merely raised her hand and said:

"God has been merciful to this house. I must go now and put the beans on for supper."

Mother Pyloon, puzzled and bursting with curiosity, called me into the other room. She could contain herself no longer. She grasped my mother's hand and pointed to me. "For him…about Reuben, what have you done?"

My mother looked pleasantly thoughtful. Then Mother Pyloon became vexed and demanded:

"And the American *orospi*!"

This brought a response from my mother. She looked at Mother Pyloon for a long time; then she spoke:

"After all, old mother, she, too, like our own children, is the child of some mother. God is the supreme Father, and like good children we must learn to love each other."

Mother Pyloon looked confused, and after a few moments of troubled mutterings, she made an excuse and left the house.

From that day on Reuben stayed home nights for a long time. And even if he only listened to the radio and didn't read books, and didn't become more than zero, it was better than the gasoline station and the pool hall, my mother said.

After a while the table hummed with all kinds of conversation, scoldings, gossip, and everything else. My father grumbled pleasantly about the sad world, and my mother gave warning after warning about wearing rubbers in the rain. Reuben ate more than anyone else. And one day when I heard one of my sisters complaining to my mother that she had put on a few too many pounds in the wrong places, eating too much, I recalled the words of my father—as he had spoken them a long, long time ago—about the rich family, with the one skinny kids, and the big family, where everybody eats and where everybody is always happy.

Tahmm-tahmm, Tahmm-tahmm

The Carusos of Revere Street were good people. There was Josie, young Nickie, Paulie, plump Lily, Grace and of course the father, one-and-a-half John; one-and-a-half because of the way he expressed himself. He never made an understatement. He gave everything he said the added benefit of his gestures and imagination...half fact, half gestures, with just his hands if he wasn't doing anything, his spoon, wineglass, or fork if he was eating, his barber tools if he was working; the other half poetry or music—or both. That was one-and-a-half John. He said things that came from his heart. Like the time I went to his shop to get a haircut; he was cutting away at someone's hair, talking with a rich Italian accent, flourishing his clippers within one inch of the customer's eye, when his brother-in-law, Charlie Pino, came in for a haircut. Charlie was a good man, but he worried a lot. People who knew Charlie said he had lots to worry about. If it wasn't his old mother and father, it was the taxes; if it wasn't the taxes, it was the dog; if it wasn't the dog, it was his health or his finances. So Charlie came into the barbershop with his usual worried face and sat down. He didn't pick up a magazine like the other customers who came there, he didn't even talk about the nigger pool or the fight at the pizza joint last night. He just sat and looked into space. When John stopped talking long enough for Charlie to get in a word, he said:

"Hello, John, how's Josie?" That was his sister, the barber's wife.

"She's O.K."

John cooled when he saw Charlie. His words didn't tumble out the way they had a few minutes ago. Instead, he went to work in earnest and the hair began to fly. He brushed his victim's neck, lathered him behind the ears and deftly arched the sides of his neck with a razor. Then he wiped off the remaining soap with a towel, rubbed some bay rum on the raw skin, powdered it and gave him the back view with a mirror.

"Awrright, my fran'?" he asked. "It's up to you if you want them a little different."

The man shook his head. "It's O.K.," he said.

"O.K." said John.

The man paid and left.

Charlie looked up at me as though to say, go ahead, you're next.

"You in a hurry?" John asked me.

"No," I said, "let Charlie go first." I liked Charlie. He looked sad and worried, a little impatient.

"Awrright, come on," said John.

"Thanks," said Charlie, and sat down in the barber chair with a sigh.

John prepared Charlie for the haircut. They exchanged a few words in curt Italian. I could see that John wasn't getting any satisfaction from his customer. Charlie stopped talking, closed his eyes and sighed.

John looked at me, shrugged his shoulders, and held up his comb and clippers in a gesture of complete lack of understanding.

Halfway through the haircut he began to talk.

"I can't understand you, young fellow."

Half of what he said he addressed to me, but he was really talking to Charlie.

"Everywhere, every day I see him he is the same. Why didn't you come for the supper last night, Charlie? We had the chaciadore and spaghetti just the way you like 'em."

"I'm sorry," said Charlie, "I had to work late. Afterwards Mamma wanted me to fix the water in the toilet."

"Ah!" John gave his comb the first unnecessary flourish. He held it in mid-air for a second, then gave himself the downbeat to begin.

"You know, Charlie, I don't want to say nothing. I'm only the barber. That's awrright. I don't get too much ejucation. What I get, I get from the old country and the newspapers. The newspapers half bull. What I get, I think myself. I get the facts from watching the people. There's no use to make worry all the time." He combed furiously for a moment. "My fran', you got the wrong idea of life. Why you worry for all the time? You got to live the full life. You can't live this kind of life all the time—the tax, the mother, the father, the money, the health! Ah, what the hell! Always your face is a mile long. All the time mmmmmmmmmm!" He made a face a mile long. "Where?" He raised his tools from Charlie's head and stood frozen in a gesture of questioning long enough for Charlie to look up and see his pose reflected in the mirror. "That's what I say to my kids. Where worry gets you?" He stooped down low to get some of the bottom hairs. "No place," he whispered. "In the grave. Look at me." The clipper was going at high speed

now. "Look at me—fifty-four years old. Not one white hairs on the head!"
He leaned over so that Charlie could see. "See? I don't make worry. I got a
few dollars. I buy the stuff for the kids to eat, I give them a home and some
clothes. The rest? What the hell! Sometimes I drink a little, sometimes I take
the wife to the show. Who wants to be like the rich people with rotten guts?
Look at me." He saw his young son approaching. "See, my kids come. He's
bring my lunch."

Nickie opened the door and placed his father's lunch in the towel cabinet.

"You brought the wine, Nickie?" his father asked.

"Yuh," said Nickie. Then without taking a breath so as to catch his father
silent for a second, he asked:

"Hey, Baba, can I go to the show?"

"The show! Jeez Crise!"

The cash register rang. He gave the boy a dime.

"What I got to lose? Tell your mother I'll be home regular time."

"See, I like to give my kids good time, too. Show, candy. What the hell.
They young once, let them live and be happy. They like good time once in a
while."

Then he got back to the old subject.

"No, Charlie, you got the wrong idea. Don't worry, you'll be happy."

Then I learned why they called him one-and-a-half John.

He was about finished with the haircut. He paused in the midst of his
work, just long enough to formulate what he was about to say.

It was late afternoon now, nothing stirred outside. Only the clock ticked
and the barber moved about.

Then in a soft voice John gave Charlie the value of the third half.

"Charlie, you ever hear the bells from the church when somebody die?"

He raised his hands from his brother-in-law's head and, with the palms
down, he made the motion of swinging bells. His voice remained soft and
melodious, distant and somber as he chanted:

"*Tahmm-tahmm, Tahmm-tahmm...*

"*Tahmm-tahmm, Tahmm-tahmm...*"

"Who die?" he asked himself.

Then in a hushed whisper came his own solemn answer, "Charlie Pino."

Charlie's eyes looked up and his mouth turned into a slow, warm smile.
John looked at me and winked.

John's son, young Paulie, was in the same class with me in school. He was
one of my best friends. One day he asked me to go with him to his house.

"Come up and see the pigeons," he said.

I liked pigeons, so I went. We played with the pigeons for a long time. Before we knew it, it was dark.

"Stay and eat with us," said Paulie's mother.

"I've got to go home," I said.

"No, no," she said, "we have plenty, you stay here."

"Sure, stay and eat with us, we're having spaghetti tonight."

He said this as though spaghetti was the rarest thing in the world. I knew we didn't have anything very good at home, and I loved spaghetti, so I risked a scolding from my mother and stayed.

Mealtime was a big occasion, here. Paulie's mother and sisters did all the work. Everybody looked busy and happy getting ready for dinner. Grace, dark and beautiful, set the table. Plump Lily sang while she stirred the sauce. And the mother did a thousand and one things as she scolded the girls for being clumsy, and Paulie and Nickie for not washing their hands now so they wouldn't be in their father's way when he came home from work tired and hungry and wanted to use the bathroom.

Gradually the noise got softer. There was a feeling of suspense around the kitchen now. I knew it was getting near the time to eat.

"What time is it?" asked the mother.

"Quarter of six," answered Grace.

"He will be here any minute now."

"Nickie, get the wine from the cellar."

In five minutes we were all at the table. John, his wife, plump Lily, dark Grace, young Paulie, and Nickie, and myself. The girls smiled at me when the father said:

"Good for you to be here. I'm glad. Lily, give me his glass. The wine is good for him."

They never gave me anything to drink at home. This was a new experience. I took a taste of the red wine. It was wonderful, but it made me cough and they all laughed.

"Here's some water," said Lily.

"He's not used to it," said the mother.

Now everyone was talking, and the father was talking to everyone. What noise and happiness! No two people talked about the same thing. Some scolded, some joked, and some tried to stick to eating, but they couldn't.

"Lily, eat," said the mother.

Lily was laughing, idly picking at her food.

A little later the mother said again, "Lily, eat." Then to me, "Have some more spaghetti." She filled my plate again.

"It's wonderful," I said. "It's wonderful!" The wine was taking hold of me. "It certainly is wonderful! It is so wonderful!" I sucked in a straggly end of spaghetti. It whipped around in the air and the saucy end struck me, leaving a blood-red mark across my forehead and eye. I thought they would die laughing.

Nickie and plump Lily laughed more than any of them. Paulie doubled up and his father had to talk to him.

John proposed a toast.

"To the Armenians," he said, "God bless them. They are just like us. I like this Armenian kid. How is your mother?" he asked.

"Good."

"How is your father?"

"Good."

"How are your brothers?"

"Good."

"How is your sister who was sick?"

"Good."

"Everybody's good," he cried, "that's the spirit!"

The mother, who was watching Lily, was vexed.

"Eat, Lily!"

"What's wrong?" John inquired angrily. He had been interrupted in the middle of something very important he was about to say. "Lily, what's the matter you don't eat? You sick?"

Lily turned red and looked down at her plate.

"It's a diet," the mother said scornfully.

"What's a diet?" asked John.

"So they won't put on fat. They don't eat so they'll be like the movie stars."

"Eat," said the father, brandishing his fork. "Eat. Are you crazy? Look at this boy." He pointed to me. "He is an Armenian and look how he eats spaghetti. Eat, or I'll show you."

Poor Lily looked at her plate and made a feeble effort to wind a piece of spaghetti around her fork.

The father was disgusted with his daughter's spiritless efforts. This child has missed the point of life.

"Lily," he said caressingly, "you got to eat. If you don't eat, pretty soon something bad happens. You will get sick and thin. Ah."

He raised his hands from his plate, with the palms turned down, and

holding his sauce-stained fork delicately, he swung them to the rhythm of
bells:

"*Tahmm-tahmm, Tahmm-tahmm…*

"*Tahmm-tahmm, Tahmm-tahmm…*

"Who die?" he then asked himself.

"Lily Caruso," came back his own ominous answer.

"Don't say those things," said the mother, making the sign of the cross.

"Now eat," said the father.

Lily finished the spaghetti; we all laughed and got up from the table.

"Now I take another drink and rest," said John. He finished what was left
in the bottle and stretched out on the couch. "I am a wise man," he said.

In a minute he was snoring.

Inside, the girls were clearing away the dinner things.

My head was feeling a little too light, so I thanked them all and went
home.

"What kept you away so late?" asked my mother. "Why didn't you come
home to eat? I thought something bad had happened to you—an accident."

She was ready to scold, but my father nodded for her to stop. I think he
smelled the wine and understood.

"Where have you been?" he asked.

I told him.

"What did you do?" he asked.

I told him.

"What did you hear?" he asked.

I told him the story of *Tahmm-tahmm*.

"He is a wise man," said my father. "Would that we could feel that way
about life. Now go to bed and sleep."

My mother looked worried and said I had been a bad boy. But my father
said, "No, he is good. I trust him." Then he helped undress me and put me
to bed.

It was late afternoon and I was walking home from school. I hadn't been
over to the Carusos' for a long time now. I didn't go there because I knew
my mother would be angry if I drank wine, and they would be angry if
I didn't. It was a quiet afternoon. The sun was setting and the sky was
beautiful. In the distance I heard the church bells from St. Anthony's. They
sounded wonderful, just like the sun looked, their tones just as golden and
as far away. As I drew nearer to School Street they sounded louder. And

now they seemed to be saying something. They seemed to be talking, saying familiar words. Yes, they were repeating familiar words. Now I recognized them; simple words as old as the world, laughter and life, whose meaning had been revealed to me not long ago by the Italian. They were the same words, singing, rolling round words—*Tahmm-tahmm, Tahmm-tahmm*—and they made me smile and feel warm, because they reminded me of a happy family and a kind and wise man, one-and-a-half John, Lily, Paulie and the merry rest.

Tahmm-tahmm, Tahmm-tahmm...

Yes, for a moment I was drawn back into the sparkling Italian world of the Carusos. But suddenly, like a dream seen in early, early youth, the picture passed away, and the happiness I had felt, the pleasant warmth, disappeared like the sun, and the corner of School Street and Eastern Avenue became a desolate land despite the squalor of dog-emptied garbage cans and the decaying structure of Epstein's tenement. I felt terribly alone.

In the quiet afternoon the bells covered my heart with new mournful meanings. *Tahmm-tahmm, Tahmm-tahmm,* they echoed deep within me. *Tahmm-tahmm, Tahmm-tahmm, and who has died this time?* came the question from a deeper place. *Who died...who died? A name, Tahmm-tahmm, a name, Tahmm-tahmm!* The compelling question forced me to think of a name. I groped for a suitable one that would make me smile warmly like Charlie Pino, or laugh drunkenly the way I had laughed at the Caruso house not long ago. But now the question came from a place deeper than the glowing mouth of one-and-a-half John. And no appropriate name came to me. Only the persistent bells sighed *Tahmm-tahmm,* never stopping, ponderous and eternal, like the beating of a large heart, like my heart, always beating, always asking, *Who died, who died, a name, a name, Tahmm-tahmm, Tahmm-tahmm!* Who died, who died,* the question to me, always to me, soft and distant, pulsating and clear, but like a pointing finger, demanding an answer...*who died, who died?*

"Who died?" I asked audibly, trying to break the silence and my growing fears. "Who died?" But my voice wasn't the voice of John, nor was my answer his answer, nor my heart his heart, nor my people his people; for he had laughed and made merry over the stupid words, he had passed them off like so much red wine. They had served to make lessons for him and to bring warmth to his heart. And now, as though angry because I had once laughed because of them, they had cornered me here and were asking a question whose answer I did not know.

What will happen to me, what will happen if I cannot answer with a name, I thought? The thought of death grew more and more abhorrent with each questioning of the bells. I must run far away so that I cannot hear them, I thought, or I will be afraid of death as long as I live. But I couldn't move. They had cast a spell over me. Over and over the mournful *Tahmm-tahmm* echoed the question *Who died?*

My fear became more intense. The horror of this question frightened me so that I felt like falling. The question is being asked of an Armenian boy, and yet the different answer is not in my heart. No one taught it to me; where can I learn it? Whose name shall I give? Who shall I say is dead? *Tahmm-tahmm, Tahmm-tahmm.* This time so oppressive, I thought I would die. *Who died, who died?*

Then quietly, as naturally as though it had been before my eyes and in my heart all my life, the answer passed before me. It was Levon Pesa, his shoulders bent, his familiar straggly mustache smoke-stained, unkempt, covering his weary lips. He was on his way home. I knew where he had been—to our house. I knew what they had been talking about, this man and my father. I knew what all old country men talked about when they came to see my father. The things they had talked about before I was born: Kharpet, Van, Gesaria and a host of other places, relations and friends, old country people, hundreds of them, all dead, all dead, even as their hearts were dead. And yet was there fear in their hearts, did they speak of death in whispers, did they tremble at the news that one of their company had died? No, no! Death to them was a friend. They spoke of him so frequently he might well have been one of them, another shabbily dressed man from the provinces of the Old World, a poor country relative to be tolerated at cards, whose move to rise from the table, whose admonition to one of them to come along it is getting late, would command the tired response of that particular one to get up and follow, to walk with him arm in arm down the dark stairway, down the deep, dark flights of our tenement stairs, into the night and out of this world.

Tahmm-tahmm, Tahmm-tahmm, Who died, who died? A name, a name?

Levon Pesa, Levon Pesa, Levon Pesa! I answered. Then I ran after the old man. Levon Pesa! I was weeping as I grasped his old hand and kissed it.

"Ah, little Levon, what is it, my son, what is it?" he begged. "Who has hurt you?"

"Oh, Levon Pesa, they were asking for a name," I sobbed, "and I gave them yours."

"Who?" asked the tired man. "Who could be asking for my name? Where is he?"

But I couldn't answer him. I just cried and clung to his hand.

"You must go home," he said, "your mother will be worried. It is getting dark."

"No, no. I have given them your name and I am afraid they will take you away. I don't ever want you to leave us. Please never go away from us."

And the old man looked at me with understanding as he held my hand.

"Where can an old man like me go? Who wants wasted Levon Pesa? Only death—and that will be welcome, my son, that will be welcome. Yes, believe me, that will be welcome, for all of us are tired."

Then he dried my eyes and said, "Come, walk with me and don't be afraid. Come walk as far as Broadway with me. It is dark now and I don't see the automobiles very well. Come, be a good boy and walk with me across the street, then you can go right home."

And I took his hand and walked with him to Broadway, and made him wait until the street was clear, always looking both ways so that nothing could happen to this good, brave man, so that nothing could happen to good, brave Levon Pesa, who had no fear of death; whose name for me had forever stopped the beating bells and the haunting question: *Who died, who died?*

Khatchik (Archie) Minasian

In his study of the Trobriand Islanders, Claude Levi-Strauss talks about the importance of the uncle figure in a young person's development. Male adolescents encountered a virtual second father in such a figure, and I think the poet Archie Minasian, who died in 1986 at the age of seventy-two, was that sort of figure in my own development. Minasian wrote for some forty years, while supporting himself and his large family as a house painter in Palo Alto, California. His only direct contact with the world of publishing was my father, his cousin and contemporary, William Saroyan. Without belaboring it, let me say that the two were friends virtually all their lives, and it seems to me that the work of each was nourished and instructed by the work of the other.

In addition to his gift as a poet, Archie was a great comedic artist. He had several personae—and voices that signaled their arrival—the most memorable of which was a figure named Archie Crashcup. Crashcup was a man who stood behind the eight-ball with endless good cheer and credence, despite encountering, in an unending flow, horrific thrashings from the reality principle. Here was a man who, stepping into his house and sniffing the unmistakable odor of horseshit, declares excitedly, "There must be a pony!"

Archie was, say, Peter Lawford to my father's Sinatra—or let's make it Sammy Davis, joyously sharing good times with a cosmic winner, who, he knew, had troubles too, even if money wasn't a central one.

Comedy was the leavening between the two, my father needing the gentle rain of laughter after his own jousts with the reality principle, not all of them so lucky, after all. What I encountered in the two of them—and similarly in

Pop's camaraderie with his cousin Ross Bagdasarian—was simply friendship, two men enjoying one another's company, with, in both cases, the signature release of laughter.

Archie and Ross were sons of my father's aunts, his mother Takoohi's sisters, and both Archie and Pop had lost their Armenian immigrant fathers early; only Ross's father lived to old age.

"What is poetry if you know what poetry is what is prose," wrote Gertrude Stein. Archie and Willie were in the way of discovering a new world at the same time that they were learning the language of this new place. Both at their best discovered a musical depth of feeling in that language, as if they could channel some of the centuries in the old place of their fathers, Bitlis, into the new place into which they'd been born, Fresno.

Both of them were bullied by *their own* uncle, Takoohi's younger brother, Aram Saroyan, who had arrived in the new world at twelve with a strong constitution—and concomitant digestive system—and a character marked by Levantine cunning. "You want to write?" he counseled the adolescent Willie Saroyan. "Learn to write checks!"

Both young men suffered under Aram's harsh tutelage, but, as in *This Boy's Life,* Tobias Wolff's memoir of his marine drill-sergeant stepfather, must be said to have gained something, too, from Aram's savvy in the ways of the new world.

As for the old world, its dreaminess, its poetry, my father's father, Armenak Saroyan, gone before his youngest son was three, had a brother, Mihran, of the same poetic familial strain, and both Archie and Willie came to cherish this man with a winking delight in his relaxed, old-world attitude, replacing Aram's ferocity with a benign, slow, deep-thinking geniality that Aram, they both knew, would dismiss as simple idiocy.

The making of Americans—Gertrude Stein again—is of course also a matter of what each of us brings to the table as a blood inheritance. Archie used humor to (partly) mask a powerful intelligence and deep pride wounded by the dissonances of the Armenian immigrant experience. Then too, he was a kind of poet-dramatist of the clash of styles between the old world and the new, and his elegance as a literary miniaturist in this arena is, I think, unmatched. Here in his poem "They Bring Me Raisins" is the young man in search of love and honor, politely riding out the waves of a broken romance in the presence of elders simply beyond the pale. Minasian is so precise and telling that he qualifies, like Saroyan, as part of the last wave of American modernists before it broke into the big postwar capitalist boom and disappeared:

> We sit, and gazing on the hills
> > my thoughts go wild.
> I see the road that led me to
> > her house in snow,
> and autumn just begun.
> I cannot bear the long months in my mind,
> > or push the drift.
>
> They bring me raisins, figs and dates,
> and press me to the wine.
> They see my father in my face
> > and ask of home.
> I give strange answers.

This could sit easily in an Imagist anthology beside the work of Ezra Pound, William Carlos Williams, and D. H. Lawrence. Built to last, Minasian's poetry, after more than half a century, remains new—a treasure for the reader to discover.

Aram Saroyan

The Snow

When winds begin to rouse the idle leaves,
> and night falls in,
And little bodies quit their favorite spot—
Reluctant till the morrow turns them out,
> I tip-toe in—
> > enchanter of the night
> > the child's delight.

Through meadows wide and little hidden yards
> I spread my charm

And turn all blemishes of land to one
Expanse of Nature's purest finery.

    With no alarm
          the gentle wood and field
          to me do yield.

Impatient till the morn, I shall expect
     some child to meet—
My first sweet blemish that shall mar my grace,
Some half awakened eye in wild surprise;
     and then the feet
          that I shall kiss in haste
          though it me waste.

The Unfortunate

In my garden
    there are butterflies.

I gather them
    to preserve their beauty.

O unfortunate women! I think.

Valley Ditch

In our ditch
    there are water skaters,
    frogs,
    tall reeds,

mud bugs,
apple cores and plum seeds,

and little naked children.

Rule 449

boy with blackspider
on hat,
and four June bugs
on new red sweater,
parades before student body
holding bull-frog high.

principal summons boy
to office,
begins with rule 173—
(not to molest fellow student)
            eye on spider;
ends with rule 449—
(becomes property of school)
            hand on bull-frog.

The Undernourished

I walk through the undernourished pasture,
see undernourished cows
      crop undernourished weeds;
I feel undernourished.

The Little Feet

We mark a patch of early snow
with little feet
quite deep and neat.

There's not a place we wish to go
with sheets of chill
upon a hill.

There's not a care our steps will show
in any track
you follow back.

There's not a thing we wish to know
with little feet
quite deep and neat.

The Cure

Restless
I pace my little room,
swing the windows and look out.

The trees on the hill are tossing madly;
I watch them,
I am thrilled at their madness.

I turn to my bare room satisfied.

We look at Goethe
        and Schiller,

huge bronze statues
    in the park,

and we think,
someday we'll be like them—
     you Goethe and I Schiller.

Then through narrow park lanes
     we crawl along,
     solemn and confident,
     eloquent and witty,
ignoring the boys that pass on bicycles
and the girls in shorts
     carrying tennis rackets.

About a Dog

the stray dog,
    to my constant beckoning,
    meekly approaches,
    whimpering
    and undecided.
soon he is tugging
    at my pants legs
    and is off with the evening paper.

how like Joe I think.

Ocean Episode

From the roof the rain tumbles
in throbs

and circles away
to the low spot in our yard.
I watch the lake widen to the barn,
disturbing the walnuts
I had spread to dry.

Now like a house boat
half submerged,
our barn stands in the lake,
and from an opening
the walnuts float outside,
like sailors fleeing from their sinking craft.
Then spin and bob
and rush and roll
they fall into the rushing of the over-flow
and hurry to the ocean
forming in the empty lot.

I look to the empty lot,
to the dark forms moving about,
perhaps the neighbors,
I watch them rescuing the sailors
in their gunny sacks.

An Evening at Home

The guests are seated in the evening parlor
smoking Izmir tobacco;
they are pleased.
The children will have dried figs
and candied nuts.
Suddenly a guest is praised for her gifted voice,
dragged to the piano

by the bearded aunt,
giggles and cannot sing.
Excitement wears to silence.

The hostess serves coffee
in the new gift cups;
the parlor becomes a tavern,
there is smoke and noise,
the sleepy children are bored,
they drift to various rooms.

The guests must go,
the children nod and fret,
and then commotion in the house
as hat and wrapper hunts begin;

farewells are shouted and exchanged,
but wait! the guests will take dried figs
and candied nuts with them.

Another pause, another word or two,
another dip of Izmir for the pipes.

They go at last,
They know the way.

How Foolish the Sweating Men

How for a long review of everything
now that old Summer plans to leave.

How comforting the fields we pass
with the slanting hay;

How pure the air we breathe
and our thoughts;

How inviting the lushy meadows,
the wandering girls by roadsides;

How jubilant each hedge
with the bird;

How dear the farmhouse half hidden
with gardens adjoining and vines sloping;

How cool the broad canal
and the lanky weeds and the weir;

How distant the brown bare hills,
the solitary trees;

How still the air,
how dense the views we pass;

How foolish the mean sweating in orchards
shaking the peach and the last ripe plum.

They Bring Me Raisins

We sit, and gazing on the hills
    my thoughts go wild.
I see the road that led me to
    her house in snow,
and autumn just begun,
I cannot bear the long months in my mind,
    or push the drift.
They bring me raisins, figs and dates,
And press me to the wine.
They see my father in my face
    and ask of home;
I give strange answers.

Parlor Talk

The guests sat on the new sofa,
they talked of old things;
we sat on old chairs
and talked of new things.

They talked of new things and grew old;
We talked of old things and dashed out.

The Holy War

We go to the meadow,
    a small army.
We are going to gather mushrooms
    and fire wood.

We carry spade and ax
    and gunny sacks.

Nothing will stop us.

The Traffic

Up and down our street
    new automobiles go
    trucks with trailers
    motorcycles
    horses and wagons
    children on bicycles
    old men walking.

Upon a tricycle a century turns the corner.

The Workers

In my presence
the men work feverishly at their tasks,
    denying themselves tobacco
and conversation.

In my absence,
    like air bags expiring,
    they sink to comfortable places
and roll cigarettes
    and discuss cheap labor.

Afternoons and Evenings

Hazy afternoons
    and workers on the grass reclining,
    ignoring the crops
    and the strong sun on their faces.
Cool evenings
    and witty city girls
    taking advantage
    of farm boys.

The Poplar

The rain brings Autumn's last leaf down
Relief! the poplar cries, relief!

The snow enwraps the naked bough,
The leaf! the poplar cries, the leaf!

Memories of My Father

the wind spoke to me
I went to the orchard,
leaves came down
        of every kind
with busy whisperings
I could not understand.

My Escort

The old man leaned upon his cane
and turned away.

I saw tomorrow—
escorting me.

The Orange Secret

I will go to my neighbor's orchard
and brush aside the wiry branches
to see the orange clusters hanging green

I will mark the tree
and return when they are ripe.
He will never know.

The Wind and the Tree

the early wind is out across the field,
it strikes a terror in the poplar leaves
and raises up the question, will they yield?

now who can tell how stubbornly the tree
will dare oppose the early autumn blow,
or what the nature of the gust will be.

I've seen the time when poplars have withstood
an awful beating and refused a leaf;
I wonder if the wind is in an ugly mood?

Water Light

It is night,
    and on the river
    lights, like banners, hang from every boat;
    and to the shore
    they join the puddles where I stand.

I watch them play in eddies
              and go on.

A Romp with the Wind

the wind threw rose petals at me,
tugged my hair
    and pushed me around.

Flattered,
I ran with the wind
    and called it names.

Unbearable

I cannot think of flowers
that I raise through months
thrown careless
like a maiden's kiss.

The Tiger Wind

The wind,
playing in the violets,
sprang upon me.

Oh! I thought,
if I could be so familiar
with her.

A Tangled Affair

See how the pond
    has caught the moon
    and grapples with her
        through the ripples
    to the reeds.

Then stealthily
    across the marshy banks
    the moon drags
    to the dwarfed birch tree.

See how my fingers struggle
    to maintain my loved one's hand.

Old Things

These are old leaves,
    do not disturb them.

The wind is shaking olives down.

These are old thoughts,
    do not destroy them.

    She is wearing out my heart.

My Summer Garden

Peaceful is my house among the trees;
and the wind is calm.
Peaceful sits my love in the garden
of my mind;
she speaks kind messages to me,
the names I called her
I have all withdrawn.

A Bit of Winter

The winter wind
hungry,
howls at her empty beds.

I watch her feeding
on leaves
the autumn overlooked.

The Message

Though I go my way calmly,
humble in countenance,
know, my love,
my soul is loud with rebuke,
my mien restrained,
my desire fierce.

Seasonal Submission

The autumn wind,
like a maddened officer,
fell upon our trees,
    jerking the leaves from their sockets.

I watch them recruiting them
for sky service.

A Bald Prospect

In our youth
neighbor Sanasar and I
passed for twins.

Now that time has passed,
I wonder if we haven't taken
too long to discover
there's not a hair of truth
between us.

Night Does That

We camp along rivers
in new canvas beds;

we are six
at night.

John plays the harmonica
with both hands—

about lovers
and sentimental things.

We crawl away
to dark places and listen;

John plays his best
by the fire, alone;

we know he is sad
when he plays softly—

about lovers
and sentimental things;

and he knows
we are smoking cheap tobacco

in dark places,
thinking.

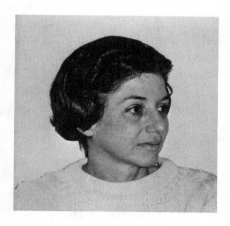

MARJORIE HOUSEPIAN

Marjorie Housepian was born on November 21, 1923, in New York City. Less than two years before her birth, practically on the other side of the world, my maternal grandmother, four of her siblings, and their mother all arrived by a horse-drawn cart in the city of Smyrna.

My grandmother later wrote of their entrance into the city:

> Night arrived. We were exhausted and sleepless. We wanted to reach the city without further delay. Tosoon (the horse) slowed down. The road gradually turned flat and finally, through the gray shadows of night, we saw Smyrna. The city's luminous domes, high minarets, and short and tall buildings stretched before our eyes.
>
> Dajad Emmi (the hired driver) turned his head around and told my mother, "Congratulations, ma'am! Here, we have reached Smyrna safe. Look, that large building is the Armenian church."
>
> "Glory to God's might! Glory, a thousand glories!" My mother crossed herself twice.
>
> Filled with joy, we looked around. We had finally reached Smyrna, the ethereal paradise, where we expected to enjoy perfect comfort and security.*

My grandmother, her family, and thousands of families like hers would not

---

* Alice Torian, *My Childhood without Spring: Eyewitness Accounts from the Smyrnian Calamity* (Monterey, CA: Mayreni Publishing, 2003).

find comfort and security in Smyrna. In September of 1922, a year and two months before Marjorie came into this world, Smyrna (now Izmir in Turkey) suffered a holocaust that resulted in the death of an estimated 150,000 people and the destruction of a once beautiful and prosperous coastal city. Greeks and Armenians living or taking refuge (as was the case for my grandmother and her family) in the predominately Christian city were raped, pillaged, and slaughtered as most of them tried to make their way to the water to escape ravaging fires set by Turkish forces. My grandmother was one of those who ran down to the port hoping to be saved by Allied battleships—including three American ships—that sat in the bay, but they just looked on, or as she says in her memoirs, "seemed petrified in the distance and did not rush to save us." Eventually my grandmother was saved, but so many were not. And the story of Smyrna's demise fell by the wayside in history. For reasons that are still debated today, in the year 2006, the year in which Marjorie will turn eighty-three, the "Smyrna affair" was swept under the proverbial Turkish carpet, ignored, denied, forgotten.

Growing up as an Armenian American in New York City's Gramercy Park area, Marjorie Housepian did not forget, could not forget, and would not forget what happened to her people, and even some of her own relatives. In 1971, already a published author—her novel *A Houseful of Love* (1957) won great critical acclaim and became a *New York Times* best seller—Marjorie would publish another, very different book. She herself stated that it was assumed she would write another novel after the success of *A Houseful of Love*. And, she says, she obediently began another one.

"Then all of a sudden one day I thought, let me try something different," she said. But Marjorie, like many good writers, had her own self-doubts about taking on the project.

Before she wrote *The Smyrna Affair* (published in England in 1972 as *Smyrna 1922: The Destruction of a City*), she admitted that her first reaction was that someone else should do it.

"We ought to get some historian to write it properly," she once said, after discovering that there was no definitive account or public record of the Turkish massacre and burning of the city of Smyrna.

"Then, like so many things, if you want it done, you do it yourself," she said. And so she did. And lucky for us too, because she did it very well. The book was called one of the one hundred most notable books of 1972 by the *New York Times,* and Book of the Year by London's *Sunday Times*, becoming a classic and going into a seventh printing. Marjorie received praise for her work from authors, scholars, academics, diplomats, and professionals. But I applaud the work most for the humanity and personal link it brings to light, so refreshing and lacking in many a history book.

Written as "vividly as a novel, and told with restraint and dignity," according to the historian C. M. Woodhouse, *Smyrna* uses diaries, letters, and eyewitness reports as sources. While Marjorie never met or interviewed my grandmother or anyone in my family, for that matter, I feel a part of it nonetheless. My grandmother's story rings true in the many eyewitness accounts included in the book and it stirs me to think how easily she could have been one of the voices Marjorie recorded. I'm not one to cry while reading a tome of historical facts, but *Smyrna* had me in tears. Tears that I believe any human being with a conscience—Greek, Armenian, Arab, Turkish, American, or otherwise—should shed.

In being able, having been chosen, or, as I like to think, being fated to write about Marjorie, I have come full circle. I had never heard of the novelist, short story and essay writer, historian, educator, and lecturer Marjorie Housepian until a few years ago, when I embarked on a personal journey of my own.

When I discovered that one of the Armenian books written by my late grandmother (books that had for many years sat in boxes in my parents' and aunt's homes) was the story of her surviving Smyrna in 1922, I began to research that part of Armenian history. The most prominent and recommended book I came across on the subject—and there were not many, unfortunately— was Marjorie's. A year or so later, I had my grandmother's book translated into English and soon after that, coincidentally, I was asked to write an essay for this anthology. The editor, David Kherdian, not really familiar with my work and certainly not aware of my recent personal journey, asked me to write about Marjorie. I could have been given any one of the writers in this anthology, I suppose, but I was destined for this.

I feel a kinship to Marjorie's fiction, as well as her nonfiction. Her novel *A Houseful of Love* is a delightful and poignant story of an Armenian American childhood in the center of New York City. Marjorie's real-life experiences were a basis for the book and made the writing so vivid and colorful that I actually felt like I was a character in the novel. I'm sure the fact that many of the characters remind me of my own offbeat lovable family members contributed to that, but I believe the book has a universal appeal. The characters are developed to the point where they practically step off the page and enter your world. *A Houseful of Love* is evocative of a time and place that Marjorie captures with finesse and charm. It really is a book that only she could have written so well.

"I write when I have something to say that no one else is saying better, as far as I can tell," Marjorie once told an interviewer. And isn't that really the best time and way to write?

Mona Ghuneim

Saturday Night

1

She told herself that she wouldn't start worrying until five o'clock, when it would begin to get dark. If he drove carefully and didn't stop at a bar, Jim couldn't possibly be back before four anyway. If only he had left Jamie at home!

By four-thirty she had scrubbed the bathroom and kitchen floors, waxed them and the woodwork, put the baby to sleep, and vacuumed the rugs. She turned on the radio before she began dusting the furniture. The good-music station was getting interference from the Italians again, and all the other stations seemed to have hillbilly music. She finally got Uncle Hugh's Houseparty. Uncle Hugh was interviewing a Mrs. Entwhistle. "Entwhistle. Is that right, madam?" That was right. Mrs. Entwhistle was from Savannah, Georgia, and she had raised eight children, all living. "Eight children! Think of that, friends!" Mrs. Entwhistle giggled, the friends applauded, and Peg turned off the radio.

She heard the baby crying and went in and picked him up and began rocking him. Soon his eyelids fluttered and closed and he was asleep again. His head was damp where it touched her arm, and his dark hair lay in small wet curls around his forehead. As she held him she marveled at how much he looked like herself. The first time she saw Jamie, when the nurse brought him in and handed him to her with that condescending smile all maternity nurses seem to have at such moments, she had wanted to cry because he had nothing of her. He was all Jim, and she might as well have had no part in him at all.

"He's his father every bit of him, isn't he?" the nurse had said. "I've never seen anything like it. It was the funniest thing to see them looking at each other—your husband on one side of the glass and this little fella on the other. I've never seen any two look more alike." She had wanted to hit her.

She held the baby in her arms awhile, watching the jerky way he drew in his breath, the quiver of the skin on his closed eyelids. She ran her hand over his hair a few times before laying him gently in the crib face down. He drew up his legs and raised his rump, like a miniature porpoise, the moment he touched the bed, and she covered him and went into the kitchen. It was five after five by the kitchen clock.

Looking out the window she could see the street lights going on. She noticed the headlights on Bob Grant's car glance off the wall as he swung into the driveway across the court. The car door slammed reassuringly and

Bob, his collar turned up against the rain and his shoulders bent, ran for the back door of his apartment. Carol Grant operated very much on schedule and at five after five she would be setting the table. She would have bathed Roger and fed him his evening cereal and changed her dungarees for one of the frilly pastel cotton dresses she was endlessly sewing for herself. "Bob *hates* seeing me in dungarees," she always said. "He likes me to kind of primp up for him in the evening. And he throws a fit if I don't have dinner ready when he gets home." Peg had come to realize long ago that Carol was endowing poor bland Bob with the one quality he didn't have; but just then it mattered very little that Carol Grant was fooling herself, or that Bob Grant was a bore—myopic, bald, and ineffectual in his middle age. As he shut the kitchen door and disappeared inside, she felt a twinge of envy, even for Carol.

She went into the living room and picked up a magazine. No use worrying until five-thirty, really. It might be snowing up the mountain. If the roads were bad, it would surely slow him up. It would slow him up despite himself. If the brakes held.

"Jim," she had said that morning, keeping her voice low, "it's bound to be skiddy on the mountain. Will you stop and have the brakes checked?"

"The brakes are all right."

"You have to step down all the way to the floorboard."

"They were tightened in September."

It's the way you've been driving lately, she had wanted to say, your damned erratic driving; and if you get one more ticket, they'll take your license away and I wish to heaven they would.

"Must you go today? It might be nice tomorrow and we could take the baby and drive over to Carey's."

"What do you want me to do, sit around here all day and go nuts?"

She had walked out of the room then, because there was too much she wanted to say. All right, take the car and go wrap it and yourself around a tree. Be sure to stop at a bar first and then drive like mad because you can't do anything halfway, and have another accident, only this time do it up right. We've got no hospital money now; you spent it on the power saw you had to have so you wouldn't sit around and go nuts Saturdays. Dear God, she thought, why is it everybody can go nuts except me?

She had waited a little, until it had worn off, and then she had come in to where he was sitting, tearing pieces out of the newspaper and throwing them into the fire. "Will you try to be back by four?" she had said, standing between him and the fireplace. "I promised Jamie I'd run him over to play with Mike this afternoon."

"I'm taking Jamie with me," he had said, not looking at her.

That was when she could have started it, she thought later. That was one of the ten thousand times she could have brought it to a head. Was it weakness, she wondered, or an aversion built up over the years when her parents' voices had come to her shrill and taut, as she lay in bed, and she had felt something within her shrivel and turn inside out? The way it did when she first saw Jamie. The way it did when Jim quit his job while she was pregnant. The way it did when Jamie had pneumonia and Jim didn't come home for three days.

She flipped the pages of the magazine on her lap. "How the Berchwassers manage on $3800 a Year," an article said. Bully for the Berchwassers, she thought. Why don't they ask me for an article? "How the Clarks Have Managed on Less than Nothing and More than Enough," or "The Ups and Downs of the Clarks—a Study in Adjustment."

"Jim Clark is a genius," the article would begin. "He can do anything he wants to do and nothing he must do. He can be witty, charming, and brilliant, and he has very often been almost successful. His faults, of course, are not his. They probably go back to a great many things his parents did to him and quite a few things his wife did not do for him, and now if he's drinking too much it's because nobody, nobody, nobody understands Jim Clark."

It's almost five-thirty, she thought, but I won't start worrying until I finish looking through the magazine. "He also has a wife who worries too much. But she can't help it either." She turned over a few more pages. "Are You Helping Your Husband?" The headline shouted at her, "Every wife wants her husband to be a success, but find your score on the following quiz to see if you're really helping or hindering him."

"Do you go to bed with cold cream on your face?" Never, never, never. Not for the first few years, anyway, and no hair curlers either.

"Do you let him know in little ways that you secretly think he's wonderful?" Of course. Always. Little ways, big ways. But you run out of things after a while. "Jim, you're wonderful. I'm *sure* you would have gotten the promotion if you hadn't quit the job."

"Do you nag at him?" Stupid question. Ask twice at four-hour intervals and then do it ourself. Any fool knows that.

"Do you interrupt him when he's enjoying himself at a party because you want to go home?" Only when he gets insulting. What would *you* do? Lord, he ought to be president of the company. She picked the magazine up and took it into the kitchen with her.

2

The clock said ten of six and the rain was splintering, half frozen, against the kitchen window. She stepped on the trash can and dropped the magazine into it. She thought, I ought to finish dusting. I ought to wake the baby—he'll never get to sleep tonight if I don't. I ought to start worrying—it's just about the time Jamie will be getting cranky and tired. "Daddy, when are we going home? I'm hungry." "We'll be home pretty soon. We'll stop here first and get you a hamburger." I don't *want* a hamburger." "Behave now, Jay, or Daddy won't take you along next time." If they weren't in a heap halfway down the mountain. She closed her eyes and held her face in her hands thinking. But *somebody* would call—if anybody happened that way.

The phone rang just then. She ran, tripping over the hall rug where Jim still hadn't nailed it down, and caught the call on the second ring.

"Hello?" she said. She could hear her voice cracking.

"Peg?" It was Susan, next door. their walls adjoined, and they had discovered how thin the wall was when she and Susan had both been in bed with the flu and they found they could converse through it by shouting only slightly.

"Just wanted to check if you were in," Susan said. "It's so quiet over there and your car was gone. I'm desperate for a can of tomatoes. The rain's so bad I can't see going out."

"Want me to run it over?"

"No, dear, thanks. I'll come over and get it."

I ought to wake the baby up, she thought again after she hung up, but she turned on the lights instead and lit a cigarette; then she heard Susan's knock and let her in, quickly.

"Lord, what a night!" Susan said.

"How about splitting a beer?" she said. "Or are you in a rush?" If she would only stay a little while. Surely Jim would drive up any minute.

"Good idea. It's a madhouse over there and I'll have to put the stew in the pressure cooker anyway. The kids go wild on a day like this." She looked around. "Jamie away? Baby asleep? Lucky you!"

"I'm beginning to get worried," Peg said from the kitchen, and her voice sounded strangely unconcerned to her own ears. "Jim took Jamie with him up to Bailey's Ridge this morning. They left at ten and they're not back yet. It's not more than a two-hour drive, is it? The roads will be fierce."

"We've done it in an hour in the summer. What in heaven's name did he go up there for in this weather?"

"He looked at that Llewellyn property last summer, and he decided he wanted to see how it looked in December. It had to be today, of course. I don't know how he thinks he's going to pay for it."

"Isn't that the truth," Susan said as Peg came into the room with the two glasses on a tray. "Bruce got the bug a year ago spring. Hunting lodges, no less, and the car hadn't been paid off. Don't worry, one trip in this weather will cure him."

You don't know Jim, Peg thought; lordy, you don't.

"Well," said Susan, settling back with her glass and raising her eyebrows, "our neighbors to the left were at it again this morning."

"Oh, goody," Peg said sarcastically, but she felt a well of nausea building up inside her.

"Honestly," Susan was saying, "I'm not going to let Jeremy go over there any more. The language! Half of it Bruce has to translate for me. It's unbelievable!"

"She seems rather nice when you talk to her," Peg said, hating herself.

"Oh, sure. Sweet as pie. You ought to come over some morning and hear them. Bruce keeps threatening to knock on the wall and referee. Oh well, it takes all kinds, I always say. I really ought to go." She drained her glass.

"No, look, the stew'll wait. One more cigarette." She looked, involuntarily, toward the window. It was snowing. The large white flakes drifted endlessly in the glow of the street lamp.

"I know you're worried," Susan said. "But you *know* they're all right. Look, if they're not back in half an hour leave a note on the door and come on over and have supper with us."

"I have to get Allen up and feed him. He'll be awake all night—he's all off schedule."

"Bring him along and we'll put him in the play pen. Okay?"

"I'll see," Peg said. "Thanks anyway. If I'm not there by seven, go ahead and eat."

3

She hadn't eaten all day, she realized as she shut the door. She was hungry, but the thought of food repelled her. Even the one glass of beer made her head light, and if she could forget about them, they would surely show up soon. Forget about them, she said to herself. You're just an old worry-wart anyway. Remember the time you were worried sick because he went to Galveston overnight on flying time during his vacation and didn't show up for four days? And he had a perfectly good reason. He always had a perfectly good reason, in those days. The boys chartered a boat and went deep-sea fishing for a couple of days. Sure, he'd called, but you were out hanging clothes and Jamie answered the phone and when you came in Jamie said, "Daddy's gone fishing." He was pretty good to remember that much when he was hardly three. And you said, "No, dear, Daddy's gone in his airplane to Texas," and Jamie kept saying, "Nope, Daddy's gone fishing." "Serves you right for taking your son for a moron," Jim had said, laughing, when she told him. "You know perfectly well Base Operations would have told you if anything had happened."

It's me, she thought, I anticipate trouble. But then that time when I didn't, they called me from the hospital; and another time I didn't they had to carry him home, drunk—he'd always managed to walk in before then. And now he has Jamie with him on top of a mountain and it's snowing. But I'm not going to think about it.

She went into the bedroom and picked up the baby. He was soaking wet and the side of his face on which he had been sleeping was red and creased. He kicked his legs and cried lustily while she changed him.

"Cheer up, old fella," she said, "chow's on." She carried him to the kitchen and held him in one arm while she put on some water, to heat the bottle, with the other.

The refrigerator rumbled and started to hum when she slammed the door. It made the apartment seem ominously quiet. It was a quarter of seven, and the snow was beginning to settle. An hour and a half to Winchester, another half hour up the Ridge. One hour—at the most one hour—to walk around the property, and two hours back. Say three, if they stopped on the way. If the car was stuck halfway up the Ridge it would be pretty cold, even with the heater on. And Jamie would be hungry. I wish the damn phone would ring, she thought.

She fed the baby and put him in the pen, then made herself a sandwich and sat on the couch to eat, wondering whether to start the mending or write some letters or straighten out the desk drawers or pay some bills; but the thought of the bills depressed her. The rest can wait, she thought, and she wrapped the baby in a blanket and ran next door to Susan's.

They were in the midst of dinner when she arrived. She declined the plate Susan offered, but Bruce drew up a chair for her by the table and brought her a drink, while they finished dessert.

"Jim not back yet?" Bruce asked it almost too casually.

"Did Susan tell you? They went up to the Ridge. I guess the weather's slowed them up."

"Sure it has," Bruce said. "It's a rough climb even in the summer. He has probably holed up somewhere till it blows over."

"Probably." Why don't you say what you're thinking? Why don't you say nobody in his right mind would go up that mountain in December?

"Jim'll be all right," Bruce said.

Jim'll be all right. She remembered Wynn Kelly at Jim's promotion party, right after the war ended. Wise old Kelly, who never did make major. How she had hated him that night!

"Colonel, suh, f'action above 'n' beyon' the call of duty—ah present you with the Croix de Guerre avec Trois Pulmes!" Joe Rocca, whose Mississippi accent veritably curled after three drinks, was sticking a toothpick speared in an olive into Jim's blouse while everybody screamed. Peg, her face a little tired from smiling, had retreated to the chartreuse settee at the rear of the club lounge and had been caught there by Bonnie Richards, who never conversed with anyone whose husband was below the rank of lieutenant colonel, though she occasionally flirted with the younger officers. It had amused Peg to see her coming toward her.

"Peg Clark! What are you doing hiding back here on a night like this?"

"Hello, Mrs. Richards," Peg had said. They had been introduced at a dozen parties since she'd been living on the post, but this was the first time Bonnie Richards was acknowledging the fact that they had met before.

"Oh, call me Bonnie, please! We're all informal here on the post. I've been meaning to call you up for the longest time, but you know how it is."

"Of course I do," Peg said.

"It's awful how little time you get to do all the things you want to. Now that you'll be putting in for larger quarters you'll know what I mean. They're wonderful of course, but much too big to take care of without the kind of help we used to get before the war."

"I hope we don't have to move," Peg said. "There are only three of us, and our quarters are almost too big now." Bonnie was looking at her as though she were a little odd.

"Naturally you'll have to move. I'll never forget the quarters we had at Hamilton. They've divided them in two now, I hear. Six bedrooms. But they even gave us a houseman in those days, and Rog was only a major. Well, times have changed."

She had finally bored Bonnie into leaving. Now Jim and Joe Rocca were singing a duet, a rollicking ditty about what the boy did on Pig-Alle. In pantomime. "Hallelujah!" Joe was shouting between choruses. "Man, ah'm gettin' *stewed* t'night!" And then she noticed Kelly standing in a corner and looking at her. When he caught her eye he came over, slowly, until he was standing by the settee, looking down at her with his twisted smile.

"Hi-ya, ma'm Colonel?" he said. "Bursting with pride?"

Why, you ten-cent runt, she wanted to say, what's the matter—sour grapes? But she had never been the type to hit back.

Jim and Joe Rocca had their arms around each other singing: "…and… they…gave him up for lost on…Pig…Alle!"

"The Colonel's in great shape tonight," Kelly said.

"You're pretty sharp-witted yourself."

"I'm drunk," Kelly said. "Mind if I sit down?" She moved over. "What're they gonna do without a war to fight? Maybe we oughtta cook up a new little war for 'em."

"What are *you* going to do?"

"Don't worry about me," Kelly said, "worry about those poor bastards. I'm only a misfit *inside* the outfit."

"You're pretty insulting," she said, "even if you were right."

"So you know I'm right! I thought you would. You're a misfit around here yourself."

"Thanks," she said.

"What's he gonna do, stay in?"

"No. Why are you so concerned about him?"

"I *like* him," Kelly said. "I like you too. I like you even better."

"Look, Captain," she said, "that's not necessary."

"Who said it was necessary? I'm merely expressing my prerogative of saying what I think 'cause I'm drunk and don't know any better. What's he gonna do when he gets out?"

"I don't know. Do you want me to lie awake nights worrying about it?"

"You have, haven't you?"

"Oh shut up," she said.

"I'm sorry." Kelly was looking pretty sober now. "I'm sorry, I was being rotten. Don't worry about Jim, he'll be all right." But he had said it as Bruce was saying it now. It sounded like a dirge.

"How about some three-handed bridge? The dishes'll wait." It was Susan talking. She didn't feel like bridge, three-handed or any other kind, but she said she'd love to play. She played sloppily, and after a while she offered to start the dishes while Susan put the kids to bed. Glancing at her watch as she took it off, she noticed that it was almost nine-thirty, and the thought suddenly occurred to her that if her phone were ringing, she wouldn't hear. She raced through the dishes, picked up the baby, and left, rather abruptly, before Susan was through with the children.

"Give us a ring if you get worried," Bruce said, looking at her with pity, she thought.

"Thanks," she said, and she wondered just at what time he would advise her to get worried.

4

She had half expected the phone would be ringing as she opened the door, but it was relentlessly silent. Her tongue felt dry and she recognized the slightly sickening feeling of panic gathering in her stomach. She put the baby to bed mechanically, and felt the panic gather momentum when he quickly fell asleep and she was left with nothing more to do. What do I do now? I ought to call somebody, she thought. Who do you call—the police? "Pardon me, have you had an accident reported? Could you send a patrol car up to the Ridge? I've lost a husband and child. They left this morning at ten and it's after ten-thirty now and they're not home yet." "Yeah, yeah, lady, we'll let you know." I wonder how many calls like that they get every night. I ought to go to bed and sleep, and they'll be here when I wake up. But how'll I get to sleep? Why did I let him take Jamie along! I wouldn't worry if Jamie weren't with him. I wouldn't care if he *never* got back. I'd wish to heaven he'd never come back!

"O ring, damn you!" she said aloud to the telephone.

She felt her anger toward him growing, almost physically. When she went in to brush her teeth and found that he had been squeezing the toothpaste from the top again, it appeared in front of her eyes like a great black blurb. She could feel the sweat forming on her chin and above her eyebrows and on the back of her neck. Her face, in the mirror, was chalk white. She took the bottle of aspirin and a glass of water into the bedroom with her, and was about to put them on the dresser, when she heard the door open and suddenly she froze.

"—in there and get to bed, Jay," his voice came through a slate wall, grating. "For God's sake," he was grinning in the doorway, "what in hell's wrong with you?"

She hurled the glass. Violently. With such force that it splintered as it struck his chin and left a diluted stream of blood running along the edge of his still half-grinning mouth. He didn't move, and she threw the bottle after it but it missed its mark and shattered against the wall, and she heard herself screaming.

It wasn't her voice. It was an aggregate of the voices that shriek from the windows of tenements on hot summer nights, filled with all the measure of the world's despair and frustration and failure. It was a wild voice; coarse, distorted, malignant. It came out in words she thought she had never known before, and he stood there and didn't move. Then she saw that Jamie was standing behind him, his eyes wild with terror and the saliva dripping down his chin, looking ridiculously like his father, even now. She ran past them into the nursery and closed the door and leaned, exhausted, against it. And then she picked up the baby and held him so tight that he began crying too.

How Levon Dai Was Surrendered to the Edemuses

It was a few weeks before Easter that Hadji read the cards for Levon Dai. "My heart is pulling for a sheep's head stew," she said one night after dinner. "It is eight years since I had *kuluk*, not since we left Cyprus, after the exile." They were sitting around the table, still, three hours after the dinner began. A good dinner—eggplant, white beans, baked fish, creamy white Greek cheese, large round loaves of bread. Well fed, perhaps, yet not quite satisfied. Kelesh there, looking moodily into his coffee cup. Kelesh wanted a yogurt factory. He wanted it badly, but no one took him seriously. Kelesh was studying the classical antecedents of Dante at Columbia, and afternoons he frequented bingo parlors to earn the carfare to attend his classes. But he wanted most of all to open a yogurt factory. It was very confusing, probably even to Kelesh.

Uncle Boghos was an artist, but no one took him seriously either. He painted from postal cards. Nostalgic scenes of the Bosphorus and the Red Sea; Saint Sophia at sundown. Everyone said: "Boghos, since when is the Bosphorus green?...Is that water, Boghos? It looks like grass...Sunset on the Sea of Marmara is never gaudy. Vivid, yes, but not gaudy. You have put in too much orange." Uncle Boghos was not a patient man, and he often collected his canvas and paints and retreated to the bedroom. But it was lonely in the bedroom and Boghos could not paint long in solitude. My mother encouraged Boghos, but he could never take her seriously. My mother encouraged everybody. She often expressed a willingness to do the worrying for everyone else in the family, feeling, I think, that it was the least she could do—not having so many of her own—but the others were not willing to shed their prerogatives so easily, so mother concentrated mostly on her concern for Levon Dai, who was away from the family circle and therefore much to be pitied. She sent him tins of Greek cheese and stuffed grape leaves and olives—the large black pickled kind that he could not possibly be expected to find in Iowa. And now that Easter was approaching he had no doubt already received the offering, sent railway express, of Easter bread and *topig*: the spicy steamed patties that no decent Armenian could be without at this season. Levon Dai was not ungrateful. If he wrote letters only at monthly intervals when he enclosed the check that provided for his godmother old Marta-mama who had brought him up, everyone knew it was because he was not articulate about his misfortunes, or given to expressing his loneliness. But one could read between the lines. Levon Dai was an eccentric: he had made money, but one understood the price he had to pay and pitied him for it.

Hadji's husband, Uncle Pousant, worried more than anyone. He worried about the janitor, and the price of eggplant, and he worried about the American foreign policy and the English and the Bolsheviks. He worried especially about Hadji's refusal to worry.

"How can you sit there, woman, peacefully cracking your melon seeds when you know how hard it is to find fresh dill these days!" Uncle Pousant owned a restaurant and he could not cook without fresh dill. Nor could he cook without chick peas, or sesame seeds, or pine nuts, and they were all hard to find at decent prices. Hadji could really exasperate Uncle Pousant.

Only Hadji seemed sure of what she wanted. Right now she wanted sheep's head. This irritated Uncle Pousant. "Now you want me to go out and find 'head'! It is not hard enough I have to rummage the town to find cracked wheat flour; it is not hard enough I have to endure the crooked looks of the fish woman as I beg her to leave on the heads of the fish. It is not hard enough I have to turn my face inside out to the butcher with pleas that he save me the liver of the lamb! Now I must go out and find 'head'!" Hadji said not a word.

"Perhaps you think that *I* don't crave head!" added Uncle Pousant. "All right, I will admit it. I lack courage. Why should I worry if he thinks I am a cannibal? They eat the foot of the pig, and I am ashamed to ask for the head of the sheep. Let me admit it, I am a coward." No one spoke.

"I am admitting it, am I not?" shouted Uncle Pousant, "Let me see you go out and ask for the head of the sheep!"

My mother changed the subject. There had been no letter from Levon Dai today, she said. This was hardly news but my mother knew it would serve.

"He cannot be coming for Easter," said Boghos. "Poor devil."

At Christmastime Levon had written that he could not come. Perhaps at Easter, he said. His hands were tied; the dry cleaning plant was thriving; he had to hire fifteen more men; it was hard to leave the factory for any length of time.

Uncle Pousant was not in a kind mood. "Levon Dai is a barbarian!" he said, "Now that he is rich, he neglects his relatives. He has a soul of a donkey!"

"It is Levon's way," said my mother, "you cannot judge him as you do others. Marta-mama understands. Perhaps he will come in the summer."

"Levon perhaps is becoming Americanized," said Kelesh, "Americans do not admit relationships with cousins after the age of sixteen."

"Behold, the authority on America!" cried Uncle Pousant, who prided himself on being the first member of the family to emigrate.

"I have read," said Kelesh, "I have talked to people."

"And I, I do not read," said Pousant, "I am an illiterate because I did not go to the University and take courses in the philanderings of the ancients. DID YOU READ THE NEW YORK TIMES TODAY?" shouted Uncle Pousant.

"Not today," said Kelesh.

"Did you read it yesterday?" said Uncle Pousant, "do not talk."

"As a matter of fact I did," said Kelesh, "Yesterday, I did."

"The horse racing news," said Uncle Pousant. "The reports of the stock market. The puzzle of words. Ha! The rotogravure! I know how you read the papers. But then, you are educated." Kelesh began to sulk.

"Levon Dai takes after his father," said Hadji. "Torcom Dai would never wear a fez, do you remember? When he came back from the German University he had become entirely European."

"Only in appearance," said my mother.

"All right, in appearance!" said Hadji, "even to the cut of his hair. 'If he went to America,' we used to say, 'he would be certain to wear feathers, like an Indian.'"

"He brought back some fine reproductions from Germany," said Boghos. "Who knows what became of them. Then I remember the stories he told when he returned from the interior, after he had been commissioned to build the Sershap road. The Kurdish soldiers, he used to say, could not tell their left from their right. They tied garlic to one shoulder, onion to the other. 'Garlic-side, onion-side' the leaders would shout, and the soldiers marched."

"He was a good man," said Hadji, "but he talked too much. He should have stayed in Europe, he would have lived longer."

"In America he would have made a fortune," said my mother.

"Of what good is money," said Uncle Pousant. "If like Levon Dai one must live in Iowa?"

"Perhaps Levon *likes* Iowa," Kelesh suggested, sarcastically.

"What is there in Iowa?" asked Pousant.

"Pigs and corn," said Kelesh.

"There is a limit to what one can endure," said Uncle Pousant.

"It must be a famine, both to the eyes and to the mind," said Boghos. "No mountains, no sea, no antiquity."

"He should at least come to New York and find a wife," said my mother. "There is Mardiros Pilafian's daughter, now. She is both beautiful and intelligent, and if the poor girl does not get married soon she must return to Rumania. They say, so far she has not found anyone she is willing to marry."

"And you are going to send a nice girl like that to Iowa?" cried Uncle Pousant, "have you no heart?"

"Iowa cannot be worse than Rumania," said my mother. "At any rate it is nearer."

"Who knows what they *eat* in Iowa," said Hadji.

"Mayonnaise on pears, probably," said Kelesh.

"Please!" said Uncle Pousant, "you are upsetting my stomach."

Hadji began to rummage in the folds of a voluminous skirt that abounded with pockets. She withdrew a deck of cards and began silently to deal them, solitaire style, on the table. "At what time will the doctor be coming home?" she asked when they were all laid out.

"Late," said my mother, "he had a call in Brooklyn and one in Jamaica."

"I have not read the cards for Levon Dai since before he bought the factory," said Hadji. "Let us see."

"You said then he would spend money, and make money," said my mother. "His letter came two weeks later. How can I forget?"

Hadji rolled her sleeves and licked the tip of her finger before she began to shift the cards systematically from place to place.

"Pick a card," she said to my mother, who uncovered the seven of hearts.

"A-ha!" said Hadji, "there is a romance. He is thinking of getting married."

"You are joking!" said my mother, "who would he marry in Iowa? Has he someone in mind?"

"You do not have a romance without having someone in mind," said Uncle Pousant.

"That depends," said my mother, "more often men do not have someone in mind until after they begin to feel like getting married."

Hadji silently manuevered the cards. "Draw another," she said at last. This time mother drew the queen of diamonds. "He has found someone," said Hadji, "a blonde."

"He would!" said Uncle Pousant.

"Oh dear, I was afraid of that," said my mother, "all the same you would think he would write us." Hadji uncovered another card.

"We will get a letter," said Hadji, "He is still making up his mind."

"Levon was never one to write much," said my mother, "but on an occasion like this…"

"We will be getting a letter," said Hadji.

"He could have come to New York and looked around, before making up his mind."

"It is too late now," said Hadji, "he has someone."

"And I did have my heart set on Satenig Pilafian," said my mother wistfully.

The letter arrived ten days later. Not being much given to words, Levon Dai told little more than the fact of his engagement and the information that his fiancee's name was Shirley Adams.

"Shiran Edemus!" snorted Uncle Pousant. "What kind of a name is that!" Mother explained that Shiran did not mean the same thing in English, and besides the name was Shirlee, not Shiran.

"Shiran, Shiree, what's the difference: it sounds obscene," said Uncle Pousant.

Levon Dai enclosed a newspaper clipping that was slightly more explicit than his letter, and a picture of Shirley. Mr. Levon Melkonian, the clipping said—the same Mr. Melkonian who owned the Tru-Clean dry cleaning plant on Kelmer Avenue and had recently been installed as High Priest of the North Gate Chapter, 2, Royal Staff Masons—was engaged to Miss Shirley Adams who was well known for her "exquisite collection of miniature glass animals." The picture showed a pixie face, smiling. Shirley was slender, and blonde.

"Very pretty," said my mother, "except that all her features point upward. It is not a sign of intelligence I'm afraid."

"She looks tuberculous to me," said Hadji.

"Did you say animals of glass?" Uncle Pousant asked when mother had finished translating the article.

"It says so," mother said, rereading the article. "Small ones."

"I wash my hands of him!" said Uncle Pousant. "What sort of foolishness is this! High Priest!"

"We can drink a toast to the occasion," said mother sadly. "It's the least we can do." She went to the kitchen, returning with the decanter of *raki* on a tray, surrounded by six small glasses. I noticed with satisfaction that the occasion warranted my getting a drop.

"To the High Priest of Iowa culture and his future bride, she who collects animals of glass," said Uncle Pousant raising his glass, "May they be blessed with long life and myriads of children."

"She does not look as though that were possible," interrupted Hadji.

"It's a figure of speech. You take everything literally, woman. May they be blessed with wealth, and yet not forget the values of the spirit." He lifted the glass to his lips.

"You have not finished the toast," said Hadji. "It ends—and may they continue the heritage..."

"Under the circumstances it is more charitable to leave that out," said Uncle Pousant.

Mother wearily collected the glasses and put them back on the tray. "There's only one thing left to do," she said. "Someone must tell Marta-mama." She looked at Hadji.

"I shall go. In the morning," Hadji said.

Hadji picked me up at the house the next morning after breakfast. Saturday was ordinarily our morning for visiting Marta-mama, who never left her apartment. Boghos and my mother would go on Monday to pay the rent and deliver the week's groceries. This morning, Hadji was dressed in the handmade brown monk's cloth garment that fell loosely about her 200-pound frame and hung almost to her ankles. She had three others, in black, navy and grey, and when one wore out she replaced it with another exactly like it. One could not imagine Hadji wearing anything else. Over her arm Hadji carried the large wicker basket filled with jars of pistachio nuts and *lochum* candy; cheese, dates and apricots which Marta-mama would much on all week as she sat by the window.

We started out walking east across Lexington Avenue, past the armory where the morning's crop of unemployed had already begun to gather for the noonday Salvation Army soup, passing the life-size wooden horse outside the livery supply store on 24th Street. The crippled beggar who indecently exposed his stumps was seated on the sidewalk in front of O'Toole's Bar and Grill, as usual, and as she usually did, Hadji stopped for a moment to greet the sculptor who sold religious art on the corner of Third Avenue. His name was Khutumian, which means Christmas Eve, and I thought how appropriate it was at the proper time, but how out of season he must feel during the rest of the year. He complained that "they"—I wondered who they might be—were murdering his art, his talents, his ambition.

"Have some *halvah*," he said to me, extending a greasy box which had been lying between two crucifixes. "The artistic taste of the masses has reached abysmal depths," he said. "What's new?" Hadji said that Levon Dai had become engaged. To an American.

"Levon Dai always was an eccentric," said Khutumian. "It was to be expected." Hadji explained that we were on our way to break the news to Marta-mama and Khutumian shook his head slowly from side to side. "Christ is Risen," he said at last. It was the traditional Armenian Easter greeting.

We continued down 24th Street under the elevated tracks, past the open markets between second and third. Hadji stopped to talk to the German lady who sold fish. "Christ is Risen," said Hadji.

"So He has," said the German lady. "Any fish today?"

"Pousant coming, little fish, big fish," said Hadji. "Keep *kuluks*."

"I *know* he wants the heads," said the German lady, "smelts, bass, right?"

"Good," said Hadji, and we continued down the street.

On the corner of Second Avenue we ran into Parseghian, the undertaker. "Christ is Risen," he said, tipping his hat.

"May His spirit be with you," said Hadji.

"And with you," said Parseghian. "Take my greetings to Marta-mama," he said. "I have not had the chance to visit her for two weeks, but tell her I will come in a few days."

"We are taking her some tidings," said Hadji. "Levon Dai has written of his engagement to an *odar*."

"The Lord give you strength!" said Parseghian. "You are serious?"

"It was in the newspapers," said Hadji. "He sent the papers."

"We are living in a sad world," said Parseghian, "but what can you do? I am on my way now to the Chinaman."

"May God rest his soul," said Hadji. "It was to be expected." We walked together to Marta-mama's apartment. She lived on Second Avenue, over the Chinese laundry. Hadji crossed herself as we passed the laundry entrance, to the right of the stairs. The Chinaman would still be there, in his small room behind the ironing board no doubt, or could he have fallen dead in the shop itself, while handing a bundle of laundry to a customer! I closed my eyes as we passed. On the left of the stairway was the opaque glass door with the sign "Society for the Prevention of Capital Punishment." The door was closed on Saturdays, but on Monday morning the stiff-looking lady with the bleached blond hair would be back, pecking at the typewriter. What did you do to prevent capital punishment I wondered. I had asked Kelesh one day what capital punishment meant.

"Killing," said Kelesh. "But they are wasting their time." How strange, I thought, to waste one's time sitting at the typewriter all week long, to prevent something that was already against the law.

Marta-mama lived on the second landing and we entered without knocking because she would not have heard anyway. She was sitting by the window crocheting a border on a multi-colored wool spread. I recognized three of my old sweaters woven into the squares. Marta-mama's sinewy fingers worked quickly while she kept her face turned toward the window. She would never admit that she could not see.

"Marta!" shouted Hadji as she placed the basket on the table by the door. I waited to be sure that Marta-mama had heard before going up to her. 'When you are ninety-seven,' my mother had said, 'any little shock can stop your heart from beating.' That had been two years before, when no one thought Marta-mama would recover from her stroke. Marta-mama put on her glasses, though we never saw that they helped her vision.

"Hadji?" She peered through the lenses. Her hair was still jet black, and from a distance, when one could not see the network of fine lines, her face looked half her age. "I thought so, I thought so, I saw you coming," she said. "*Yavrum!*" as I touched her arm. "Take off your coat, you are not going to run out quickly. I have waited all week for you." I was not wearing a coat, but I sat on the arm of her chair. "Let me see what I have for you today. Ah, I know. Close your eyes." I closed them. "Here!" she handed me a pomegranate. "You see? I saved one for you, I know how you like them."

Marta-mama's room was small, but it was pleasantly cluttered. When you opened the door of the corner cabinet postcards and pictures fell out in heaps; pictures mostly of Levon Dai at various ages. There was a water pipe which had once belonged to Marta-mama's husband, and it sat beside his fez next to the large tinted photograph of Levon Dai. There was a victrola of 1917 vintage, and on this was a box filled with every size and color of rag imaginable.

While Hadji unpacked the basket Marta-mama pleaded that she would just complete the border on the spread. Levon Dai would no doubt be coming for Easter, and she wanted him to have it to take back with him. Hadji handed her a dish of pistachio nuts and she took one, opened it, and began munching on her bare gums.

"I am getting old," said Marta-mama.

"Nonsense!" shouted Hadji.

"I am, I am," said Marta-mama. "Ten years ago I would have finished this spread in a week. Do you know that this has taken me three months? But I do not begrudge the time. At Christmas I made a pact with myself to work the spread until Levon Dai arrives. It will be finished just in time. Old age, Hadji, is no more than a prolonged period of waiting. It is better when one does not wait idly." She crocheted silently for a moment. "Did you hear the excitement downstairs?" she said, "The poor man went last night. I could see from here he looked poorly yesterday. Poor fellow, he could not have been more than seventy." Marta-mama put down her work and took out a cigarette from a pack in her lap. "At seventy, I was riding horseback from Aintab to Kessab," she said, as she groped for some matches.

"Didn't they have trains?" I asked.

"Trains!" exclaimed Marta-mama, "who would have believed such things could exist! One had to be rich even to own a horse, otherwise you walked." She shook her finger in my face, "Do not believe them," she told me, "When they say that the olden days were better. People who speak like that have no memories. Think of your Levon Dai—he has a factory, he has machines—in one hour he can do what would have taken five men a day. Only empty-heads wish for the olden days. Well?" she added, looking at Hadji, "have you a letter? You are not saying anything." Hadji drew the letter out of her pocket.

"And you did not say anything. *Vayreni!*" said Marta-mama.

Hadji took the letter out of the envelope. "He says he is busier than he has ever been before," she said, pretending to read. Marta-mama sighed. "I understand," she said, "he cannot come."

"Perhaps in the summer," said Hadji. "They are not so busy then."

"Perhaps," said Marta-mama. "What else does he say?"

"The check came," Hadji said, stalling. "Boghos and Maryam will bring the money Monday."

"He always sends too much money," said Marta-mama. "What does he think I will do with so much money. Buy ball dresses? Give a banquet? What else does he say?"

"He says he is getting lonely there. He is thinking that he is not getting younger. He thinks perhaps he ought to be looking for a wife."

"About time!" said Marta-mama. "He was thirty-six years old last December. Why shouldn't he come to look for a wife? Does he say when he is coming?"

"He says he has met some very nice ladies right where he is. One, especially, he says, is a real *dandigin*. He sends you her picture to see how you like her." Hadji handed the picture to Marta-mama, who studied it carefully through her glasses.

"Eh? It's hard to tell from a picture," Marta-mama said at last. "Does she look bright enough to you?"

"Very intelligent," said Hadji.

"Nice deep dark eyes, hasn't she?" asked Marta-mama.

"It looks that way."

"What did you say her name was?"

"Shirlan Edemus."

"Edemus—Greek name, isn't it?"

"It must be," said Hadji, avoiding my eyes.

"Eh," said Marta-mama, "we cannot be old-fashioned about these things. The Greeks are fine people. They cook much the same way we do."

Hadji looked relieved. "Parseghian is coming to see you next week," she said. "He sent *parevs*; we saw him downstairs." Marta-mama had not heard. She had stopped crocheting when Hadji produced the letter. She began now to unravel slowly and deliberately the border of the spread, winding the wool around her fingers.

"What are you doing...?" I started to shout, but Marta-mama did not hear, and Hadji waved at me to be silent.

"It will take me a week to undo the colors," Marta-mama said at last, and she seemed to be talking to herself, "and three more months to make it up again. That will bring us to July. After that," she said, "I cannot have much longer to wait, I suppose, one way or another."

PETER SOURIAN

Born in Boston, Massachusetts, Peter Sourian moved with his family to New York City as a teenager and still calls Manhattan's Upper East Side home. A graduate of two of the country's most elite schools, Phillips Academy Andover and Harvard University, at an early age Sourian was aware of cultural and class divisions and he explores many of those issues in his writing, sometimes using his own experience as an upper-middle-class Armenian American but often through the prism of other American cultures, whether Greek, black, or Anglo.

As if to round out his education, Sourian studied briefly at universities in France and Spain, and it is obvious he relished those continental sojourns. He is a Francophile through and through, and for a brief period in the late seventies and early eighties he produced radio reports for the French-language Radio-Canada on everything from Matisse to the contemporary American novel.

In 1957 he served a two-year stint in the U.S. Army in Germany. When he returned stateside, he taught at New York University's Extension Division, City College (CUNY) and the Writers' and Teachers' Collaborative in East Harlem, and for fifteen years instructed budding fiction writers in courses at the New School for Social Research—becoming a member of the faculty. In 1965 he established what proved to be a long relationship with Bard College, in upstate New York, first as an instructor and in ten years becoming a professor of English. He is currently co-director of Bard's Writing Program in Fiction and Poetry and enjoys a superb reputation as a writing coach.

In his three novels, which were published during a compact period (1957 to 1965), Sourian riffs off what could be largely autobiographical material and creates languid narratives that meander through the lives of their characters: *Miri* (1957), *The Best and Worst of Times* (1961), and *The Gate* (1965).

Two years out of Harvard, Sourian was on the fast track to literary stardom with *Miri*, which was published by Helen and Kurt Wolff at Pantheon—the Wolffs were, remarkably, Franz Kafka's first publishers. Sourian was the Wolffs' first American find and the novel was translated into Swedish and German and appeared in Dell paperback.

Critical acclaim arrived quickly for Sourian. *Time Magazine* called the book, "the season's most appealing U.S. fiction debut," and the *New York Herald Tribune* wrote that *Miri* "is an impressive example of the novelist's art and sensitive understanding."

A straightforward narrative refracted through the eyes of each of its three main characters (Miri, Josh, and Lexy), *Miri* is a coming-of-age story that takes place at a New England college. The stories are filled with awkward and clumsy youthful tales, as well as the clash of Greek-American and Anglo-American sensibilities.

His second novel, *The Best and Worst of Times*, is perhaps the best written of all three novels. Its language is fast and easy but its story, in which two Harvard men, Jack Gillan and Tony Chase, reflect on their past and current lives, seems to fizzle as the novel stalls, relying on the characters' psychological reflections rather than a dynamic plot to drive the storytelling.

If *Miri* and *The Best and Worst of Times* are successful at charting the young adult emotional lives of their rambunctious characters, his third novel, *The Gate,* is as memorable for its literary mastery as it is for its focus on the Armenian Genocide during a time when no one, not even Armenians, uttered the word outside of their then ghettoized communities. As if to overcompensate for the long silence, the pioneering book overflows with stories that retain the raw edges of powerful narratives.

There is a sense of quiet frenzy in the story, as if Sourian was desperate to purge himself of the heavy, burdensome stories that appear on each page. Four decades after its publication, *The Gate* is forgotten to most but its impact as the first book to dive headfirst into the juggernaut of the Armenian Genocide is not.

The story of three generations of the Stepanyan family (primarily its patriarchs Vahan, Sarkis, and Paul), *The Gate* jumps from stories of escape and exile from the genocidal Ottoman Empire to the life of writer Paul Stepanyan and his sister Grace, both New Yorkers with the emotional baggage of a complex history they don't have the tools to understand.

When the book appeared, the Armenian American community finally had a mainstream voice that discussed the issues that defined them. While other Armenian Americans had already made huge contributions to the worlds of literature (William Saroyan), art (Arshile Gorky), and cinema (Rouben Mamoulian), Sourian was the first to transform the communal albatross of the Genocide into the material of art without sublimating it into abstractions. With such a daunting and unenviable task, Sourian's book comes across as cathartic, like a literary scream that wanted to lay to rest the tortured souls of the 1915 generation.

That being said, the myriad of stories and narratives that make up *The Gate* are uneven, but its peaks are superb, including the poignant scene of Grace wandering the theatre district, half-dazed, or is it confused, until she breaks down and calls a therapist for help, and the awkward moment when Paul is given the manuscript of a man who wants his family's genocide story told to the world. Paul discovers it to be parochial at best.

Unfortunately, the novel ends in a fit of violence when the fanatic Hagopian kills Paul, reiterating American stereotypes that regard ethnicity as a crucible of backward rage and nationalism. But to read the novel's shortcomings as Sourian's alone is wrong; it was written at a time when the Armenian American community lacked the language to define itself. Sourian's book was a starting point for a larger discussion that continues to this day.

After his three novels, Sourian published short stories and much cultural and literary criticism. He says that he destroyed, without regret, over a thousand pages of fiction which he believes had no value. He is, however, decidedly sanguine about his recent intensive surge of work: two long novels, presently in manuscript, and a third, nearing completion (his three recent unpublished novels are entitled *Twice Upon a Time, A Comedy of Property,* and *We You They*).

His short fiction is different from his more labored novels. The characters in his short stories come across on the page as quick and agile with more of a zest for life than a mission. This is a rich collection of tales that explore a multitude of lives and voices.

"The Calfayan Collection," published in *Playboy,* conflates two common literary stereotypes of Armenians, the affluent businessman and the erotic sage, and presents a portrait of a highly sophisticated if sympathetically manipulative millionaire who comes across as part-Rasputin, part–Sixties radical. Calfayan is a looming, frustrated character who with an appropriately exotic sidekick exudes a certain reserved sexual prowess afforded him by his wealth.

In "About Kenneth's Education," Sourian finds a perfect pitch of character and narrative, recounting the life of one African American student who is confronted with a world very different from his own. The tone is not nostalgic but raw. He sketches the Bronx teenager's world with a vivid narrative voice that captures the tension of the characters. It is a lively piece with a strong visual component—an element that consistently appears in his best short fiction.

Sourian's nonfiction is altogether different from his fiction. Not because the writer's voice shifts radically, but rather because the haze that can hang around his fiction gently lifts when he writes critically of books, television, or life. It is as if in the world of his imagination his thoughts get lost in the infinity of the vista, always taking the scenic path rather than the most direct route. The finite task of reviews provides the perfect canvas for his urbane, wry, and often insightful prose.

Writing in *The Nation* about television coverage of the 1976 Republican Convention, he wisecracks, "It also had funny hats, an Invocation which actually mentioned Jesus Christ, a U.S. Secretary of State with a terrific German accent, a President's wife looking unwell, glum black conservatives, and clever NBC cameras alternating shots of Rockefeller having a grand foxy time with shots of a heavy unhappy Happy [Rockefeller]." There is exuberance in a sentence like this that never surfaces in his fiction.

In the sixties, he began to contribute to the *New York Times Book Review.* Later, from 1975 to 1980, he became the television columnist for *The Nation* and wrote dozens of pieces during a pivotal period in the history of television as it asserted its role as the agora of American life.

Since then, he has written for various publications, including the Armenian American quarterly *Ararat*, for which he has served as a board member since 1975.

In 1992 Ashod Press published his first, and so far only, collection of nonfiction works, *At the French Embassy in Sofia*, which bundles most of the notable pieces from the last three decades as well as a hefty essay about the transformation of Bulgaria from communism to democratic socialism. In this large, sprawling piece, Sourian shows off some of his literary muscle, using arcane vocabulary, a smattering of italicized foreign expressions, and observations that make him seem more like an eighteenth-century traveler on the Grand Tour, rather than a modern tourist. Most recently, in 2000, *Ararat's* long-time editor Leo Hamalian decided to honor Sourian by devoting a whole issue of the journal to Sourian's published and previously unpublished short fiction. The result is a sweet and absorbing collection that reflects his decades of exploration in prose.

If Virginia Woolf is right and "Every secret of a writer's soul, every experience of his life, every quality of his mind is written large in his works," then I would suggest that Sourian's writing reveals a pensive soul that is always looking for truth. His work is the record of this search for the genuine and it is filled with quiet moments of surprise that appear when he finds it in unexpected places. The fact that he has been able to live a full life in words that chart that journey is a credit to his intellectual energy and a testament to his curious mind.

Hrag Vartanian

Death of an Art Dealer

On Wednesday afternoon I packed my father's things for the stay at the hospital. It was dusk out the window. The weather had become relatively mild. We had a long evening ahead of us. I sat down glumly and stared out the window.

"Bring me that mail from over there," he said.

I fetched some mail from the top of the bureau and brought it over to the bed. He looked at each piece of mail as I stood there, and then tore some of the envelopes in half, putting each torn envelope on the blanket. I took each one as he did so and put it in the wastebasket.

We continued doing this. A certain amount of junk mail had accumulated. I began straightening and tidying various things around the room. I emptied the ashtrays. When an envelope was especially thick I tore it for him.

"How about some of that old mail over there you haven't touched?"

"Yes, yes, bring that to me as well."

"How about this old string on the desk that you've been saving?"

"I'd better save some of that. Cut it about in half."

"You don't need to save it, father, really!"

"I want to save half of it."

"All right, all right," I said, and cut it in half with a scissors from the desk, and threw one half away.

"Now put these fire insurance papers in the desk."

I did, moving smartly. Then I had another idea. I went into the living room and brought back a large sheaf of Christmas cards which had been in a silver tray on the piano.

"Don't you want to throw these away too?"

"Yes. No, no. I want to keep those," he said. "Put them back."

"All right."

"Bring me my checkbook," he said.

I brought him his big checkbook, bearing it like a crown upon a pillow. He opened it, and began writing a check.

"This is a real estate tax payment. Get an envelope."

"How about your opera tickets?"

I had been thinking about his subscription to the Metropolitan Opera. I'd thought about getting him to write the check to renew it, because I didn't know whether or not you forfeited your right to the subscription if you let too much time lapse without sending them a check. I imagined hordes of people wanting it, waiting for it out there, waiting to take it away from me.

The phone rang, and I answered it. It was a high-pitched woman's voice.

"Hello? This is Mrs. Kenneth Basford. Is Mr. Tigranian there?"

"Yes, I'm his son. Can I help you?"

"Well, I'm in town very briefly, and I've just purchased a lovely blue Rayya bowl from Charles Epler. I've met Mr. Tigranian several times—at the Jacobs'—and I wondered if it would be possible for me to bring it over, if perhaps he wouldn't mind taking a look at it."

"Just a moment," I said, and told my father what she had said.

He looked up at me, his eyes alert. "Tell her she can see me in an hour."

Mrs. Basford sounded very pleased at this. She could come.

"I wonder what Epler charged her for that piece," my father said, smiling.

He had me dress him in a blue pinstripe suit, with a vest, and then adjusted his pocket watch and chain himself, as well as the tiny red boutonniere of the French Legion of Honor on his lapel. He called for Leroy and told him to dress and be ready to answer the door. Then he had me turn most of the lights off in the house. The living room was dim and quiet.

"Nicholas, I may ask you to bring that Rayya bowl down from the shelf and put it here on the coffee table at some time during my conversation with Mrs. Basford."

"All right," I said. He looked at his pocket watch and bade me help him over to his armchair.

"Set that standing lamp back just a few feet," he said. I did, and with difficulty he turned his head to see if the new position of the lamp was satisfactory. Then he waited, motionless, for the doorbell to ring.

Leroy led her in, bowing with exaggeration and then retiring downstairs. Mrs. Basford entered, followed by a uniformed chauffeur carrying a box in his hands. She was about fifty, with a heavy body and fleshy yet attractive face—blue-grey eyes, childish ones, gray suit, and silver fox furs, which I hadn't seen in a long time. My father rose slowly and touched his lips to her hand. He gestured for her to sit on the sofa and sat down himself.

Mrs. Basford smiled engagingly, "Such a pleasure to see you again," she said, the fresh out-of-doors still in her hearty face and in her voice. "I know I shouldn't have disturbed you, but I'm staying up the street at the Carlyle and really couldn't resist."

"You should not have hesitated. My time belongs to anyone with a real interest in art. Well! How is Mrs. Jacobs? Remarkable woman! Intelligent woman!"

"Edith's fine."

"Now about this piece you have from Charles Epler."

"Yes, I brought it along."

"Unwrap it please."

The chauffeur stepped forward with the box, placing it on the coffee table in front of Mrs. Basford, who began hurriedly to unwrap it.

"I *do* like it," she said.

My father leaned forward and grasped her wrists firmly. She looked up in surprise. His smile erased his emaciation. "Slowly, my dear girl."

He finished unwrapping it himself, with sure hands. He turned it in his hands, his face expressionless, except for a calm gravity.

"It *is* authentic, I suppose," Mrs. Basford said, with a tiny laugh. "Of course I know it is authentic, literally, but I hope it's all it's cracked up to be!"

"Of course. Epler is a reliable man. This is from the collection of Lord Sedley."

"Why yes, it is."

The Rayya bowl had a blue-green background, and was crowded with riding figures, and harpies around the edge—similar to the bowl on the shelf behind Mrs. Basford. My father had managed to make Epler seem obscurely unreliable, without any discernible irony in his voice.

"This bowl is easily worth five thousand dollars today," he said.

"Oh," Mrs. Basford was visibly crestfallen.

My father changed the subject, speaking of their mutual acquaintance, Mrs. Jacobs.

"I admire her taste enormously," he said. "At the rate she is going now, in another few years she will have one of the finest collections."

"Edith's so clever."

"She is also a wise woman."

"Mr. Tigranian, if I may ask, what is your opinion of Charles Epler?"

"He is a reliable man. His interests are eclectic, and I approve of that. Our tastes differ, especially when you come to the contemporary, but it seems I am very wrong about some things. Picasso, for instance, was never my dish of tea."

"You know, I've never really appreciated his work. I've tried."

"I find little feeling there. It's cold, somewhat thin, and perhaps finally vulgar…Of course you and I must be very wrong."

"Oh, Mr. Tigranian, I can't tell you how grateful I am that you should have been willing to bother having a look at this bowl of mine," Mrs. Basford said. She was looking better now; in fact she now looked almost pleased.

"Mr. Tigranian, I wonder if you have anything which might interest me particularly." She smiled bashfully.

"Not really. I have one or two pieces which might be right for you, but I am reluctant to part with them."

"Couldn't I see them? It would be an honor to see them!"

My father offered Mrs. Basford a cigarette from the box on the table, which she refused. He took on himself, and I lighted it for him, knowing he hadn't smoked in weeks.

"Nicholas, I would like to show Mrs. Basford the shallow blue Rayya bowl, please."

I took the bowl down from its place and handed it to him. He regarded it and we looked at it with him. It was similar to Mrs. Basford's pottery, except that the colors were much more vibrant, and there seemed to be an endless multitude of horsemen, a crowded, thronging, never-ending procession, in extraordinarily rich trappings.

"Ohh," exclaimed Mrs. Basford. She was right. My father's face glowed, young in the dim light.

"How much is it?"

"Twenty-five thousand dollars."

"I'll take it," she said, and added in a smaller voice, "if you'll let me."

"I like to see someone who really loves a piece like this."

"You mean I can have it?"

"Yes."

I enveloped it in tissue paper and put it in a box.

"I almost forgot. The check. I'd make a good thief, wouldn't I?"

"You take this home with you," he said, in rather a gentle voice. "Don't write a check now. Go slowly, go slowly. You send me your check sometime later."

Mrs. Basford took a step toward my father with quite a lovely smile on her face. She seemed to lean or drift toward him. He did not stand up, but took her hand, touched it with his lips, and then sat slowly back. I said I would return in a moment, and escorted Mrs. Basford out to a black double-parked car.

She didn't seem to have noticed how emaciated my father was. Like Gatsby's Klipspringer, she seemed to have arrived from the end of the earth.

When I came back to the living room, greenish fluid was coming from his mouth onto his vest. I went to him quickly. He was also urinating. I carried him into the bedroom; he was so light now. I undressed him and washed and cleaned him with sponges, and then got him into his pajamas, and settled him under the covers. The pillowcase was crisp and fresh. He seemed comfortable.

"I'll call Dr. Rice," I said

"No."

I felt good somehow, seeing him looking comfortable now.

"I feel wonderful," he said.

"I'll be right back," I said, and went to the bathroom with the sponges and the basin. I squeezed the sponges and washed out the basin.

I came back into the bedroom.

"Father?" His eyes were closed. He seemed peaceful under the light. I stepped forward and looked into his face. I bent forward and stared into his face. It was a delicate face, really. He was dead. I turned my face and my body into a corner of the room, and I put my hands up to my face.

from *The Gate*

1961: I stopped. I was already late for supper at my parents' house. I lit a cigarette and looked at what I had written, concerning my grandfather as a young man, concerning a massacre—one in a long series of Turkish Muslim massacres of the Armenian Christians in Asia Minor. I got up from the table—a drafting board, borrowed from my father's architectural office on East Forty-sixth Street, laced across two wooden horses.

My parents' house was only a few blocks away from my place, westward, between Madison and Park Avenues. At first I walked rapidly, then slowed down. Although it was early spring, the street lights had already come on, and shone pleasantly through the leaves of the many trees lining the side streets. On Third Avenue, couples were trying to catch taxis; one man looked nervous, even frightened, about being late.

When I reached the house I ran up the stone steps and, using my own key, opened the heavy front door. I passed the unused fireplace in the public front hallway, and an old oak sideboard—there for as long as I could remember, its legs carved into a maze of harmless dragons' heads and bodies. Opening the door to the apartment, I heard laughter, and then I could see my father in the living room at the end of the long vestibule, sitting deep in his armchair, but leaning forward, pouring gin into his martini pitcher.

As I came into the room Lew Johnson, my brother-in-law, stood up; still talking to my father, he extended his large hand to me, smiling broadly. My sister Grace sat curled up at one end of the green couch, and my grandmother at the other, a knitted rose shawl about her bent shoulders. I went over and leaned down to kiss them. My father, in salute, made a little comic drum-major flourish with his cigar. Ash fell onto his vest and he brushed at it vigorously with the side of his hand, staring down.

"I was hoping Julie'd be here," I said. Sometimes, if Lew and Grace came over to supper they would bring their child and stay overnight, leaving her with my mother during the next day. There was plenty of room in the apartment, a duplex.

"We got a baby-sitter," Grace said.

"Sarkis? Is that Paul?" my mother called from the kitchen downstairs.

"Yes, it's me."

"I hate to ask you, but would you mind running around the corner and getting a loaf of bread? I forgot."

"O.K."

When I came back, I ran downstairs, leaned over the wooden banister, and handed the bread to my mother. "Tell Sarkis supper's ready."

"Let me just have a drink first," I said.

"All right, but come down pretty soon."

We spent a long time over the supper table, arguing politics, interrupting each other, especially Grace and I. I wanted to tell them about the book I had just begun, but I had already been writing one for some time now, supposedly. Then, over grapes and cheese, my father, perhaps because Lew was there, began to speak about his first days in America.

I was anxious to get back to my book, and left early, with a warm feeling.

It was windy outside. I walked back to my place, but went on past it, my mind racing toward all sorts of possibilities: designs, episodes, character—a harehound in high grass. I walked over to the East River and gazed down at the swirling water currents there, all moving out to sea in the exciting darkness; and then after a while I went home.

1920: Ellis Island. Herded down onto a launch from the liner, taken to Ellis Island. Ordered to walk two by two. Ordered to sit down on the sticky benches. Ordered to get up. Ordered to take off all your clothes. Ordered on line to be examined. Waiting over twenty minutes, naked, with other naked people. Ordered to follow, no explanations. Locked alone, uncomprehending, naked in a small bare room. Fetched, still no explanations. Ordered to dress. Ordered to follow a man with a slip of green paper in his hand. Living. Living there for three days, but not knowing the limit of time, in a place of detention, a large, rumor-glutted, locked room with many other people in it, bars on the narrow grime-caked windows, dirty mattresses down on the floor. Taken at last to the city by launch, and set loose under the terrifying roar of the elevated train.

Sarkis, later, after his arrival in America from Constantinople via Piraeus, heard this sort of description many times—what happened to you at Ellis Island, how terrible it was, how even a Turkish official would not order people to undress in public.

But for sixteen-year-old Sarkis himself, arriving after twenty-one days at sea, it had not been so. Yes, they had walked two by two from the launch, after one day's quarantine aboard the slow Greek liner. But he had walked sprightly, singing. As they waited to be examined they were each given a basket of lunch with fresh fruit in it. The doctor looked into his eyes for trachoma, and found none—winked at him. He was patiently instructed how to get to Boston on the boat that left New York each evening. Although the light-haired American at a desk could speak no Armenian, nor Turkish, he was friendly; by drawing a sketch, and by means of gestures, he made himself understood to Sarkis, who had handed him Boghos Boghosian's address, grinned, held his palms open, up, and shrugged.

Sarkis bought himself a hat in Manhattan, like the ones the passing men wore. With twenty dollars and some bright American change left in his pocket, he stood under the elevated train and gazed up at it, shuddering delightedly as it passed over him. He dropped his hat. A gust of wind blew it across the cobblestones. He ran after it and rescued it from the wheels of vehicles.

Shortly before five o'clock that September evening he boarded the white boat, slept deeply between glistening sheets, and the next morning, Sunday,

he was in Boston. A bell was ringing someplace, but how quiet—a peaceful
God-loving world.

I went into the front room of my apartment. The apartments were all identical.
Two railroad flats to a floor. I stood there and listened. The sound was less
obtrusive in the front room, so with furious energy I began to move the
worktable in there, then my large heavy bed and my dresser back into the room
just off the kitchen, which was at the rear of the building. I sat down at the table.

Now my telephone was still in the front room, but my bed was not. If
the phone rang while I was in bed I would have to dash naked, barefoot,
through the apartment from my bed to the phone. If asleep, I might not hear
it at all. Now it sat on my working table; if it rang while I worked I would
most certainly hear it and have to answer it. I had often thought that while
working I should turn the ring down low, bundle the phone in a blanket,
and hide it under the bed so as to ignore it all the better. But there it sat
now, where it had always meant to sit, squat and evil on my working table. I
dialed my father's office number again.

"You know, Yervant showed me a whole trunkful of stuff Grandfather
wrote, in copybooks. He said there were two thirds of a history of Armenia
Grandfather had written, and half of that had burned in some big fire that
destroyed a whole section of the city, and that Grandfather started writing it
over again, but never finished."

"That was just before I left."

"Anyway, there were also translations of French plays and novels into
Armenian—Les Misérables—and little skits he wrote for the school, and
nursery rhymes. Yervant gave me a couple of books to bring back with me,
and one, he said, is a kind of journal Grandfather kept when he was in exile;
it's made up of all kinds of different paper bound up together. Here, I'll get
it." I stood up and looked around.

"Your mother put your things in our room."

"Oh," I said, and went to tiptoe into the darkness.

"Sarkis?" my mother murmured.

"No, it's Paul."

"Paul, don't stay up too late. Your father's tired. What is it?"

"I'm looking for my stuff."

"It's next to your father's chest of drawers. The bed's made up in Grace's
room for you."

I rummaged around in the dark, found the book, and began to tiptoe out.

"Do you want me to wake you up in the morning?" she said.

"No. I'm so used to getting up at five-thirty I'll probably be out of bed when it's still dark. Good night, Mother." I stopped and went over. I knelt down and hugged her and kissed her hard on the cheek.

"It's so nice to have you home, dear," she murmured in a sleepy voice, and in the light coming through the partly open door I could see her smiling, her eyes closed.

I tiptoed out with the little book. I handed it to my father, who put it down, put on his glasses, picked it up, and opened it with care. Although he hardly read anything but the newspaper, he had a respect for the printed word that bordered on the ridiculous. When I was little he would fly into a rage when he saw notes written in my schoolbooks, and dog-eared pages. Once he saw a number underlined in the phone book and demanded to know who had done it. Scared me half to death. It took days for me to muster the courage to tell him I had. But now I write in books anyway, and scribble numbers on the cover of my phone book.

His face was now quite still, but not in repose. I watched it, holding my breath for some reason. He was holding the book away from his eyes, squinting, turned toward the light.

"Would you translate some of it now? Just a few lines? I'd like to get the feel of it," I said, curious, wondering if it had any literary merit.

"It's hard; the pencil is faded. Let me see."

I scrambled over behind him, my hands on the back of the chair, and I kneeled, looking over his shoulder, thinking, I ought to get myself a suit like his, wondering foolishly if it would impress Lila. His suit looked good.

"With God's help I will come back along this road again."

My father stopped. "It's hard to translate," he said, and reading on while he turned the page, he said, "I'll try something else." Then he sort of froze. I could feel it.

At last, in a slow soft voice, trembling with an age which I had never heard, old and yet a chastened boy, he read: "Sarkis...Sarkis is..."

He closed the book.

My father began to weep. His shoulder trembled. It must have lasted no longer than ten or fifteen seconds. Once I heard a sort of *aohh*-sound come from him.

I saw him bite his lip. Tears were touching it now. Then he set the book blindly down on the black coffee table, pushed his glasses back on his forehead, blinked, and began to wipe his eyes with his hands, clumsily. He stopped and pulled the handkerchief from his breast pocket. "I can't any more." When he hade wiped his face, he looked up clear-eyed, his gaze resting on a painting he had once made, of silvery blue mackerel lying on a table outdoors under a shading tree.

"Your grandfather was a wonderful man."

I kneeled there. He turned his head as far as he could toward my eyes, without having to move his body. I moved, crouching up now, so he could see my eyes. We said nothing.

"I guess I'll go to bed," I said, wanting to listen to him, but thinking, Some other time, sensing also that he did not want to talk.

"Good night, Paul."

I stood up, bent to kiss him, and went into Grace's old room. I tried the light switch but the light didn't go on. I saw the back of my father's head, rising motionless, just above the rim of the broad-backed chair. I closed the door and took off my clothes in the dark. I didn't go back out to brush my teeth; I often skipped that at night anyway.

I had never in my life seen tears in my father's eyes before, nor have I since, except outdoors, walking in the face of a winter wind, or when he laughed particularly hard at something.

I lay down naked between the fresh sheets, and while already noting coolly what I had just witnessed, I knew that a full dark oceanic tide, crimson Lila floating brightly upon it though no larger than a bobbing cork, was rising from depths in and around me I could not fathom.

About Kenneth's Education

After handing Kenneth back his book review of *The Martian Chronicles*, Mr. Freeman put his hand on Kenneth's flattop, kind of pushed his head around, and said the review was excellent.

"I guess your hair's not the kind that tousles," he added. Kenneth looked up at him immediately, putting sass into his eyes, wanting to say what was wrong with his nigger hair you white fuck.

"What does that mean?"

"T-O-U-S-L-E. Look it up," Freeman said, passing on to the next row and handing Eric Walker his paper, saying he hadn't read the book now had he? Freeman always said Look it up when you didn't know a word. Kenneth figured he had to be the absolute only kid in the class who ever did.

He walked home with Eric Walker and Archie M. Sinquefield, who both lived on the same floor of the McCann Project, nine flights down from Kenneth on Seventeen. McCann was supposed to be one of the worst projects, drugs and rape and stuff, but Kenneth had heard it was s'pose to be getting much better. Eric and Archie M. were in the same grade but older. From way back he'd always wanted to be like them but figured he'd never make it. It was like he'd never make it, no matter what. But they'd been hanging out with him more and more.

He waited impatiently for the slow elevator, went up and got his basketball and came down to meet them and shoot a few before going over to the FINAST where he bagged groceries. He was shorter than they were but maybe even just about as good.

"Now watch this. Best shooter in the worl'," said Archie M., leaping elaborately and missing. Kenneth laughed. Archie M. did make you laugh. "Say hey, Freeman's gay," he said. "Right, Eric? I mean feelin' up Kenny's beautiful flattop an' like that."

The next afternoon Mr. Freeman asked Kenneth to stay after class for a minute. Eric winked as he went out and Kenneth grinned back, shrugging, happy about this new complicity.

Freeman went to close the door, came back and sat on the edge of his desk. Had Kenneth done something wrong?

"Where do you figure on going to school? Clinton?"

"Yeah, I guess."

"Why don't you try for Bronx Science or Stuyvesant?"

"Nobody can get into those places."

"I think you have a shot."

"Nobody ever went to those schools from here. Stuyvesant's way down in Manhattan anyway."

"Bronx Science is one of the best schools in the world, and it's right next door to Clinton. You can walk there, the way you do now."

"Yeah."

"Tell you what. That exam is in December. If you stay after school forty-five minutes twice a week, I'll give you some tutoring, and extra assignments. Even if you don't score high enough, you come close and they let you go to a summer program for minority kids and then they take you if you do well there. You're an exceptional student. You realize that, don't you?"

"Huh."

"Of course you realize that."

"I guess."

"You're interested in the work."

Kenneth wanted to say it was because Mr. Freeman made seventh grade social studies interesting. But how many teachers did Freeman think were like that? Zero. He agreed to give it a try if his mother let him. He would go a half-hour later to the FINAST.

"I'll be happy to talk to your mother if it's necessary," Mr. Freeman said.

When he got home Eric and Archie M. were sitting on a bench smoking. Eric looked up and squinted. "What the man want from you?"

"Nothing."

"Wants your ass," said Archie M. "Wants to stick it up your ass."

"He's married," Kenneth said. "That blonde English teacher in 8-408. Ms. Greenberg."

"Don't make no difference."

"He doesn't act gay," Kenneth said. "He's more like some kin' a cowboy." Freeman was tall and rangy, and almost bald. Strong.

"Don' mean nothin'."

"True," Kenneth agreed thoughtfully. "He wants me to stay after school to give me extra tutoring to take the test for Bronx Science."

"Oooh!" Archie shook out his long bony hand as if it were a wet-mop.

"You look up that word he said, mussin' whitcha yesterday?" Eric asked.

"Yeah. Tousle. To muss or disorder."

"He gonna disorder you," Archie M. said.

"Ain' gonna disorder me," answered Kenneth, putting sass into his eyes, indignant at the idea of Mr. Freeman mussing with him.

"Now if Freeman's so great what's he doin' teachin' seven grade?" Eric said. "An' why he take his time to tutor with you when he got that nice blonde piece of ass headin' straight home husself right after school lets out."

Kenneth nodded.

"Exceptional paper, Kenneth," Archie M. said, mimicking Freeman aptly enough so Kenneth laughed as he left for the FINAST. Now he felt uncomfortable at the idea of staying after school with Freeman.

Kenneth's mother, Mrs. Morey, was well-respected. She had a good job as office manager for a small exterminating company on the Grand Concourse. Kenneth's father, Bobby Morey, had been away in the Air Force for as long as anyone could remember. A check for the family allotment part of Bobby Morey's pay arrived every month, but it had been reduced a year-and-a-half ago because Airman Third Class Bobby Morey, Mrs. Morey figured out, must have been demoted for some reason, some kind of trouble.

Kenneth told his mother about the tutoring and that Mr. Freeman had said Kenneth was exceptional.

He had been afraid his mother might hassle him but she only said it was very nice of the man to give of his time. It was all right with her so long as he could arrange his hours at the FINAST so as to continue helping at home with his little brother and Aretha, his sister. Sometimes his mother had to work late and he gave them supper.

Kenneth did his homework at the kitchen table, as usual, while everyone sat in the living room with the TV. He always went to bed last. His mother didn't always feel so well and often went to bed early. She was a big woman, a large woman.

When he was done he put his books into his backpack, arranging them with care, and quietly brought the backpack into the room he shared with his little brother. He got in bed and lay there thinking of himself as a big lawyer with a lot of money and a beautiful white wife, like Ms. Greenberg.

The next afternoon he couldn't go fooling around with Eric and Archie M. He had tutoring.

"Tutorin', *shee-it*," said Eric.

Mr. Freeman didn't leave Kenneth much time to fool around with Eric and Archie M., but he told himself he could hang out with them after the test was over. Mr. Freeman explained things very well, very clearly. He spent more time on Math than English, which surprised Kenneth. Mr. Freeman told him that he'd majored in Math in college before switching over to English. Kenneth could never have understood all the algebra without Mr. Freeman. In his regular Math class you didn't ask questions when you didn't understand; you knew dumb Mrs. Getz didn't like questions, and you figured you knew why.

He found a book of vocabulary words in the school library: *Lists for NYC Competitive High Schools Tests*, but Mr. Freeman wasn't so interested in that. He gave Kenneth *The Adventures of Sherlock Holmes*, an old book with *Dick Freeman* written in pencil on the flyleaf, which was okay once you got used to it, and *The Red Badge of Courage* and *Ethan Frome* which were very boring, and a paperback, *Essays by George Orwell*, mostly very terrible. Mr. Freeman said that Kenneth would develop his vocabulary better by reading than by memorizing like a monkey. But Kenneth studied a few words from the lists every night just before going to bed anyway.

The test was on Saturday morning, December 8, at Bronx Science High School. There were hundreds of kids, mostly white and Chinese, and he didn't have a chance.

But the test was easier than he had expected. He had time left over to check his Math answers. Bronx Science was clean, and light, and airy, and Kenneth began to hope he might make it. He was going to tell Mr. Freeman on Monday that he'd maybe done okay. You didn't find out the results until February 11.

On Monday there was a sub. Mr. Freeman was out sick. And he'd been out twice the week before. He was usually never absent.

They had a different sub every day for the whole week and then after that they got a regular sub, an old lady, Mrs. Rosen.

Mr. Freeman had leukemia. *Galloping* leukemia, Kenneth heard. From the beginning of January, even before Mr. Freeman was absent, Kenneth realized he'd seen Ms. Greenberg on the stairs a few times, with her eyes red.

He died very fast. He died the week before Kenneth got the notice in the mail that he'd passed the Bronx Science with a 558, two points above the regular cutoff that year, so even without the extra minority points he wouldn't have to go to the summer program and could work all day at the FINAST. Mrs. Rosen had everyone in the class write a note to Ms. Greenberg saying how sorry they were.

"We want to shoot a few?" Kenneth said, coming out of school a few days later.

"Unh-uh," said Archie M.

"How come?"

"Got no time," Eric said, and they walked away, going the opposite direction from the McCann Project.

Saturday, just after eleven he looked out the window and saw them playing down there. He got dressed and went down, and stood in the trashy dried-up grass at the edge of the court.

"Howsa goin'?" They had a brand-new ball.

"Nothin' much," Eric said, so he could hardly hear it, then concentrated, and made a nice set-shot. The ball came Kenneth's way and he went in for a layup.

"Where'd you get a new ball?" He passed it to Archie M. and rubbed his hands together against the cold.

"Archie M. got it," Eric said.

"Guess you won't be at Clinton next year with everybody," Eric said.

"Nope."

"Bronx Science."

"Yeah," Kenneth said, feeling ashamed not going to Clinton with everybody else.

But Eric just said, "pretty good," in a friendly voice.

"Yeah," Archie M. said, dribbling.

"I gotta go over the FINAST."

"Yeah," Eric said.

"Best in the worl'," said Archie M., leaping up for the shot.

The next Saturday Kenneth came out to get some medicine for his mother and saw Eric sitting out on the bench alone, looking thoughtful.

"Hey, Eric, wanna shoot a few? As soon as I get back from the pharmacy I'll go up and get my ball."

"Man—"

"Yeah?"

"—We don' wanna see you any more."

"Huh?"

"We don' wanna hang out, unnestan?"

"Why?"

"Thassa way it is."

"The way it is?"

"We goin' diffren' paths, man. Diffren' paths."

"Okay man," Kenneth said, his voice cool. He marched to the pharmacy. He was hurting bad.

Then on Monday the new manager at the FINAST only needed him an hour, so he got home at 4:30. Coming out of the elevator were Eric and Archie M. and he said hello but they said nothing. He turned and asked were they looking for him and then the elevator door closed and it went right up to Seventeen, when it was usually so fuckin' slow. What were they doing here in his entry if it wasn't to see him?

There was something on the floor in front of the apartment door, some kind of mess. He bent down. It was two broken eggs, broken neatly like in a frying pan waiting to be done. He looked down at them, his hands on his knees, and they looked right back up at him, two round yellow eyes in the whites. Then he went in and came back with a rag and wiped it up. They had put it there on purpose, someone.

Why did he ever listen to that white Freeman? He wanted his friends. He didn't want no Bronx Science. He was going to change it back. After one semester you could change back to Clinton, but then it was final you stayed in Clinton. He'd be at Clinton like everyone else. *Exceptional.* That Freeman. That Freeman was dead.

That night he could not sleep. The sheet was all twisted and he kept arching up his back and straightening the sheet under him and flopping back down, and then getting it twisted all over again as if it just didn't want to be straight. He had done Freeman *wrong.* He'd wanted to shine and show off and so he had to act with Eric and Archie M. as if Mr. Freeman was gay. He couldn't exactly remember his words, but it seemed to him for sure that he must have gone and said Mr. Freeman was gay. And then laughed. He tried, but he couldn't seem to remember exactly. He wished he hadn't done laughed. Maybe he hadn't, since he couldn't remember. But come on, be honest and admit. And he didn't even thank him for what he had done in the note Mrs. Rosen made them write in class to Freeman's wife. Why had he joked with them about Mr. Freeman? But it was too late now. Too late.'

Too late. Tears started coming out of his eyes while he lay on his back not moving, tears just flowing out of him for a long time. He thought of what a fine man Mr. Freeman was. He felt alone, except for Mr. Freeman, who'd cared about him, his friend. Then he began to feel good, when he least expected it, glad the tears were coming from his eyes, so he was smiling and crying at the same time. And so after a while he turned onto his side, and fell sound asleep.

There was another black in his home-room at Bronx Science in September, Roy Davis, along with three girls. Roy came all the way from Brooklyn on the subway, like a lot of the kids. Roy's mother had made him take the test and he'd gotten in under the summer program for minorities. Kenneth was lucky, getting to school walking in less than ten minutes.

He got along with Roy, but the person he liked best was Paul Conover, who sat next to him in History and in English. He had a big grin. He was always raising his hand to answer the questions, and to ask questions too, and the teachers respected him. These teachers usually explained things pretty well (because they knew what they were talking about) and Kenneth could see from watching Paul that they usually didn't mind your asking questions when you didn't understand. The thing was, as long as you were trying to do the work they respected you.

But you could have a fun time with Paul too, and Kenneth and he laughed and fooled around a lot, sometimes like a bug got them and they couldn't help it and the teacher would straighten them out and they'd fly right. It was just they forgot themselves sometimes. The work was a thousand times worse than Junior High but Kenneth was determined to make it.

Paul had blue eyes. He lived downtown, on the East Side of Manhattan, but Kenneth would often walk him to the subway which was only a couple minutes out of his way.

One afternoon Ms. Nash asked for someone to relate the events of the French Revolution and no one was about to raise his hand. It was very hard to keep track what happened in the French Revolution. But Kenneth had been up until 2:30 AM; just because it was so confusing he had to sit down and work it out. He'd kept pinching himself on the thigh and slapping himself in the face to keep awake until he maybe had it kind of straight.

So he looked around him and then raised his hand, and he went right through it: The Estates-General of 1789, the Constituent Assembly and then the Legislative, the King going to Paris, the arrest of the King, the Convention and the Terror with Robespierre guillotined. And Kenneth explained each event as he went along, surprised he could do it, because when he'd gone to bed at 2:40 AM he didn't think so. That was *Excellent*, Ms. Nash said, surprised, and Kenneth knew it was.

"What's up?" Paul said, catching up with him after school. "I still have a lot of trouble with the French Revolution," he said.

So a few days later Kenneth didn't have the FINAST and he brought Paul home and they studied for the test together. Kenneth could tell Paul didn't think it was a great place to study; it suddenly was a little messy and the kids had TV on.

"Wanna Pepsi?"

"No thanks—uh, yeah okay."

"Bring us a couple Pepsis in the refrigerator," Kenneth told his sister Aretha.

"No, I'm watching this."

"Girl don't talk back to me."

So Sassy Aretha shook her head and got the Pepsis, muttering how he was such a big man now, Bronx Science.

After they'd finished working Kenneth went down and walked Paul over to the subway. It got darker sooner now and colder, and Paul probably wasn't too sure where the subway was from the McCann Project.

When he got back, Eric Walker and Archie M. were standing under the light bulb by their entry, leaning their backs against the rail.

"Hey. What's up?" Kenneth said, before he had a chance to think.

"Hey Whitey," whispered Archie M., and Eric laughed softly, and Kenneth went right on past.

The next afternoon Paul said he was staying after school and wouldn't be heading for the subway right away.

"What's up?"

"I think I may join the Debating Club. There's a meeting."

"I saw that...I guess I'll come too," Kenneth said, a little timid.

It sounded interesting. Bronx Science had an excellent debate team known all over the country. The novices got to go to Newark and White Plains and Scarsdale, and the Varsity went to Massachusetts and flew to Virginia and Iowa, and five or six seniors got to go to California. Of course it was a lot of extra work. He decided he would go from fourteen hours a week at the FINAST to ten, maybe even eight. The debates were on weekends so if he made it he would have to arrange for someone else to take his place on the Saturdays when they had debates.

The first novice debate was going to be in Newark. RESOLVED: *There is no meaning to life except for the meaning Human Beings give to it.* Before going you had to write out your opening statements, though some of the more experienced kids just made a few notes on file cards. You had both Affirmative and Negative, you had to take both sides, no matter what side you believed. In your opening statement you put in your own logic and also quotes from philosophers and thinkers. Where would they get the quotes? In the library of course. But Paul had a different idea.

"My parents have a lot of books," he said. "Look, why don't you come down with me to my house and we can work out our opening statements there? Go through the books and get some quotes and stuff."

"Yeah."

"And then we can show our opening statements to my father and he can check them over."

"I'd really like that," Kenneth said.

✳ ✳ ✳

Going down on the subway Kenneth was excited. He'd only been to Manhattan twice in his life. The Conovers lived on East Eighty-fourth Street between Park and Lexington Avenue. As they went in the man at the door smiled and said hello to Paul and put two fingers to his cap.

"Hiya Carlos," Paul said.

The Conovers' apartment was awesome. Awesome. It had a big living room with a whole wall full of books, a dining room with a long dark polished table and a chandelier. Paul and his older brother Billy each had their own room. Billy's room was quiet and very neat. He was away at college—Swarthmore. He was interested in Astronomy and there was a brass telescope on a stand looking out the window at the city, and there was a computer in there—IBM. Paul's own room was big and had wall-to-wall carpeting. He had the Encyclopedia Britannica, complete (though Ms. Nash said she never wanted them to use the encyclopedia but go to the sources themselves).

Paul was explaining some sculptures from India and some pottery from Iran in the living room when a slim woman came in.

"Mom, this is Kenneth Morey from school, I told you about, we're gonna do some work."

"Hello Mrs. Conover, I'm very pleased to meet you," Kenneth said, stepping forward immediately and putting out his hand. But then he had to stand there and wait until she got off her gloves, and the way she looked he wondered if he'd done something wrong. But then he told himself, No, he had done nothing wrong.

But Mrs. Conover was really nice. Later, when they were working away, she brought them cookies and hot chocolate. Paul explained to her what they were doing and she came in later with some book by the Existentialists, especially an essay three pages long, *The Myth of Sisyphus*.

They didn't waste time. Kenneth turned the pages of the books, hunting for good quotes.

"Can you stay for supper, Kenneth?" Mrs. Conover asked, from the doorway of Paul's room. He looked over at Paul.

"Sure you can, right Kenneth?"

"Yeah, I guess."

"Should you call your mother?"

"That's okay, I can call later." Kenneth wanted to keep working.

"Good," she said in a firm voice and went away and they went right on working.

Later on, Mr. Conover came in and said, "Hi, kids."

"I've heard a lot about you from Paul, Mr. Conover," Kenneth said, getting up quickly, stepping forward and putting out his hand.

There was steak for dinner, and baked potato, peas, and salad, with ice cream for dessert. Mr. Conover was talking business or something with Mrs. Conover but after awhile he turned to Kenneth.

"Well, how do you like Bronx Science?"

Kenneth said he liked it a lot, the kids and everything.

"He's very good in History, but he's having a little trouble in Math. Mom might be able to help him, the way she does with me."

"My wife's in an accounting firm," Mr. Conover said.

"He knows," Paul said. "Can we go get some more ice cream?"

After supper, Mr. Conover stayed at the table, sipping his coffee and listening attentively as Paul and Kenneth read their Affirmative and Negative statements.

Then he and Paul read his Negative again, and they quarreled when Paul refused to make a change his father suggested.

"I'm telling you, Paul, it isn't right the way you have it. It just isn't logical."

"I like it that way."

"You can't have it that way."

"I like it."

"You like it. Well then, don't ask me to criticize!"

"All *right!* I'll change it," Paul said. Then they suddenly both laughed, and after Paul had changed it, he said, "I see what you mean. I guess you're right."

Then Mr. Conover had Kenneth read his Affirmative again and criticized it bit by bit as he went along. Kenneth made each change he suggested, especially the conclusion, which Mr. Conover thought was weak. At first it made him mad that Mr. Conover said it was weak. But then he nodded. Mr. Conover dictated a couple of sentences to him and said that they were really just the logical outcome of what Kenneth himself had been saying in the statement as a whole. Kenneth thought it sounded much better now and he said to himself that he felt grateful for Mr. Conover's help.

It was late. Paul walked him to the subway at Lexington Avenue. "Your parents are so great. They are so great," Kenneth said.

On the subway he began to feel tired and he sat there patiently with his backpack on his knees, his hands clasped around it. The weather had gotten colder and he ran all the way home from the subway. He felt very tired but he felt happy too.

"Is that you?"

"Yes."

"You come right in here!"

"Yes Mamma."

"Hurry up!"

"Okay! Just have to go the bathroom!"

Mrs. Morey lay on top of her bed in her pink bathrobe, her hair in pink curlers. Her eyes looked up at him out of her round black face. He had never seen her look so fat.

"I was going to call and I forgot."

"I come from work bone-tired and the children all alone and you just gone. I told you I was coming home late."

"I didn't hear you say that."

"You don't hear a lot of things, boy. It seems like you don't know what's going on." She reached back and pulled her pillows toward her so they propped up her head. Aretha watched from the little bed, swiping at her runny nose with the back of her hand. Kenneth kept having to tell her not to do that, but she never listened.

"I was all the way downtown in Manhattan, working with that Paul Conover I told you about. His father was helping us, a lot."

"You have got no business whatsoever running around and not taking care of things up here!"

"I wasn't running around. I was working. This Bronx Science is work. It's like a job."

"Sitting and reading books is no job."

"Yes it is."

"That is NO JOB, I told you."

"I'm tired Mamma. I got to go to bed." He turned around went out and closed the door behind him.

He could hear her in there. How she had to put up with Bobby Morey all these years and now his son. Kenneth's brother sat up in bed.

"What's wrong with Mamma now?"

"Nothing. Go back to sleep."

"Before I only had Airman Third Class Morey to contend. Now I got General Morey. General KENNETH MOREY!"

"She's screaming," said his little brother.

"Go back to sleep I said."

Kenneth himself slept fitfully. He awoke having been beset by some long heavy dream. He dressed, made himself some Instant, and sat staring at the bedroom, where his mother and sister slept. After a minute he got up and headed out the front door, but stopped, went back, and went in to see his mother. He knew it was crazy but he had this sudden fear she might be dead.

"Hey, Mamma?"

She opened her eyes, very wide, and then relaxed, seeing it was her Kenneth.

"Hey, Mamma," he said tenderly. He bent down and kissed her.

"Good morning, Honeypie." Her hand held his neck down firmly as she kissed him back, smelling of warm sleep.

He rushed out, and as he waited for the elevator he thought comfortably of his Affirmative and Negative Debate statements all neatly written out, and his assignments for today all completed. He was all set.

Then abruptly—seized with panic—he ran back into the apartment just as the elevator had at last arrived, put his backpack down on the kitchen table, and got out his Affirmative statement. Quickly he crossed out the sentences Mr. Conover had suggested and neatly wrote above them pretty much what he'd had in the first place. Mr. Conover had maybe seemed right last night, but now he seemed all wrong. Kenneth now thought that his own first ending was better than Mr. Conover's ending.

He didn't do too well in the Newark debate. Paul did a little better. On the bus going back home, with some other kids rapping in the dark, he felt pretty discouraged after all that work, but Paul said they were just beginning, just learning, and they had to be patient. Kenneth agreed that that was right.

But things were going along well otherwise. He got his midterm printout. It said *Highly Motivated* next to Ms. Nash's grade, and *Perseveres* for Biology. His lowest grade was in Math and Paul said he could get some help from Mrs. Conover. Kenneth's mother said she was happy about his grades, and she seemed to understand things from Kenneth's point of view better now.

Paul invited him to stay overnight the next weekend. Mrs. Morey had to see the doctor Saturday morning so Kenneth came back from the FINAST at noon and heated up three cans of Franco-American for the kids before heading downtown.

Mrs. Conover explained the Math even better than Mr. Freeman. Kenneth knew he was going to pull up his Math grade now and he was really excited about that. The Conovers were so nice. *Awesome.*

Saturday afternoon he and Paul just played; then they went and got a movie to watch after supper. Paul's parents were going out, to a dinner party.

In the morning Mrs. Conover made them pancakes and around 11:30 she sat down with Kenneth at the dining table to go over his Math assignment with him. Then he and Paul had to start working on the next debate, which was at White Plains next weekend. RESOLVED: *That mandatory drug testing of public officials is justified.*

The seniors, who coached the novices, suggested they get hold of John Rawls' *Theory of Justice* and Locke's *Second Treatise on Government*, and Rousseau's *Social Contract*. So Kenneth and Paul took the bus down to the Donnell Branch of the library which opened at one on Sundays, and took the books out with Paul's library card.

After they'd worked on that for a while it was time for dinner, and they still had a lot of homework for Monday. Kenneth hadn't even started reading his History.

"Why don't you stay overnight and we can go to school together?" Paul said.

"I don't know. I'll call my Mom."

His sister answered.

"Aretha, why you talking so soft?"

"Mamma went to bed. She don' feel well. When you getting home?"

Kenneth explained, and after he hung up he went straight to work at the desk in Billy's room while Paul worked over in his room. But they put Billy's mattress on the floor in Paul's room so they would be together. Paul was going to sleep on it and Kenneth up in Paul's bed. He tried to concentrate.

He had so much work...

He awoke with a start. His head had been lying on the History book open in front of him.

"Kenneth, it's almost three in the morning." It was Mr. Conover patting him gently on the shoulder.

"Oh."

"You'd better go to bed."

He was okay in school next day. When he got home his brother was there in the kitchen, nervous.

"Mamma's acting real crazy, Mamma's acting crazy, watch out Kenny."

She lumbered out of the bedroom and into the kitchen. "You don't listen. Nobody listens to me, nobody ever listens to me."

"Mamma."

"You never listen to me. NEVER LISTEN TO ME. Year after year after year and I keep on screaming and no wonder I scream why because NOBODY EVER

LISTENS TO ME. ARE YOU LISTENING? Do you HEAR me? I got diabetes and I am dying. You hear THAT?"

"No Mamma, you'll be all—"

"I'm TELLING you to LISTEN to ME."

"I am."

"I got diabetes and I am dying right now. And you don't listen. You got to listen to me. Are you listening?"

"Yes Mamma, yes."

"No. And they going to fire me from my job. I got eleven and one-half years on that job and now they firing me and I won't have my job."

"You won't get fired, Mamma."

He felt so badly for his mother, her hair flying out every whichaways, and she was so frightened. He knew she would be all right. He just knew it.

And then she changed. She drew herself up straight and very big and large and pointed a finger at him and looked at him with a wicked, wicked eye and said, "And you cut back your hours at the FINAST! How you think we gonna live with General Morey cuttin' back his hours at the FINAST, huh?"

"I'll get them back, Mamma."

"Too late. Too late boy. You know what I'm gonna do now?...I said do you know what I'm gonna do? Whyn't you listen?"

"I'm listening," Kenneth said softly.

"You're no good to me here. You don't help with the kids. You cut back on the FINAST. You think you're so big at the Bronx Science, you know what I'm gonna do?"

"I'm gonna send you to Airman Third Class Bobby Morey, thass what I'm gonna do, take you out of the Bronx Science and send you to your father in Wiesbaden or the Philippines or wherever he is since you just like that Bobby Morey and you will go to the gov'ment dependent high school out there and you'll be outta my hair, you understand?"

"I want to stay here with you, Mamma," Kenneth said, and he really meant it.

"I hate that Bronx Science, it ruin you. I—" His mother stopped, grunted, wiped her nose with the back of her hand, exactly the way Aretha always did, turned and went into the bedroom, shutting the door behind her, calm now, as calm as the sea with not a breath of wind.

Kenneth's brother and sister looked up at him, but he said nothing. Still, he decided they would need for him to spend more time with them from now on.

✳ ✳ ✳

He didn't get very prepared for the White Plains debate. In the middle of his first round he got stuck, he just stopped and couldn't go on. Then after a few seconds he started up again, but he ended up using only four minutes of the eight minutes for his second rebuttal. He was embarrassed about going back to the Bronx with the team but everyone in the bus turned out to be really nice. Paul had done real well this time. He hit the octofinals and got a trophy. Kenneth knew that Paul was going to get better and better from now on.

Kenneth was back to his old schedule at the FINAST, and he took the kids out to Burger King a few times, and spent more time at home. But his mother didn't really let up on him. She started making him get out of the kitchen where he did a lot of his studying late at night. He quit the debate team. That was a relief, even though he saw less of Paul, who was always with the other guys from the team.

But he went down to Manhattan and spent some weekends at Paul's, where Mrs. Conover helped him with Math, the weekends when Paul didn't have a debate. So his Math wasn't too bad, but History and Biology had been his best subjects, and they were going down. A new Biology teacher had come in who called on Kenneth a lot, and a lot of the time Kenneth didn't know the answers. He knew that the Biology teacher—Mr. Stonehill—didn't like him. He knew what that Stonehill was thinking. He was thinking here is a black got in on the special program and couldn't handle the work, probably wasn't even trying to do the work! At first he wanted to say he'd been doing well in Biology before, but after a while he told himself why should he do that and he just put sass into his eyes every time Stonehill called on him, or even looked over at him.

One afternoon, walking Paul to the subway, Paul asked him how come his work had been falling off lately. He didn't even mention the fact that Kenneth had quit the debate team. Kenneth told him what had been going on at home. He tried to explain it.

"But doesn't your mother realize how well you've been doing?"

"I'm not doing so well."

"Hey, how about spending the weekend at my house?"

"Okay," Kenneth said, after a couple of seconds. He wanted to go, but for some reason he didn't feel too much like seeing Mr. and Mrs. Conover. The thought of having to see them depressed him a little for some reason.

"There's no novice debate this weekend," Paul said. "Maybe we can just fool around."

"That'd be good."

Kenneth felt like taking it a little easy this weekend. He'd been planning on staying pretty much at home; Roy Davis had some fantasy books he'd always meant to read: *Castle Roganoff* and *Giant Ogre*, both by Piers Anthony. He'd already read *On a Pale Horse* and liked it and Roy said the other two were even better. Roy had a big collection of fantasy books and he was really proud of them, and Kenneth had been meaning to borrow some when he had a chance.

So after finishing at the FINAST on Saturday morning he took the subway down to Paul's. They had a good time and even did some work around 5:30, which was good.

Then around a half an hour before supper Kenneth was coming out of the bathroom off the living room to go back to Paul's room, when he heard Mrs. Conover mentioning his name. She was in the kitchen with Mr. Conover and the door was closed but you could hear them. He stood there without moving a muscle and listened.

"His mother just has no idea how important it is that he's got into Bronx Science. It will make all the difference, to his whole life, and I think we should have him stay here with us. Paul says he's started doing badly in school. He cannot work at home. It's just not fair. She wants to take him out of Bronx Science! She'll destroy that boy. He tries so hard. It's a disaster!"

"I know he does," Mr. Conover said. "But you're being unrealistic. You're much too much of an idealist, Leslie. We'd better just have him free to come here on weekends as he's been doing."

"He can stay in Billy's room. Look at all the help Billy and Paul got from us. This boy gets no help. And then people say what's the matter with these blacks…"

Kenneth ran quietly away from the door and back into Paul's room and about twenty minutes later it was time for supper. What do they know about my mother. I love my mother stupid ignorant muthafuckahs.

On Sunday evening around 7:30 Kenneth was getting his things together to go home, and he could not find *Castle Roganoff* and *Giant Ogre*. Paul hadn't given them back to him. He was looking at the TV.

"Where's *Castle Roganoff* and *Giant Ogre*?"

"Huh?"

"You heard me," Kenneth said. "Where's Roy's books?"

"Search me!"

"Maybe I better do just that. Remember I gave them to you a few minutes after I came in yesterday afternoon. I put them right down there on your bed and said take which one you want."

"No you didn't!"

Kenneth sighed. "Remember you told me you were interested in reading some Piers Anthony stuff?"

"Yes."

"If you want to read them, you can keep them for a couple of weeks and then give them back, or give them back to Roy yourself." Kenneth almost went on and said, *You got enough money from your father to buy them yourself and not go around borrowing stuff.*

"I don't have them," Paul said and kept watching TV.

"Well, if you're going to keep on just watching TV I'll have a look around myself. Roy's going to be mad. I gotta return those books. That's his collection, his pride and joy."

"You never gave them to me, Kenneth," Paul said.

"Yes I did," Kenneth said, his lips close together. He went over and looked in the top drawer of Paul's bureau, where Paul kept some of his best stuff, but the books weren't there.

"Anything wrong?" It was Mrs. Conover, standing in the doorway to Paul's room, her slim body against the door frame, a good-looking woman.

"No," Paul said.

"Yes there is. Paul has my books, that I borrowed, and I have to return them tomorrow," Kenneth said, and then he pointed his finger at Paul.

"Paul, why don't you try to find them instead of just sitting there," Mrs. Conover said.

"Because I don't have them. They're not HERE!"

"You don't have to shout, Paul."

"What's going on in here?" It was Paul's father, out in the living room, in a nice voice. Kenneth would have to explain to Paul's father. So he went out to explain. Mr. Conover was watching TV in the living room—the Knicks—but he turned it way down and listened to Kenneth explaining.

"Kenneth," he said, when Kenneth was through, "I want you to do something for me, will you? Just one thing."

"Yes," Kenneth said, warily.

"Just do me one favor. Call up this Roy Davis and check out whether he actually lent you the books in the first place."

"He did lend me the books. Why do I have to call him up? I know he lent me the books, Mr. Conover!" *One hundred percent sure he lent me the books. One MILLION percent.*

"All right. But I want you to call him anyway, just as a favor to me, please."

Kenneth shrugged and said, Okay, if Roy was home.

Roy answered the phone. "Roy, it's Kenneth Morey."

"I know your stupid voice," Roy said. "What you want?"

"Yeah, well look, remember those Piers Anthony books you lent me?"

"Which?"

"What do you mean which?"

"I never lent you any Piers Anthony books."

"Yeah?"

"Yeah. You were gonna borrow some, but you didn't actually borrow them yet."

"Oh. Oh. Okay. Thanks Roy. See you tomorrow."

When Kenneth hung up, Mr. Conover had gone back to watching the Knicks game. Kenneth ran over and stood between the TV and Mr. Conover.

"Oh my God, I'm sorry. I'm so sorry," he said. Then he got down on both knees on the floor in front of Mr. Conover and said he was sorry again.

"Kenneth! Don't do that!" Mr. Conover jumped up and was pulling Kenneth off the floor onto his feet. "Don't ever get down on your knees like that to anyone," he said urgently.

Kenneth pulled through all right at end-term. His grades could have been better, but they were all right. Things settled down a lot at home. It turned out Mrs. Morey didn't have diabetes, and she wasn't fired. In fact she got a small raise at the Exterminating.

Kenneth and Paul are as good friends as ever, but they don't have any classes together now. There's a new system, to make things more efficient, where if your foreign language is Spanish, for example, you have the other classes with the kids who take Spanish and if it's French you have the other classes with the kids who take French. Since Paul takes French he has all different teachers from Kenneth. With that and Paul's debating they don't see a lot of each other.

Mr. Burns, the new manager at the FINAST for the past few months, thinks highly of Kenneth and said that if he wants to work full-time this summer he can probably be in charge of deliveries to replace Joe Rivera, who will be on vacation in Puerto Rico for the whole summer. Kenneth has gotten interested in fantasy books and has started a pretty good collection himself—not yet as good as Roy's of course.

HARRY BARBA

Born in 1922 in Bristol, Connecticut, to a family of Armenians from Iran and the Caucasus region, Harry Barba has risen from humble working-class beginnings to his present status as one of the doyens of Armenian American literature. Over a lifetime otherwise filled with writing novels, teaching, and raising a family in various parts of his native New England, Barba has also achieved the enviable feat of mastering the short story. In the preface to his 1976 collection *One of a Kind*, Barba advocates "socially functional writing," in which writers are to act as "legislators to the world." The writer is meant to present, analyze, and provide some sort of positivistic resolution to a given situation or problematic: "The reader…rise(s) from his book either a better man…or with insights into how he may better handle himself in a social encounter." A tall order for any writer, and especially so in a post-structuralist and post-deconstructionist world, where any statements affirming literature's regenerative or reformative powers seem innocent at best. Good old-fashioned humanists are in short shrift these days, thus making Barba especially relevant to both present and future generations.

At least two of Barba's most accomplished short stories take place completely outside any Armenian context. In "The Plum Tree Plunderers," a tale of youth, sexuality, nature, and conflict, plums mature and ripen like the breasts of one of the story's protagonists, Amy Lou. Barba's sensibility and milieu in such stories—white poverty and country roads—liken him to Southern writers, or perhaps Carolyn Chute in *The Beans of Egypt Maine,* but the ending of this short story, I would suggest, harkens back to more Middle Eastern, mystical roots: "I saw Amy Lou standing with her face up, like a blind mole trying to feel out the moment."

"The Man Who Did Not Want to Box Muhammad Ali" takes the reader into a different context altogether. Its protagonist, Nomans Meier, wages an Oedipal battle against the memory of an abusive father, as well as an opponent that he at first refuses to fight. When the delirious, tragic climax to his bout arrives, Meier is also left to face the void: "In the background, the din of the crowd from the arena. Before him, the gaping maw of the locker and its familiar odors."

"On a strong breeze smelling of spring timothy grass, fern and woods came the hoot of the church owl." Thus begins *For the Grape Season* (Macmillan, 1960), Barba's best-known work. Essentially an Armenian, Eastern-seaboard version of Steinbeck's *The Grapes of Wrath*, it narrates the story of a group of seasonal Armenian grape pickers who move into a Vermont town of Anglo Protestants. The predictable happens: the Anglos at first reject their swarthy guests; then hosts and guests begin to fall in love with each other, which causes problems on both sides. A flood of near-Biblical proportions threatens to destroy the valley, at which point the Armenian grape pickers display uncommon courage and save their hosts. All's well that ends well and *For the Grape Season* enters the annals of both Armenian American and New England regional literature.

Barba's writings pose several questions of interest to Armenian American literature, not the least of which is what it means to an Armenian writer when one is writing in English and not Armenian and when the majority of one's stories revolve around non-Armenian, or *odar*, characters. It's hard to ignore the elliptical way in which Barba approaches both his own identity and those of his characters. Barba—né Nahabed O'Hanessian—suffered from being part of what he terms a "minority's minority": the author clearly grew up at a time when being Armenian represented a handicap, when there were few Armenian novelists to model oneself after, and when assimilation provided the model to follow for a generation of immigrants and their children.

The fact that we are at first unsure as to the specific identity of the immigrants in *For the Grape Season* (Tatar? Armenian? Iranian? all three?) plays into the general unease that Barba must have felt at coming clean as an Armenian. In his obviously autobiographical short story "The Ikon," Barba identifies Professor Hart as a Middle Easterner but never specifically as an Armenian. During a classroom crisis, Hart calls on a dark girl, the only student who will speak up. One of the Arab students yells out: "Anyways, Siir…that girl, she is not real *Arabi*—is Armenian." The Armenian is thus positioned as an outsider even within a Middle Eastern context, a minority within a minority, always displaced, never really fully at home.

Barba's second novel, *Round Trip to Byzantium*, offers a prescient view of a contemporary Middle East rife with corrupt oil sheiks and Westerners playing petro-politics. Shepherded into the 1985 Pulitzer Prize finals by Edward Said, *Round Trip to Byzantium* also features an American professor on a fellowship year, and is thus both a reprise and expansion of "The Ikon," a clever parable of corruption and political intrigue that has in fact come to pass. Barba's prose marries acute satirization and recherché prose with rich colloquialisms. The reader also joyously meets up again with the raunchy Barba first encountered in his short story "Love, in the Persian Way," where a randy teenage protagonist beds in quick succession his aunt, his father's mistress, and her barely pubescent daughter before being caught with his proverbial pants down. In *Round Trip to Byzantium*, the object of the protagonist's affections symbolizes both miscegenation and feminine oppression, an Armeno-Byzantine *Lolita* of sorts,

> She undoes the burnoose from her chin and unloosens
> an *abeyid* within. Then, with several deft movements
> of shoulder and head...she shakes the covering from
> herself to the rug. As she does, her hair tumbles about her
> shoulders, breasts and back. A black waterfall drenches her
> to her waist. Emerging in sweater and skirt, gym stockings,
> and by far the most expensive item of her clothing, jogging
> shoes with deep blue scalloping, she seems an exotic small-
> town American co-ed hatched from a most extraordinary
> egg of brown and white shells...An Americanized Baghdad
> Venus on a half-shell, but fully clothed and afloat on an
> Aladdin rug!

It is entirely to Barba's credit that he can combine such evocative prose with the acute social commentary that follows. Barba more than fulfills the premises of socially functional writing: in and of itself, that is already quite an accomplishment.

Christopher Atamian

The Ikon

JohnnieHart woke up all at once. There had been a vibratory sound, as of a
man in his last agony. Stiffening, he lifted his eyes to the blazing morning.

The room was octagonal and the hotel was downtown. That much he was
sure of. He was also sure of how he got to be there. But he could in no way,
beyond the superficial, account for the reason he was there.

He wanted to teach a year abroad.

Yes, but "Why in the Middle East?" his former wife repeatedly shouted at
him.

That was the question on which their separation pivoted until the heat of
contention swept them into divorce proceedings.

Why indeed? He took in the photograph of his family, his six children
and his ex-wife: Peter, his oldest, a schoolboy athlete with knotty biceps like
wild apples, his man Friday, reminding him when he became neglectful of
his responsibilities; Mary, raven-haired but white, white skin, a Mommy-
mimicker; black-eyed Stephen, the boy's boy, a frequent rebel with endless
causes, the main one being bringing up father; Martha, thin and willowy all
the way down; his nine-year-old, valentine-faced Esther, who addressed him
as her "Diddy-Daddy"; and finally Paul, a Daddy-mimicker in everything but
stature and voice, age five. His eyes lingered on his wife, until he had to look
away. It would not have helped matters much had he answered her as he
once was sorely tempted to shout, "Because my Goddam immigrant parents
were born and spent their youth in the Middle East, that's why! Because I
want more than the ikon they passed down to me from the past as a way of
understanding their heritage, that's why! Because I want to see for myself
where they came from so I can understand myself a little better—that's why
too! So I know who I am and how I might grow and become! Is it really all
that hard for a nonimmigrant mainstreamer to understand this?" It would
not have helped because the reply was self-understood, and, as such, the
fuel under the flames. And they both knew this. For he would not have been
able to stop at that but would have added the quip, "When it comes to that,
the primal parents of all of us came from—the Garden of the World! And
even you know where that is!"

Suddenly the sound again, harsh and vibratory. It was unmistakably
not part of a nightmare. That is, it was a nightmare, a real one, and he was
determined to know what it was.

He leaped from the coarse sheets and rushed to the balcony. In the street, wildly honking automobiles, taxis, and buses. On the sidewalks, bustling street peddlers and pedestrians. The scene was like a turbulent river cut by spurting motorbikes.

And right in the midst, a donkey braying its guts out under a load the size of a small house.

His stomach leaping, JohnnieHart broke away from the balcony and rushed through his room into the European john. Thank heavens, not Arabic!

A half hour later, he managed to dress: sportscoat, oxford gray trousers, and white pigskin shoes. Black-eyed, pot-bellied, and big-arsed, a former collegiate boxer turned novelist, humanist, and teacher, he was now ambassadorial.

But what if funereal?

He went galloping down the stairs.

In the lobby, he decided he would try starting the day without breakfast. Who could tell?

He bolted out onto the street and yelled for a taxi.

Ten minutes later, Damascus University. The center of a thousand eyes, a half-hundred grins, and a few scowls, he walked through a mass of students leaning against cement buildings and squatting on cement sidewalks. Inside the stucco two-story building, a scattering of girls, staring as he hurried by.

He trotted into the teachers' room and plopped into the remaining empty overstuffed chair. There were more than eight against the walls, and now all were filled. Conversation was at a polite drone, but again he sensed all eyes were on him. He remembered his colleague's monition of the night before, giving JohnnieHart the benefit of a previous year of experience, "In Damascus, chairs in a circle mean conviviality; chairs in any other configuration mean business." But in Damascus, one might drink coffee and tea while doing business. So he looked up to the servant and begged, *"Chai."*

"Desirez-chai?" the mustached servant grinned. And there it was again, first the Lebanese taxi driver, then the help in the American Embassy, and now—

JohnnieHart looked at him quickly. *"Vous parlez Français?"*

"Swaiesh! Swaiesh! Arabi, vous?"

A speedy learner of cultural ways and byways, JohnnieHart raised his nose and eyebrows in the Arabic sign of negation. The room exploded into harsh sibilants and throaty consonants. Churning back and forth freely, Arabic Syrian! Arabic, at its most vigorous! *Arabic to command the multitudes, to keep women in their place, and to give orders to a donkey!* His colleague's summation.

Arabic to eat olives, leek, and radishes by! Arabic to eat fatty lamb stew and acridly garlicky chick-pea sauce and clabbered milk by! Arabic to throw up by! And Arabic to squat eternally over Arabic johns by!

Arabic! Arabic! Arabic!

JohnnieHart retreated to his thoughts. *I must remember to speak slowly, distinctly, and even oversimply, whatever happens.*

Whatever happens? Whatever can happen, anyway? He put his *chai* glass down, retrieved his notebook and books from the floor, and rose to brave the corridors.

"Have a good clahss!" An Anglofied Arab, his avian features gigantic behind horn-rimmed glasses, afloat in an overstuffed chair.

In the corridors again, "Hello, Siir!"

"Good morning, Siir!"

"Let me carry your books, thank you, Siir!"

They parted before him like the waters of a biblical sea.

His eyes searching to decipher the extraordinary markings above doorways, he thought, *Arabic numbers?* Finally he yelled broadside, "4!" And helped them to help him by holding up four fingers.

Grasshoppery eyes ablaze, a young man fell in at his side. Together they tracked down the classroom. Parting reluctantly, JohnnieHart ducked away from the joyous young man into the room—only to find himself facing a dozen students jumping to their feet to stand stiffly at attention. The insistence of his two hands unavailing, he vaulted the steps to the platform and dropped himself into the chair behind the desk.

Ahhh! He smiled to their gigantically attentive faces, "I-am-Dr. John Hartyon—American Ful-bright pro-fes-sor. This-is-a-class-in-ex-po-si-tion—En-glish ex-po-si-tion—" Slowly he focused in on them: All but one were thick-nosed and had skin that was oily and pimply. Most faces showed innocence, as though life had not touched them in the least. A girl with black shoulder-length hair and marble skin watched him with sloe eyes that never left his.

"If-we-are-patient with each other—we-will-soon-find-out-we-have-more-to-learn-from-each-other-than-words." That was it, to forget everything of caution and to love each face into intelligence and understanding.

"Tea-sher, is class to be in this manner the rest of year?"

JohnnieHart studied the youth's intense face. *No insolence here!* Less insolence—impertinence?—impudence?—than even one of his own sons, Stephen, might have shown from the small arrogance of his boyish outbursts of rebellion.

"You must forgive me—I am searching ways to teach you."

"We are not like the others, Sir. We are the pick of the crop." The intonation, the crispness of handling of the unaccustomed idiom indicated the Anglofied-Arab teacher was present by influence.

"That you are, indeed!" JohnnieHart smiled big. And wonder of wonders!— they smiled big in return, eye to eye, smile to smile.

An hour later, he was the last to leave the classroom. Behind him, the blackboard scratched with the history of his first teaching assignment in the Arabic world (the cuneiform of the fool he had almost made of himself as he scribbled and erased and then scribbled and erased again). He tried to smile at the fool he had most certainly made of himself until he had stood up as tall as they. He had talked down to them, he had taught down to them and bent down to them, only to find himself scrambling wildly to save face. And they had all come out of it together, smiling. An initial debacle turned into a small victory! A good retrieval!

He might yet keep down his bile.

Returned to the teachers' room, he took his *chai* from the servant with a dip of his head, a smile, and a *"Soochran."* To the old man's soft *"Afwahn,"* he had one glass, a second, and then a third like a camel needing a fill-up. He gave a whinny after.

Finally, up and venture forth! Still two hours before lunch. His stomach lurching again, he headed straight for the Arabic john.

He risked a lunch of *shorva* (vegetable soup), bread, and yogurt (*leben*, they called it). He even tried fruit, *mishmish* (apricots?—plums?—who knows?).

Reentering the campus, he saw again the university grounds were thronged with students. Arm in arm and hand in hand, boys walked with boys and girls walked with girls. Many seemed to be going everywhere, anywhere, nowhere as they chattered and milled around. The university seemed to be their first, not their second, home.

In the university yard, the sea of eyes now all showed recognition, interest, or curiosity.

The word has gotten around, he thought. As he scrambled into the building, the sea opened before him, then closed behind him. A young man took him by the arm. Another took his notebook and books. A third took him by the hand and led him. Girls offered him smiles from a distance.

Escorted all the way into the amphitheater auditorium, he saw a multitude of students standing at the front and rear. Those seated surged to their feet.

"No!" He waved his arms wildly. But they remained rigidly at attention.

Vaulting onto the platform, he charged to the blackboard. Snatching up chalk and about to stroke, he remembered—

Swinging around, he saw they were still standing. Frantically he threw himself into the chair. As he grabbed the armrests, chalk and eraser went clattering across the floor.

As one, students standing at empty seats sat down, leaving a half-hundred and more standing against the walls and crowding his desk down front.

"My name is Professor John Hartyon," he panted. "From now on, please— please do not rise when I come into the room." Attentive, their faces were yet blank.

"You, up there in heaven!" he called high. A general whispering followed. And then low, "You down here in hell!" More whispering. Still more whispering.

He plunged on valiantly, "Sit down!—On the aisle steps!" And so it had once been that he took command of his family sprawled in great disarray in the rear of the station wagon as they ventured forth on a Sunday afternoon drive. His wife acting as go-between, order always emerged from chaos.

But nobody in the amphitheater made a move. Was there no one, not even a Peter, to help him make adjustments? He was willing! He was eager!

"Sit—sit down! Like this!" He rose and sat down on the edge of the platform. One, two—one, two! His legs swung in a most comfortable casualness.

In the past it had always worked—teaching by example! So a man ruled his family! So a teacher—

"This not the way we do in Damascus, Siir!" Her voice was high and violinny. He thought of his Mary, the Mommy-mimicker, as he recognized the girl of fine skin and long black hair and quiescent eyes. *She likes poetry too*, he thought. Forgetting himself once when Mary had sassed him gently the way her mother often did, he had been about to whack her on the rump, as he sometimes did her mother, when he remembered, just in time, to put her in her place with a pinch of the cheek instead, and a "Now, Miss Hart— Get me a glass of milk like a good Daddy's girl!"

"We are in Damascus, yes," he smiled his thanks to the girl of alabaster skin. "How can I forget this as I look at all these beautiful *Arabi* faces?" He grinned freely in response to his reward of smiles and delighted laughter. "But we are also in Professor JohnnieHart's classroom, yes, too." Those who did not laugh this time turned and chattered to those who did.

"Anyways, Siir," an anonymous voice ululated from the rear of the auditorium, "that girl, she is not real *Arabi*—is Armenian."

Now everyone laughed, and the small amphitheater reverberated. Sometimes, at Stephen's instigation, his family seemed in sibling league against him. So The Brothers and Sisters of the World united against the Father, leaving the Mother astray in the No-man's-land between.

"Please!" He even tried with his hands. "Please, wait until after class— there are too many of you to manage at once." The chattering again, the whispering and overconcerned looks to each other.

"I'm going to have to insist!" He stretched to the limits of his muscle, meat, and bone. He waved a taut finger as he had never dared wave it in his family—for he believed in authority by example, by doing and so leading to do. Never by edict! Proclamation! Or insistence.

"Why not?" One of his fellow graduate assistants had asked him during a time when his household seemed to be bursting around him as his attention, his mind, and finally his heart became more and more taken up in his graduate work. "Why not snap the whip now and again? Just to let them know you're still there!"

But he had never been able to resort to that desperate substitution (confessing failure?) for what he knew they all needed, his attention and his active love.

But now, in a classroom, after everything else has been tried and found wanting, why not?

Tall and commanding, he waved his index finger, greatly!

Still the chattering! Still the whispering and the zealous looks!

Agonizing the amphitheater with his eyes, he pulled the textbook from his sportscoat pocket, raised it above his head, and then brought it down exploding onto the desk.

The report was almost as loud!

The chattering died, faces emptied! Eyes turned to him, haunted.

"All right." He gentled the moment with his open hands. "All I ask is that you—that we—try to understand each other in our time together." He smiled face to face. There were many attractive girls, the flowers of any class. And the young men and those not so young, the look of bruised innocence.

"If only you give me and yourselves a chance!" In one of his marathon letters that had brought JohnnieHart running to the Damascus post, his colleague had advised, "You're going to have to forget everything you've learned in graduate school about teaching. Leave yourself open to learning how to teach these ones from themselves." And more, "Learn a few words of the language, serviceable phrases—" Ah, that was it.

He fished for words picked up with bags of pistachio nuts, with food ordered in little olive-rancid restaurants, from street peddlers, and from his colleague. Finally he came out with, "You're human beings—not *hemars*." He all but brayed the word. The amphitheater opened wide with laughter. One student even brayed outright.

JohnnieHart's glance went from face to face. The happy wonder of it!

"All right!" he said through his grin. "*Sicout!*" Now, the class seemed entirely his—beyond his wildest dream. Like an *open sesame*.

Through delighted grins, "Yes, tea-sher!" "We silent, Profes-sor Siir!" And then, to each other, "Si-lence!" "Si-lence!" "Si-lent—Don't talk!" A hundred teachers to a hundred students.

Even the girl of black tresses and alabaster skin smiled at him with shy ardor. Venturing from the home base of her face, he generalized his knowledge of the moment. He would play the situation by ear—he would teach them by heart!

"In this class we will be studying—what we are sharing right now— POETRY!" Calling over the waves of delight, he pushed aside his notes.

"The first kind of poetry we are to enjoy is called by name the LOVE LYRIC!" Thinking to himself, *Too wordy! Too damn wordy!* he yet managed to smile face to face. "The love lyric!" Turning slowly, he picked up chalk and filled the entire blackboard: "L-O-V-E L-Y-R-I-C!" Turning about, he smiled broadside. Their faces radiant, the students bent their heads to their notebooks. The amphitheater waxed with a sibilant scribbling.

JohnnieHart waited out the bowed heads patiently. When every pair of eyes was on him again, he knew he had them. He was certain this class would be the darlings of his stay in the Levant. An invisible filament seemed to connect him with them. Glowing, he opened the book of verse and started reading:

> "Love bade me welcome; yet my soul drew back,
>   Guilty of dust and sin."

He read it to them as he had intended to read it to his wife and family at the height of his graduate studies, to explain himself to them, and to beg them for their understanding and forgiveness.

"'Love,'" he said, feeling redundant—then sure he was compounding an intruding discord he could not understand, "By the seventeenth-century English poet George Herbert." He risked a glance about the auditorium— strained attentiveness, anxious concern, and even befuddlement everywhere. Chattering again, this time a virtual babble. He knew he had lost them.

Surely the subject matter was not alien to them. As a graduate assistant he had been able to reach even the dullards on the poem's simplest level of meaning. For who was there who did not respond to love? Even the word itself, "Love! Love! Love!" was enough to inspire emotion followed by comprehension.

There could not be that great a distance between what he was and what they were.

Then what was it? Did they mistrust him? Were traditional Arabic taboos operating here?

Or was it something more commonplace?

"What's the matter?" he addressed the class, but his eyes held the girl with sea-washed eyes and black waterfall hair.

"We're not understanding you, Siir!" He pulled his eyes away from the girl to the speaker, a determined front-row sitter—he had sparse blond hair, a blond moustache, and hesitant blue eyes. They say crusaders settled in the Holy Land.

"Did I read too fast?"

"We're not understanding your words, Siir." Jiggling, the pale blue eyes eluded JohnnieHart's eyes terribly.

"Why, it's a simple poem—expressing a simple feeling—"

But he pondered the interruption. Was the young man to be his Levantine Peter or his Stephen? But even that comprehension did not yield itself up right then.

His sense of failure in his face, he searched the amphitheater. What he saw was unmistakable. He was in the quagmire now, and once in—

Still, a man had to make his efforts. He would try the young man out as his Peter.

"How many of you do not understand?" His emotions rasped with a warning—"No—How many of you understand my reading of the poem?" That was it.

Was there a providential vine he might grasp?

"Please, raise your hands. Please!" He looked to the alabaster girl.

As her hand rose hesitantly, he breathed, "Yes!" He turned to the others.

One hand, then another and another. He smiled eager. Still another and another.

"Oh, yes!" His face opened to the auditorium as the few hands became a score, more than a score, a half hundred, and then a forest.

Feeling benevolent, he faced up to the number of students who had not raised their hands—fifteen—but in a classroom of more than a hundred! He was out of the quagmire. The eternal teacher again, he would drive home the very first lessons they had undertaken together. From this point on they would journey together. Ah, Peter! Peter!

"The name of the poem I have just read is—"

"Lies!" Jiggle-eyes turned on his classmates. The rest was lost in Arabic.

"All right!" He tried to speak firmly but benevolently as the new moment threatened.

"All lies, Siir! They are not understanding one word you are saying." The face became livid. He was Stephen, not Peter.

"That'll be enough of that!" He shook his finger.

"But they all lie! They lie!"

"If you don't quiet down!" He struggled with his emotions.

"You swallow your words, Siir!" But Stephen had never been— impertinent, impudent, rude. Stephen always talked back, but never insultingly.

"Will you leave the room? Right now!"

The eyes jiggled wildly now.

"I said, *Leave!*"

"I will not, Siir!" The livid face became rigid.

"Either you leave or I do!" He gathered up his notebook and texts. They say that in every teaching assignment a teacher faces a moment of truth.

The amphitheater buzzed. Faces turned this way and that. The whey-faced student babbled at them. They babbled back!

Finally Jiggly-eyes turned back to the teacher, but the eyes ever shunting.

"Do not be leaving, Professor, Siir!" The look of fury now quashed, the eyes were finally steady but still avoided a showdown.

"All right! It's going to be all right!" The culprit at least displayed honesty in unclothing his own ignorance. An emotion stirred: How much did the rude honesty of the young nemesis represent the true feelings of the others, and of how many?

But there was teaching to be done. He picked up the book of verse. A second reading, laboriously slow, unbelievably loud. Drawing upon every shade of emotion left him by the encounter, the moment to be conceived, the emotion to be felt, the teacher spoke the poem in capital letters:

"LOVE BADE ME WELCOME; YET MY SOUL DREW BACK."

As he read, he knew he was doing what he should have done in his attempts to reach his ex-wife and his children from behind the wall that his graduate studies had thrown up between them. He filled his mind with the thought of his listeners. He returned the ardor of their eyes, smiled to their smiles, and shared their emotions. He would be their mother-bountiful, their father-provider, their lord and savior offering forth the harvest of his life to their gigantic needs. They were starved and he would translate his inner resources into a manna that passeth understanding. He should have done this with his ex-wife and children. He should have done this with his family. He should have! He should have!

When it was all over, his voice diminished to the size of the emotion left him, he suggested to them, but dared not insist, that they read the poem aloud at home, to their mothers and fathers, to their sisters and brothers, to a friend (he dared not say "girl friend" or "boy friend"), to enjoy the experience all the better, to know it at its best—never mind how much ("how little," he meant to say, but he feared it would offend their ardor which had been fanned by the second reading). The next time, then, the same poem and enjoyment again— but enjoyment of a new kind, on fire with the sunrise of understanding.

His eyes turned and head bowed away from the sight of students rising and facing him. The thunderous applause breaking against him, he busied himself gigantically with his notebook, his texts, and the unabashed scribblings on the blackboard: "P O E T R Y" "L O V E!" "Y O U A N D M E!" He knew, he knew—he sensed the decision in his nerve-ends, he felt it in his mind. He pulled in as the mass of cloth and flesh surged down the aisles.

But one student, then another and another stopped at the desk, surrounded him on the right, blocked his escape on the left. Faces were raised to his; eyes searched contact with his.

He looked up with panic.

"Shall this be how we learn very day, Siir?" He had heard the question before and answered it too.

"Siir, is needed to carry books to class all occasions?" This also!

"My notepaperbook is with fixed paper, Siir. Is this forbidden, Siir?" Also this.

The boys' faces within inches of his (the girls in the background, always the girls in the background), questions clattered on soaring voices. He saw how large their eyes were, how black their eyebrows and hair, how thick and oily (when not pearly gray and fine) the texture of their skin. Fleetingly he had glimpses of the girls' thick lips, the brilliance of their teeth. When they came to him as smells—the garlicky and sour smells of mouth, acrid smells of old sweat and crude cleaning fluids, the intimate smells of hairy armpits and unwashed bodies—he tried to back off while still holding fast to their avid eyes, their warm faces, and the hunger of their minds.

Still they thronged upon him. Still the questions. Still the boys' faces rising and falling before his. He felt awash in the dark froth of eyebrows and hair, in the tide of oily skin and a sea of odors. He felt smothered in the smells. Suddenly they seemed to be rising from himself.

Peter! Mary! Stephen! Martha! Esther! Paul! If he had yelled his anguish aloud, would it have mattered? Would they have heard?

Finally, they let him go.

And it all went out of him.

Fussing with his books and notebooks, it came to him how lucky he was—to have the rest of the day, that afternoon and the entire evening too, to himself.

"Oh, thank you, Siir!" a pair of dark glasses, an empty face, and olive-pulp lips pushed up to his.

"Thank you, Siir."

"Thank you too much, Siir!"

"Thank *you!*" He snapped his notebook closed.

Smiles flickered and a few eyes lit up. The young men withdrew before him as one, yielding him a way. Young women waited at the doorway. Upon them, he held back a moment and gestured to the open door. But they stood firm with their eyes ablaze to him. He let his chin sag and hurried out.

The vestibule turbulent with students, he gripped his books all the tighter.

"Dr. Hart-yon—Professor, Siir!"

He started to run for it, but, then, risking a backwards glance, he took the assault of the whey face and the jiggly eyes.

"Would you be minding if I walked with you?" The chin jutted and eyelids fluttered.

"Be on guard with the boys after class," his colleague had warned. "They are as nosy and as impertinent as raccoons."

"Have to hurry!" He began trotting.

"Oh, I do not mind, Siir!" The youth fell in behind him.

"*Ça va?*" the smiling servant tried to engage his eyes as teacher went by with student at his shoulder.

"*Ça va!*" He returned a token wave.

"*Ça va! Ça va! Ça va!*" the servant's thin voice died joyously behind in the university yard.

"Siir," the student's voice pulled through the moment. "Are you minding very much if I am asking a few questions?"

He did not have to glance back to know the white-white face would be greatly sincere.

"No, I don't mind if you ask—a few." He spurted ahead.

"Siir, why are you residing in a hotel, Siir? Do you not like us, Siir?"

Balked for comprehension, he retreated to his colleague's scotch-'n'-water lecture on Arabic hospitality. Entertaining was the most accessible and least expensive diversion in the Levantine, "the hospitality syndrome."

"I plan to spend part of every day looking for a suitable apartment," he emerged, slowing to a walk.

"Oh, I hope you succeed, Siir!" He felt chin bone brush his shoulder as the student drew alongside, wedding the two of them by smells again.

"Siir, Professor Hart-yon, Siir!" The acidy face was turned full to his, the lips overconscientious with consonants and syllables. "How old are you, Siir?"

"Over forty!" He pulled ahead again, dodging taxis, motorbikes, and pedestrians. Out of a blind alley, an overloaded donkey came trotting nimbly toward him. He started trotting too.

But the student clung like Levantine sweat. Valiantly, the teacher plunged ahead. Determinedly the student came after.

"Siir," the student was all but shouting over his efforts to keep up, "why is it you never married?"

With a frantic look backward only to meet gigantically sincere eyes, he cried out, "Have to hurry!" and bolted into the thronging avenue. A bus careened and tilted to miss him—a motorbike crowded him onto the sidewalk. He waved wildly for a taxi.

Climbing into the vehicle, he looked away from the image of the student standing immobile with incomprehension amidst the hurtling traffic as though abandoned.

It was Paul, Paul! Not Peter, nor even Stephen! But Paul, his needy and vulnerable youngest one he thought of now.

At the hotel, he threw the taxi driver a handful of pounds, dragged himself up the stoop to the lobby, and then took the stairs to the second floor on his hands and knees. In his wake the manager and desk clerk, open-mouthed.

Pulling himself to his feet, he made it into his room, slammed the door, threw the bolt, and fell onto the bed.

Suddenly the distant braying of a donkey, again and again! His eyes widened, traveled the interminable expanse of white walls—looking, searching.

Finally, they fixed on the photograph on the dresser.

He had loved her so much once! The photograph was testament thereof.

They had had "such a yen for each other," as she had put it. But they were also sensible, and had planned—only to discover what was felt so deeply could not always be controlled.

"You were a natural," his wife had said to him once they were safely married. "You reek with it—love, marriage, fatherhood!"

And now?

And now?

And now?

Now that had all changed. Five years of intense application at his stall in the university library had converted him into a mind whose—yens were preempted by books pored over endlessly, by essays and critiques crimped into shape at an aseptic desk, now to come flooding forth as a most adulterous and polygamous love affair with students in a Levantine university far from family and home. And all he had left of what he had known of personal passion and private love was the single ikon of a photograph.

The Man Who Didn't Want to Box Muhammad Ali

"How's he now?" Nomans Meier says. Thick, his speech might be the victor over ice floes of feeling. Nude before his open locker, he sniffs—a familiar whore. He reaches in and grasps a large sponge in thick fingers.

"Not better," Breeze Line slams the door after himself. "Doc says can't tell yet."

Nomans Meier's hand begins to work the sponge.

"The heart of a bull, Doc says." Breeze Line watches Nomans Meier's hand, the sponge drowning therein. One of those casual bluffmen whose very glance bespeaks confidence, Breeze Line always believes this fight is the one.

Looking away from his manager, Nomans Meier turns his eyes away from his wife too.

Lela watches Nomans Meier's hand swallowing the sponge.

"It's all gone, Meier!" Lela says,

"Wha?" A look at the tiny woman, quickly—then at his hand—only his tight fist, the taut fingers whitened.

As though with a will of their own, the fingers let go and the fist opens like a flower—the sponge leaps and falls to the floor. Watching the wobbling skeleton, absently Nomans Meier crosses his left leg over his right—his most comfortable stance.

Six feet four, Nomans Meier weighed in at two hundred sixty less than an hour earlier—fighting weight. Also, the patient training camp sun had made him a dark contender.

At the weighing in, Lela said, "You look one of them—Now all you need is their—goose." She twisted her hand with the idiom, foreign on her tongue.

"One wallop!" his father had once said, "and they'll all fall down, one, two, Jack Dempsey—Rocky Marciano, Cassius Clay, even Joe Louis himself in his heyday."

Yet, four years and a hundred fights later, Nomans Meier was still no more than a promise, not even a title contender.

He drew crowds all right, the greatest. Once, he was even put on exhibit at Madison Square Garden.

Tonight, he is to fight nowhere near the Garden. Tonight, he is to fight in the suburbs again, eighteen miles north, a third less than that south of the farmhouse in which his father, Old Hemans Way, lies fighting pneumonia and death.

"When'll they know?" Nomans Meier offers his hands to Breeze Line for the last taping.

The warning blinker wildly red, Breeze Line pulls the door open and holds it for Nomans Meier, who has to bend his head to go through. Nomans Meier goes out before Breeze Line and also before Lela. On the way to the ring, Nomans Meier always goes first, glorious in his wine-dark trunks, but his purple bathrobe a collapsed tent across his shoulders. Breeze Line's mouth is all teeth.

Returning from the ring, it is just the reverse. Also, after a fight Breeze Line's mouth is always a pinched slit, his toothy smile vanished.

Echoes of their steps funnelling behind them in the corridor, Nomans Meier stops at the arena entrance. Drawing up quickly to his side, Lela's face rises.

"Just listen to them, Meier!" Her nostrils furl. "And smell them! Feel them! Feel them!"

"Whatta they wanta me anyways?" Nomans Meier muttered across the fallen crest of his chin to Lela.

"Just you, dar-ling!—To show them how good you are!" Lela makes herself even smaller at his side, opens the gate and looks in. The din jumps into a mingle-mangle shouting.

Riding the turbulence from foot to foot, his weight shifting, Nomans Meier feels the floor give and then come back. He feels how easy it would be to bring his feet down, smashing through the floor.

Looming over Lela's head, he listens to the crowd yelling at the prelims, urgefully.

Should he do it now? So easy!

"O.K.?" Breeze Line pulls alongside. Nomans Meier watches the two prelim fighters leaving hastily by the far gate on the ocean of boos and caterwauls. Someone in a yelping falsetto, "How's about a frug, baby? Then, how's about a dance?"

"You brute, you!" Falsetto too.

Breeze Line tries the crowd with his eyes and ears, the lift of his face, the angle of his head, then steps in, then motions Nomans Meier ahead.

Momentarily Nomans Meier hesitates, tall and dour, then he breaks the resistance barrier, and then walks straight on in, eyes straight ahead.

"The Vandal Samson!" Someone yells.

"Lookit them soul-jers, willya!"

"The build of a hippo!"

"Lookit, willya—lookit!—King Kong!"

"Show them! Show them! Show them, Meier!" Hands sprouting betting money, his father's cronies present at the ringside. They know, everyone knows, it is rare that Nomans Meier scores a knockout even in late rounds, yet as always they take odds from all comers on an early knockout.

As he stands astride, the canvas, ropes and the stadium, the yelling becomes fast and furious.

"Pull any pillars down lately?"

"Kill any lions today?"

"Gonna show us something tonight, Meier, Baby?" Again the vague echo of a taunt.

"Schmangle him—bangle him!" A jackal might have been cackling to the moon.

His long arms like broken limbs down his sides, Nomans Meier stands in his corner as Lela sits down on the stool giving him her special hot look, intended to make him feel he was a really big man. Knocking the dousing pail and water bottle together, Breeze Line looks out into the crowd as though to sniff something.

When the opponent appears in the opposite gateway, Nomans Meier listens to the shouting rise, and then fall off, slowly, not abruptly.

The opponent is young and under six feet, just over two hundred pounds. When the bell sounds and they move out into the center of the ring to receive the referee's instructions, Nomans Meier towers like a mammoth Philistine over a trim and athletic David. They could be three entirely different species from, perhaps, entirely different planets—the opponent from the sun, or Venus, the referee from the moon or Mars, and Nomans Meier from faraway, dark Jupiter.

After the briefing, Nomans Meier holds astride the ropes with his gloves, waiting.

"Tell Lela, keep calling," he yells over his shoulder.

"Just put this boy away for us—that's your job, Meier, Baby!" Breeze Line knows Nomans Meier doesn't like being addressed by his last name only. "Watch for his left—He goes for the throat!"

Nomans Meier looks away from Breeze Line to Lela, still smiling her urge of heart. Quickly he looks back to the opponent and the referee.

The opponent has his elbows on the ropes, cool and relaxed. Right then he looks fine, how Nomans Meier would want to look if he had his way about it. He is a wonder boy as a fighter too, Nomans Meier knows this. Within a year he has taken on everyone the Commission threw at him as he made his way up the secondary ranks. Now, he is at the gateway to the top ten, across which Nomans Meier stands astraddle, eliminating the lesser boxers and watching the promising ones slip by.

With the clang of the bell, Nomans Meier bunches his gloved hands at his chest and shuffles out into the ring. The opponent's body becomes taut and alive, as if a small dynamo is going within him, and moves about Nomans Meier, one side, then the other. It is obvious the youth is not just another callow jockstrap the Commission has dug up to round out the usual Barbarian spectacle.

A lean mountain lion stalking a bull buffalo, the youth strikes Nomans' face, then slips away, only to strike again seconds later. He moves with ease, yet is taut, quick, and sure. With each hit, his pale eyes glint. Nomans Meier has seen the look once or twice before, and then only when he was fighting the best. Someday, perhaps—

The bell clangs sharply.

"Hold him off!" Breeze Line sponges his body and face. "The long-arm,

Meier, Baby." One of Breeze Line's fingers slips, touching a raw spot alive in Nomans' face.

Nomans Meier looks at Breeze Line and then at Lela. Still smiling, Lela smokes a cigarette, bird-like, a way she has learned in the cabarets of Europe where, a singer of love ballads, she was seen and loved by Nomans Meier. It was curious how Nomans Meier had taken to her the moment he heard her throaty, flat voice, the next moment he saw her tiny, jewel-hard face. What was even more surprising was the way Hemans Way, the father, had taken to her instantaneously too, when, weeks later, she was presented to the big man as his son's wife, Mrs. Nomans Meier, daughter-in-law of Hemans Way Meier. Yet, perhaps it was not so surprising. In her high spirits and ambitiousness, she reminded the old warrior of a part of himself and a part of his newly departed own wife, both. Hemans Way likes such people as Ms. Nomans Way Meier. That is why he likes Breeze Line too. Breeze Line is also a reminder of a part of Nomans Meier's father, the public part. Together, the pert Lela, bright-eyes and clever, and Breeze Line, affable and confident, make up an alter image of Nomans Meier's father, the magnificent Hemans Way. Neither reminds Nomans Meier much of his mother. In the Hemans Way household, Nomans Meier's mother was always something of an unknown, except in matters of her duties. Hemans Way is that kind of man.

"Tell Lela to call now," Nomans Meier breathes with difficulty.

"Just keep him off—the long-arm," Breeze Line says as though he hasn't heard Nomans Meier. "He'll tire by the seventh—"

"Wanna know after this round!" Nomans Meier says again, still watching Lela.

The bell clangs. No sooner is Nomans Meier in the center of the ring than the youth is at his body from all sides. Nomans Meier glances back to his corner—Lela's seat is empty.

Flurrying through Nomans' defenses with jabs and hooks to the face, the youth's glove glances off Nomans Meier's adams apple. Gasping panic, Nomans Meier grabs the youth in his long arms and clutches as though a buoy. Through agonized sucks of air, he feels the flat muscles of the youth's chest rise and fall like waves. He feels the bands of the youth's arms and chest ripple like corrugated steel as the youth's gloves pound him with a rapid, unrelenting tattoo through the intake and expulsion of their married breaths.

The referee's hands insistent on his shoulders, Nomans Meier shoves the youth away from himself as his agonized mouth breathes solo again.

The youth backing off from him cleanly, Nomans Meier sees an opening.

And he knows, right now, if he wants—

But, he hesitates—and the moment is lost.

At the end of the round, Lela has not returned.

"How about that opening?" Breeze Line's voice goes at him as his hands tear Nomans Meier's skin with a towel. "He was wide as a barn door! You did it again, Meier, Baby!"

Nomans Meier winces violently.

Breeze Line throws the sponge and towel into the dousing pail, "He got at you worse—Long- arm him! The long-arm, Meier, Baby!" His voice dips with finality. "The long-arm!" He stabs the air with his fist and arm and snaps his head with clean affirmation.

In the third round, Nomans Meier pokes and pushes the opponent away from himself but with a simpering smile. It is as though he is trying to avoid his due, what the opponent, the crowd, and he himself know is coming to him.

Nomans Meier learned the arm trick when he was a boy. First he had used his long legs, then his arms to ward off his father. There was always a part of his father that was still of the old world, middle European—Beat a boy, not hard but properly, if he is bad. And if he lacks spirit, then really beat, wallop him, schmash him—it was never too soon to show a boy how hard the world he was born into is and what it would do to a weak one. Hemans Way Meier believed that. Near death, he still believes it—all the more, Nomans Meier is certain.

And so, Nomans Meier discovered the usefulness of his long legs, but not to run away—he was not that bright. And of his arms—he would keep his arms out and keep jabbing his father as though with sticks....

At the end of the round, Lela still has not returned.

Nomans Meier's mouthpiece sticks as he tries to spit it into Breeze Line's hand.

"Thatta boy, Meier, Baby!" Breeze Line's voice is easy and soothing. "Ya just listen to Poppa Breeze Line—have him in no time flat! And then—" Breeze Line busts the air with his hand and explodes breath with his puckered lips. "Bingo!"

His breath dragging down deep, Nomans Meier feels the long muscle of his midriff rising and falling like a truck tire abarrelling on highway ruts.

His eyes fix Lela's empty seat.

When the bell clangs for the fourth round, the seat is still empty.

Nomans Meier pokes the youth away, long-arming him again. He manages
to move about briskly, with style, or with what might seem style to the viewers
as he does so. Every now and again he hits the youth's body resoundingly, not
one of his great blows but one enough to shake the smaller man up. Nomans'
perfected punch, it made him look good to the fans, made the opponent feel
him, and satisfied his own needs to strike back every now and again—and so
he resorts to it.

With the clanging of the bell, he breaks away clean, skipping.

"Whoya kiddin'?" Breeze Line whips him with his tongue. "Take a good
gander at that crowd—Ya think ya goosin' them?" Breeze Line's hands go at
Nomans Meier's body with the towel and sponge, vigorously, harsh.

"I'm tellin' ya, Meier, Baby, they're onta ya. From here on, it's either come
through, or—"

Lela's seat was still empty—Nomans Meier's stomach gnawed vaguely.

"If ya couldn't lay your hands on him—" Breeze Line pushes the bottle
into his mouth, the pail shoved under where the reluctant gladiator can spit
into it while his mouthpiece waits in mid-air, ready to be slipped in like a bit.
"But you and I know—and every last mother-sucker one of them out there
knows—"

Nomans Meier jumps to his feet a hair of a breath before the bell clangs.

His face grim, the youth gets at Nomans Meier again instantly. Boxing
through Nomans Meier's defenses from all sides, he pounds Nomans Meier's
chest, jabs his jaw, and batters his face. Nomans Meier's head snaps back and
his mouthpiece jars loose...

That was it—his father beat him so much when he was a boy, and not
only with the broom handle but also with his big hands. His father also beat
his mother—accidentally when she put herself between the man and the boy
during a beating. But also, sometimes, intentionally. He beat her rarely, but
enough, and always after he'd been in a deep wine drunk or a beer souse with
his gambling friends. Saturday afternoons, Hemans Way went into town in
his roadmaster and stayed the rest of the day and night. When he returned
the next morning, he was still drunk and sullen. The least thing made him
grumble and at any excuse he hit out at Nomans Meier and Nomans Meier's
mother. Nomans Meier tried to take his father's anger for both of them on his
feet and arms...

At the end of the round, Nomans Meier's face throbs and his chest and arms
feel overlarge.

"You sure look a beauty, Meier, Baby!" Breeze Line swabs the cuts as though
stabbing Nomans Meier. "Looks like the end of the line—a shute-shute ride all

the way down!"

Still Lela does not return.

In the sixth, the youth gets past Nomans Meier's long arms almost at will. Nomans Meier feels certain if the youth doesn't tire, it'll be a topheavy win. From there, a quick climb to the top. The youth could be the champion soon. Nomans Meier is sure.

But this doesn't bother Nomans Meier. What does bother him is the incessant flurry of blows. Whichever way he turns, the opponent's gloves batter him, bruise him, and cut him. If he goes into a clinch, the opponent works steadily on his ribs and midriff, a jolting uppercut to the jaw every now and again. If he tries to back away, the opponent is quickly upon him, forcing him all the way back until Nomans Meier feels the ropes cut into his back.

As the opponent's pounding dominates him, battering him relentlessly, Nomans Meier finds himself infuriated with the thought that no other boxer had ever got at him like that before. Before, it was mostly always Nomans Meier missing chances. Now it is the opponent making the most of his, mercilessly.

The bell comes as a rescue.

As he works the cuts, Breeze Line says nothing. Behind him, returned, Lela waits.

"Tell me!" Nomans Meier gasps.

Lela looks at him.

"I gotta know!" Nomans Meier pushes Breeze Line off and tries to rise.

"Dawktor says crisis will soon come!" Lela inspects his face, then touches one of the cuts with her fingertips. Slowly, deliberately, she smoothes the raw edges.

"Keep calling!" Nomans Meier flops into the stool and against the ropes. He has to know, about his father. At the same time he has a feeling close to certainty that he would know as soon as he lumbers out to the opponent in answer to the bell.

The opponent is at him again instantly. Nomans Meier stumbles to get out of range but the opponent's gloves flurry punishingly. If only Nomans Meier could get him in a clinch—if only he could hold on!

Suddenly Nomans Meier's face splinters and feels spongey with pain. His head feels split open from forehead to his upper lip. The taste of blood, warm and choking in his mouth, his nose feels crushed. Clutching his opponent desperately, he wonders wildly what he should do. But what, what at all can he do? As with his father, he knows there is nothing he can do but protect himself. But he cannot do even that any longer now. Of course there have been times when his father attacked him and always when the big man attacked Nomans Meier's mother, a simple, dutiful woman who was as much servant as she was wife, Nomans Meier wanted so much to be able to strike out wildly. But somehow he never did. Even the thought of striking his father made him feel unclean. Each time he had such a thought, the moment after, the thought vanished, his emotions became tangled and he felt another layer of hopelessness settle on his life.

His opponent works on his body now, on his heart and midriff. Every now and again a glove swipes Nomans Meier's face, then flurries on his jaw, his forehead and cheeks. Nomans Meier's cheeks and forehead feel gigantic. Spitting blood to get his breath, he has a sharp sensation of a sliver on his puffed lips.

If only he had struck out at his father once!

His opponent's gloves cut him again and again, opening the raw hurt of his nose, scraping flesh and skin from his cheeks. Through the blooded sweat, Nomans Meier watches his opponent's eyes narrowing.

Nomans Meier remembered he struck out at someone finally. But not at his father. An adolescent then, he was almost at his full growth. In the pasture nearest the farmhouse, a young bull, worked on but hours before to turn it into beef stock, lowed its agony broadside to the world. The slit the vet had made had been botched. Running amuck, the animal charged the stone wall blindly again and again.

Hemans Way Meier tried everything to pacify and corner the horrendous creature. Deciding there was no other way finally, he went off in his roadmaster to a neighboring farm to borrow a gun. Before Hemans Way returned, raging with unbearable pain, the bull went over the wall. Bawling raucously, it trampled a half dozen hens and tossed everything in its way as it charged, its snout scraping yard gravel, for the farmhouse where Nomans Meier's mother looked out, fascinated by dread, from a kitchen window.

Quickly Nomans Meier rushed into the path of the bull's charge. Its head lowered, its eyes googling with pain and rage over a dust smeared snout, its hooves squinting angrily in the gravel and chickensand, the swart bull came at Nomans Meier in a seething line...

Nomans Meier's opponent worked on his face again, belaboring his face, pounding his forehead and thrashing his jaw. Through the raw hurt of his nose, Nomans Meier felt his left eye closing into a puffed slit like a flower struck by hail.

As the bull thundered for him, Nomans Meier braced himself, his back against the kitchen door, his feet planted firmly against the threshold. The bull's head lowering still more until its horrendously snorting nose scraped dirt, Nomans Meier watched the newly sprouted horns coming at him. He saw how silken the fur about the bases of the horns were, how new the bone looked at the tips. The head fur and hide of the young bull looked silken too, a rich jade nap. The ridge between the two horn tips, the mature horn still buried beneath, was firm and proud. He saw how the bull's eyes smoked with rage, how its syrupy nose was caked with the mud of yard dust.

He waited until he had the taste of the dust from the bull's hooves in his mouth and felt the torrential breath of the bull's gaping nostrils on his face and mouth and felt the torrential breath of the bull's gaping nostrils on his face and hands—then he made a fist, drew his arm back and waited just a second more. When the horns were about to lurch upon him, he let go.

He felt bone and fur give way beneath his knuckles, between the seething eyes, just above the smoking muzzle. He could almost hear bone crunch and the flesh underneath squinge. As he hit the bull, he stepped to one side.

The young bull hurtled past him, grazed his leg with its flank, and clattered onto the stairs. As its hooves went upon the stairs, it stopped suddenly and collapsed. Its hind legs kicking furiously, it tumbled off the stairs into yard dirt on its side.

And it was over. Experiencing awesome fear, Nomans Meier did not feel the pronged hurt of his hand.

When his father returned with the gun, the bull had stopped kicking. Its legs up in the air, like a monument of black iron, its eyes were blooded and glazed. Blood trickled thickly from its muzzle into yard dirt. Hens had flocked at its flanks and head to peck strands of haygrass; the farm dog snuffled at its brook of blood.

His father looked at the bull and then at Nomans Meier. Nomans Meier just stood there with his hand hanging swollen at his side. His father came to his side, took the hand up in his massive hands and squeezed.

Nomans Meier winced and drew his hand away.

"It's broken, your hand," his father said.

Nomans Meier looked down at the bull. His sense of awesome unreality made him delirious with fear. After, when his hand started to jump with pain, he felt secure in the knowledge that it was hurting.

"Good boy, Nomans! My boy, Nomans!" his father said. Nomans Meier looked at his father dumbly. A moment later, he turned about and walked into the farmhouse....

His opponent's left hand opens a cut on Nomans Meier's left eyebrow, filling his eye with hot blood. His face feels bloated with raw pain and he can see and hear the crowd only dimly.

Scraping his face, his opponent's glove carries away skin and flesh from his right cheekbone. The raw flesh beneath itches maddeningly and Nomans Meier claws at the wound with both gloves. The same moment, a wild flurry pierces Nomans Meier's heart with ragged pain and bursts his lungs of breath.

Gasping, Nomans Meier feels his adams apple explode, leaving him in an agonized breathlessness. The cartilage of his throat feeling shattered, Nomans Meier is frenziedly famished for breath within the smothering balloon of his face.

Through the fuzzed torrent of the arena, Nomans Meier's opponent comes at him hot and furious, walloping his body with cold deliberation, cutting his face relentlessly. Nomans Meier tries to bring his guard up, but his arms are almost too heavy to move. He tries to stumble out of reach as he peers through a haze of blood, looking out, looking out for his opponent. Head carried high and mouth half open, his opponent haws and snorts as he forces the fight pell-mell into the final onslaught that would finish off Nomans Meier. His face is thrust forward eagerly.

The moment seems inevitable to Nomans Meier, to the fans, to Nomans Meier's opponent.

On the crest of the moment, eager to drink up success, Nomans Meier's opponent lets his guard drop as he cocks his right hand at his knee, ready to hammer the big man to the canvas.

In the same moment, Nomans Meier brings his right arm back as though cocking a cannon. Shouting horrendously, he strikes out blindly at his opponent's face.

He feels his glove explode against flesh and bone, splattering him with blooded sweat. He feels bone crackle like stiff plaster board under his glove and then give way as the skins of melons his father held up for him to practice on when he was a boy.

Head jolted, snapped, and twisted back, the youth's face has a look of surprise and anguish as he totters, then sinks to his knee as though kneeling for prayer, then falls over on his face and stomach. Crumpled, he lies like an empty fodder sack, still. His right leg is caught under the dead weight of his body.

As the din in the arena explodes into a mingle-mangle, Nomans Meier feels the referee's hands shoving him into a neutral corner. The moment feels curiously awesome through his labored and painful breathing, through the sweat and blood suffocating his eyes.

Bent over the youth, the referee counts methodically and emphatically as at the stations of the cross in a rural cathedral—or as the final dozen moves of an inevitable chess game played by a grandmaster against a novice. As the beads on a counting board—one, two, three—five—and ten. Out.

His breath coming easier, Nomans Meier experiences an extraordinary calm. The arena is tumultuous and all the spectators are on their feet as the referee raises Nomans Meier's hand abruptly and walks off.

Nomans Meier sees Breeze Line's face through the haze of blood, shouting with surprise and joy. And Lela, her staccato voice sieving through, reaches to him urgefully, "Nomans Meier! Nomans Meier! He will be champion soon!"

When Breeze Line and Lela lead him out of the ring through the bellowing faces of the clamorous arena, the youth is still lying on the canvas. Nomans Meier aches with the image of the twisted leg pinned under the young body.

The spectators swarm about Nomans Meier, buffet him, and drown him.

"Thatta baby, Meier!"

"We knew it! We knew it! We knew it! All the time we knew it!"

"That's murdering him!"

And stridently over the shouting, "Bravo! Goose-oh! You are the king of the world-oh!"

They have to shove, sidle, and scamper to get back to the gate, back into the corridor leading to the dressing room.

In the dressing room finally, Breeze Line is jubilant. Lela's face is feverish, her voice thrumbles, and her hands fly from gesture to gesture.

"My boy, Nomans Meier! I knew you could do it, boy!" Breeze Line cries, all teeth.

"Nomans, my lover," Lela touches his face with the tips of her fingers. "They will be singing songs about you in the cabarets of Berlin next week!" On tiptoes, face to face, her eyes glow furiously.

"My father?" Nomans Meier murmurs through his swollen lips.

"Yes, dar-ling!" Lela mouths into his ear. "I will this minute call." She turns her head and kisses him with the scalding fullness of her mouth. Giving him a great look over her shoulder, she settles on her heels and goes through the door into the corridor, her spikes sounding like a triphammer in a vacuum of plastics.

Right after, a small balding head pokes in.

"Looks serious—" the man says to Breeze Line. Breeze Line's wide-open mouth closes slowly, masking his teeth.

A moment later, sober-faced men come in and inspect Nomans Meier's gloves, first the right, then the left, one by one. They have Breeze Line cut Nomans Meier's bandages, inspect Nomans Meier's hands and then, without looking at either Nomans Meier or Breeze Line, start out again. One of them says over his shoulder, "It looks bad!" And they leave.

His mouth a sullen slit, Breeze Line studies the closing door and then goes out too, following the men into the tunnel.

Nomans Meier begins flexing and massaging his hands. They don't even hurt this time, he thinks. He picks up the sponge and sops his body of sweat and blood.

When he hears Breeze Line returning down the corridor, he knows Lela is with him by the sound of the quick, insistent clickings of her heels. At the door, her voice comes loud, uncontrolled.

When they come in, they look at Nomans Meier. He looks at them.

"He's dead!" Breeze Line says and looks away. Nomans Meier feels a nauseous delirium. He keeps looking.

"My father?" he says, the delirium becoming awesome as it whorls within him. The sponge feels large and loose in his hand.

"Your opponent!" Breeze Line says.

Suddenly Nomans Meier feels emptied.

He just looks at Breeze Line.

"And my father?" he finally mutters.

"He came through the crisis all right," Lela says, looking at him and then quickly away. "Dawkter says he will live to be a hundred."

Nomans Meier feels his hand beginning to work at the sponge. When the sponge is all gathered into his palm, he closes his fist tight on it. He looks again to Breeze Line and to Lela. They are looking at each other, not at him.

He opens his fist—the sponge comes springing out. Dropping to the floor, it bounces about for seconds and then wobbles crazily. In the background, the din of the crowd from the arena. Before him the gaping maw of the locker and its familiar odors.

Diana Der-Hovanessian

Diana Der-Hovanessian was born in Worcester, Massachusetts, into an Armenian home that was filled with poetry, history, and fantastic tales, both real and imagined.

Her father, Hovaness (John) Der-Hovanessian, a native of the village of Tadem in the Kharpert region of Western Armenia, had been the secretary and first lieutenant of Sepastatsi Unger Murad, the Armenian general. In the 1918 battle when Murad was killed and his famous horse Pegasus shot, Hovaness Der-Hovanessian's horse was also killed and he himself was shot in the forehead. The bullet was never removed and Diana remembers as a child climbing into her father's lap to touch the spot where the bullet had entered.

After the founding of the first Armenian Republic, Hovaness was sent by the government to study agronomy at Michigan State University. He traveled east on the Trans-Siberian railroad and in Japan was put on a steamship to America by Diana Aghabeg Apkar, the Armenian woman diplomat for whom Diana Der-Hovanessian was named. When Armenia was annexed by the Soviet Union, Hovaness stayed in the United States and became a part of the Armenian Revolutionary Federation's "government in exile," which entailed frequent traveling. While speaking at an Armenian community picnic in Worcester, Hovaness, described by Diana as handsome and charismatic, met Marian Israelyan, whom he later married.

Marian Israelyan's parents, Hagop and Helen, were also natives of Tadem and knew the Der-Hovanessians from there. Hagop Israelyan immigrated to the United States as a young boy, a trajectory recreated in the poem "charm against inertia." After graduating from Lowell High School he worked in a

Worcester wire mill by day and studied immigration law at night. On one of his trips home to Tadem, his parents persuaded him to marry a local orphan girl, their goal being to prevent him from marrying a non-Armenian, as many young Armenian men in America were doing.

For the first four years of her life Diana lived in Worcester with her maternal grandparents in an apartment too small to house the whole family. Her parents and sister were in an apartment a few streets away. Diana describes her grandfather Hagop as "my favorite person in the world," who recounted the plays of Shakespeare on their afternoon walks, and she says that her grandmother Helen "told me Armenian folk tales."

Eventually Diana's parents bought a house and settled with their children in the suburbs of first Auburn and later Marlborough, Massachusetts. There were no other Armenians in either of these communities. To support his family, her father founded a dairy, the first in the state to homogenize milk. Diana says:

> It was a great childhood for a while: wandering in the
> woods, picking blackberries, blueberries, and climbing
> trees. But our house was on a highway, a busy highway.
> And one day in March when I was five, my sister and I
> were crossing the road, we were hit by a car and she died.
> That changed everything. I kept waiting and waiting for her
> to come back.

This traumatic experience is memorialized in the poem "White Lamb, Blue Mulberry" as the poet stands before her sister's grave in the Armenian section of the Hope Cemetery. Diana muses:

> Perhaps writing poems was a way of talking to my sister.
> Writing poems was something we did at home anyway.
> My father wrote poems for us to recite in public when we
> were very little. Both parents went around reciting poems
> all the time. My father in Armenian and mother in English.
> And we were expected to give each other poems for our
> birthdays.

As an undergraduate at Boston University, Diana majored in English. When her grandfather asked her what career her degree would prepare her for she told him she wanted to be a poet. He replied that the Armenians already had enough poets, but what they truly needed were journalists to tell their story.

Diana followed his advice. She worked at the student paper and after graduating took at job at the *Medford Mercury*, a local daily in a Boston suburb.

She soon moved to New York, where she started at the Associated Press as a messenger, eventually working her way up to Near East Editor at *Young America*.

In the meantime, she was writing poems and submitting them to magazines for publication. She married, moved back to the Boston area, and was selected to participate in the last poetry class taught by Robert Lowell at Harvard.

When her father needed English versions of some poems by Daniel Varoujan for a lecture he was preparing, Diana provided them—and thus began her career as a translator.

Even though she was raised in a family that was steeped in Armenian culture, Diana says, "I didn't become Armenian until I went to New York and sang in a chorus, and joined a dance group."

As an adult—living away from her kin—Diana gravitated towards a group of young, politicized Armenians and began to feel consciously Armenian, an identity that increasingly informed her poetry.

Diana's poems are filled with family stories, as well as references to Armenian history, proverbs, and folk tales. Her poetry is also inhabited by the ghosts of the dead: her sister Sona, her grandparents, the poets Varoujan and Siamanto, and the countless Armenians who died during the mass deportations and executions of 1915 to 1922. The grandchild and child of survivors, Diana—who says there was very little talk of the Genocide in her household while she was growing up—has devoted much of her writing life to telling the story of her people.

Diana's unique contribution to American and Armenian American poetry comes not simply from her engagement with the large forces of history, but in the domestic detail and precise, empathetic observation that give her poetry its sense of intimacy and warmth—an intimacy that paradoxically amplifies the scope and scale of her voice. In poems such as "Teaching a Child to Dance" and "At Twilight" she writes from the point of view of a mother, with tenderness and melancholy, balancing a specific and unique maternal regard with an underlying expanse of public, shared remembrance. In the poem about her sister, "White Lamb, Blue Mulberry," she says, "This poem is my child," and in a sense, all her poems exist both as tightly held progeny and as wandering, independent expressions. In "Angel in Somerville" a bag lady is transformed into the poet and the poet herself is "a mother / feeding her children, dispensing grace"—a perfect example of how Diana transforms the impersonal public space of contemporary America and revisions it, through intensely personal imagining, into an almost Whitmanesque emotional vista.

Diana is an award-winning poet and translator, has been the president of the

New England Poetry Club for more than twenty years, and is a revered lecturer and teacher. She has taught workshops at Boston University, Bard College, and Columbia University, among others. She has twice been the recipient of Fulbright Fellowships to teach at Yerevan State University, in Armenia. Three volumes of her poetry have been translated into Armenian and published in Yerevan: *Inside Green Eyes, Valley of Flowers*, and *Recycling Today*. Her poems have also been translated into Greek, French, and Romanian.

Armenian poetry and American poetry are made richer by Diana Der-Hovanessian, who continues to dispense grace with her words.

Nancy Kricorian

Once in a Village

Once there was, and never was,
my grandmother's stories began
the way all Armenian fairytales
begin: Once there was
and never was, a village,
at the end of the woods,
a small village roofed
with cranes and smoke.

One there was, and never was,
at the foot of a mountain
a village called Tadem,
where everyday, a shepherd boy
passed the house of a woodsman
at the edge of the town.
The woodsman lived there with
his wife and little girl.
And when the boy took his goats
to graze, the girl would watch
secretly from a window, making

up names for the goats, and the boy.
She was not the daughter of the woodsman
and his wife, but had been sent
to live with them by her real father
a mysterious king, with a mysterious name.

Once there was, and never was,
a village with a shepherd boy,
and a witch's curse. In this village
lived a woodsman, his wife
and an orphan girl who thought
she was the daughter of a nameless king.

Years passed and the king never came
to take home his little girl
and so she was sent far away
to America to marry.

And after she was gone the boy felt lonely
and unwatched. But not for long
because a strange thing happened.
His goats, the school, the children,
their teacher, the church,
priest and parish disappeared
in a terrible way. Too terrible to tell.

One morning there was an Armenian village
that turned into a Turkish fire.

Once there was or never was
a little girl who thought
she was the lost daughter
of a lost king who would go back

for her and thank everyone
in the village for taking care '
of her. He would thank woodsman,
priest, teacher, baker, shoemaker,
children, tillers in the fields
for singing their songs to her.
And she would go with him
to thank them for being her friends.
But they disappeared.
Once in a village, a rooster crowed
and no one stirred.
Once there was a village
with wild hedges, a goat boy who never grew up
and a princess who never woke.

Notice

Once, the Greek writer Vassillikos
said, a writer's worth is measured
by the size of his country.

I laughed and didn't agree.
What about the British Isles?
Don't be flip, he said. You know
I speak of readership and power.

Last week, mourning an Armenian poet
I sent the death notice from
the Armenian press to the Boston Globe
obituary writer.

But he did not think the loss
of a poet from such a small nation
worthy of space. A car wash
operator. Yes.

Dear Maro Markarian, tiny woman
from a small land, writer of small poems,
maker of true gems, transformer of
tears into songs, songs into knives,
knives into petals of apricots,
dear Maro Markarian, defender of
children, activist poet, nourisher
of souls, tall on the page, large
voice of a small people, giant
shadow, what can I say to you,
you now beyond the borders
that kept you small.

It's Hard To Be the Child

of a revolutionary, Father. What can
I revolt against? The poems of Varoujan
and Siamanto which turned you into
what you were?

No. That boy you were did not need
Varoujan to drive him on.
Wasn't your own father taken in 1896?

Didn't your mother stand
holding the hand of her small son,
your older brother,

to scream at the Turk as he raised
his scimitar to finish them,
didn't she shout, "Use your gun,
use your gun!"

You still inside her and almost born,
didn't you hear her shouting
Use your gun! And then
her sigh of relief.
The Turk, not wanting to waste
a bullet, let them go.

You knew how to use bullets;
you had one lodged inside your forehead
from the battlefield where Murad fell,
you who grew into a diplomat
with skills that could put anyone at ease.
Where did you learn that ease?

I remember the TWA flight to Cairo,
when the pilot's voice
over the loudspeaker asked if anyone
knew Turkish, to help a Turk fill
in his landing card. You offered.
(We, your children, were amazed
at your kindness to one of "them"
and how serene you were with someone
at whom I wanted to spit.) My dear,
you said, there is a time and place to spit.

Angel in Somerville

Once Sona gave me an angel or I should say
her drawing of one sprinkling stars
like snow, inscribing it "Diana scattering
light." Not mother, not mommy, not mom—
she used my name. I taped it to the door
of her old room and there it stayed until

it came to life today. Walking in
Somerville I saw a woman in
an empty parking lot scattering
crumbs St. Francis style
to swarming pigeons at her feet,
Sona's angel strewing stars,
chatting as regent, angel, queen,
—bag lady no more, but a mother
feeding her children, dispensing grace.

The Proverb As Warning

Don't walk on hot coals
unless you have consulted your feet.

Save your breath when you
make a request of the deaf.

Don't press hands too tightly
at parting unless you mean hello.

Before you devote your life to song
find out who wants to hear you sing.

No one can live up to
the fantasies created by
long distance courtship.

Silent love sounds
the same as indifference.

In 1979

While arranging a poetry reading
at Boston University for a Russian poet
I was assigned help from Elena
from alumni administration.

My first book had come out.

"Do you know how good you are?"
"Well," I said, "I would have stayed
in advertising if I thought I were bad."

"It's the same thing," said Elena.
"Poems advertise the poet."

"No," I objected. "That's not the point.
The reader has to find himself in…"

"It's all show biz. And I could do a lot
for you if you'd let me.
You dress all wrong for a poet."

I looked down at my little tweed
skirt, my loafers. 1979.

"You should wear long peasant skirts,
heavy jewelry. And a cape. Always a cape."

I laughed.

"You laugh too much." she said. "People
don't take you seriously. You have to
wear a black cape and arrive late.
You're always early. Make people
wait. Have heads turn."

"But that wouldn't be me."

"Of course it would. Your poems say
'Hey, look at me.' Why can't your clothes?"

"My poems say, I hope this speaks
to you."

"No. Poems say, Look at this cape."

Teaching a Child to Dance

Move with the music but
as if through water
with knees bent imperceptibly,
just barely, for grace.

Move your arms in joy
and let your fingers float,
following wrists as if through
waters that flow.

Let your hand trace a moonrise;
let your fingers harvest grapes
while we glide forward
walking like queens.

Bend slightly, move sprightly
with a springing step
in rhythms of the heart beat
with Anahid and Naneh
guiding your feet.

Move your hands
through the waters of Arax,
palms down, then palms up.
Move with small glides,
magnificent child,
gift of waters and light.

And if you wave a kerchief
wave it leaning back smiling
as if greeting hello and good-bye.

Look over your left shoulder
I am beside you.
And over my left shoulder
my grandmother and hers.
They walk like shy Christian
brides but behind them marching
their pagan mothers
parading with shields.

Look toward your right shoulder
and into your future where

a mother-in-law smiles beckoning
you into a life to be.
The Armenian dance is a dance of women,
friends in a circle that opens
and closes and never ends.

May I Have This Dance?

May I have this dance? Father would bow.
One of us would leap on Father's feet,
hanging on to his hands as if we knew how,

riding his shoes as if on the prow
of a huge ship journeying into the deep
rhythms of dancing. Father would bow

thanking one partner and then allow
another to leap on his toes to sweep
into a waltz as if knowing how.

We'd follow the steps of polka or loud
march. Whatever the tune it was always sweet
and brief until Father would bow
toward Mother laughing (I hear her now).
They never danced; it was our treat.
We didn't realize he didn't know how.

His childhood was stolen, but he endowed
ours with laughter as we rode his feet
lifting us over the past somehow.
Father would thank us and solemnly bow.

Recycling Today

So this is the day we get back
at the end of our lives
the day we can have again
to relive twenty four hours?

"Recycling Today" says the banner
across the gate of the University
of Massachusetts, Boston
where I drive north on the Southeast
Expressway past the glittering bay.

Today recycled?
Not a bad one
with its intense sun.
I smile at drivers passing me
who scowl at my pace, not realizing
they frown on recycle day.

"What day will you have back again"
Antranig Zarougian wrote,
"on your dying day,
if it were given, if it were given
to relive again?"

"Not my wedding day,"
he answered himself. "Not the day
of the birth of my child.
Not the hour of my greatest success.
But one day from my lost
childhood. Any day."

Any one day,
when there was such a thing
as childhood.
Before the genocide.

Before the nation
was orphaned. Any day
before we know we are cut down.

And this is the day,
driving, rolling along
not cut down, smiling in the sun.
The day we'll have back.

"Don't choose a special day"
Thornton Wilder advised.
"An ordinary day
will be extraordinary enough."

I will telephone everyone
to tell them the good news.
When all else is lost
we will have this day.

Charm Against Inertia

I fight listlessness
with energy from the steam
rising on the Black Sea.

My grandfather,
Hagop is walking

toward it, through Kharpert
to Samsun,
and the boat for Marseilles
and America.

He is thirteen.
He enters a dark forest
of brush and snakes
to pass water and gets lost.

He runs. He falls,
cuts his leg against
a stump. The scar will last
sixty three years past
1879.

But wait;
he finds the others
and they all reach the port.

The Turkish boatman
paid by their families,
demands another payment
to row them to the ship for America.

What shall we do?
Hagop has a plan: We will pay him
because we must get on the boat.
Trust me.

The oarsman delivers them to the ship.
He holds out the paper
for signatures he needs
to get the rest of his fee.

No, says Hagop, once aboard.
We won't sign.
Unless you give back the money
you cheated us of, on the shore.

It is returned with a shrug.
The mist rises from the water
like gauze, and I watch
the boat sail toward me.

What If

What if all the poets were rounded up and killed?
What if all the priests were executed?
What if all the men in the country
were drafted and then shot in front of ditches
they themselves had dug?
What if the government said: In two days
you must leave your home and belongings
taking only enough for two days on the road?
What if all the pretty girls were raped?
What if small children were taken
by families who wanted slaves
or pets? What if everyone in your family
was pushed into the Euphrates?
What if you alone, with an older girl,
made it to Baku?
What if in Baku you met compatriots
who had been there for centuries
and there you grew?
What if you lived until old age
with your children and then again
eight years ago men came

and burned your home again?
What if you were forced again to leave?
What if you reached other Armenians
in Karabagh?
What if they were being bombed and maimed
and blockaded?
What if you were asked again to leave?
What if you were over eighty
and everything that had happened to you
was happening again
and again the world did not believe you?
What if it were you and not me.

Every Woman

Every woman who has loved you, every hand
that pressed, caressed, shaped the man
you've become, every female—mother, child
who claimed, tamed, calmed or drove you wild;
every woman in your life I bless,
thanking them for this happiness.

Whether redemption or temptation to your soul,
whether she pulled you apart or made you whole,
everyone you've loved I love from your past,
everywhere you walked, every shadow cast.
But I can't promise to care for (should there be)
a successor. Let her love me.

Shifting the Sun

When your father dies, say the Irish,
you lose your umbrella against bad weather.
May his sun be your light, say the Armenians.

When your father dies, say the Welsh,
you sink a foot deeper into the earth.
May you inherit his light, say the Armenians.

When your father dies, say the Canadians,
you run out of excuses. May you inherit
his sun, say the Armenians.

When your father dies, say the French,
you become your own father.
May you stand up in his light, say the Armenians.

When your father dies, say the Indians,
he comes back as the thunder.
May you inherit his light, say the Armenians.

When your father dies, say the Russians,
he takes your childhood with him.
May you inherit his light, say the Armenians.

When your father dies, say the English,
you join his club you vowed you wouldn't.
May you inherit his sun, say the Armenians.

When you father dies, say the Armenians,
your sun shifts forever.
And you walk in his light.

Diaspora

"Children of massacre,
children of destruction
children of dispersion,
oh, my diaspora…"
someone was calling
in my dream.
Someone was explaining
why Armenian children
are raised with so much wonder, as if they
might disappear
at any moment.
"Tsak. Tsakoug."
Someone was explaining
why Armenian sons love
their mothers to excess,
why daughters-in-law are
cherished, why mothers-
in-law are treasured,
why everything
is slightly different
in an Armenian home,
stared at,
as if it might melt.
Someone was telling me
why Armenians love
earth and gardening so much
and why there is a hidden rage
in that love.
Someone was explaining
why I surround
myself with green plants
that do not flourish

in spite of great care.
"The slant of the sun is wrong."
Someone was gently chiding
for the strange angle of
my outside plants.
Someone was saying
I spoke English with a slight accent
even after three generations.
Someone was calling
in a forgotten language.

This Is for Zarif

who used to draw
in the mud of the water bank
with a stick and weave marvelous
stories for her little boy
in a village called Tadem,

who used to decorate
the tops of pastry with cut outs
of fantastic figures;
this is for Zarif
who did needlework
passably well
and figures faster than any man.
This is for Zarif
who prayed with two hands
and who wrote to her son
that although she could not watch him
while he was away at school
she knew he would want to be
like the other good men in his family
who did not smoke.

This is for that simple woman
who did not teach her son
to be a revolutionary
but when revolution came, hid a gun for him
in the garden, against bad days.

This is for Zarif whom the Turks beat,
asking the whereabouts of that son;

for Zarif who said over and over again
I do not know,
although she did.

This is for Zarif whose arm was smashed
then made raw then broken to pieces
then cut off while she repeated when she waked
she did not know.

This is for one-armed Zarif
who lived through hell;
who lived to see her grandchildren
in another world,
this is for her
who once held my right hand in her left
and never told me what I must do with mine.

Horses on the Roof

My father in a storm
of pigeons
in San Marco's Square
points up,

"Now look at those
horses well." His words
bring back Browning's
Last Duchess.

"They're yours,"
he says,
"They came with
Tiridates to Italy
in Nero's day
overland, not
to pollute the sea.
Perfect symbols
of our craft.
They blend bronze
with our tales
of fiery steeds.

"On such a beast
Sanasar flew
into the sun.
Just how these four
were planted
on this roof
is a mystery
to all except tourists
with Armenian blood."

We move in for a closer
view of horses
that can be seen
only from far away.

Songs of Bread*

You think I wrote from love.
You think I wrote from ease.
You imagine me singing as I walked
through wheat, praising bread.
You imagine me looking from my window
at my children in the grass, my wife
humming, my dog running, my sun
still warm. But this notebook is
drenched in blood. It is written in blood
in a wagon rolling past yellow,
amber, gold wheat. But in the dark,
in the smell of sweat, urine, vomit.
The song of blue pitchers filled
with sweet milk, the song of silver
fountains welcoming students home,
the song of silo, barn, harvest,
tiller and red soil, all written
in the dark. The Turks allowed it.
What harm in a pen soon to be theirs,
a notebook to be theirs, a coat,
theirs, unless too much blood splattered.
You read and picture me in
a tranquil village, a church, on
the Bosphorus, on a hillside, not
in anguish, not in fury, not wrenching
back the dead, holding the sun still
for a few more hours, making bread
out of words. This notebook you ransomed,
dear friend, postponed, delayed my storm.
You see only its calm.

---

*   Title of a volume of poems by Armenian poet Daniel Varoujan published after his death,
from his prison notebooks, kept while he was awaiting his execution (by stoning) at
the outset of the Turkish massacres of the Armenians in 1915. The notebook, *Songs of
Bread*, containing sunny, pastoral poems, was sold by his jailers to an Armenian priest.
The title poem was missing.

Translating I

I am sitting in a café in Prague
in my 1960 dancer's body
next to the table
where Marina Tsvetayeva,
tears in her eyes, waits
for you, anticipating
the kiss you will give.

She lights her cigarette
and looks up at you, hurrying
toward her, impatient
for the sweetness
to be transferred from
her tongue to yours.

I tense against the sight
of you rushing toward her.
You see only the blue lake
of her eyes where illusions
ride out the storm.

And I on the edge of despair
taste as much joy as you
on the brink of a poem
making much of time.

On Being Asked to Supply a Date of Birth for a Literary Encyclopedia

I am thirteen years old.
Forever. Pasternak said
he was fourteen. But I am
younger. Just starting
but no longer a child. And
aging fast. Although
the world stays new and
wet behind the ears. I just begin
to understand that I will never
understand. And I am in love
as if for the first time with
the written word. This affair
began when my grandfather promised
me that true love would always be
returned. I was conceived in 1915
when the blood of my other grandparents
soaked through the earth of Kharpert
and seeped, seeped until the thirties
when it reached Worcester, Massachusetts.
I was born in a garden when war cracked
the face of the earth that had not listened
to the 1915 blood. I was born in the New
York City subway when everyone turned
to stare at my American legs.
I was born in the Boston University
Mugar Library the first time
I heard Gerard Manley Hopkins
playing with words. I arrived
after difficult labor in the seventies
attended by physicians named Narek,
Siamanto and Varoujan who decided I might be
worth saving. That was thirteen years ago.

Translating II

I would run, run
to escape your blood
filled poems which
my father would recite.
I would dodge the ash
and smoke that hid
in your songs, Siamanto.

And who will bring,
who will bring
one handful of that sacred
ash to bury with
my exiled bones?

I ran
from tattooed skin that
bore the blue cross, ran
from numbers on the wrists.

I did not want to know
the poetry of wrongs.

And when my father died
and strangers came to say
your lines, a stranger
sprinkled sacred ash,
men who had heard the words
I would not hear.

And now I take your poems
and pound, pound them

into a raw new language
using all the force
of unshed tears.

Secret of Life

Once during the war
on a bus going to Portsmouth
a navy yard worker
told me the secret of life.

The secret of life, he said,
can never be passed down
one generation to the other.

The secret of life, he said,
is hunger. It makes you open doors.

The secret of life is food
and size decides clothes.

The secret of life, he said,
is hate. You become what you hate.

The secret of life, he said,
is water. The world will end
in flood.

The secret of life, he said,
is circumstance.

If you catch the right bus
at the right time
you will sit next
to the secret teller

who will whisper it
in your ear.

From Ruin to Ruin

Hospitality was bred
into our blood and bones.
Our doors were always open,
our ovens always warm.

Even when invaders came
we welcomed them until
we learned they were a fury;
they were a scourge and storm.

We loved the little piece of land
left to us, and our tongue.
We praised dry gullies, crags,
and scarfs of soil with song.

We honed cathedrals out of rock,
worshiped valleys greened by flood.
We thought the land would love us back,
soaked as it was in our blood.

We never expected it to fall
on both sides of our life,
nor roads to lead to darkness,
for those who worshiped light.

Are those who love life too much
the best beloved of death?
Do those who sing with too much joy
have measures on their breath?

We will not praise you anymore,
mountains, rivers, cliffs.
Not toast life except to say
how brief is every gift.

MICHAEL J. ARLEN

Michael J. Arlen was born in 1930 in London, England, and came to the United States in 1940. He attended Harvard University (1948–1952), worked as a reporter for *Life* magazine (1952–1956), and for many years was the television critic for *The New Yorker*. Parts of *Exiles* and the entire text of *Passage to Ararat*—his only work dealing specifically with Armenian themes—also originally appeared in *The New Yorker*.

The son of the Armenian writer Dickran Kouyoumdjian (1895–1956, pseudonym Michael Arlen), Arlen repeatedly explores the father/son relationship, one of the central themes of twentieth-century literature. D. H. Lawrence, Franz Kafka, Charles Bukowski, Thomas Wolfe—all devoted considerable thought to the meaning of fatherhood. As Henry Miller wrote of D. H. Lawrence:

> Why is the Oedipal so dominant in Lawrence's work—not
> only in Lawrence but in so many men of genius, noticeably
> the moderns? Because it is the central theme of the artist's
> conflict with life, the root-pattern of his struggle to
> emancipate himself, to raise himself to fatherhood—that is
> to restore the great religious motive of life....This search for
> God and fatherhood is only the expression of the search for
> one's true self.*

This is also true of Armenian American writers such as William Saroyan, Peter Sourian, David Kherdian, and Peter Najarian. In the case of Arlen, the relationship is further complicated by the fact that his father sought to suppress

---

* Henry Miller, *The World of Lawrence: A Passionate Appreciation* (Santa Barbara, CA: Capra Press, 1980), pp. 133, 134.

all aspects of his Armenian identity. Kouyoumdjian's own father, Sarkis, had fled Turkish persecution and brought his family from Armenia to Bulgaria and thence to England in 1901. Yet in order to "fit in" with literary life in England in the Twenties—Kouyoumdjian knew Lawrence, Aldous Huxley, H. G. Wells, Arnold Bennett, and W. Somerset Maugham—he essentially erased his own Armenian heritage. The success of his novel *The Green Hat* and subsequent novels enabled him to live the high life as a sophisticated, well-dressed dandy at European hotels, to send his children to private schools, and to drive a yellow Rolls-Royce through the streets of London: completely "assimilated," more British than the British.

Yet the greatest literary genius of the time—D. H. Lawrence—found things to like about him. In a letter to Lady Ottoline Morrell, 12 December 1915, he wrote:

> Kouyoumdjian seems a bit blatant and pushing; you may
> be put off by him. But that is because he is very foreign,
> even though he doesn't know it himself. In English life he is
> in a strange, alien medium, and he can't adjust himself. But
> I find the core of him very good. One must be patient with
> his jarring manner, and listen to the sound decency that is
> in him. He is not a bit rotten, which most young cultivated
> Englishmen are.

Lawrence modeled the character Michaelis in *Lady Chatterley's Lover* after Arlen—the Irish playwright with whom Connie has an affair. Lawrence catches here quite accurately Kouyoumdjian's inability to "adjust himself" and it is precisely this sense of exile and alienation which he bequeathed unknowingly to his son.

In *Exiles* (1970), Arlen fils traces his family history, his time in boarding schools, his mother's (a Greek-American countess) alcoholism, his doomed affair with a girl he met at Harvard, and the increasingly fraught relationship of his parents. Arlen describes in some detail the upper-class life of a famous English writer of the times among the "beautiful people": the stays in hotels in Cannes, servants, swims on the beach. All is related without commentary, in a detached style which seems to float off the surface of things. There is an ambivalent aspect to the narration: it is as if the author is present in these events, but in a sense they are merely happening to him and he seems at times an uninvolved observer. The "Anglo-Saxon" cool, analytical personality of the father pervades the son's style. The question of Armenian identity appears here only fleetingly when we are told that his father was glad to change his name: "[it was] a change I think he was fully pleased to make, he was never much for Armenian pride, at least when he felt it limiting."

The Armenian theme, however, takes center stage in Arlen's best work—*Passage to Ararat* (1975)—which appeared at the time in American history when ethnicity began to emerge as a key concern among immigrant groups. Until that point in the United States, it was common for "foreigners" (the term often used quite unselfconsciously when I was a child in the fifties to describe those from other lands) to change their last names in order to erase the traces of their cultures of origin.

Arlen—like Armenian American writers such as Peter Najarian, David Kherdian, and Peter Sourian—is involved in a search for his own buried self and the meaning of the suffering of his ancestors. He combines personal memoir with the quest for self-education—through travel and reading about Armenian history. He learns that history in order to discover his own past and in the process communicates this newfound knowledge to the reader, who thereby shares in the process of self-discovery. The effort of Armenian writers to confront the Genocide recalls Suren Bartevian, who struggled to write "the great elegy, the splendid epic poem...the divine and eternal 'Book of Blood'"; Armenian American writers have also struggled to create the great elegy.

Arlen describes his own effort to come to know his Armenian ancestry and recalls feverishly devouring Xenophon's *Anabasis,* which he had read thirty years earlier without noticing that "much of the retreat of the Ten Thousand took place through the Armenian high country." He describes reading, among other volumes, Movses Khorenatsi's *History of Armenia*, Dickran Boyajian's *Armenia: The Case for a Forgotten Genocide*, Robert Curzon's *Travels in Armenia*, and Avedis Sanjian's *Colophons of Armenian Manuscripts, 1301–1408*.

As he delves more deeply into Armenia's history, he begins to learn about the Catastrophe about which his father had remained silent. He confesses, "I knew I should begin to read some of the 'difficult' books about the Armenians—namely, the post–First World War literature on the massacres—but I found it hard to do so." However, he goes on to read Grace Knapp on the killings in Van and *The Treatment of Armenians in the Ottoman Empire, 1915–1916* by Viscount Bryce and Arnold Toynbee, as well as *Ambassador Morgenthau's Story*.

But in Yerevan, Arlen encounters an Armenian named Sarkis: "I walked along and thought, Sarkis has been trying to define me as an Armenian—but a certain kind of Armenian. Those damned massacres, I thought. That chauvinism, such a chauvinism of misfortune!" Arlen struggles with the legacy of Armenian impotence and self-hatred left by the Genocide and recalls sentiments very similar to those of the architect father of Peter Sourian's *The*

Gate: Armenians are trapped unhealthily and neurotically in the tragedies of the past.

Yet Arlen also tries to free himself from aspects of this Armenian self-hatred. During a trip to the Yerevan museum he writes:

> I remember staring dumbly at an enormous orange-colored
> wine jar, peering at it studiously, and thinking, my secret
> is that I have always hated being an Armenian. I haven't
> ignored it or been shy about it—I have hated it. Because I
> was given the values of the Europeans and they despised
> the Armenians. And I have hated my father not, as I have
> thought all these years, for being too strong a figure or too
> authoritarian—but because he, so to speak, stepped back
> and gave me to the Europeans.

It is sobering to remember that it was only recently that multiculturalism has become an accepted idea in American educational institutions: "The glory that was Greece and the grandeur that was Rome" unfortunately left out the rest of the cultural heritage of the entire globe. Arlen begins to connect his sense of identity-less-ness with the fact that his father deprived him of his own cultural heritage. After all, the Armenians—as my own grandfather Vagharshak Galoostian used to laughingly tell me—had created an alphabet and a magnificent literature at a time when "the British were painting their bodies blue."

Arlen describes his relationship to his father not only in *Exiles* and *Passage to Ararat* but also in his novel *Say Goodbye to Sam* (1984), in which a ferocious, dominating, and cruel movie scriptwriter named Sam Avery is unsparingly depicted. Tony Avery and his wife Catherine travel to the American Southwest to visit Sam and the father/son conflict is painfully documented, culminating in Sam's making a pass at Catherine. It is difficult after reading the nonfictional works not to see this novel as a continued working-out of the themes which appeared earlier, for again the son makes futile attempts to make contact with the father whose domineering ways leave little room for emotional closeness.

Arlen's work compels the reader to consider the intersection between social class, ethnic identity formation, and the important question of the Genocide in the development of Armenian American literature. What does it mean to be an Armenian in America? What is the process of assimilation? Does one choose to be an Armenian? Is it in fact an act of existential choice in which one decides to preserve the language, music, literature, and culture of one's ancestors? Arlen grew up in an emotionally constricted environment where the choice was clearly to pretend to not be Armenian.

Arlen's work ultimately sheds a complex light on the Armenian American experience and on the ambivalence and ambiguity of the relation to the Father/Homeland. Leon Surmelian, in an astute essay on Arlen, wrote:

> The inner tensions, most likely, are greater in the half-Armenian, who is more of a marginal person, belonging to a kind of third dimension in his makeup, neither wholly this or wholly that, but richer and sturdier for that reason, despite the agonies in the early phases of this split. These tensions are valuable for the artist. I hope they never fully relax in Arlen. He should nurse them as a poet. (*Ararat*, Autumn 1975)

In his best work—*Passage to Ararat*—Arlen succeeds in bringing to vivid life this "third dimension" and fathoms the poetic depths of the Armenian tragedy in ways that would have made his father proud.

David Stephen Calonne

from *Passage to Ararat*

Fresno, California: *"Fresno"* is a Spanish word meaning "ash tree." There are still some ash trees here, scattered far out of town, but the Spanish influence, as they call it, is pretty well gone by now, unless you count the roadside Margarita places and Taco Pete's. The Armenian presence is a little more visible, but not much. There are two Armenian churches. An Armenian bakery. Two or three Armenian restaurants. There used to be an Armenian community—"Armenian Town"—but it has largely disappeared, torn up to make way for the new expressway and the shopping center. There is a Basque presence, also an Italian presence, and a Japanese presence, but mainly a Wasp presence, for this is a California town, a micro-city. "Fresno: Pop. 180,000," say the big green signs. What is going on here is agribusiness, which means the great earth factory of the San Joaquin Valley: untold acres of farmland, fruitland, vineland. Trees and vines and pastureland extending for miles between the invisible Pacific and the dimly visible Sierra: snowcapped blue mountains seen through a bluish haze. Over on the coast is Monterey—John Steinbeck's Cannery Row and Tortilla Flat. Here was William Saroyan's hot, flat valley filled with fruit and crops and poverty and life. "A man could walk four or five miles in any direction from the heart of our city and see our streets dwindle to land and weeds," Saroyan wrote in the nineteen-thirties. "In many places the land would be vineyard and orchard land, but in most places it would be desert land and the weeds would be the strong dry weeds of deserts....Our trees were not yet tall enough to make much shade, and we had planted a number of kinds of trees we ought not to have planted because they were of weak stuff and would never live a century, but we had made a pretty good beginning. Our cemeteries were few and the graves in them were few. We had buried no great men because we hadn't had time to produce any great men, we had been too busy trying to get water into the desert." I don't know what I expected it to be like now. I know not like that, because nothing is like that any more—certainly not in California. I think I expected to see Armenian faces at the airport or on the street. I think I expected to walk off the plane and see Armenians hanging around the car-rental counters, behind the car-rental counters. Armenians—for it was our town, wasn't it?

I stood one afternoon in a field on the outskirts of the city and looked at the fruit trees, which were bare in the March wind, and looked at the grapevines, which were also bare—brown tendrils close to the brown soil, stretching out to the horizon as far as the eye could see. The man who owned the field was an Armenian named Gadalian. He had thick, graying hair and a wide, leathery face and thick hands. He was about fifty years old, but an outdoor fifty—square shoulders and a large, tough belly. He was worrying about frost. "The frost is strange here," he said. "It comes in waves across the valley. In one place there may be frost, but on the farm across the road there may be no frost. Look at this." He held up a grapevine that had been bent or broken around another vine. "Nobody knows how to work the vines any more," he said. It was a modest farm, about eighty acres. There was a comfortable small farmhouse on the edge of the property, just off the dirt road, with grapefruit trees in the front and a kennel for two or three large dogs in the back. We were standing next to a ramshackle old house or hut of dark redwood, weathered by rain and sun—a place for tools and empty boxes. "My father lived here," said Gadalian, pointing inside. "This is where we grew up. He was a good man, my father. He worked very hard."

My father committed no crime. The bare trees stretch out everywhere. Bare branches against the metallic gray sky. Plums. Peaches. Apples. Grapefruit. Grapes. Fertility. The bluish mountains swim in haze against the sky.

"Did you know the Armenians brought the melons to California?" said Gadalian. "The melon they call the Persian melon. The casaba melon, whose seeds come from Kasaba, in Turkey. Most of the melons in this valley were grown by Arakelian. They called old Arakelian the Melon King."

"Where is he?" I asked.

"He is dead, I think. Anyway, his sons have moved to Los Angeles."

"Are there many Armenians here?" I asked.

"There are some," he said. "There are not too many any more."

We stood beside stacks of empty raisin crates. Old boxes, weathered like the hut.

"Look at this one," said Gadalian, pointing to a box so old that its sides had started to split apart. "This one goes back to my father's time. Look at the way they made the corners."

"How is it your father came here?" I asked.

"I don't know," said Gadalian. Then, "I think he and my mother came from the old country around 1900, some time like that. For a while, they were in the East, around Worcester, Massachusetts. They worked in the shoe factories. There were a number of Armenians who worked in the shoe factories. Then they heard about California, where they could grow things."

"Was your father happy here?" I asked.

Gadalian seemed puzzled. "I don't know," he said. "It is hard to tell if a father is happy." Then, "He worked very hard. I remember that."

Little farms scattered around the great valley. These were some of the names on mailboxes: Pirogian, Kavanessian, Agajanian. A sign on an abandoned warehouse: "SIMOJIAN RAISINS, THE FINEST IN THE WORLD." I thought of Bud and his tropical fish in New York. I thought of my father, who had journeyed to Hollywood a number of times in his career but never to Fresno. What was here in Fresno? What had been here?

I thought of the simple warmth of a Saroyan story: "Walking along Alvin Street he felt glad to be home again. Everything was fine, common and good, the smell of earth, cooking suppers, smoke, the rich summer air of the valley full of plant growth, grapes growing, peaches ripening, and the oleander bush swooning with sweetness, the same as ever....This valley, he thought, all this country between the mountains, is mine, home to me, the place I dream about, and everything is the same."

I thought, too, of what a friend of Gadalian's had said when I asked him where most of the Armenians in Fresno lived.

"Oh, now they can live anywhere," he said.

"What do you mean, anywhere?"

"There are no more restrictions," he said. "Before, it wasn't always so easy. Of course, you have to understand that a lot of the first Armenians here were country people. Farmers. Rough people." He smiled. He had enormous hands, fingers as thick as roots, palms caked with dirt. "They took away the restrictions at the end of the war," he said. And "This valley is my home. It's the place I dream about." Sometimes the dreams of people make one gasp.

And now William Saroyan himself, standing in the lobby of the Fresno Hilton. William Saroyan at sixty-six. The hair thick but graying. A burly man. Stocky. A fine mustache. Also large hands. A laugh. Good eyes, a good face.

"I was out in the country," I said.

"It's beautiful, isn't it? You should come back in the summer," said Saroyan. "Of course, it is terrible in the summer. You sweat all day long. But then everybody is busy."

We drove through side streets, past the sterile glass office buildings of the new downtown, past the immense modern convention center. "Everything has changed," said Saroyan. "But of course it has changed. Look at that shopping center. Nobody comes to it. Do you see that street? I used to deliver papers up and down that street. It was a good job, too. The paper was called the Fresno *Republican*, and it was edited and published by Mr. Chester Rowell. Both are gone now, though there's a statue of the paper's founder in Courthouse Square."

We drove under a viaduct over which the new expressway was being built. The land ahead of us was mostly desolate from the bulldozers, but here and there a few small frame houses remained. "I'd show you where I grew up, but they tore that down, too," said Saroyan. "I hope for their sake more people use the new expressway than use the shopping center."

"There don't seem to be very many Armenians around," I said.

"There are still a few," said Saroyan. "Maybe ten thousand in the valley. But the town has grown, and the Armenians sold their land and moved to the cities."

"What about you?" I asked.

"I got tired of knocking around too much. One day, I decided to come back. Once you like a place, you always like it."

We drove away from the little streets and little houses, and out past the familiar landmarks of modern California: the endless strip of car lots and Mexican restaurants and bowling alleys and garden-supply stores and farm-hardware warehouses and motels with banquet and convention facilities.

I thought of a story of Saroyan's that I'd read long ago, which began, "I don't suppose you ever saw a two-hundred-and-fifty-pound Filipino." It's hard to forget a story that begins that way. I had read that story in school, when my favorite writers were Ernest Hemingway, Robert Benchley, and William Saroyan: Hemingway because he was so sexy with those sleeping bags; Benchley because he was so funny; and Saroyan because nobody could write to a person (me) the way that William Saroyan wrote.

There was another story, which I'd read on the plane to California—a story called "Five Ripe Pears." It began like this: "If old man Pollard is still alive I hope he reads this because I want him to know I am not a thief and never have been. Instead of making up a lie, which I could have done, I told the truth, and got a licking. I don't care about the licking because I got a lot of them in grammar school.... The licking Mr. Pollard gave me I didn't deserve, and I hope he reads this because I am going to tell him why. I couldn't tell him that day because I didn't know how to explain what I knew.... It was about spring pears." It was not an important story, but it was a lovely story—a story with a voice. It made one think with a kind of pleasure that J. D. Salinger must have heard that voice, and Richard Brautigan, and Jack Kerouac, and all those writers of the personal sound, the flower-writers, the writers of our modern Era of Feeling.

"I'm glad you decided to find out about Armenians," said Saroyan. "They're a crazy people, you know. Or sometimes they seem that way. But they're a very simple people."

We drove on awhile. Saroyan talked about his children—a daughter in New York, a son in San Francisco. Family talk. He asked me about my wife and children, about my sister, about my work. I felt something surprisingly paternal in his voice. It was a strange, deep feeling, as if we had known each other all along, when in fact I had met Saroyan only once before, briefly, a few years ago in New York, and had called him in Fresno only a week earlier to arrange our meeting.

We stopped to have dinner at a roadside restaurant, a roadside Armenian restaurant called Stanley's. A nice place, too, with bright lights and the ubiquitous Olde Steake House furniture and a photograph of Mt. Ararat behind the cashier's desk.

"Sometime, I hope you'll meet my Uncle Aram," said Saroyan. "He's eighty-two now, and a fine man. I've written a lot of stories about Aram. People would ask me, 'Are they true stories?' I'd always reply, 'Of course not.

I am a writer. I make things up. I embellish.' But it's been hard to embellish Aram."

Saroyan began to tell some stories about his Uncle Aram in a loud, resonant voice. The waiter brought some Armenian bread and a bottle of wine, then shish kebab. Saroyan laughed as he spoke. I looked at him and thought, My father was sixty when he died; he would be seventy-nine now. I thought of my father's frailness, his thin elegance; it seemed like such a different presence.

"You know, your father was a fine man," Saroyan said, as if he were reading my mind.

"Did you think of him as an Armenian?" I asked.

"Of course I did," said Saroyan. "An Armenian can never not be an Armenian. But your father went about it differently. I think he had other things on his mind."

"What kind of things?"

"I don't know," said Saroyan. "The truth is, I didn't see him often. We were different. But we were also close. I can't quite explain it. I remember the first time I met him. It was just after the war. I heard he was in New York, and I was passing through, and so I telephoned. We met at some hotel—the Hampshire House, or maybe the Pierre. I remember how we embraced; that is what I remember. Another time, this was a few years later, we had dinner at that restaurant—did you ever go?—the Golden Horn, and afterward we went back to where I was living. I had an apartment that winter on Central Park West. We talked about writing and families, I remember. Your father was about to start another book; at least, that is what he said, although I guess he never finished it. But it was a close time. I remember him standing in the corridor and looking in on our children, who were sleeping. The children were very young and they kept stirring in their sleep, and your father kept saying 'shhh,' the way fathers do."

I thought of that photograph in the Golden Horn. The two comrades, the two Armenian writers—both of them in fact then passing the peak of their fame, my father putting on a graceful front of having "retired," Saroyan both more and less fortunate in not being able to retire but, instead, turning out a stream of novels and plays that critics were beginning to say did not compare to the early work.

A waitress came over to Saroyan with a menu she wished him to autograph. Saroyan signed it with a flourish and then asked her to sign one for him.

"I will tell you," Saroyan said to me. "If you want to know about Armenians, then you must go to Armenia, or what remains of it. You must go to Erevan—in Soviet Armenia."

"Have you been there?" I asked.

"Yes, I've been there. I went there the first time I earned any money. This was in 1935, and it wasn't much money, either. I went to New York and took one of those beautiful ships they had then. The *Berengaria*. I went to Europe and then to Soviet Armenia. They didn't have much in Armenia in those days, but it was a trip I had to make. I went back once again, in 1960."

"What did you find out when you went there?" I asked.

"I found out that there was an Armenia," said Saroyan. "Of course, it isn't what it used to be, but it *is* there; it is something."

We went back to Saroyan's house: a small tract house on one of the new streets—a modest house, on a street lined with perhaps a hundred similar houses. Inside, there was an extraordinary jumble of objects: not so much a disorder as a plenitude of things—books, and cartons, and suitcases, and boxes of this and that. In a large room off the kitchen, a tiny portable typewriter stood in the middle of a table piled with books and paper and manuscript. "I've always worked, and so I work now," said Saroyan. "Besides, I have to live."

"What are you writing?" I asked.

"I mostly write plays now. Sometimes people want to produce them, sometimes they do not. But that is what I do. Besides, my writing is better than my painting." He pointed to innumerable bright-colored abstract designs that had been pinned or Scotch-taped to the walls. Then he bent down in front of a pile of dusty magazines and pulled one out. "Did you ever see this?" he said. It was a copy of an old English-language Armenian magazine. Saroyan opened it to a picture of my father; in fact, it was reproduction of a photograph that had appeared on a cover of *Time* in 1927—now with a short note beside it on the "popular Anglo-Armenian novelist, formerly Dikran Kouyoumdjian." Saroyan held the magazine open for a moment, and then put it down on the table. "It's a good photo of him, isn't it?" he said. "Such confidence."

"How is it that he never wrote anything serious about Armenians?" I asked.

"I think he wasn't that kind of writer," Saroyan said. "He liked to be entertaining. He made a couple of good jokes about Armenians, as I remember."

"Yes," I said. "But how is it that you wrote all the time about Armenians and he never did?"

"I don't know," said Saroyan. "Except that we all go on different journeys. Just like you. Now you come here. And soon, I think, you must go to Erevan."

We stood in the semidarkness of Saroyan's small house, surrounded by the clutter, the books, the magazines, the cartons, the jars of "treasures" that Saroyan had picked up on his travels or on the street. "I am a writer," Saroyan said. "It is something to be a writer. All my life, I have written. Also talked and drunk and gambled and everything else." He laughed. "They say that Armenians live to be very old. Did you know that?" My grandmother Lucy Saroyan died at eighty-eight. My father's kid brother Mihran died at eighty. Come on. Let's go and look at the graveyard."

It was now midnight, or a bit later. We got in the car and drove through the silent streets of Fresno. It was hard to tell in which direction we were going—out toward the country or in toward the downtown. Darkened houses flicked by in the night. "It is too bad you don't know Armenian," Saroyan said. "Although you will survive. But it is a marvelous language— marvelous sounds. Do you know their songs? I shall sing one for you."

Saroyan sang, rolling down the window of the car. Outside, it had begun to rain—one of those fine, sprinkling nighttime rains. Saroyan's voice filled the car, the countryside silent except for the sound of our tires on the wet road. "It is a song about love and injustice and about pomegranates getting ripe," said Saroyan. "In other words, about the important things in life."

The car stopped beside the road. "Come on," he said, getting out. The rain was pouring down more heavily, but the air was warm and had a kind of fragrance. "Now, over there is the Protestant graveyard," he said. "And somewhere down there are the Catholics. And right here are the Armenians." Saroyan was wearing an old hat, a kind of old newspaperman's hat—a hat from *The Time of Your Life*, maybe. Now he began to run at a trot through the graveyard. We passed dim gravestones in the darkness. "Over there is Levon!" he called. "I think one of Lucy's sisters is here!" the grass was soft and slippery underfoot. Saroyan kept up a steady jog. "I think somewhere over there is Uncle Mihran!" He stopped, breathing heavily. "You know, everybody seems the same in a graveyard—Protestant, Catholic, and Armenian. But still there is something different. I don't know what it is." He wiped his forehead, which was damp with rain and sweat. "Come on," he said. "It's wet here. It's time to go home."

Later on, when we said goodbye, Saroyan embraced me. I could feel his rough cheek scrape against mine. His rough, robust cheek. "Fathers and sons are always different," he said. "But they are also the same. Maybe you will find out about that, too. Anyway, I was truly fond of him and now I am fond of you, and that is something, is it not?" He clasped my hand, and put the newspaperman's hat back on his head, and tugged his jacket about him more closely, for a cold wind was blowing now, and stuffed his hands in his pockets, and turned back to the car, and got in and drove away across "the valley full of plant growth, grapes growing, peaches ripening, and the oleander bush swooning with sweetness," to the house with the cartons and suitcases and the small portable typewriter.

I watched him go, still feeling the roughness of his face against mine.

Our hotel was oddly gracious, or almost gracious: a large, old-fashioned place, also built out of the ubiquitous pink stone, and fronting on the central square. Lenin Square, although apart from the predictable and rather modest statue of Himself—not in the middle of it, either, but off to one side—there were few signs of Soviet style either outside the hotel or within it. There was the standard Soviet watch-lady on our floor, but she had a classic Armenian face. An ample, dark-haired woman seated upon a wicker chair, looking at television.

Our room was also large and old-fashioned: the usual bedroom and, in addition, a studio room—doubtless provided by the Cultural Committee—containing some simple wooden furniture and a piano. I sat for a moment in a chair in our room. Our room with the piano—our room in Armenia. Oh, I had mixed feelings. I knew not which.

We went out onto the street. There was a small park near the hotel. An ice-cream stand at the entrance. A bootblack with an elaborate "customer's chair," made out of leather and brass, each part of it finely polished and shining in the sun. Inside the park there were more men playing chess, and children swinging on a half-dozen swings. The children with large brown eyes. Armenian children! It was a gay scene, a summer's scene. The dust from the dirt paths rose beneath our feet. Children's laughter sounded in the leaves. I wanted to embrace them—to embrace somebody. But I could not. A voice inside me spoke: You have come this far. You must make a connection. But I could not. I knew, too, that it was a question not of my having to rush and embrace some stranger—for my temperament always stopped me short of such gestures—but only of my *feeling* something: of feeling real warmth as opposed to the pale heat of (in this case) literary sensibility. Old men and children in a park! A summer's scene! An Armenian scene! But I felt frozen.

"Now, *there's* an Armenian!" I heard my wife say.

I looked where she had been looking—toward a group of people gathered around some chess players. On the outside of the group were some young men, perhaps in their early twenties. One of them stood out from all the rest:

tall, curly-haired, quite fiercely handsome. I knew which one she meant, but I said, "Who?"

My wife laughed. She was easily made shy. "Oh," she said. "You know which one." Now she was embarrassed. "The one with the blue shirt. Isn't he striking?"

I looked at him again. Yes, he was striking. He was a fine young man. But somehow I felt incapable of replying, of responding. It was quite startling. I knew that it wasn't on account of some simple jealousy—it didn't seem to have much to do with *him*. It was as if I had been found out in something— something that had to do with how *I* cared about the way Armenians looked, and that I couldn't bear to admit.

Just then, a voice behind me said, in English, "I thought I'd find you here. It is a lovely park, is it not?"

We turned to see a square-shouldered man in a brown suit—a man of medium build, of medium age, with a hard Armenian face, which seemed to be smiling.

"Permit me to introduce myself," he said. "I am Sarkis. I am not your guide. Your guide is an excellent young man who is always occupied. I am your friend." He paused, then stepped forward and shook my wife's hand in a vigorous and awkward grip, and then threw his arms around me in an embrace. "Welcome to Armenia!" he said.

How to describe this Sarkis, who had arrived apparently from nowhere, and who now walked beside us—a bustling, short-legged figure in a brown suit (an unusually warm brown suit for the season), gesticulating, talking? Our friend? In reality, the mystery of his appearance soon became less mysterious, yet it was still fascinating, for, although neither officially a guide nor precisely an interpreter, he was in private life a teacher, a teacher of English at a local high school, who maintained, as he put it, "connections" with the Cultural Committee, and who periodically offered his services to visitors—to sympathetic visitors.

"I knew right away that you would be sympathetic," he said as we walked across the street toward the central square. "Besides, you are Armenian. All Armenians are sympathetic to one another, are they not?"

I nodded. I could see my wife smiling, walking lightly. She was pleased that we had found a friend—at least, a "personal contact," not one of those mechanical guides we had dreaded. It occurred to me that she liked Armenians better than I did.

"Is your father still living?" Sarkis asked me.

I said no.

"I understand he was a writer, also," Sarkis said. "Unfortunately, I have never read his work. Did he ever travel to Soviet Armenia?"

"He never did," I said.

"What a pity," Sarkis said. "I am sure he would have liked it. He would have admired the achievements of the Armenian people."

"Yes, I'm sure he would have," I said.

Sarkis turned to my wife. "Did you know his father?"

"No, I didn't," she said. "I wish I had."

"I am sure he was a wonderful man," said Sarkis. "Armenian men make wonderful fathers. They worship their families. They would do anything for their families."

We stood now in the middle of the square, beside some fountains. I thought, Why won't this man stop about my father—about fathers, Armenian fathers? I knew it was a childish thought, and disliked myself for thinking it, and Sarkis for making me think it.

My wife apparently noticed a new expression on my face. "What's the matter?" she asked.

Sarkis overheard. In some ways, he was obviously very agile. "Is something the matter?" he said. "Probably you are tired after your long voyage. Forgive me for talking so much, but in these parts one rarely has a chance for such international conversation."

He was so singular and charming I couldn't imagine what anger, or peevishness, had possessed me. "I think it's mostly hunger," I said.

We walked over to our hotel.

"You have lunch," said Sarkis. "I have some business to attend to. Afterward, I am going to take you somewhere very special."

My wife and I found a table in the hotel restaurant—a large, high-ceilinged room crowded with customers and waiters (Armenian customers! Armenian waiters!), all of them speaking not Russian but Armenian. A beaming waiter presented an enormous menu with virtually all the items crossed out. We ordered a dried-beef dish, some kind of greenish salad, and a white wine. Four men at a nearby table were drinking brandy and singing—a soft and almost dainty melody.

Once again, everything seemed gay though somehow oppressive. My wife talked excitedly of her impressions of the new city. I felt myself silent, trying to listen, trying to listen to everything.

"What happened to you out there?" she asked.

"It was nothing," I said.

"Was it all that about your father?"

"Perhaps that was a bit of it," I said. "I don't know why."

"But Armenians always go on like that," she said. "You told me so yourself. You mustn't mind it."

"I know," I said. Then, because it was what I felt, I said, "You know, I don't think I really *like* Armenians."

"You know you don't mean that," she said. She smiled. Beside us, the singing rose into a kind of march. The waiters clapped their hands. We had more wine and finished off the greenish salad, which was mostly scallions, with a kind of bitter pungent taste.

Sarkis reappeared outside. He was in command of an ancient Russian touring car, a definitely imposing vehicle of unnamed manufacture and of vaguely czarist inclinations: faded limousine upholstery, remains of a lap-robe cordon in the back (without the lap robe), and little, tattered curtains on the side windows, bespeaking a romantic past of modest bureaucratic trysts or kidnappings, or both.

"Naturally, it is not mine," said Sarkis, seeming very pleased. "I have borrowed it from the Committee. Naturally, it belongs to the State."

"I had hoped it was Armenian—an Armenian car," my wife said.

"I do not think so," said Sarkis. Then, "You are not joking?"

"No, I wasn't," she said.

"Armenians make many valuable things now in Armenia," said Sarkis. "In America, how do you call them—products? Armenians make electrical products. They make computers. Armenians make excellent computers. Look!" He pointed to a cloud of dark smoke on the horizon. "You call that pollution, but we are still poorer than you. We call it industry."

"Are we going to a factory now?" I asked, for I had come prepared to visit many factories.

"No," said Sarkis. "Not today. The Committee will arrange for you to visit factories. Today, on your arrival, I am taking you on a special trip—to a place that all Armenians would want to visit. I am taking you to a *hallowed* place. We call it the Monument—the Monument to the Armenian Martyrs."

We climbed into the front seat of the limousine, squeezed in beside Sarkis, who handled the old machine with a classic pedagogic mixture of vagueness and speedway fervor. "I do not drive very often," he said disarmingly, "although I had a motorcycle for many years."

It didn't seem right to inquire what had happened to the motorcycle.

We drove down one of the wide boulevards, a long, straight roadway lined with trees, which led toward the semicircle of low hills.

The olive-colored leaves were deep green as we came closer. There were flowers beside the road, and a few houses. It seemed suddenly as if we were in a different country—as if we had left the Balkans behind us in the dusty city and were now motoring through some familiar minor bit of Europe. There were orange-tiled roofs on the poorish stone houses, red flowers in the skimpy gardens. Some goats wandered beside the road.

Then even this feeling of Europe died out. Meadows of yellow-green grass extended on all sides. The fields were flat and dry and full of stones. You could see clusters of trees against the horizon, far away, and a few scattered houses, far away—and, yet farther away, the mass of Ararat, not quite in front of us but dominating the land, its summit of snow on a level with the clouds.

"Every Armenian in the world should visit this monument," Sarkis was saying. "Every Armenian should know what it is to stand before it and feel in his bones the tragedy of Armenia." He turned to my wife. "The suffering of the Armenian people has been enormous," he said. "Enormous. Incomprehensible. Are you acquainted with the suffering of the Armenian people?"

"I've read something about it," she said. "It seemed truly terrible."

"Ah, you've read about it," he said. "Your husband must be a good Armenian. He understands that it is necessary for us to speak out about these things." With one hand he reached out and clasped my arm. "Have you told her what happened at Van and Bitlis? Have you told her how the Turks clubbed our poor people to death? Have you told her how they tortured our men and raped our women?" He turned to my wife. "Did you know, my dear, that they burned priests on crosses and killed small infants with their bayonets? Yes, that is right. Small infants. They killed small children with their knives and bayonets. Oh, it was surely horrible, the most horrible of deeds."

I was conscious of the dry straw of the fields floating past us. Sarkis stared straight ahead. Ararat was a dream.

Sarkis said, "To be an Armenian is to have this intolerable weight of sadness on one's soul. That is what one of our Armenian poets said. Is it not true?"

In a moment, he said, "Armenians can never forget what happened to them. Armenians must never forget. It was a genocide. Do you know, it was the world's first genocide."

It seemed as if we drove for hours, but it was less than one hour. The heat was everywhere. There were no people—only yellow fields shimmering in the sun. Sarkis stopped the car—our destination.

We climbed some stone steps. There was a stone walk. "You should take off your coat," Sarkis said. I took off my coat. I felt oddly grateful that he had said that. In front of us, about a half mile away, was an unusual structure. It had the appearance of a kind of Stonehenge—columns, metallic columns rising out of the ground, but angled inward. A Stonehenge of slanted slabs.

"How beautiful!" I could hear my wife saying. "How extraordinary!"

"Of course it is beautiful," Sarkis said. He walked just a step in front of us. For some reason, I was conscious of his stride—a stolid, heavy gait—and of his belly, which seemed not so much fat as hard, a politician's belly.

Suddenly he stooped down and plucked a little flower from the grass beside the walk. He looked at me. "For our Armenian martyrs," he said.

I was conscious of his eyes on me, my wife's eyes on me. On all sides of us I could see fields stretching away into the distance. I knew there were flowers beneath my gaze, but I could see no flowers. I kept on walking.

In the center of the slanted columns stood a large vessel—a metal bowl—with a flame burning inside it.

We stood beneath the columns looking at the bowl and the flame.

"Think of the Armenians who died," said Sarkis, almost in a whisper. "Think of your martyred countrymen. Think what it is to be an Armenian."

Sarkis's voice was only a murmur, but it seemed to roar in my ears. I knew that I felt nothing. An image flickered through my mind of soldiers in a First World War movie advancing in slow motion across a muddy field, being mown down in slow motion by machine-gun fire, turning, falling, falling in silence. Sarkis reached out toward me and put the flower he had been holding into my hand.

"I save this for you," he said. "For your offering."

I looked at him. "I can't," I said.

For a moment, we looked at one another. I could find no meaning in his glance or mine.

"Please..." my wife said.

The flower—it was a kind of buttercup, I think—was in my palm. I took a few steps forward and placed it—gently dropped it—in the flaming bowl. And turned and began to walk back slowly, away from the bowl and out from beneath the overhanging columns.

Sarkis and my wife were a step or so behind me, then beside me. They were talking about the Monument. "Each year in April," Sarkis was saying, "our people come down here from Erevan to bow their heads. Some of them even make the journey on foot."

I thought, I have come this far—so close—but I seem unable to go further, to make the connection.

Over my shoulder I glimpsed Ararat in the distance: a blue shape in a bluish haze. It seemed as silent as the dry fields, as the yellow flowers, as everything in sight. I thought quite simply, How strange to have no country. Just then, a breeze from somewhere rippled the fields. I heard my wife's laugh. The flowers swayed in the breeze from the blue mountain.

DAVID KHERDIAN

Over a writing career spanning some forty years, David Kherdian has published fifty books in nearly every genre, including poetry, children's books, memoirs, novels, biographies, and bibliographies. He has also edited nine volumes, co-founded two journals, edited another, translated and retold ethnic stories from the Armenian and allegories from the Chinese and the Gnostics, and started three literary presses. He is the most prolific Armenian American writer of his generation, and one of the most important of any generation.

David Kherdian was born in Racine, Wisconsin, in 1931. Both of his parents were survivors of the Armenian Genocide. Veron was a homemaker, and Melkon a blue-collar worker for J. I. Case Company, a machine manufacturer that was also the largest employer in Racine. The town was typically Midwestern, low in high culture, small enough to keep kids safe, big enough to satisfy their appetite for adventure. To the west end was "Island Park," to the east Lake Michigan, and through the length of the town the Root River ran. Kherdian wrote, "Ours was a city of parks and bridges: tiny parks, short bridges, with each representing a span in fact and in time."

Kherdian was not a bookish kid. He shot baskets on the sandlot until dark, spent Saturday afternoons at the movies, fished for perch off Lake Michigan's piers, and in the fall and winter hunted with his friends for small game in the neighboring woods. Upon leaving high school he became a door-to-door magazine salesman for Crowell-Collier Publishing Company, and then he was drafted into the army for the Korean War. The soldiers were shipped overseas, and for most of the thirteen-day trip young Kherdian went AWOL— impossibly, right on the boat. When they finally arrived in Japan, Kherdian was told he would be among five hundred soldiers who would remain there. The balance of the five thousand men would be dispatched to Korea.

Straight out of college, he'd landed in San Francisco. It was 1960 and the city was the hotbed of a poetry renaissance that was beginning to spread across the country. He drank beer with Lew Welch and Allen Ginsberg, shot pool with Richard Brautigan, and roomed across the way from Philip Whalen. He wasn't writing poetry at the time, but instead putting together a bibliography of William Saroyan. Kherdian published the bibliography in 1965 (the first such resource on Saroyan and still definitive). Soon to follow was *Six Poets of the San Francisco Renaissance: Portraits and Checklists*, comprised of the Beat poets Snyder, Meltzer, Ferlinghetti, McClure, Whalen, and Brother Antoninus, published after Kherdian had moved to Fresno, where he set up The Giligia Press. Under that imprint he published his first book of poems, *On the Death of My Father*. Saroyan titled it and wrote an introduction, calling the title poem "one of the best lyric poems in American poetry." Though Kherdian was obviously at the "heart" of the Beat movement, and in the late sixties taught one of the first courses ever on the Beats—at Fresno State College of all places—he never joined the club. What attracted him to this movement was its energy and nerve. When he published, in 1995, *Beat Voices: An Anthology of Beat Poetry*, he explained: "They were authentic poets who had something urgent to say, and were willing to pay the price for their assaults on the status quo." For the rest that followed—the long hair, psychedelics, and moonbeams—Kherdian had no interest, and turned to go his own way.

He has never allowed the latest trends in literature to dictate his direction as a writer, but in several instances he has anticipated those trends. In 1995 he started the journal *Forkroads*, one of the first journals to champion multicultural writing, but nearly twenty years earlier he had published what is likely the first anthology with the same theme, titled *Settling America: The Ethnic Expression of 14 Contemporary American Poets*. *The Road from Home*, a somewhat fictionalized biography of his mother's survival of the Genocide, paved the way for similar books, including Nancy Kricorian's *Zabel*, Micheline Marcom Aharonian's *Three Apples Fell from Heaven*, and Adam Bagdasarian's *Forgotten Fire*. Another seminal work was *Down at Santa Fe Depot: 20 Fresno Poets*, a 1970 anthology that helped put the Central Valley poets on the national map, and began an explosion of small press books devoted to regional writing.

Kherdian's own place, Racine, has been the focus of twelve books that make up his Root River Cycle. The first book in the cycle, *Homage to Adana*, was published in 1971, and the last, titled *Letters to My Father*, was issued in 2004. Whatever form they take—novellas, short essays, poems, memoirs—

the books amount to a rich and detailed tableau of the town. Kherdian moves from places (the Armenian Coffee House, the Danish Old People's Home) and persons (the Greek Popcorn Man, State Street Harry, United States Tony) to outings (crab catching, fishing) and relationships, and tells about them all in a clear and conversational style, as if he were sitting down with friends and family after a long absence in order to acknowledge the unspoken vows and taken-for-granted intersections that gave their daily life together its solidity, dignity, and rhythm. In these books, we also find Kherdian acutely tuned to the preconscious mood of the town—the way lamplight falls upon a barren street, the humming sound of a bus taking men to work at dawn, the waves lapping at the lake's shore. And as it wends through the town, under bridges and past parks, the deep and silently running Root River seems to stand for the unconscious, the ever-giving yet unpredictable source that gives Racine ("root" in French)—and indeed Kherdian's writing—its very life pulse.

Many of the episodes in the cycle are written from the perspective of a mature man looking through the eyes of a young boy, and others are reflections on childhood itself. In "The Child," from *I Called It Home*, Kherdian seems to sum up the entire project and its vital necessity for him: "The child's world is numerous, but the place of his birth is the only place there is. Faraway places do not figure in the life of his imagination, for the other side of the city is already beyond his comprehension." Kherdian continues:

> Thrown into the pool of life, we follow the concentric
> circles out, little by little, and each of us stops at a different
> place, with some of us never able to stop, until, having
> circled the globe, we return to our one spot and look at it
> again, carefully, within the perspective now of time, and
> wonder again what it was that brought us here, and what it
> was that brought us back.

Kherdian has worked over the years in several styles, from lyrical poetry to short prose to Haiku-like bursts of observation. He is hardly a philosophically showy writer, though one can sense a quiet mystical strain running through much of his work. Neither is he formally experimental. He goes straight to the heart of the matter, often urgently, and rarely pauses to strike a pose. Self-conscious irony, pastiche, parody, and cleverness—the four lethal horsemen of contemporary American fiction—have never found a foothold in Kherdian's writing. Like his mentor Saroyan, his clear and open-handed style gives much to the reader, but perhaps not surprisingly, it leaves little for the critics to chew on.

In 1971 Kherdian edited the Armenian American literary journal *Ararat*, and he has written much about the Armenian American experience through the eyes of survivors and their children; but it has hardly been his primary concern. He seems to see the experience of victimization as part of a cultural and even spiritual condition that a vast part of humanity shares, and for which the universal remedy is compassion and forgiveness—toward the aggressors but also toward oneself. From 1974 to 1986 Kherdian, with his wife, the Caldecott-winning illustrator Nonny Hogrogian, entered into a period of intense reflection and spiritual training in line with the teachings of Gurdjieff, the Greek-Armenian mystical writer of the early part of the last century. They established Two Rivers Press to publish, together with their own writing and illustrating, material that was in line with their beliefs. Later they would publish *Stopinder: A Gurdjieff Journal for Our Time*. One issue of *Stopinder* concludes with a quote from Gandhi which seems to sum up Kherdian's worldview: "We must be the change we wish to see in the world."

This attitude also best describes the crux of his life's work. Kherdian's writing over the years amounts to one man's quest to examine the affinities between himself and the world in order to draw closer and closer to what matters most. He has also nurtured affinities wherever he has had a chance. Since the start of his career, he has been a tireless and forward-looking editor and anthologizer, a job that almost every writer knows to be as thankless as it is necessary. At the age of seventy-five, he is still writing as energetically as ever. In 2004 he published no fewer than three books: *The Buddha: The Story of an Awakened Life*; *The Song of the Stork and Other Early and Ancient Armenian Songs*; and *Letters to My Father*, a penetrating collection of verse on the bonds between father and son, and perhaps his best book of poetry to date. His twentieth book of poems, *Nearer the Heart*, was published in London in 2006 by Taderon Press.

Aris Janigian

from *The Road from Home*

We often talked about Grandma. Papa said that he had written her that we would be coming home just as soon as we could. He said the war was still going on, and that we couldn't go home until it was over.

The days would become dull and monotonous again when Papa went away. When I mentioned this to him one day, he said that I shouldn't feel sorry for myself, that instead I should find ways to make my aunties happy. He said that we were all more exhausted from our journey than we knew. I sensed for the first time that he was lonely and worn out. I realized that he had never let me see this before, but somehow I saw it now, while he was speaking to me, and it made me feel very sad for my Papa, and at the same time very grateful for all that he had given me. I thought of all the people who had sacrificed for me. I gave thanks to God, and I made a promise then and there that I would always find ways to make others happy, too.

One day Papa said, "Come now, let's take a walk to the top of the city and get some sun on our faces while there is still time."

We sat alone on a large rock for a long time, enjoying the silence. The brown and yellow plain on the other side of the river stretched on forever, and a few of the large black birds could still be seen, flying back and forth.

"Azizya is still our home," Papa said, breaking the silence, "but the Turk and the Armenian can never be friends again. I worry about the future. I have one worry for me and Grandma and Auntie, but I have another worry for you and Hrpsime and the other young ones who have escaped death and must begin life all over again, with an obliterated past and an unknown future. I think a way must be discovered to refound the race in another land, and I believe it should be far from here—far from our sufferings and our scars and our torment, in a world in which our sons and daughters may be free of our wounds. Try to remember this, Veron, even if it means forgetting everything else I have ever told you. Try to remember my words today."

The leaves were beginning to fall from the trees when he left, and this was how I remembered his departure—the chill in the air, as the sun began to set, and the swirling leaves under my father's wagon.

On the Death of My Father

Dead now, and forever,
ceremony release him to the ground,
where once he played in tales that
have been handed down.

Cupped upturned hands
lower thru your spreading fingers
this soil-splashed man.
You knew him first that touch him last.
His circling fading time
hovers over my head,
his life my own to lose or live again.

Take him earth
in final release.
Toss him and catch him
in your cloudy hands.
He'll know your touch, his
feet, when he comes to you
are sure to be bare.

My Mother and the Hummingbird

As the green-winged hummingbird
        darts sideways into the
        leaves of our baby apricot tree
Suspended, taking sugar with his
        quivering bill
I move in around the palm tree
        to have a better look ·

But my mother pushes open
    the window and says
    right now write a poem

Chuck Pehlivanian

We had certain lunacies in common,
but the one I remember best was the
idea of digging our own fish pond
in your family's backyard. We went
so far as to consult Old Man Cook,
who ran the bait shack by the pier.

He wasn't the first one to laugh at us,
but he was the only one who took the
trouble to explain why it wouldn't work:
no running water meant no oxygen, and
even if the fish survived they'd soon
be swimming in their own shit.

Never mind. We decided to build a boat
instead. At this point our mothers
brought our fathers into the act.
Your father had a car—very unusual—
and together they took us fishing.
We supplied the gear and enthusiasm,
they got to provide everything else.

None of us knew where to go or what
to do once we got there. I think they
figured we couldn't all fish out of
one boat without at least three of us

drowning. And so, not finding a place
to fish at Brown's Lake, we worked our
way back towards town, finally settling
for a tiny pond at Johnson's Park.

There was this big concern over the minnows
that kept splashing onto the floor in back.
First one of our dads, and then the other
would turn around and say, "Watch it out
the minnets," or "Be careful, don't spill
it, the winnets." Neither one of them
could speak English worth a damn.

They dropped us off and went searching
for grape leaves, figuring we'd only
get wet, and maybe decide to quit.
The pond wasn't deep enough to drown
a good sized fish. We made a game of
throwing first the winnets and then the
minnets into the pond, imitating their
accents, and then cracking up and falling
to the ground.

We didn't catch a single fish, and they
didn't do much better with grape leaves.
We were wet and miserable driving home,
and they were sad and disgusted—but also
relieved to have it done. We drove back
in silence, staring out our private windows,
filling the landscape with our different
dreams and losses.

Your father broke the silence with a sigh,
saying, simply, "Where we are, where we are,"
meaning, not this ordinary day with its
ordinary losses, but the time of his life,
that had taken him all the way here,
America, from all the way there, Armenia,
the bewildering and inexplicable passage
of our mysterious life on earth.

Dedeh

Dedeh, I was to find out much later, meant grandfather in Turkish. It could also mean Father of the race, in which case the name could be taken as a title, or as an earned honor—an acquired name that effaced the given name of the man.

I was not aware of it at the time, but Dedeh, I am sure, had been named in this way.

He was in no way noble or outstanding. Nor was he distinguished, or in any way special. And yet, as the accumulation of lived moments coalesce and pass gradually into memory, what emerges from my own remembrance is a man who possessed all of these qualities, along with the still greater quality of humility.

He was, I believe now, all of these things because he was none of them. He was none of them because he thought of himself as nothing. I don't think he even thought of himself as simple or unimportant. Perhaps he thought of himself as insignificant.

It was because of this right attitude—that is possessed by so few, and understood and valued by even fewer—that he was able to find his function, which he had assumed, I am sure, without appointment, and had fulfilled without any special thanks.

I don't remember if I ever spoke to him, but whenever I rode my bike up State Street, he would be there, sitting on his metal folding chair, mornings and afternoons, in front of the doors of St. Mesrob Armenian Church.

Traveling west from home, I would pass first the fire station, and wave to the blue uniformed firemen, sitting in threes and fours on their sturdy wooden chairs. They would wave back and call out, and I would be proud to be recognized by men whose badges flashed so brilliantly in the sun.

And then, just next door, I would see Dedeh again, in his old clothes, seated, serene and silent, and I would look away and bicycle on.

Sundays he would stand in front of the church and enter with the last of the parishioners. But all week he kept his vigil alone, nodding to his countrymen as they passed, as he did to those who occasionally entered the doors he sat beside.

The meek shall inherit the earth, the Bible says. Dedeh had inherited his portion of it while he lived.

He grows more understandable and cherishable with each passing year.

My Father

My father always carried a different
look and smell into the house when he
returned from the coffee houses in Racine.
Playing in the streets we would stop,
walk quietly by, and peer in thru the
cracked doors at the hunched backgammon
players, their Turkish cups at their elbows.

Years later, reading the solemn and bittersweet
stories of our Armenian writer in California,
who visited as a paperboy coffee houses in
Fresno, I came to understand that in these
cafes were contained the suffering and
shattered hopes of my orphaned people.

Calling My Name

Remember when
Superior Street
held the world
swaying in its arms
wafting innocence
for miles
down that block
elm trees and fences
to carve & kiss behind

brother of many names
sisters in the night
come now and add your
incense to the hour
while I sing of a lost
child's fireflies.

Our Block

There were a number of streets that had as many Armenian families living
on them as ours, but only in our neighborhood—or, to be more exact, our
section of the city.

The Armenian children, many of whom were playmates of mine, were
the easiest for me to understand. For one thing, we spoke the language of
Armenia in our homes—with different accents, and varying mixtures of
Turkish blended in (or spoken exclusively by our parents, when they didn't
want us to understand), and we sometimes spoke in the mother tongue to
each other, when we wanted to keep something from our non-Armenian
playmates.

Also, we ate the same foods at home, slept under the same covers—called
yoreghans—shared the same values of frugality, suspicion, common sense,
truth telling (within reason), respect for our elders, honesty (up to a point),

shrewdness, and above all we valued money, education, family solidarity, and love of God.

Despite all this, we fought with each other anyhow. But not seriously, because, being members of a common tribe, it was difficult to hold a grudge, or even to stay mad with one's friend when you liked his mother, or respected his older brother, or had once received a favor from some other member of his family.

We also believed in gratitude and manners.

It was different with the *odars*, who we usually referred to as the "Americans." Anyone whose parents were born in this country, if they weren't as dark (or darker) than us, we called Americans. We were of course the Armenians, although when the Americans were angry with us, or wished to insult us, they called us Harmones, or Dirty Armenians. The latter expression both pained and confused me. Why dirty, when our living habits—based on my observations, at least—were far cleaner than were those of the Americans, who were often defeated by poverty, and were—very often—the last to own radios, telephones, refrigerators, and other "modern" appliances. Our next door neighbor not only used our telephone, they sent their child over to our house once a week for a tub bath, as well.

So why were they insulting us in this way? I finally concluded that it was because we were dark, and dark in their minds meant dirty.

I didn't want to be blond. On the other hand I didn't want to be any darker than Tyrone Power. He was, in a way, dark like us, although lighter complected, and with features not at all Mediterranean. But he did have black, black hair.

One of our neighbors, Zary Kaiserlian, announced one day that Tyrone Power was an Armenian. *Blood and Sand*, in technicolor, starring Tyrone Power and Rita Hayworth, had been showing at the Venetian Theater for the second straight week. Rouben Mamoulian, who *was* Armenian, was the director. "Why he give such big role him, if he not Armenian, ha! Explain me that." Her *odar* neighbors took no notice of her, while all her Armenian friends were eager to be convinced.

But it was no use. We couldn't make ourselves more desirable by making Tyrone Power Armenian. We were stuck with ourselves the way we were. We could maybe change the color of our hair, but never the color of our skin.

I had no choice in the end but to begin to live with these feelings of inferiority that were being imposed on me, and there were times when I was tempted to believe the slander, but two things kept this from happening: one, the Americans were notably not special in any way (their only claim to superiority was their majority), and two, our parents were so haughty and superior in their belief in the Armenian character—in its integrity, resilience and fortitude, that they were somehow able to instill in us a pride in our heritage.

But stretched in this way, between two quite distant poles, our sensibilities were strained, and we became awkward and apologetic and self-effacing, despite ourselves, and the membrane of sensitivity, having developed too soon, was forced either into a posture of bragging, lying, or withdrawal, which often manifested in wounded pride.

Some of us pushed too hard, fell on our faces, got up and pushed again, while others withdrew into the safety and shelter of their homes, and were never able to re-emerge and engage again in the great American experiment and dream.

None of us were normal.

And yet our parents would admonish us in their inimitable English, "Don't be abnormal (pronounced *ahpnormel*). "You going grow up be zero."

Had we only been Armenian we might not have become *ahpnormel*. But had we been only Armenian we wouldn't have been forced to be more than we were. We were being pushed into a larger world, and it was the other children of our block who were our entry into that world, like it or not.

There was a great deal to be gained or lost.

I gave up all hope of feeling entirely good or entirely bad about myself, and threw myself into the life around me with abandon. And yet, the best part of my life, the secret part, the part I kept for myself alone, I opened only to nature. For my love of nature was something beyond like and dislike, as well as beyond my immediate comprehension. Nature was the source of all mystery and wonder. I never tired of it, and it seemed never to grow tired of me.

Histories

What do we gain from our parents
that was never ours
but in being theirs was ours.
I wonder about the food and music
and especially the tongue

that never ceased to make me laugh or weep—
because I realize now that our tongue
has always been a member of the heart,
not the head;
a language for histories and passions,
spent, perhaps, but alive
alive always in the body of each man.

I put all that aside because so many
others could say it as well—
and take one thing, one thing alone
that is mine, that no one else can touch
or want to understand:
my father at an Armenian picnic, dancing,
round and round and round,
his whirling arms in a speech I could not
understand
with a knife tightly clenched in his teeth
held fast forever
in his bald and spinning head.

Thompsondale

We will never leave the picnic
    at Thompsondale
      our mothers ever beautiful
      in their summer dresses
Our fathers with straw hats
    and colored suspenders
A blanket spread upon the meadow
    cane poles strung
      with bobbers dancing over
      the slow moving stream

The grapeleaves gathered
    in the basket
    will never be taken home
    the sandwiches will be eaten
    again and again
And clouds will gather and part
    the sun will rise and recede
    night will come
And then tomorrow again and again

from *My Racine*

I didn't want to protect myself
by seeking perfection against the
accidental onslaughts of time—
but instead to move imperfectly
through it all, not to be the best
or the only, or the one to watch,
but rather the beggar of mercy
and grace, finding new hope
in each disappointment,
believing against reason
(against what the senses said
could not be) that there was
an order beyond this
disorder, that there was
a truth beyond this lie:
and that I was included
in its design
that could not be seen
or named
but could be believed in,
if one believed that one
was loved

from *My Racine*

The closest we came to being
    in the old country
    was attending church
    on Sundays, and also
    evening lessons in our language,
    as well as plays, recitations,
    and skits in the downstairs hall.
It was the hub around which
    we turned.
    Or didn't. Or barely
    turned.
I watched it all very carefully,
    and mostly from the outside,
    unable to organize myself
    into a pattern
    or system of belief
    that I didn't have a hand
    in the creation of.
But the choir touched my heart
    and the ceremony resonated
    with something in me that
    was older than race,
    while the incense,
    the wafer on the tongue
    and the gathering with
    children all of my blood
Kept me moored to the sorrow,
    the pain of the past;
    our present situation
    that I wished to escape from
    as our parents had not from theirs:
    our victimized past
    that all of us shared.

I was troubled, uneasy, proud, ashamed,
  and not yet old enough to
  experience the joy that sorrow
  often brings,
  only the heartache
  I hadn't earned and didn't
  deserve, and therefore
  could only deny.
Rejection was my salvation for a time
  until I was able to return
  on my own
  to absorb what I had refused
But consciously
  and to shed as consciously
  what impeded the needs
  the requirements
  the daily bread
  of my immortal soul.

Our Sparrows

The tall, very tall yellow brick chimney
aged into darkness by soot and time
that stood down below the end
of our deadend street
beside the woodwork factory it served—
held, in its four tiny squared apertures
near the top (made by the removal or
absence of one or at most two of the bricks),
the homes of many sparrows;
and always, coming home, or just standing
on the porch, I would look up
and see them flying in and out,

or just perched there, waiting and watching
before leaping into flight.

We are known by what we remember,
what we noticed.
Each poet must find his own objects
in the sun.
And so I remember this
as something of significant beauty
that is gratefully beyond the need
of any words
although words must sometimes be used
to indicate the real.

The chimney, the little window openings,
and the sparrows that made of it their home,
were simply there, mingling
their time with ours,
and this is what time meant:
the keeping of the rituals of the eyes
and heart.

Sparrows would always be my only nightingales.

Melkon

Father I have your rug.
I sit on it now—not as you
did, but on a chair before
a table, and write.

It is all that is left of
Adana, of us, of what we
share in this life, in
your death.

In my nomadic head I carry all
the things of my life,
determined by memory and love.
And on certain distant nights,
I take them one by one.
And count.
And place them on your rug.

from *My Racine*

Next door to Garfield Elementary
just above the playground, lived
the Mikaelian family. Abby, the
third son, stood alone on their lawn
and roared at the top of his lungs.
It was not an hysterical or angry
cry, just a bellow, loud and strong
and clear, and though it may have
had an intentional meaning, being
a specific call to someone or other,
what it meant to me, simply, was one
brave man calling out his anonymous
name to the unresponding universe.
It was a call I relished, because here
was someone, half mad, I thought, but
with a joyous inner freedom, reveling
in his own humanity—vulnerable, unsecured,
but fearless and undaunted. He was

for me the first Armenian to punctuate
the American landscape with a signature
that was his alone. Some day, one way
or another, I would add my name to that.

Our Library

Built by Carnegie to fit our city's needs,
it stood there—as it does today—a solid,
square, yellow brick, two story building on the
corner of 7th and Main, just one block up
from Monument Square, and within sight of that
great lake, that I never failed to look out
upon each time I visited that place.
I went there first with my mother to the story
hour Saturday afternoons, and then for books to
take home, until I was old enough to have my own
card, searching the shelves with my growing needs,
fascinated by the hushed silence of the place,
the circular stairs that took me to areas I browsed,
standing on the thick glass floors I marveled at.

Downstairs there were books for older readers,
along with the newspaper and magazine racks,
beside the table where so many sat, who were there
to escape the elements and to find in the
journals and dailies some hope for their lives, or,
barring that, an excuse for their presence in that holy
atmosphere, beyond the wind and rain and cold of day.

My library card was free and it would never date,
for it was as renewable as my need. It was second in
importance only to the streets, where my first education

took place, that I would finally give shape and form to
because of the learning and knowledge I found within those
walls, where the spirit was aided to weld body to mind
from a grace that only the printed word could provide.

When These Old Barns Lost Their Inhabitants and Then Their Pain and Then All Semblance of Human Construction

1.
They began to sway to the
forms of nature, desiring
some final ruin; desiring
some final ruin and return

Their bodies ache and sway
to the rhythms of the
beckoning hills

3.
They carry in their burnt
wood the descending rays
of the setting sun

4.
Their windows are as small
as eyes

5.
They wish again to be a falling tree

Darkness

The stillness of the night
when you are alone,
can anyone say it. The dark
breathing, the dark crackling
silence, the dark death of night.

And where am I in myself.
And what after all these years do I know
and what have I become.
To sit here like this is to be
reminded of one's life,
the strangeness of being who
I am, and all that I am not.

The day picks you up and takes you
but always it leaves you here,
here where you remember yourself
and see again the same desperate life.

We are not big enough for the dark
we do not know enough for the light.
Something else must enter here before
death does, death that cracks
us open, dispersing all color and sound.

Celebrating Gurdjieff's One Hundredth

January 13, 1978   *Aurora, Oregon*

The fog lifts, falls
    is penetrated by invading
    lights of cars.

I imagine candles in procession
    walkers in Asian mountains
    chanting as they come to prayers.

Here their descendants arrive
    in shields of tin and glass
    over mended gravel roads.

O brothers, our fathers
    in the distant firmament,
    with our drum the silent wheel
    that turns
    and our prayer beads rattling
    in the engine
    that hums under the hood

We   Affirming   Come

Poem

In the great firmament
the eternal world spins on—

The summer pear blossoms
will make a perfect mat
for the autumn frost—

The days slow to a crawl
or speed past quicker
than the heart can follow—

Still, all the stars are present
if one will only look up.
Now and then, with right timing,
I catch them
casting their white nets of light
against the indigo night

from *Taking the Soundings on Third Avenue*

held for an instant
in the taxi's passing
lights—two drunks in
an archway—one with
hardened, mangled face,
and the other, younger,
with a bottle paper-bagged,
tapping a shivering leg

*

the wing-set lone seagull
floating in the sky
takes the city's pulse

*

the hidden foot
dancing
finds the earth that prays

*

gliding with the tide
the barge is pulling
a piece of the city
out to sea

*

the Armenian grocer
staring out his window
sees the old country

*

A halo of silence
just brushed past me
on the sidewalk
A Peruvian Indian couple
with the jungle still
in their hair

from *Letters to My Father*

It must have been 1950. Racine, Wisconsin.
Was I nineteen. Was my father sixty
or sixty-one—the age I am now.
It must have been my first car, a Plymouth.
My father never drove, nor my mother.
Only one Armenian family,
as I remember, owned a car back then.

It is evening and I am driving him
to the Veteran's building for some event
or meeting that he is attending.
We are downtown before I realize that

he is uncertain of the address.
He is used to walking everywhere,
and has become disoriented in my car
(but I don't realize any of this
at the time). I am being impatient
with him. I don't like being his chauffeur,
I want to get on with my life, not
be a helpmate in his.

Pull over, he says, reading my thoughts.
Which I do, feeling a little
uneasy, my conscience fighting
with my impatience. But I
pull over. He gets out and quickly
begins his hurried walk—
the walk I will always know
him by, and that I will always remember
when I think of him and think of myself.

He gets out in front of Woolworth's.
It is dark out, but the street lights
are not on, and I am there, alone
in the semi-darkness,
unable to move, my car stationed at the curb.

And I am there still, watching,
staring at his back as he moves away,
knowing the Veteran's building
is just three blocks away,
I would call if he could hear me
but he is on his own and alone
as I am
with whatever this is that I am.

from *Letters to My Father*

Is there a natural antagonism
    between father and son
    that cannot be avoided
Does he lose his wife to his son
Does he lose his life to his son
    slowly giving over the very
    earth he stands upon to be
    replaced by the thing he made
    or had a part in making—
    however different his original
    intent
Is he jealous, inevitably, if it
    turns out the son has attributes,
    abilities, good fortune, luck,
    or whatever else he sees in him
    whom he sired
    that he cannot find in himself
    should it turn out that the son
    is making more of the event
    of life than he ever did
Has he forgotten his own chances

Has he given up on his own possibilities
    does the son even care or notice
    these things
Is that part of his anger, his
    disturbance
Does he wish the son would notice
    and help, or does he wish he had
    not noticed, and will therefore
    not demean him further with his help

Does he miss the old country
    and is his son's English a terrible
    reminder of this loss
Or does he wish he had never married
    never left the old country and
    died instead, as he surely would have
Or is he grateful for everything
    but sad, lonely, disillusioned, worn
    out from work, confused by America,
    in love with his son, but angry
    with everything at the same time
And must therefore take it out on his son
    because he is available
    in the way that everything else is not

And does he worry that the son is lost
    to him, does not understand him
    does not care to, but has worries
    and concerns of his own that he
    the father cannot help him
    his son with
Because this is a new country, not
    his country
    and he does not know its ways
And can see that the son is not
    interested in his ways
    and even mistrusts him and
    looks down on him
    for not knowing better
    for being an immigrant,
    an embarrassment
So what can he do but shout
    at him, lose his temper
    and find ways to get under
    his skin

For which he is justified
    for hasn't the son done the same
    thing to him

They stare at each other
    unable to communicate,
    aware of the abyss,
    on one side father Armenia
    on the other, son America

There is so much more here
    than they know, and yet all
    there is to know they sense
    uneasily, wary of each other
    and the possibilities
    that exist, that are contained
    in each of them, to be
    mined before they explode

Nonny Hogrogian

Hogrogian means earth carrier
in the language of our ancestors,
and now Nonny takes up the tools
of her new trade, putting the
tools of art aside for the moment—
to actualize something new, that
is as old as our people, whose
beginnings precede Biblical time,
knowing, as she has always known,
that to work is to enter mystery
(the oldest mystery being earth
and its turning), by making new

forms out of combinations of old
materials. A garden, an idea as
old as Eden, from where the
beginning of knowledge moved out
into the coming, as yet unmade world.

The Two

I married an earth-carrier.
My father spaded his garden.
She often says she would have
liked him, understood his ways,
like the daughter who brings
her father things, smiling,
expecting nothing, already
receiving heart exchange.

He would have been at home
with her, forgetting even
the ocean breeze of his country
settling in the plain where
the storks made their homes
in the village trees.
But he died before she came
into my life, returning
to earth years ahead of my
earth-carrier's time.

20:XII:72

stillness
snowfall
in the valley
across the mountain
a bird flies
in the cathedral
of the wind

Mulberry Trees

When
as a small boy
I saw them ripen against
the early summer sun
I stopped alone for an hour
and ate until my fingers
took an ancient purple stain

until something remembered
a smaller, knotty tree
in a barren, rocky landscape
before an older, quieter sun

and I went home a little
sadder, a little gladdened
and standing on the porch
my mother and father
saw their Armenian son.

HAROLD BOND

Harold Bond, whose family name is Bondjoukjian, was born in Boston in 1939 and educated at Northeastern University and the University of Iowa, where he received his M.F.A. degree in poetry. For many years, until his death in 2000, he was a member of the staff at the Cambridge Center for Adult Education, where he taught poetry workshops and was considered a legendary teacher by many of his students who went on to establish writing careers of their own. In his forty-five-year career as a poet, he published but three books of poems, the first a chapbook, yet these three books reveal to us a writer whose voice has been a notable, if sometimes unacknowledged, presence in American poetry written during the last half century.

What is immediately impressive about Harold Bond's poems, the early ones as well, is their urbanity: they are stylish, attractively musical, elegantly idiomatic. His language has none of the halting, uncertain missteps one might expect from a first-generation Armenian American who grew up in a household filled with Middle Eastern resonances. Even in the poems which suggest his discomfort with himself, exiled from the mainstream and normative culture by both his ancestral past and his physical disability (he contracted polio as a child), he retains an attractive formal distance from all that might spiral him into bouts of self-pity. In "That Routine," for instance, he maintains his even temper and his linguistic refinement as he struggles with bringing his legs back into working order:

> At the rehabilitation
> center, I am taught the
> principles of coordination,

how, in the good name
of physiotherapy
I will restore my
self to that society
from whence I came.

And in "The Recognition," though he identifies the flaws which set him apart from others, he nonetheless allows himself, however provisionally, the possibility of being a flashy, cosmopolitan jetsetter:

I am debonair, my friends
tell me[...]

[...]In my
faded pink ascot and my
Saroyan mustache, I am

an Armenian Romeo,
a gilded gigolo gone

big-time. I am in Paris,
in Yerevan and Dublin,

and the change in my pockets
jingles of its own accord."

This notion of identity seems significant to him through his first two books, most especially in his second, *Dancing on Water*, whose title itself describes the way his "drunken sealegs" must walk, "woozily down the street" in their "clumsy fashion," terrorizing children because of their damaged condition. But the evocative title also implies that his ungainly legs are perhaps lovelier for their resistance against giving up, their acts of faith toward movement and life, their singular gesture of "dancing on water." Poems such as "The Birthmark," "Acrophobia," and "HP" further heighten Bond's obsession with the damaged self as something to regret. Other poems, reversing that conventional inclination, hold it dear and make it sacred. In "The Glove," for example, the lost half of a pair of gloves "[i]n its absence...become[s] beautiful," and when found soiled and damaged, "fits like a good metaphor," skintight, outlining the fingers beneath its surface, the stricken body giving weight and heft to the pure, untouched body beneath. In "The Hook," the one-armed elevator man's prosthetic contraption becomes an object of power, pointing, accusing, indicting, "shriveling" the hands of refined ladies who pass by his station.

How does one define oneself, Bond seems to be asking in every poem, and should one's vulnerabilities be as equally treasured as one's strengths? Poems like "Him: The Roach," a metaphoric, Kafkaesque exploration of the ubiquitous insect self, and "Breakthrough," which sees the secretive self as a rat about to tunnel out an apartment wall into the clear light of day, give primacy to our hidden lives and ask us to readjust our responses to what is suppressed and dark and other. Even in poems about sexual stirrings and discovery, there is the sense that the self to be prized—at the cost of losing the possible lover, is the one that is private, hard to get to know, even hard to love. "You do not read my poems," Bond addresses a possible love interest in "To the Girl Who Photocopies My Manuscript," realizing, of course, that the sleek, shiny, all too available photocopier turns her head more than he does. But the copier only copies; it does not write the poems, and though that is small consolation in this romantically charged instance, it nonetheless serves to show us that what's of value comes from within and is difficult to duplicate in any profound way. "I will squat here / among the rats forever," he says in "The Old Maid," affiliating himself with what is cursed and flea-ridden rather than with those who clear house of all that's thorny to live with, as the old maid in the poem has done, leaving herself sanitized but alone. What he valorizes as a whole is a life freely lived, without imposition or notions of propriety, a life that Sonny Stitt seems to live in "The Gold Tooth," gunning his Cadillac down the street "like a gazelle...like the wind...his big bag of brass / flashing like a gold tooth."

What is intriguing, finally, is how markedly Bond's style has changed in his last book, *The Way It Happens to You*. Discounting the poems that are included here but have appeared in the earlier collections, one gets the general sense from the work of a wholly new way of maneuvering through a poem, integrating into its linear structure unpredictable shifts of thinking and imagery, in a style that has lost its constraints and propriety. It's almost as though Bond has given himself permission to be scandalous with language, forgoing the precise, deliberate, cultivated tones of the earlier work and igniting his lines with electric vitality which flares toward the surreal:

> Leaving, for where it was that
> I was going, I cocked my tongue deep
> inside my cheek. Arleta, California

was swirling around me
like an ocean. My rear-view mirror
grew amniotic, my shirt sleeve
became a pearl, brilliant and probable.
                    (from "The Way It Happens To You")

Sensuous and visionary, the lines intimate a traveling away from what is customary toward promising new states of being where the commonplace is transmuted into the extraordinary. The first section of the book, in fact, is a travelogue of a kind, driven by Bond's limitless desire to experience the United States in its entirety, from Oregon to New York City, assimilating himself into diverse landscapes with more ease than before. He no longer seems, for instance, the misfit Armenian wary about his place in the mainstream culture, the shy schoolboy in the classroom worried about embarrassing himself by not getting things right ("The Chance"), the physically stricken outsider whose wounds single him out ("HP"). Nor is he oppressed by the constrictions of the immigrant identity, or the postures of the *poete maudit* whose outcast self keeps him apart from the rest of the race. He seems less worried about who he is, projecting a persona that is, in fact, far more socially comfortable than before. Even in his intersections with the opposite sex, he seems more daring, fully open to the notion of admiring women with "lithe, exquisite ankles," touching them, having them "whisper to you what they know" ("Girls Who Wave at Cars from Bridges"), or mooning over the iconic Dorothy Malone, with her "solid curves and bountiful hair," and with whom he can't help but fall "in love, love, love" without the slightest hint of mortification or self-effacement ("Falling in Love with Dorothy Malone").

If he courts awkwardness, if he errs in any way, he does so out of a fearless disregard for what is conventional, going against the grain of the literary fashion of his time. His language has become decidedly unrefined, jagged, more idiomatic. His rhythms are rhythms not of the parlor but of the underground café or hip gallery, and the formal concerns of meter and rhyme have given way to a jangly music that evokes the street:

[The graffitist] cocks his ear lobes,
inviting in the resultant
sonic boom. His hands massage

the conflagration. His eyes squint
into the sun for the last time.

Harold Bond wrote, of course, before the postmodern poetic explosion of the 1980s, before the disjunctions of experimental writing and language poetry would come to light, offering us an alternative view of where poem and reader intersect and what each brings to the venture of experiencing a poem. Yet for all his early refinements, how postmodern Bond seems, eschewing a familiar and comfortable lyricism for an aesthetic that asks us to engage ourselves wholeheartedly with his poems, and to feel the world as it is embodied in them: as harnessed chaos, bridled disorder. We may criticize him for abandoning his early lyric interests, since they were so fruitful and engaging. But there is such excitement to the later work, and a certain irreverence of all that's canonical. *We are on the cusp of all that's to come,* Bond seems to be insinuating in each poem, and with him, we ride out each wave, each exhilarating turmoil and crash of idiom and tongue.

Gregory Djanikian

Dancing on Water

Mothers who clutch the hands of your children,
what fable can I claim to assure you
these are not drunken sealegs I walk on?
If there is an unseen line I follow

woozily down a winter street, this is
the only act of faith I know. You walk
distances around me, winging like hens
protectively over your broods. I take

these intricate steps only in the dance
I do. I balk gravity by timing
the one disjointed knee that will collapse
predictably as a jackknife. Something

is special in the way I walk, sealegs
to be sure but drunken only in what

blue waters will not buoy me up. These rags
of kneebones for my fable, can we not

call it beautiful that I move over
such fathoms in this my clumsy fashion?
We will say I am dancing on water
in my faith. Ladies, I must dance or drown.

The Chance

First grade. I am the skinny
one with the foreign accent. I am
so scared I think I will wee
in my pants. Miss Breen is teaching us
colors. We are cutting out
strips of paper in the fashion of
Indian feathers. We must

order them in descending hues on
a black headband. I cannot
understand Miss Breen. It is not done
the way it should be: blue with
yellow and black with white. Unless I
do something soon Miss Breen will
say I am a dumb Armenian. So

without looking I shuffle
my feathers in my hand. I paste them
over my headband. I spill
my pastepot, and I know I will wee
now because here comes Miss Breen,
only Miss Breen says, Good, Harold, good,
blue after purple and green

after blue. It happened, it happened
like a rainbow, like a swatch
of oil on water, eight feathers thieved
in perfect succession one
on the other. Miss Breen did not say
I am a dumb Armenian,
and I do not even have to wee.

The Recognition

I am debonair, my friends
tell me, being my friends and

not less than candid. They are
playing their scene, and I am

playing mine, and I like it.
I am making it. In my

faded pink ascot and my
Saroyan mustache, I am

an Armenian Romeo,
a gilded gigolo gone

big-time. I am in Paris,
in Yerevan and Dublin,

and the change in my pockets
jingles of its own accord.

Would you believe it? My friends
are everywhere. They are arm

in arm, and they are saying,
Did you see that guy? Did you?

And I do, walking along
in my herky-jerky way,

making it, believing it,
the flow, the recognition.

The Glove

In its absence it has become beautiful,
        my black-leather, my rabbit-fur-lined glove,
given over to the foreignness of strangers,

        of mad dogs thieving away to the deep woods
            with my lost glove. I imagine even
the hunger of hobos and the coveted taste

        of leather in their infamous mulligan stews.
            I consider my lost glove. I consider
the copulation of rabbits, the precise instant

        of conception of that hapless mother's sons
            who would inhabit my lost glove. I think
of the busy, unknowable chain of commerce,

        the wholesale and the retail of my lost glove.
            And today I leave my home uncertain
which will effect attention to itself—the one

gloved hand or the one gloveless. I revisit
   my itinerary of the night before:
Huffy's Sinclair, the Eagle Mart, and Tic-Toc Lounge;

no one has seen my lost glove. Later I find it
   grease-stained behind the cash register of
the Campus Grill. I put it on, my slipped skin,

and it fits like a good metaphor in that
   fortuitous gathering of elements:
cowhide, rabbit fur, the five fingers of my hand.

Postscript: Marash

The Armenian is an historical
phenomenon. He should have
been extinct decades ago.

Out of Marash and
Musa Dagh, Aintab
and Ourfa, it is

the same story of
the bloodbath: the Turk,
mounted on his black,

oversexed steed, his
scimitar poised and
thirsty. And in our

secret family
archives, my father
poses in a fez,

a conscript in the
Turkish army at
eighteen. The year my

mother's brother was
beheaded, the Turks
issued religious

tolerance for the
empire. In England
William Watson was

writing his purple
sonnets for the lost
nation. He became

promptly famous. From
Egypt, from Cyprus
and Lebanon the

Armenian Legion
fought under General

Allenby for the
homeland. Now the old
grow wrinkles over

their scars. They picket
the UN building
in memory of the

massacres. They demand
justice for the one
million dead. And in

Fresno, the dark-haired
youngbloods bury their
guns. They are eyeing

their fathers' daughters.
Two by two they have
disappeared into

the vineyards. Under
the grape-heavy frost
they are making love.

The Birthmark

> ...*some inner war*
> *of chemicals and nerves and cells.*
> —*Joseph de Roche*

Father called it his rose. Mother, who
owned it, called it nothing I can
remember. They agreed from the first
to take it from her, box it perhaps,
freeze it and put it on the market.

Photographs came back, the film retouched,
the right cheek perfect as the left.
Salesgirls in the department stores
besieged her with Max Factor, promising
to make it disappear. And always

the dutiful doctor through the years
insisting on the operation,
on maximum cosmetic effect
with minimum pain. Relatives came,
and it was the other cheek turned for

the embrace—the scarlet, vascular,
perpetually blushing side of her face
touched only by the hands that loved her.
Later, to her sons and her sons' sons,
it grew apparent she would keep it.

They battered down the tarpaper walls
at homecoming, and leaping over
fathers, flowerpots, family albums,
they seized her, they kissed her and loved her,
and they believed how it would be there.

Letters from Birmingham

Birmingham. The city bell tower chimes one.
I write letters from an all-night diner,
telling of the four hundred miles I've done
this day: rubble of roads and the weather,

the repairing of tires gone thin and flat.
The hawk-eyed waitress watches me writing.
She says I write with a fine hand except
for the extended slant. I cringe and bring
myself to straighten up beneath her eyes,
loading my letters with her smalltalk home.
What else is there to write of if the pose
of Birmingham, my hours in Birmingham,

the slick city hot on a Sunday night.
That my righteousness will overwhelm me?
That the intensity of my fire is great
and will sustain us all? Not that, I pray.

But from the bell tower I hear the singsong
pealing of 'Dixie' windward by the hour,
the bell-rattled refrain of 'Dixie' hung
blessingly over Birmingham, sky and spire,

tipping the Sabbath with hallelujahs
to worshippers spun from their homes at dawn,
hearing church organs grind out canticles
for all souls dynamited into heaven.

                                        1965

The Way It Happens to You

Leaving, for where it was that
I was going, I cocked my tongue deep
inside my cheek. Arleta, California
was swirling around me
like an ocean. My rear-view mirror
grew amniotic, my shirt sleeve
became a pearl, brilliant and probable.

Leaving, I left only to return.
The myriad little second
cousins washed back into view,
a seascape of ragdolls fluttering above
the waves. For half the day
I had driven the maximum distance,
returning at night, to Arleta, California.

So it was I spent as much
time leaving as returning, each day,
each morning, by dint of leaving sooner
instead of later, arriving closer
to where it was that I was going,
before returning, by nightfall,
to Arleta, California.

So it was until I left so early
I saw myself returning
from the night before. This was the day
that I would be arriving
beyond the maximum possible distance.
The myriad little second cousins
would flutter below the browbeating waves;

and turning over in her bed of water,
her tongue uncocked, across America
the woman, awakening only
to mark the time on a calendar
so beautiful she will keep it forever,
would hear my footsteps, and hear
the brilliant pearl dropping outside her door.

Girls Who Wave at Cars from Bridges

You have seen them. Above the freeways
they hang from bridges, their velvet eyes

yielding secrets which you cannot know.
They wave to you hello and goodbye.

They wave this one time and forever.
They wave at old men who no longer

believe girls wave at them from bridges.
Sleek-finned convertibles drag and cruise

and bargain for a spot below them.
You look up, and you can see through them.

Their faces are creampuffs; their skirts are
so high their billowing hair appears

as streamers on a skyful of kites.
Were you to reach up and seize their white

ankles, their lithe, exquisite ankles,
you could spin them on the antenna

of your car. And were they to reach down
and cup their hands lightly on your chin,

they would fly off with you. Together
you would be a solid bet, a sure

pie in the sky. You would touch their noses,
and they would whisper to you what they know.

To the Welcome Wagon Lady

Little lady of the Welcome Wagon
in the suburb I now call home,
I waited eight months to hear your voice
chirping across my telephone,

and when you came, and when you came,
I heard your wings flap you away
before I could reach my door to see
what love sent you here, and why.

There was no feather of you in sight.
You *must* have been little to vanish so.
Because I keep no woman at home
your welcome basket was all I found.

What I have kept of all you left
are one potholder, one cookbook,
two coupons and a shoehorn,
a four-blade knife and one yardstick.

I took one coupon to the florist
who offered me a styrofoam rose.
I took another to the locksmith.
He confiscated half my keys.

I looked, and found no love inside
your welcome basket, found your name
but not your face or half a song
to listen to or shape a dream.

I promise I will not stub your toes,
I promise I will not tell your man
if you come back, I promise that
and promise never to cage you in.

Falling in Love with Dorothy Malone

There she is like manna traipsing
down a staircase, Dorothy Malone:
those tweaky eyes, that flash of leg.
It's Irwin Shaw's whodunit thriller,
Tip on a Dead Jockey. Robert Taylor
plays her swarthy husband who's hell-bent
to smuggle whatnot through the Alps.
It's 1957, vintage Dorothy Malone.
I switch channels. There she is again.
It's 1969, *The Pigeon* with old salt
and pepper Pat Boone and Sammy Davis.
She's mobster's widow. She keeps
his black book. The mob's after her.
It's car chases and fist fights.
Boone's a pushover, Davis is camp.
Dorothy's herself, possibly better:
solid curves and bountiful hair.
Where is she now, O horn of plenty?
I fumble for the switch again.
Somewhere in those twelve years I know
that loveliness is lonely, and time
will keep her for anyone falling
in love, love, love with Dorothy Malone.

The Gold Tooth

That was Sonny in the big
red Cadillac, Sonny Stitt
in Newport. I was bug-

eyed to see Sonny. I caught
Sonny at the next light. I
yelled at him. I waved out

my car window at him. Sonny
waved back as if we were old
friends. He laughed. He made a

musician's joke. Sonny's gold
tooth flashed in the sun. The light
turned green. Sonny Stitt gunned

his Cadillac down Newport
like a gazelle. Sonny blew
alto for the Bird that

night. It was Charlie Parker
night in Newport. I thought how
they called Sonny a poor

man's Charlie Parker all those
years. Well, Sonny clipped his wings
in Newport. Sonny was

like the wind. That night all you
heard was his big bag of brass
flashing like a gold tooth.

The Birthday Present

The lawn has not been
cut now for years. My
lungs are stuck with grass.

It is June. Finally
it has stopped snowing.
My car needs a new

engine, and I need
a new car. My rugs
curl at the edges

like magic carpets.
For my birthday I
have bound one copy

of my unpublished
manuscript. The boy
who is so small he

cannot cross the street,
asked me today if
I were American.

Thinking he said *a
miracle*, I called
back to him, yes. I

hoisted him on my
shoulders. I gave him
my book of poems.

I carried him to
the river. Ungulate
beasts descended

the hills. Together
we drank the sapphire,
newly melted snow,

saying, Goodbye, spring,
my thin loins girding
for the invasion.

Calculations

Carcasses of victims
of the black widow spider
are strewn over the beach house.

His webs compose a slaughterhouse
or a mosaic.

The giant-winged luna moth wants in.

He cannot tolerate the crickets
and desires a soft light for his cocoon.

The purring tortoiseshell scratches
the screen door for a second
offering of milk and tuna.

Her nipples are swollen
and her belly sags with life.

I have stacked the fireplace with driftwood.

Termites are chiseling tunnels in the heap
but I need only to touch a match
to kindling to ignite us all.

In moments the teapot will be singing
and I will ride out the lost moon.

The Last of the Free Samples

(for R.)

Even as the mail truck wheels
out of view, there are those
who will not possibly
believe it is everlasting,
while there are others who will
believe it is Rosalind Russell's
fantastic ostrich-feather hat.

It is postmarked Addis Ababa
and addressed in a handwriting
that is almost familiar.
It has taken a year
to reach me, escaping Customs
and quarantine, and by now
it is drifting into sleeplessness.

I am holding it for all
it is worth. You could not
buy it if you wished to,
being the last of its kind.
Herein lies the beauty
of it, and of the dream
to be partaken, such as it is.

Though I could describe it
to you, I am afraid no one
would listen. Where would I begin,
it having previously begun?
Now I am carrying it like
a vendetta. Look: already it is
finding a place in my heart.

Limbo

Witness how at the rotary the man
revs the engine to his posh, low-number-
plated sedan. Cars flank him on either side.
He will acknowledge his presence over

the hubbub of the home-moving traffic.
He will assert how he only is there,
beautiful, ushering the van of stopped cars,
his car windows closed to the city air,

the summer heat. The man in the blue suit
motions him forward. He does not unsheathe
his handcuffs, billyclub, thirty-eight. The man
in the sedan waves back. He smiles beneath

that unmistakable passing of favors,
nuzzling his baby home now, runaway
and ragtag, thinking it all clean, clean like old
men who bathe day after day after day.

The Graffitist

Huddled on a rooftop,
he is burning a discarded
harpoon. His tongue never spoke

the syllables of anyone
he knew. Hieroglyphics
also was his forte.

Across the alley a broomstick
is dressed in leotards,
all swagger and bravura.

He cocks his ear lobes,
inviting in the resultant
sonic boom. His hands massage

the conflagration. His eyes squint
into the sun for the last time.
In a hundred years or two

the smoke signals will be
deciphered, and in that time
such things about him will be said.

The Menagerie

You say you know me. I am the one
who appears suddenly at parties.
When I am late, which I am always,

you cry *procrastinator*, and flap
your ears like any old basset hound.
Your jellyfish women take my hand,

feeling the hoofed fingers stuck with glue.
In our various wars of attrition
you come paddling up your Rubicon

with nothing but a jackass' jaw
to lay me under. You cry *stopgap*
over the potatoes I have dropped,

the fumbled passes, the killed small talk.
And when I huddle in some corner
and hunch my shoulders against your clear

plastic tombstones for warmth, sir, you cry
schizophrenic. I am your burlap bag
of glue, your palomino frothing

at the mouth. You carry me around
with you always. Do you understand me?
Say it. You understand perfectly.

Another Rescue

Any time now the waters
will open. Somewhere a bullfrog
has all but swallowed
the river. Preholiday fireworks
are croaking in the distance.
I carry a dime and an ID.

I descend the cascaded steps
and walk under the old
stone bridge. A patrol car's
high beams flood the walkway.
Should anyone ask, I will say
I am thinking beautiful thoughts:

the calves of women or the hooves
of mountain goats. I have come here
to discover what troubles me,
or to forget, I am unsure which.
It is a night for all seasons.
Something is dying here.

Helene Pilibosian

During the Poetry Society of America's "Tribute to Marianne Moore" at the Boston Public Library in 1997, critic and professor Bonnie Costello referred to Marianne Moore's "sense that poetry should affirm life or help us to endure." Not too far away in Watertown, Massachusetts, Helene Pilibosian may have been considering those very words while crafting her own sense of poetry's purpose. *At Quarter Past Reality*, her second full-length collection of poetry and a Writer's Digest National Self-Published Book Award Winner, was written in 1998, and, although certain facets of Pilibosian's work differ from Moore's in terms of aesthetic sensibility, the collection and much of Pilibosian's work is very much concerned with helping us endure the complexities that inevitably come with exploration of identity and history, place and time.

Moore is a good starting place for entering Pilibosian's work. Who knows: perhaps Mrs. Pilibosian was in attendance that night at the Poetry Society tribute. Their writings share the same natural kind of prosaic structure, attention to sibilance and syntax, and transformative quality. The first time I read her work, Pilibosian was, for me, Marianne Moore with a genocidal past. While the inventive feminist of early twentieth-century modernism mined catalogues of exotic animals with scholarly precision, Pilibosian is interested in how digging the mountain of a past can help shape the present.

Pilibosian belongs to that unique category of "in between" Armenians, a generation that, as a result of being children of Diaspora parents, is neither entirely American nor entirely Armenian. On the one hand we have survivor stories. On the other, we have the grandchildren of Genocide survivors, who often are too young and too far away from the trauma to feel its effects. Pilibosian falls in the middle of these two fields, and the tensions that accompany this specific territory, if you will, become the material for her poetry. She grew up within the Armenian community of Watertown, Massachusetts, and her ethnic roots can be found in her poetry as well as in her Ohan Press, which she established with her designer husband, Hagop Sarkissian. In addition to her poetry, they published her father's memoir, *They Called Me Mustafa*, and translated her husband's father's memoir, *From Kessab to Watertown*. From 1964 to 1966 Helene was the editor of the *Armenian Mirror-Spectator*, later writing book reviews and feature articles for the paper as its co-editor.

She began her exploration of her Armenian identity with her first book, *Carvings from an Heirloom: Oral History Poems*. Titles like "Sako of the Village," "The Apricot Songs," and "A New Lake in Anatolia—1980" evoke a sensorial vernacular of "the old world." The poems themselves feel familiar to Armenian readers. And for non-Armenians, the duality is nicely explicated in poems whose trajectory is more obvious, such as "Less Than a Pinpoint":

> Our Armenian vision was
> a baseball street with teams
> that outran the occasional cars,
> so spare that their
> existence was not a fear.
>
> Inside the walls of home
> was Armenian, was another me,
> elemental and untested.

What's "elemental and untested" and what isn't in Pilibosian's first book, through a reductionist lens, becomes a metaphor for what is from the "old world" and what isn't. And what is from the "old world" is charged with electric memory. "Armenians," Pilibosian asserts in "Game of Languages," "drew luck in dice / from mountains, stars, earthquakes / of history." In another poem, smoke from a "shish kebab" at a picnic is smoke from another time, is transformative, is "elemental," enough to bring the past into the present. A study of contemporary cross-cultural writers or, in this country, "hyphenated Americans" would reveal that this type of connectivity—of history to things of the earth and sky and water, and the present to modernization, technology, artifice, and daily domestic life—is prevalent in writers who are trying to make meaning of their pasts. Pilibosian's poems are "tellings" of, as the title suggests, oral histories, and a necessary first book, I think, for a poet interested in reconciliation. Eventually, what's beyond the present is addressed in "With the Bait of Bread," the poem from which the title of this anthology was drawn. A child is told that "If not already, Armenian will / ring in one of your ears someday," and we hear some distant bells.

Fifteen years after the publication of her first book of poetry, *At Quarter Past Reality* was published, and in it we see a writer who has moved away from the sad and dark tapestry of genocide and towards a New England kind of domesticity filled with motherhood, middle age, and a "House of Toys:"

> The past
> is such a show,
> a dream with a window
> to open and close,
> screened, cleaned.
>
> I adjust
> its cadence
> to the song of life[.]

This poem lends the book its title and is a good example of poetry in the poet's "new world." Poetry, it seems, with its capacity to "affirm life" and help us "endure" the changes in our lives, now marks the tidings of a new reality. As the poet moves away in time from a past she only partially owned and understood, a psychological distance also develops, making the past a dream, and, for Pilibosian, "dreams are toys / here." Time is examined closely, as is its relation to the past and, subsequently, this psychological distance culminates in the declaration that, for the poet, "it is a quarter past / the dream" and finally, the inevitable, "quarter past / reality and / crickets of an August / that hugs us / are chirping." There is a Stevens-esque imaginative leap in this poem and once again, Pilibosian, now at a different point in her life, places herself as a successor of modernist ideals and attentiveness to image.

Although there are shifts in topical content (poems about motherhood, poems about chores, poems about getting older, dealing with illness, etc.) and experiments in form (list poems, concrete poems, etc.), Pilibosian's primary concern throughout these poems is still the tension between the old and the new. In this new round of struggle, however, the poetry has greater scope and suggests more wisdom towards issues outside the realm of genocide and reconciliation. In "A Plain Green," the poet meditates on the nature of beauty, and more specifically, the nature of what is beautiful in a woman. The "green dress" that the speaker explains made her look "thin as a mountain stream" is the ghost of the elemental past for the poet. Her assertion that this is what makes her beautiful—not adornment ("icons of gold") or attitude ("I scrawled / some graffiti / in my time")—is a simple yet powerful statement of gender as connected to ancestry. The closer we get to our heritage, our past, and all the complications that come with that proximity, the closer we get to an almost spiritual contentment, a "warmth" that Pilibosian describes as implying "what might have been / was." And in "After Staring at an Owl," the poet contemplates the politics of power, how logic and reason and evidence can be circumvented by deception and injustice, an unfortunate and too-familiar theme in scholarly genocide study:

> What would an owl
> know about wishes
> that turn to silver dew
> in the moonlight,
> to the shine of gold,
> or to the mud
> of sludge upon
> the river of reason?

In these final lines we see Pilibosian now consider truth itself as something natural and pure, and falsity as unnatural and "sludge," conjuring images of governmental denial of genocide for the Armenian and poor journalism for everybody else.

Helene Pilibosian is the kind of poet who is inspired by the complicated music of her history in conversation with her reality. In a newer poem, "The 39 Letters," she personifies the sonorous characters of the Armenian alphabet, writing, "they'd never forget the songs / like lullabies." And like lullabies, she delivers these big poems quietly, mostly self-publishing from her lighthouse in New England to the world. And when all is said and done and Mrs. Pilibosian's body of lyrical work situates itself in the ever-growing world of American letters (if it hasn't already), we won't forget her songs either.

Alan Semerdjian

With the Bait of Bread

Child, you were and
you learned to be.
For a while, Armenian was
a wish you could not fathom.
It is still a sea
and we fish in it for food
with the bait of forgotten bread.
The moon will be less specific
with the sun and the tides
if you wish it, Child.

You are yeast scattered upon
the ground and the rising dough
will grow into tomorrow.
You are the yeast of
your friends in one language
or another.
If not already, Armenian will
ring in one of your ears someday.

Less Than a Pinpoint

House of my childhood,
my rented rest,
stood, still stands
upon less than a pinpoint
of America. I had no claim
except to the sights
of a store-back alley lolling
on one side and the strong shoulder
of the Kimball house on the other.

The Coolidge School nearby
complemented the corner theater
that made the century light,
lighter because we, its children
had not yet tried its weight.
Our American vision was
a baseball street with teams
that outran the occasional cars,
so spare that their
existence was not a fear.

Inside the walls of home
was Armenian, was another me,
elemental and untested.
I thought it elementary
until I graduated from life.
Kaleidoscopic surprises
brought me back near
that primary focus
of my reality.

The Other Sun

Woman,
your gold teeth
speak through the veil
that veils the Eastern world.
Woman,
the blue velvet
that clothes you
to your ankles
declares a Kurdish style
that was part

of my parents' past,
a rote cross made over bread
before it was baked in ovens
that had known Armenian too.

My Western stance
walks by that pride
curious of that other time
that still rides upon its own sun.
What worldless moods
had told me of other ways,
of other times,
better forgotten, but not.

Game of Languages

Two tangled in a game,
one calling it backgammon,
the other *tavloo*. One American
land, they each had their own
law, umpire, preacher,
speaking often to air pockets.

The Armenian drew luck in dice
from mountains, stars, earthquakes
of history. The other was
ready for the instant,
the change with sustenance
of muscle.

The game was their generation,
those who kissed the ground
for its freedom

and worked with arms and legs
more than with sentences;
it was emotion.

A set outlined one
profile, another set took
the players to a third final
where a weary handshake
wondered who would win
out of playing in two languages.

The Anti-Rebel

He would not sit
upon the park bench
of meditation
nor watch the children
of the primal force
repeat the cycle again.
He would not walk lazily
upon a quiet street
unless his watch
ticked like a hammer
dedicated to building.
In his leisure
there was music
as sound
deluding itself.

He was anti-rebellious.
One would wonder
if he felt pain,
if he saw

the dark moon brood sometimes
upon a monotonous night.

He was a paradox
with women,
unromantic,
unrebellious
(rebellion is
romantic, emotional).
His face was composed
but not elegant,
because elegance too
is a shade of emotion.
He stared at abundance
but envied no one
and avoided the park bench
of the deluded, as if there
were guilt in thinking
of pleasant things.

His schedule was arranged
in the shape of his mind,
had been since the beginning
of time, his time.
He was Mr. Ordinary.
What else could one call him
unless he said his name was Smith.
But it was not Smith.
It was Sissian,
who had forgotten
his third dimension.

He would look in the mirror
and not see the hyphen
in American-Armenian
(or should it be
Armenian-American?)
He would worship
all that was typical,
not knowing
even that could change.
Not knowing,
not knowing.
"Oh, a woman could change that,"
the ladies would say,
though they never chose
the right one,
the one who could work
Eve's spell.
But she walked
into his life one night
dancing a kind of folk dance.
He found himself meditating
upon the children
of the primal force. Then
his watch stopped
rebelliously.

Armenian is rebellious.
Armenian is emotional.
He found the third dimension,
the hyphen,
the woman,
the primal force,
the music achieving itself.

Sincerely

My relative,
are you still
Mediterranean
or has your mind
    as I suspect
assumed the geography
of the country
on which you stand?
    My mind is American,
    they say,
    but I say,
    perhaps half.
You are
no doubt
too busy to search
as I, as we,
trying not to think
too much
of the Mediterranean
that was for us
younger days.

After Staring at an Owl

What would an owl
know about toothbrushes
or mirrors or lipstick
that we must wear
to meet some scrutinies?

What would an owl
know about the friendship
that is an ampersand,
the circle of discovery,
all-connecting?

What would an owl
know about the ritual,
about church and its
sometime incense and
debates about it?

What would an owl
know about wishes
that turn to silver dew
in the moonlight,
to the shine of gold,
or to the mud
of sludge upon
the river of reason?

What do I know
about the eyes of the
owl except that they
follow the moonlight
that follows me?

To My Daughter

I'm in the kitchen where
we so often puttered
in the living space that
is now your absinthe.

I crunch on symbols
where we learned and
unlearned the ritual of
flour that made us palpable.

That frosting fight
of how many years ago
was fair. We never did
need an umpire.

I pour some parody
into my coffee and
read a book of hours,
each page like a slice

of blueberry pie that
always added up to
family. What yeast
there is in the cupboard

often remains a myth.
There is more mystery
these days in the
aisles of the supermarket,

my particular forest
of plastics. I no
sooner find a point
of energy than I have to

change my pace and
find a panacea,
an orchid under the sun,
terrycloth at the shore.

My favorite is
the container of
thoughts that taste
like breakfast flakes.

I deny the
prescription for
early middle age given
in the threat of the thirties.

I have a cardboard box
and will send you some things,
like lights and shadows
and a coat of dew.

Charcoal Sketches

Watertown is sketched
on the paper of my mind
like a drawing by the Charles River
in a younger frame of time.
A charcoal pencil had no doubts
of stores on Mt. Auburn Street
that still rearrange wares
according to waves of immigrants.
The unleavened rounds on the shelves
break like biblical bread,
soften when wet
to adjust the cracker-crunch
of the sun-baked questions:
who are we
and why are we here?

The East Side could be
the East Side of anywhere
that flour, salt and water
mix for bread, of everywhere
there is a practical river.
Legend like a boat
floats down the Euphrates,
river of my forebears.
The Charles too draws my stare
in blue or shades of gray
depending upon the delicacy
of unrelenting weather.
All for local tender.

I have softened
like the cracker bread
with the water of that river.
I carry a cane of regret
having missed serving a piece
of that bread to those first here—
Sir Richard Saltonstall
and his Massasoit friends,
long gone to their final dugouts,
forms of revolutionaries
winking like sobering rays,
their guns, relics.
They were attuned to the trees
as well as a horse's trot
on the banks of the river;
so much later bread
was of a changed flavor.
They paved the land
I walk on, tap with my cane.

A Plain Green

It was the
green dress that
made me look
thin as a mountain stream.
It was a cool
color but not cold.
Cold is meant
for the heartless.

I didn't wear
icons of gold.
My shoulders
rose and fell
with the usual
human brawl.

I must admit
that I scrawled
some graffiti
in my time.
But time erased
the rebel with
the color green.

The dress was the smile
that no one believed,
beguiled some as
worship does
(or is supposed to).
There was no pattern.
It was a silent green.

It implied
the rule of
spring and summer,
the warmth that
followed me.
It implied that
what might have been
was.

House of Toys

I

I crank
the old phonograph
in a dream,
the song of Caruso
having slowed.

The past
is such a show,
a dream with a window
to open and close,
screened, cleaned.

I adjust
its cadence
to the song of life,
putting time
under a microscope
and spinning
with the stars.

II

The room is
large enough,
painted an accurate
shade of pink
to complement the lights.

Dreams are toys
here. They
run on batteries
or they pretend
to prattle
at the children.

I throw a net
over those dreams,
metallic as the old
black stove that
seemed so perfect
when the trolley
ran on its track.
The clock strikes
midnight as children
of mothers become
adults and mothers
become grandmothers.
The clock strikes
upon the hour
of a life that is
wound for measure.

III

It is quarter past ten.
Business of the day
stirs baseball talk,
the exercise walk,
a change of counters,
calculations of painted
rooms and canvases
that draw lines
around the bronzing
of the sun.

It is quarter past
the dream
and a Magnificat
is playing,
praying,
evaporating into
a mystical mist.

It is quarter past
reality and
crickets of an August
that hugs us
are chirping.

The 39 Letters

of Armenian words,
their 39 swords,
their 39 favors,
locked fingers in the group

like 39 dancers.
They'd never forget the songs
like lullabies
in and out of mountain crags,
on pollinated afterthoughts,
in the rain of chance,
in the clearing after snow.
They'd never forget
the enchantment of candles
stacked like stems
with fire the flowers,
fire the ancient worship
of a simpler earth.

Even the earthquake learned
the 39 letters
and all the words that spelled
a fractured vista,
learned the dances too,
the chances of blankets,
the trances of food.
The four flowers—
summer, fall, winter, spring—
learned the 39 letters best,
endowing them
with the mood of weather.

Silent Call

A darkness separates
a tiger from its stripes.
A forest of buildings,
of countries, separates

me from Yerevan.
Its envies mellow
my night, as dark
swallows me here
while I hide from light.

Don't snarl,
I tell the city
as if it were a pet.
I pat its head,
muzzle its snarl.
I muffle police sirens
here for its benefit.
I rail at threatening
sticks. I try not
to be so shy.

Yet Yerevan calls.
We both have ambition
as the tiger has instinct.
It doesn't call
by phone, nor by letter.
It simply is,
exists, Armenian,
a word that defines me
again and again.
And I exist, simply,
Armenian…

Years of Glass

They'd left the farms
ancient Hittites had spaded,

left Armenian trees
with fruit as sweet as moons
in the esthetics of the tides.
Necessity had goaded them.
Sweet fruit of forgetting!
1930 was the year
of their marriage to each other
and to America, its meanings
often as vague as dictionary words.
Through the decades,
tales of the old huddle together
as their houses had
when candid flames of wood
in the dugout stoves
had spoken of food and kitchen.

Daily talk was of family
or factories and stores
they spent their days in.
Parents and their friends whittled
the sharp edges of complaint
down to round wooden blocks, smoothed
and polished for an end table.
It was the decoration of the 40's
with neat, sandpapered edges,
put together on points of need
that were not on sale.
There was always a serving
of details like fruit
contrasting flavors, cultures.
The table stood like praise
for their hands and psyches,
strong with the varnish
of equality for workers

and on it there was a dish
made of American glass.

They were paid in the currency
of contentment for that work.

First Names

The elders,
the mild men
of stern white hair
and the stubborn strength
of warriors,
forbade
with the old world
what the old world
would miss.
The younger
stubborn echoes said
"We are phasing out
the customs,"
and became a group.
Alive,
the useless current
struggled
against itself,
struggles still
like a habit
of lost love,
and the elders speak
new names of choice
without shame,
empty for them.

Seasonal Dust

Clipping spearmint and grape leaves
of a conscious green,

soil dripping from my fingers
in fingerprints,

the pith of the ritual of
Armenian women

preserving the leaves
like old customs,

the frail stems
of planthood

cast like the pattern
of puns in a letter,

washing my hands of green
and my mind of pollen,

seasonal dust
for my conscience

sneezing at the trees
that try to sleep,

washing my eyes of summer
and wiping them

with a towel
but not apology,

pouring tea made
from such dried conversations.

PETER NAJARIAN

Roughly thirty years ago, my father gave me a copy of a slim purple dust-jacketed novel called *Voyages* by Peter Najarian. In my early teens at the time, I didn't get around to it and I'm glad I waited. In all the book's brilliant subtlety and in my own youthful impatience, I would not have been able to appreciate it nearly as much as I did. My father did not offer me many books. Looking back, I think I know why my father gave me *Voyages*. He was at the end of his life, dying of Lou Gehrig's disease. After growing up in a world of survivors, not far from where Najarian was raised, he fled to New York City in the 1940s, much like Najarian, in search of himself. My father had difficulty dealing with his parent's memories of the Armenian Genocide.

Upon finally reading Najarian's works, I knew it wasn't simply about being Armenian, or reconciling the past with the present culture. I think my father must have admired Najarian's unflinching candor in dealing with life.

Najarian seems to carry history with him at every moment. There is one passage in *Voyages* that amusingly connects the various turns and twists of time to the lusty loneliness of the moment: "the generations descending from the high plateau where once Urartu girls opened their legs to Armens, their daughters fucked by Medes, semen starting its long journey downstream where Greeks came and Mongols came and Arabs came, to end nowhere in America, the struggle of ten thousand pricks futile in America, ending in a bald sterile creature masturbating in the mirror."

In reading Peter Najarian's works back to back, four patiently written books over a period of thirty-five years, I wondered if I wasn't inadvertently doing him a disservice. Instead of considering the integrity of each work on its own merits, I hooked so thoroughly into his style and rhythms, it was as though I was reading a single six-hundred-page epic, divided into four parts.

There is indeed an organic growth to his fiction. His works take on a life of their own, growing where they will, like a wild garden.

Voyages is a touching portrait of an artist as a young man. It is about Aram, whose father dies suddenly when he is young. He is raised by his mother, Melina, whose own amazing tale of survival is included in the book. Aram grows up in Union City, New Jersey, and attends college, only to get tossed out for stealing books. Aside from being ironic, this is also a serendipitous act, compelling Aram to leave the comfort of his childhood world—the Armenian community of eastern New Jersey, including and contrasted by Yero, a brother who is slowly sinking into a swamp of petty bourgeois values. Aram ventures into an artistic/spiritual wilderness, first in the Greenwich Village of the 1960s.

As is common when writers are first starting out, Najarian lets his stylistic pyrotechnics explode. In italics, he creates voices of the past that are so authentic it's as though he's transcribing first-generation witnesses. He forges streams of consciousness, interspersed in parentheses, rich with mythological allusions:

> (You were forced to marry but not to split my brother's
> home. Yet where's blame in the spontaneous war
> between man and woman?...But Atum created cities
> by masturbation, and Gilgamesh spurned Inanna.
> Finally Eve revenged her mother and sent us all to Hell.
> Where's Demeter in our Fatherland, Jehovah in our
> Motherland?...)

Then just as quickly he returns to the linear narrative of the present.

The second half of the book is all voyages. It reads like a spiritual travelogue across the ocean, to England, Spain, and then back, hitchhiking to the far-flung outposts of America, where he finds flashes of love separated by longer introspective periods of loneliness. Slowly, though, we feel the artist stirring and growing as he defines himself against so many other characters he encounters.

His second novel, published nearly ten years later, *Wash Me on Home, Mama,* is probably his most novelistic work. Najarian appears to have conceived it in total, leaving all traces of Armenian heritage behind. Our narrator slowly dissolves into the narrative until we are left with a repertoire of half a dozen people in a Berkeley commune. Having lived on the West Coast during the tail end of the seventies, I was able to easily recognize how thoroughly he captures the spirit of the times and the sensibility of its quirky characters, each encapsulated in a chapter, such as Daphne:

> She never did get a degree. Instead lots of leaflets, acid,
> tripping and canvassing, marching among burning draft
> cards and jungle music in the street of flowers, of pellets,
> of incense and broken bottles...until someone turned her
> on to yoga through whom she met someone who took her
> to her first encounter group...until People's Park became
> the last stop...settled into the great calabash, potpourri
> of Gurdjieff, Guevara, Shambhala, scientology, electoral
> politics, liberals with long hair, radicals with short hair,
> food stamps, falaffel...

All of the characters have their own dreams, but it is how their dreams interrelate that makes the work most poignant. From his powerful descriptive details flow all the verisimilitudes that create any given moment, whether he's describing a compost heap or the ingredients that go into a lamb stew. Sometimes he's almost Whitmanesque in capturing all the aspects of a single holistic moment: "he watched...roofs opening with skylights, streets flowering into playgrounds, bicycles on every corner, all chimney pots painted bright colors, sidewalks shining with mosaic, utopia, like a child building a fort out of fruit-crates..." Yet he's never wordy. The prose is far more inclined toward the austere, even Buddhist in its simplicity.

Daughters of Memory returns full force back into his heritage. The great matriarchal book would be well worth the cost for the art alone, stunning charcoal sketches done by Najarian himself. Like the sketches, the writing wonderfully balances a dreamlike quality with the realistic, the erotic, and at times, the classical.

In a series of mini-chapters, largely through spare dialogue, the book explores various female archetypes. The voices of grandmothers, mothers, daughters, wives, and prostitutes converse with an idiosyncrasy and tenderness that keep any of them from falling into stereotypes.

The dialogue of elderly Armenian women, which runs through the book like a coda, interplays the past and the present. Frequently they discuss matters that are heartbreaking and difficult, but so matter-of-factly that they seem maudlin or sentimental:

- She has a beautiful body, your granddaughter.

- I hope it's not too beautiful. Look what happened to
  Lucia.

- It's not easy to be beautiful. My mother had to smear
  herself with shit so they [the Turks] wouldn't rape her.

The dialogue of these women make the issues of contemporary America seem trite when compared to the unbearably horrific past that they survived.

This quiet message, which is repeated throughout Najarian's work, comes across loudest here: How can we brutally lose our land, our people, and our heritage, simply to flee to America where we take up office jobs, move to the suburbs, and anesthetize ourselves with creature comforts?

Perhaps his most mature and writerly work is *The Great American Loneliness*—a terrific title, as all his books have a beautiful loneliness to them.

In the book's preface I realized the full extent of Najarian's own fictional Diaspora: "[I] got a short work published in an anthology, *New Voices*…and this would grow into a book called *Voyages*. My second book, *Wash Me on Home, Mama,* was written in the first half of the seventies.…The first two narratives in this book are from an unpublished book I wrote in Detroit in the second half of the seventies. Puer Eternis [another chapter of *Loneliness*] was written while I was visiting a friend in Montana…"

Many of the chapters are about his travels, first to India, then to Armenia in 1989, the painful time of the earthquake. Interspersed, but mainly at the end of the book, we get his early years, including the powerful scholastic forces that shaped him during his formative years.

His list of friends is an impressive slice of recent contemporary literature. We get brief and touching glimpses of William Saroyan, alone in his last days.

Najarian sketches two writers unfairly neglected today, Richard Brautigan and Richard Yates, both of whom also died sadly. Scholars like Francis Fergusson, John Ciardi, and Paul Fussell shaped his young life while he was attending Rutgers. *Loneliness* is loaded with great tidbits, such as a wonderful portrait of American Poet Laureate Robert Pinsky as a young man. There is a brief chapter that could easily have been expanded (or exploited) into a sensational youth market memoir. He hangs out with Ken Kesey, and briefly meets Kerouac's great muse, Neal Cassady, in his final days. Later he spends time getting high with members of the Grateful Dead and acquiring free tickets, through Bill Graham, to a Doors concert.

Najarian is not, as my first literary agent used to phrase it, "manufacturing a product." Quite the other way, his books, after *Voyages*, are published by small presses, in limited printings, far from the madding corporate crowd. The good news is that in the age of the Internet most of them can still be obtained at a reasonable price online. Though they're not beach reads or edge-of-your-seat page-turners, these polished gems offer candor, grace, history, and dignity, qualities in short supply in today's fiction.

Arthur Nersesian

The Aki

Travelling through Turkey years ago, I came to Adana on the circle back to Istanbul, but my foot was swollen from a bad burn and I stayed only two nights, nothing left of my mother's childhood except the bridge. The aki had been on the other side of the river and she had often told me of sitting on the donkey when her family went there in the spring. "Look for the bridge," she had said before I left, "and you will find it." But when I hobbled there it led to more highrises and traffic, so I just sat on a bench to rest my foot and I watched a boy fishing in the sundown. "You stayed in Adana only two days?" she would say. "My foot was bad, Ma, and I had to get back to Istanbul." "Well, at least you saw my Adana."

Not really, except for the bridge and the boy fishing from its ancient stones, the river flowing fresh from the mountains through the gentle arches to the sea, the boy and the stones and the river all glowing in the long rays. "I remember the bridge," she always said. "I sat on the donkey and we crossed it to our aki on the other shore.

Tas Kopru, said the guide book, and she too had used the Turkish word, kopru. It was built by Hadrian and later restored by Justinian. The Crusader, Geoffrey of Bouillon, crossed it on his way to Palestine. It was the bridge of history and the aki lay buried in its nightmare, but the river was the same and the same light shined on the boy with his line in the waves. Here now in this screen, I fish with my own lines as if they could be a movie of the lost aki with my longing like a zoom.

Here, in my movie, are my mother's family and their donkey crossing the bridge, their figures silhouetted in the morning sun like a Daumier. She can't remember their faces, but she remembers her mother had red and freckled cheeks, and her father was a gentle man whose heels were cracked like hers are now. They were peasants like those of Daumier and Millet and Van Gogh, and their clothes were in earth tones and patches of primal color, the little Zaroohe and her younger brother in a donkey cart and the donkey's hooves clicking on the cobbles, the wheels creaking in counterpoint.

But there was no cart. She doesn't remember any cart, she was alone on the donkey. Then how did her little brother come? Maybe there were two trips, maybe she came on the second trip? Yet there has to be a cart so they can be filmed together. They are returning to their place in the sun after huddling in a tenement all winter, the rains have ended and the fields are splashed with wildflowers in the new green.

What kind of wildflowers? Are they the lupine and broom of California and Provence, and are there poppies too? A Faulkner or Tolstoy could find the details of their stories in the world around them, but mine are buried under highrises and gas stations.

Yet the climate is the same as California and Provence and the rains are only in winter, the fields full of fruit and cotton and sesame and flax. It is like a happy day in childhood before my loneliness began, the father a whole man like a thriving specie before the clear cut and genocide, the mother like a glowing dream before the day brought back the night. Shut your eyes to see, they say, and come home again.

The road goes east to Urfa and Hadjin where the parents were born. They probably met through relatives and settled by Adana after they married. Who knows how they got the aki, but it is theirs now and all it needs is hard work.

Home again, says the young mother in Turkish, the bubbly syllables I never learned now translated in subtitles. Parkes-der—Praise the lord, says the father in Armenian, though like his wife he spoke only Turkish.

He was a church-going man, but there would be no church until they returned to the city. The metal and the fabric are from the city, but not the wood for the fire nor the food from the vines. Nor is there a dome or a spire or a priest or a mullah, the sons not yet men who will kill each other and the daughter not yet a prize, there is just love and light and the need to live in them, for this is the home in the dream that says we don't have to wander anymore.

"Look, Papa," says the oldest boy, "the fig tree has grown." It is as if he is looking at himself in the new green of his life. His Armenian name is Boghos, like the Greek for Paul, and indeed this is the home of the famous Paul of the very religion that would lead to death, the very naming and the tongue itself a part of death. Death is everywhere, and this is their last year in the aki, the fig tree to fall like the orchards in Fresno now paved with developments. Yet here in this vision it curls its limbs with new leaves as if in welcome, and the billowing clouds are an ecstatic white in a brilliant blue.

First comes an open space lined with mulberry trees, then the cabin at the end of it. No, not a cabin, she said. They didn't sleep in it, they just kept their things there, they slept in the open on the deck.

"But what about the road, was it like our roads or was it a dirt road?" "You ask too many questions, be glad I can remember this much."

So it is just a road as in a Ruysdael or a Bellini, its vanishing point an eternal au revoir. And here now in the aki itself, the peach and apricot are in bloom and soon the quince and mulberry, or is the mulberry already blooming? What do mulberry trees look like, mulberry as in Hemingway's story where the silk worms feed in the middle of the night when he couldn't sleep? And did they wake with petals falling on their faces?

They are falling now, pink and white and stippled with yellow and a delicate red, the young Zaroohe and her younger brother let loose to play and maybe her older brother as well, for loving parents would let their children play as long as they wanted, the time for work will come later, if they live long enough.

They unpack, and the young mother—she couldn't have been more than thirty if her oldest boy is twelve—airs the bedrolls on the line. Did they bring the bedrolls from the city, or did they have two sets, one for the city and one for the aki?

And the shack, who built it and with what kind of wood? They don't sleep in it because there is no rain, and the nights are as pleasant as in Avignon or New Delhi. Mosquitoes? Maybe a few but not a hindrance in the cool nights, so they sleep in the open with the deck raised high and the donkey underneath. What a pleasure it must have been to sleep under the stars with no streetlamps of insomnia, the love of stars zooming like a Voyager into a sparkling infinity! Listen, it says, listen to the crickets like their echo on earth, their incessant rhythm like a Tibetan prayer wheel. How peacefully my humble family sleeps on their bedrolls.

What kind of bedrolls? Where they of the wool the immigrants brought to America like the quilt here now on my bed? How magical it was one summer when my mother washed the wool and I helped her card it on the roof, the forked branch like a tuning fork as if I were making music. How bountiful it was, like a gift from sheep to protect us from the cold darkness. Feel it, says the sense of touch no movie can simulate, touch the woolen quilt to be part of life and never be alone again.

But maybe the blankets weren't wool.

"I don't remember seeing sheep, we lived in a land of cotton."

Then let them be of cotton, the same as on the way to Fresno in the autumn with tiny puffs bursting from their starry husks, the cotton of this shirt and a weary seamstress in a sweatshop.

"One night I saw my mother and father making love. I never told you this before because I was ashamed, but now it doesn't matter. We all slept together and when I woke one night I saw them, but I didn't know what it meant."

They sigh in counterpoint to the humming crickets, two small people with their genitals together like hairy animals.

"My mother was pregnant when we started the march, and the baby died on the road."

Not yet, not yet, let the petals fall on their sleep once more, let me guard over them like a god with the moon in his hair, my zoom rising higher until not only they but all such families come in view, their dreams purling into the clouds that blanket our tiny planet. They dream, they dream the dream of life as if it is a movie for an audience of stars, all dreams a cinema in a giant dome of wish-fulfillments, the crickets leading to birds like strings to woodwinds in a symphony and the darkness dissolving into a luscious blue, the morning star cradled by an old moon and the silhouette of trees embroidered in the glowing crimson. Wake up, it is not time to die.

The father is the first to rise, or maybe the mother or one of the children who stands on the platform as if on the deck of a ship, the dawn like the other shore. And now the long rays of the new sun are shredded by the leaves. Come, says the need to piss, let the piss flow in the vineyard and then wash from the pump with the water of life, it is time to break bread around the teapot.

"We sweetened the tea with syrup, our breakfast was sweetened tea and bread."

It is the syrup from last year's harvest, the big ceramic jars sealed with fig leaves and mud. But were they left here over the winter? Did no one come and take them?

There was another family who lived in a tent by the road and they must have guarded the aki during the winter. They were black and landless, yet life is home to those who share it and make more. "I remember their children."

"Paint my aki," she said when she saw me struggling with a canvas in her garage one day. "I'll describe it and you paint it."

"I can't paint like that, Ma, I need something to look at."

"What kind of an artist are you if you can't paint from imagination? Be like that painting teacher in the television, she just paints and leaves it, but you keep wiping it away."

"I'm not as good as she is."

"Oh you always say you're not as good as someone, you don't have to be as good as anyone, you just have to do it."

"You do it."

"All right, give me that brush, and I'll do it myself."

And so for the first time in her life, she held the brush like a ladle and dabbed with her fearless and matter of fact way a few marks on the primed paper as if she were a kindergarten girl.

"What's that, Ma?"

"What do you mean, what's that? That's a tree, don't you know what a tree looks like?"

"Okay, it's a tree. Now let's put some more paint on the brush."

"No, I don't like that color, it's too grey. Give me some yellow for the shack."

And so with the yellow she made a little shelter like children everywhere, then she added the road with the primal flatness that is always fresh and alive.

"There," she said, handing back the brush, "you see how easy it is?"

"That's pretty good, Ma. Why don't I leave some paint and paper and you can do more after I leave?"

"What's the matter with you, I don't have time for painting, you see all the cleaning I have to do."

"You said your brother used to draw. It will make you remember your brother."

"I already remember my brother."

He sits under the mulberry tree like a young Siddhartha practicing for enlightenment, his daily lesson the lights and darks and his delicate lines like the fine hairs above his lips, Uncle Boghos, the gh pronounced from the back of the palate as if clearing the throat, the Bo and the os like a call from the deep, the boy who never became a man and nothing known of him but that he loved to draw.

"Make lines, my boy, make lines," said Ingres to the young Degas, "keep making lines." What for, said an old artist who had saved them all, what for when no one will see them? "For Eden," said Blake, for Uncle Boghos who is the love of drawing and seeing a pattern in the lights and darks.

But why is he not helping his father tie the vines or weed the seedling vegetables, how will he survive if he doesn't learn how to farm, what future is there under a mulberry tree with a pad and pencil? Yet his father must have encouraged him, for he too must have been a dreamer.

"I remember my father saying, '*Gyun dolmazdan, nahlar doghar.*'"

"What does it mean?" "It means 'Tomorrow is happening while we sleep and dream.'"

In the vineyard now, he ties the vines and....And what? What was a real father like, a whole man whose hands could tie a world together, who could actually speak instead of groan? Can a movie be made with a shattered memory like the scraps Picasso made into people and animals, a tool for a face and a jar for a torso?

"I remember my brother Boghos telling me to tell him the truth after I broke his pencil. 'If you tell the truth I won't hit you,' he said, 'but if you lie, I will.'" And I told him the truth. 'Yes,' I said, 'I broke your pencil.'" "Is that all you remember?" "Be glad I can remember that much."

She naps in her living room eighty years later, my own pencil following her wrinkles like the map of her life. Who would her brother have been had he survived, he and the others who disappeared under the great eraser?

He sits under the mulberry tree with his little sister playing nearby. She doesn't remember him playing with her because he probably didn't, she was in her own barefoot world with leaves and bugs.

And over there in an open space her mother is sealing another jar with fig leaves and mud, her father picking the last of the tomatoes in the garden. For already in just a few pages the summer is gone and the harvest a syrup to sweeten the winter tea. It has been another summer of details now hiding behind her eyelids like rare species from extinction, the vegetables cooked on an open fire and the yoghurt from the milk of the neighbor's cow, the cracked wheat boiled into bulghur and the dried syrup stripped from sheets like edible leather, a mere minute of flashbacks that must somehow flower from an old woman's nap and come to life in a storyboard.

The father turns the compost and the mother empties the mash, the sun low and the light soft like in Millet's *Gleaners*, the yellowing leaves like a warm dream of life's lushness. There behind her wrinkled eyelids a summer has ripened into glowing ochres and the shadows pulse in violets and reds. It has been a summer like a long life and there are still more grapes on the hairy vines, their juice so sweet it could erase a millennium of bitterness. It has been the summer of life for all who have known its bitter winters and its labor in the vineyard.

A summer as in my own childhood when she treated my father and me to the fresh air of a chicken farm and the odor of chickenshit. She was only forty-four then, and she had saved enough from the factory for two months in Dickran's little chicken farm in Freehold, which was about an hour from West Hoboken in the truck Vahan drove on his drycleaner's route. Dickran was Vahan's older brother and Vahan was the husband of Manooshag who was my father's niece. Manooshag and Vahan tried to live on that chicken farm during the Depression and when they couldn't anymore they let Dickran have it. Dickran lived alone in that big house and was glad to have us. He was only around sixty then but he seemed ancient, and with my love of father figures I went with him to town to sell his eggs in his ancient pickup with the crankstart, his husky hands on the wheel of the old jalopy as it chugged along the road at the pace of a Buddha's breathing. It was the last summer of my golden age and I can still smell the chickenshit and the tomatoes heavy on the vines, I can still see the haughty chickens walking on the porch and my mother chasing them with the broom, my paralyzed father sitting silent with his hand in his lap. It was the last year in which I can remember a happiness and I was the same age as my mother when she was torn from her own little Eden.

There were fruit trees on that farm and the sap would drip and harden into a lovely amber on their limbs. She peels the same sap from her own trees now and chews it like a jujube. "What are you doing, Ma?" "Oh, I used to do this on the aki."

It has the amber glow like a late Degas where the features blur but the forms are solid, it is in this glow that my little family sits on the ground for their last meal in the aki before their return to the city and the start of the genocide.

They all eat from the same pot and the donkey munches in the background, their dialogue like the voices of silence in a museum without walls.

The mother, Tirfandah, like all the figures from Hatshepsut to Matisse, her freckles a glaze to the eternal feminine.

The father, Haritun, like El Greco's old man in the Met, though he is only in his thirties in the death march.

The brother, Boghos, staring back like a young Picasso with eyes in a mirror as if in a skull.

The child, Toros, unremembered except for his death in Damascus, his grave like a last supper in a peeling fresco.

The little Zaroohe, the sole survivor, her passport photo the only view of what she may have looked like, yet how girls change after nightmare in puberty.

They sit now, still glowing in the sundown, the trees embroidered in the gold leaf of the long rays.

"What are you going to do today," she asked over the phone this morning.

"My work," I said.

"Me too," she said. "I have so much cleaning to do."

Following are excerpts from Daughters of Memory, *a novel in the form of short episodes punctuated by a chorus of four old Armenian women who survived the Massacre in 1915 and are now sitting together near a vineyard in Fresno, California, where they have retired after living Back East. The main narrative of the novel is largely concerned with the narrator's grandmother who died in the Massacre.*

Selections from the Chorus

The Garbage Man

- I'd like to get a job in one of those hamburger places.
- She's got more money than a pasha and now she wants to be a servant.
- You don't even know how to write. How are you going to write the orders?
- I don't have to work in the front, I can work in the back. I can wash dishes.
- They're not going to hire someone your age.
- This isn't the village. Old people don't work in this country. Young people can't even find work.
- Diamond Ring Zakar owns some of those places. Maybe he can give you a job.
- I wouldn't work for Diamond Ring if I were you.
- He's not an easy boss.
- He was a slave himself when he was a child.

- Was he one too?
- His mother left him under a tree before she was slaughtered. Some Kurds got him and made him a slave. He lived with them for some years before he escaped.
- He's a good boy. He can't help it if he loves money.
- So what good did it do him? He waited till he was fifty to marry and then to one who couldn't have a child.
- I wonder who he'll leave his money to?
- The government will get it.
- Let them have it, they were good to him.
- Why should they get it? They don't know how to use it.
- I don't care what happens to it, just don't give any to me. I have enough trouble giving away what I have.
- Then why do you want to make more?
- It's not for the money.
- She wants to be around young people.
- Young people don't want to be around us.
- They think we have some kind of disease.
- My garbage man is young and he always stops for a cup of coffee in my garage.
- In your garage?
- Why sure, didn't you know my garage is a coffee house?
- That was a good idea putting a stove in your garage.
- Why sure, who wants to sit in the house? I pull the door up and I'm open to the street.
- That's what everyone does on my street. They live in the garage all the time.
- I wouldn't be able to talk to my garbage man if I was inside. I give him coffee and *choreg* whenever he comes. He's good to me. He takes all my garbage no matter how much I have.

The Lag-Lag

- Tell me the truth, do I smell like piss?
- No, not so far.
- Thank goodness. I used to smell it on Agavni before she died. I wanted to tell her but I didn't want to hurt her feelings.
- I used to smell it too. She used to wash her underwear every day but it was not enough.
- I go through twenty pair of underwear a week. Good thing I have a

drier, what would my neighbors think if they saw all them on the line?
- Well thank God you can still wash them yourself.
- You said it, I'd rather leak piss in my own house than wear a diaper in one of those others.
- My children say they'll never let me go to one of those places.
- They all say that.
- I never heard of those places when I was young.
- Whoever started them, let the dog shit in his father's mouth.
- They're not so bad.
- They stink and you know it.
- Everywhere stinks if your ass is shitty.
- Just like the lag-lag.
- What lag-lag?
- The lag-lag with the shitty ass. Every time he'd fly to a lake he would say, 'It stinks here.' And everywhere he went would stink because he would stink.
- Let's talk about something else.
- Bring some pumpkin seeds. I want to do something else with my mouth.
- No, we must keep talking. Talking is good for us, no matter what we talk about.

Where Was Your Mother Buried?

- I don't know where my mother was buried.
- My mother was buried in a ditch outside Damascus.
- I don't know where my mother was buried but I know where her brother died. He went to the Soviet Armenia and then he starved to death.
- I remember my mother a little. I remember she used to hit me a lot.
- She must have been a young mother.
- I remember my father saying, 'You hit a donkey when it doesn't move but you don't have to hit a child.'
- I wish I could remember my mother. I wish I knew what she looked like.
- She didn't look like us, I'll tell you that. She was too young to look like us.

Beautiful Bodies

- I remember Lucia's body in the bathhouse. She was so beautiful she felt ashamed.
- She didn't feel ashamed. The old women made her feel ashamed.
- What mouths they had.
- Now we have them.
- Do we? My granddaughter doesn't even wear a brassiere and do I say anything?
- When I was her age I couldn't even shave my legs without the old women calling me a whore.
- What happened to the bathhouse?
- I think it's a Cuban restaurant now.
- I remember the horse-stables in the back of it and the smell of horseshit.
- How much fun we had there.
- Now men and women sit together. Everything showing, even between their legs.
- They just sit in a big tub.
- Do they make music?
- I don't know what they do.
- They smoke dope.
- Good, let them smoke dope.
- My son-in-law put one of those jacuzzis in his bathroom.
- Oh yeh? I want one too.
- I don't need any jacuzzi. I like a good *keesah* on my body.
- You can't get that flaxen cloth anymore.
- My granddaughter wants one. She likes old-fashioned stuff.
- She has a beautiful body, your granddaughter.
- I hope it's not too beautiful. Look what happened to Lucia.
- It's not easy to be beautiful.
- My mother had to smear herself with shit so they wouldn't rape her.
- My granddaughter doesn't have to do that.
- They learn to fight now. They do that Japanese stuff. I saw on the news a woman who broke a man's nose when he tried to rape her.
- Good for her.
- Did they catch him?
- Yes, they caught him in the hospital when he went for his nose.

History

- My grandson's girlfriend came the other day to write recipes. She wanted to cook for him, but she's an *odar*. I told her, 'You have to live with me and cook with me to learn these foods.'
- What kind of *odar* is she?
- I don't know, she says she's American.
- They all say that.
- I asked her what kind of American and she said a little of this and a little of that as if she were a recipe.
- There are no Americans. They just say that to make themselves feel like they're somebody.
- There won't be anymore of us either.
- Not if we marry a part of this and a part of that.
- We will be gone when we lose the language.
- Why should anyone want to keep the language?
- The language is everything.
- It gives us history.
- I don't like history.
- Let us be part of this and part of that.
- It's safer.
- What are you saying? Did my father die for nothing?
- I don't know why your father died.
- He died because he would not become a Moslem.
- So they ripped his nails out and slit him open with a butcher knife, that's better than being a Moslem?
- They would have done that even if he did become a Moslem.
- They ripped my baby daughter from my arms and threw her in the river. Do you think I could ever be a Moslem after that?
- They did something else to me.
- Christians do those things too.
- I'm not Moslem and I'm not Christian.
- What are you then?
- I'm a grandmother, that's what I am.

Turkish Coffee and the Airport

- Read the mud in my coffee cup and tell my fortune.
- Old Oghidah should be here, she read good fortunes.

- That's because she was the best gossip-monger around. She used to go around smelling everyone's dirty laundry and then when she read your fortune she would know everything about you.
- But she always read a good fortune. Whenever she would read my coffee cup she would say, 'See this cloud in the corner, my girl? That's good luck coming.'
- Then one day I said, '*Deegin* Oghidah, how can I believe you when you say everything is good luck?' '*Yavrim*,' she said, 'If you don't believe me, who are you going to believe?'
- After what she went through everything else had to be good luck.
- She loved coffee. She loved to roll her own cigarettes and drink coffee with everyone.
- With cardamom seeds. It was good luck if it had cardamom seeds.
- So what about my cup now?
- See this cloud in it? That's good luck coming.
- I don't care about any clouds. Just tell me if I'm going to Hawaii. I want to go to Hawaii on one of those love boats.
- I don't see a boat but I see an airport.
- Of course you see an airport. That's because you know I go there for lunch.
- You go for lunch at the airport?
- Why sure, I like to believe I'm going somewhere. You want to come?

Big Noses and Chechens

- Askig has a cousin who grew up in China. She speaks Chinese with her children.
- I heard there are some of us who made it to the end of Argentina.
- Where is Argentina?
- It's at the end of the world somewhere.
- Did they keep their names? Some of us don't keep our names.
- My name isn't my name anyway. It comes from a Moslem word.
- As long as it has our ending it's okay. Everyone knows who we are by the *ian*.
- Some of us in this town didn't want the *ian*. They took the *ian* off or even changed their names.
- How come?
- We were like dogs in this town while you and I were living back east. The signs here used to say, "No dogs or Armenians."

- Now we are the ones who own the signs and they say, "No Blacks and no Mexicans."
- They do?
- Why sure, you think we're any different?
- The Blacks and the Mexicans will own the signs someday and I wonder what they'll say then.
- Some of us could pass for Blacks or Mexicans. Jack-knife Nishan had hair so kinky he could pass for a Black in the summertime.
- The way you eat hot peppers you could pass for a Mexican.
- What about Indians? We used to play Indians in the movies.
- That's because of our big noses.
- I wonder how we got these noses.
- Once there's a big nose in a family it never goes away.
- Maybe the Indians got their noses in the same place.
- The Chechens were like Indians.
- You lived with the Chechens, didn't you?
- I lived with them for three years. After my family was slaughtered they took me for a slave. I spoke Chechen, I ate Chechen, and I would have had a Chechen child now if I hadn't escaped.
- How did you escape?
- I didn't really escape. There were merchants that passed over our plateau and I would give them notes to take with them. I would write my name and where I was.
- I did that too.
- I would have done that but I couldn't write.
- I learned how to write just in time. I had already been in school when that Chechen grabbed me and took me away on his horse.
- So did anyone find your notes?
- You know who found one of my notes? You know old Harry, the iceman?
- Why sure, he used to come to my home all the time with his pick in the ice and the burlap dripping on his shoulder.
- Well he found my note and he came to get me. But he had no money when he came and they would not give me to him so he had to go back and I had to wait another six months before he had enough to buy me from them. I think he gave them about ten dollars.
- Can you speak Chechen now?
- Not a word. Sometimes in my dreams I speak Chechen but when I wake I can't remember a word.

Killing and Sex

- They shot another diplomat.
- Who?
- Those who come from Beirut.
- They grow up with shooting in Beirut.
- Did they kill him?
- No, they just wounded him.
- They should have killed him.
- What are you saying? Do you know what you're saying?
- Of course I know what I'm saying.
- What good is it to kill the poor man?
- He's not a poor man, he's a Moslem.
- He doesn't know what happened. He wasn't even born then.
- Then he should know. They should all know.
- She's right, something must be done. Too many years have gone by and nothing has been done.
- What do you want to be done?
- I want them to admit what they did.
- What for?
- So everyone knows.
- So everyone knows, so what?
- So then it's a beginning. They can begin to pay us back.
- How are they going to pay us back?
- I don't care if they pay us back or not, as long as they know.
- My granddaughter knows. She wants to join the underground.
- Does she want to shoot diplomats?
- She wants to fight for her race.
- She just wants to fight.
- No, she grew up with the stories.
- Who told her those stories? What kind of stories are they for children?
- They like to hear those kinds of stories. The Jews play their stories over and over again.
- They're our stories. Our grandchildren should know them.
- So they can hate and kill?
- Not to hate and kill. To know where they come from.
- They all come from television.
- They all come from killing and sex.
- Not all of them.
- All of them and all of us. We all come from killing and sex.

Loneliness and Gossip

- I got a call from Zevart the other day.
- How is she?
- She's miserable. She can't take the loneliness.
- She has to take it.
- What else is she going to do?
- She can move in with her children.
- Would you move in with your children?
- I can deal with the loneliness.
- People die from loneliness.
- Zevart's not going to die from it.
- It's only a few hours at night. During the day she can keep busy.
- We're not the only ones who are lonely. The young are lonely too.
- My nephew is lonelier than I am.
- Your nephew doesn't have to be lonely. He can find someone.
- We can find someone too.
- I can't live with anyone anymore.
- I can't even live with my children anymore.
- I visit them and they sit in their den watching television.
- No one talks anymore. They all watch television.
- I'm glad. I used to hate all that talking. Everybody talking about each other.
- The television gossips even more.
- The television is all gossip. Even the news is gossip.
- I like gossip. It keeps us together.

Oil and Fat

- There's a sale on olive oil in my supermarket.
- Buy me two gallons. I'll pay you back.
- My daughter says safflower oil is better.
- Now your daughter is an expert on oil too?
- First it's sugar and then meat and now they want to change the oil.
- They worry about their health.
- Let them worry about what comes out of their mouths.
- I like olive oil. I never use fat anymore.
- I like fat but I use butter in my *choreg* now.
- It's not the same. The old *choreg* with the fat had its own taste.

- Agavni still uses it but she doesn't tell anyone. She boils it and keeps it in her second refrigerator. Her son's a millionaire but he still likes fat in his *choreg*.
- I used to get it for a nickel a pound from the butcher.
- I used to get it for free.
- You can still get it cheap.
- No one wants to boil it anymore. They don't even know how.
- You don't have to know. You just throw an apple in and when it's brown the fat is ready.
- They say it gives you heart trouble.
- Everything gives you heart trouble if you sit on your ass all day.
- That's why they all run.
- My daughter gets depressed if she doesn't run.
- Your daughter looks like a skeleton already.
- She likes to look that way. It's the new style.
- Do men like it?
- They don't care what men like.
- Good for them.
- They don't get old so fast.
- What's wrong with getting old? So they look young, so what?
- So then they can go out and have a good time.
- Do they have to run to have a good time?

Turkish Songs and Armenian Moslems

- I saw Satenig last week. She just came back from Russia.
- It's not Russia. It's Armenia.
- It's still Russia.
- But we have our language there. All the street signs are in Armenian.
- They may use our language but I can hardly understand them when they speak.
- Half of their words are Russian.
- It's still our language.
- People make too much of language.
- To tell you the truth, I enjoy speaking Turkish more. It was my first tongue.
- Some of us hate it. The Dashnaks even want to change the words in the songs.
- They can't change the words. All the pleasure is in the words.
- No, they say the words are filth.

- Listen, I know what filth is.
- I know you know.
- They lay on top of me and they left me for dead. Every one of them lay on top of me and I was only fourteen and I will never stop hating them. But when I hear their songs I love their strings and their words.
- You can say that?
- I can say it.
- Because she loves music.
- It isn't only their music. It's our music too.
- They invited my uncle to play for them. My uncle Vosdanig played the zither and my uncle Mateos sang. My uncle Mateos had the best voice in the whole city and sang for the Pasha himself, but when the massacre started his head was cut off.
- It's our music more than their music.
- It's our land too.
- It's no one's land if no one lives on it.
- No one wants to live there.
- Everyone wants to live here.
- There are still some of us left back there.
- Those who are left are Moslems.
- So even if they are Moslems, they're still Armenians.
- How can an Armenian be a Moslem?
- Nubar's sister is a Moslem now, if she's still alive. After her husband was killed a Moslem took her for his wife. She had four children with him. Nubar went back and wanted her to leave, but no, she said, how could she leave her children? Her children are Moslems now but they're still Nubar's nieces and nephews.
- Isn't that something, Nubar who was such a passionate Dashnak?
- He hardly knows the difference anymore. All he does is sit on the porch and tell his childhood stories.

The Ghosts

- I wish I could write. I make marks on paper to help me remember and then I forget what they're for.
- That's okay, just keep trying. Don't lose your memory. If our memories go we're finished.
- I forget everything now. I can't remember yesterday and sixty years ago seems like this morning.

- Call me up and I'll tell you the difference. You remind me and I'll remind you.
- We have to keep remembering or we'll be like Zarzavart in the nursing home. If you go there now she won't even know who you are.
- She doesn't want to know who I am. I never really liked her to tell you the truth.
- She lost touch with her family, that's how she got like that. There was no one to talk with but the walls.
- There's always someone to talk with. You can talk with the plants, you can talk with the cat, you can talk with the old Chinese man around the corner who's half dead and can't understand anything you say, but at least he pretends to.
- Zarzavart didn't want to talk with just anyone, she was always too private.
- She talks with ghosts now. She looks out the window and talks with the ghosts in her head.

Flesheaters

- There's no taste in meat anymore.
- Not to young people. They love it, they eat it twice a day.
- Every once in a while I have a craving for a piece of steak, but it doesn't taste like what I wanted.
- What kind of steak you eat?
- I eat the senior citizen special and it tastes delicious.
- I'm going to eat cheese. They're giving cheese away downtown.
- I went down there. There was a line two blocks long and the old people were fainting on the sidewalk from waiting so long.
- Nevertheless I see people in Cadillacs coming to get it.
- I miss the cheese we used to get from the Dough-eaters.
- The Dough-eaters here don't make it, they buy their mozzarella in the supermarket.
- I had a lot of friends who were Dough-eaters.
- They're Christians. They drink the wine and eat the wafer.
- I had friends who were Jewish too. They have their own wine and wafer.
- It's all the same grapes and the same wheat.

From the Main Narrative

She Begins to Reveal Herself in Fairyland

At the border the Turkish guards searched the bus and there was a long wait by the river, the lush green of the other shore filled with poppies and lupine. Come, it seemed to say, come through the gate of flowers and bones.

It opened into a landscape like a dream, the same glow of soft sienna and new spring grass, the boys on the buses sprinkling lemon cologne in everyone's palm and the faces everywhere seeming to smell as fragrant. Were these the faces that raped Aunty Zabel, were these the eyes that slaughtered Uncle Avedis?

They stared back like innocent models. Nowhere else, not even in India, were they more friendly and hospitable. They heard of the past but it was not theirs, it was erased from their history books.

Should they have owned it, should they have paid for it? They sat like Harlem and Benares in homemade scarves and brightly colored caps, the empire of the Golden Bough reduced to unemployment and Saint Sophia gutted and crumbling, the great mosaics another page in a guidebook.

Yet the land was rich with abundant streams and the road unravelled into a wild interior like Wyoming before the white man. Kayseri was the frontier town at the edge of the wilderness and from there on the bus was empty. It climbed the snow-ribbed mountains as if departing from civilization, the chubby gold-toothed driver tapping his steering wheel in rhythm to the vibrant music on the scratchy radio, the ancient sas and zither twanging into the new green cottonwoods and exotic storks, the mud homes nestled in the high rocks like pueblo adobes.

Suddenly in the middle of nowhere the bus stopped and the only other passenger got off.

Where was he going, his plastic slippers trodding in the snow in the middle of nowhere?

He disappeared as if into fairyland.

As if into Uncle Jacko and Mano who used to play backgammon in Mano's little grocery shop in Weehawken, nothing to do but sit on the barrel of olives and watch them slap the board and roll the dice with their hearty *yalahs*.

As if into Aunty Shooshanig who had a cross tattooed on her hand when she was a girl in Jerusalem and so she was called *Haji* Shoosho like all other oriental Christians who visited the holy sepulchre.

As if into Aunty Lucinah who had that wooden camel from Alexandria where she lived before she could come to America.

As if into all those who were left behind. All those who were driven through these beautiful mountains with the weak ones slipping or jumping to their deaths, their screams echoing in a passionate lovesong from the nearest radio station, the jolly driver tapping in tune with the exciting lament and the twang of the *sas* waving through the air like a suicide falling to the rocks below.

Arlene Voski Avakian

Arlene Avakian occupies her dual roles of activist and writer in ethical, artful ways. Professor and Director of Women's Studies at the University of Massachusetts at Amherst, she is the editor of *Through the Kitchen Window: Women Writers Explore the Intimate Meanings of Food and Cooking* (1997); co-editor of *African-American Women and the Vote, 1837–1965* (1997); guest editor of a special issue of *Ararat* (August 1988) on Armenian feminism; featured in the independent film *Hamburger and Dolma* (1999), and the author of numerous articles and poems. But her most significant literary work is her landmark Armenian American memoir of 1992, *Lion Woman's Legacy*, in which she writes about her life as a feminist, displaying how her political consciousness gradually developed over time, while also allowing the reader to comprehend, on his or her own terms, the question of "how a particular life is shaped, in part, by cultural and social forces."

Lion Woman's Legacy was the first book to fill in the void that exists between growing up in the traditional Armenian American community and discovering an adult self through feminism. A clear, articulate documentation and consideration of first-person experiences, the book is structured much like a novel, dependent on narrative and containing vivid scenes that represent the major life shifts of the protagonist. Born in 1938 to Armenian immigrants from Persia and Turkey, Avakian grew up in multi-ethnic Washington Heights, in New York City, daughter to the Avakian Brothers carpet store family. The memoir chronicles her early childhood among her closely knit family, including a maternal grandmother who was a survivor of the Armenian Genocide; her move to the predominantly white New Jersey suburbs with her family in her teens; her college years in the socially restrictive 1950s; marrying young to escape her family, followed by an unexpected pregnancy, just when she wanted to pursue a "life of ideas"; depression during young motherhood and life as an academic's wife in the sixties; her own burgeoning career as an academic; her awakening as a feminist in the seventies; divorce; and her first love relationship with a woman.

The writer carefully depicts passages that were pivotal in developing her consciousness of oppression, set against a background of race relations in the United States. Early in the book, she describes an aborted friendship with a black friend because she can't envision the friend coming to her Armenian home, nor she, Avakian, going to the friend's place. Later, she becomes intrigued with white marchers of the Civil Rights movement and finds herself initiating racism awareness in Sheboygan, Wisconsin. When she becomes critical of the way the schools in Ithaca, New York, worked with her son Neal, a special-needs student, she further questions authority and relates it to the Black Power movement, and then, her own life.

> It also became clear to me that when black students
> spoke about the very real needs of black children to see
> themselves in the curriculum that my life might have been
> very different if I too had had that opportunity. Perhaps
> being an Armenian might not have been so difficult had I
> heard about my history and culture in the schools.

She soon integrates readings on racism into English composition curriculum as a writing tutor at Ithaca College. Later, in an attempt to diversify the women's studies offerings at the University of Massachusetts, Avakian takes black studies classes to further her education. The lessons she learns further affect her thinking on her Armenian identity, spawning confusion ("It was true that I did feel very different from all the whites I knew, but I also knew that I wasn't black") and arguments with her lover, Martha, a white woman:

> One day, when we had been yelling at each other for some
> time, I heard myself saying that my grandfather's power had
> been very limited. There was no doubt in my mind, I said,
> that he had oppressed my grandmother, but he had been
> killed by the Turks nonetheless. I screamed my uncle had
> been put into a camp because he was an Armenian, and
> had my grandfather been alive he would have had no more
> power to save his son than my grandmother had had. I

> continued, now through my tears, to say that I understood
> the oppression of a people and that oppression had an
> impact on patriarchy. I was well aware that Armenian men
> were male chauvinist pigs, and it was impossible for me
> to live near my family because of the way women were
> treated, but there was something about our common pain
> that would always connect me in some profound way to
> Armenians, women and men.

Avakian's development of consciousness leads her away from Armenian culture because of its restrictions in her life, but then it brings her to a reunion with her Armenian roots, eventually to a new understanding of feminism through her culture, through her grandmother's life, in the second-to-last chapter of the book.

These kinds of passages of realization are rooted in the times in which Avakian has lived. The writer does not exposit or interject, but tries to show what she was thinking and experiencing: Avakian the writer stays out of the way of Avakian the subject. It's a strong creative choice which gives the reader room to relate and to reflect on his or her own life. But it also displays both restraint and bravery, when considered in an Armenian context, since the reader can also take license to judge—not hard for traditional Armenians to do when presented with a feminist and a lesbian. In addition, Armenian stories are so rarely heard, and so many people don't know we exist, that to resist the pull to define and control the way others understand us seems like an act against history.

For this reason, another striking quality of Avakian's prose is the absence of quoted dialogue. Rarely does a person speak for him or herself in *Lion Woman's Legacy*; rather, the writer reports in her own words what was said to her by friends, colleagues, family. Avakian explains in her prologue:

> I tried, as much as possible, to recreate my response to
> events and people in my life as I experienced them at the
> time. The people who appear in this work are characterized
> from this perspective, as their histories are filtered through
> my memory. I wanted to tell the truth with this narrative,
> but I understand that my truth is only one of many.

There exist other perspectives, other voices, Avakian acknowledges, but the truth in this book is hers.

But there is another voice, another truth that appears later in the book:

that of the Lion Woman, Avakian's maternal grandmother. It's clear that the lack of dialogue is deliberate; here are two voices that matter, that of her own, and that of her grandmother, keeper of a repressed history of the Armenian Genocide. This approach gets at the core of Avakian's early life: she did not have a means to expression, growing up female in an Armenian household. A pivotal section of the book takes place when Avakian sees a psychologist, and feelings begin to emerge.

> Before therapy, I was only minimally aware of my feelings, though I had been the screamer in the family in my early teens.…When I got into a rage generally everyone left the room, and my grandmother always said, in Armenian of course, "The temper has a hold of her." Her statement made me angrier. She denied everything that had made me angry.…By the time I was eighteen my feelings were so well repressed that I hardly felt them at all.

After this point, the reader watches Avakian gradually express herself more and make active decisions about the direction of her life. The book itself seems to be an offshoot of her self-actualization and activism.

But Avakian has poetic gifts, it is clear. Her poems "Connections" I and II, originally published in *Forkroads,* are evidence of this, powerfully combining images and sound; ideas of inheritance and anger reverberate together. The most sensual and detailed passages in *Lion Woman's Legacy* are the ones on food, which is telling, since it was the main means, Avakian reflects, by which her family expressed love towards her: "my grandmother sat at the kitchen table for hours trimming dozens of artichokes, reaching into the cactuslike vegetables to scoop out the chokes, and then cooking them with potatoes and small white onions in olive oil and lemon." But it's an artistic choice to keep the poetry limited to the culinary, since it's more urgent to Avakian to articulate thought, to "scoop out" the truth and meaning from her prickly familial experiences of repressed emotion. It's notable that later, with her anthology *Through the Kitchen Window*, Avakian critiques women's forced relationship to cooking, but also reclaims Armenian food both as a longtime link to her Armenian identity and as an expression of creativity. And with *Hamburger and Dolma* the circle seems to complete itself; Avakian and her Armenian feminist friends cook food, not because they are expected to, but for their own enjoyment.

Avakian came into her own, as an adult woman, after reading Doris Lessing's Children of Violence series; literature became a major means through which she changed herself. Never before had Avakian seen her life, of compromise and limitations, of loss of self through marriage and motherhood, represented in words. Once she was able to find someone who spoke her reality, she launched into action, "fully committed to working to change my life and the world."

I met Arlene Avakian three years ago, when she came to read at the inaugural reading of Gartal, a poetry series I coordinate in New York City. The evening also included a gay Armenian man and a woman of mixed Palestinian and Armenian heritage. The goal of the event is "to bring together diverse Armenian constituencies, from the traditional to the progressive." After I introduced her, Arlene stood at the podium and announced, "It's a new day." It was something I had hoped for but it hadn't seemed real until Arlene put it into words; her lifelong work had helped to make that day come true for us, activists, writers, Armenians. Reading the work of Arlene Avakian, one can clearly follow the shaping of a self by the forces around it. But one can also see a spirit that could not be kept back by the mores and standards of the times she lived in, and this spirit is hopeful, powerful: part legacy, part lion.

Nancy Agabian

from *Lion Woman's Legacy*
Chapter 21

Shortly after Martha and I had finished reading *Passage to Ararat*, women's studies sponsored a lecture by Andrea Dworkin, "Women and the New Right." Since I was interested in the topic, I decided to go, and Martha joined me. The large auditorium was almost full, but we found two seats near the stage. Shortly after we sat down Dworkin was introduced, and when she rose to the podium the audience responded with thunderous applause. She began her talk with general comments on the oppression of women and finally focused on Anita Bryant, who had just begun her campaign against gays and lesbians. To my great surprise, Dworkin asked the audience to empathize with Bryant—to see her as a woman, like ourselves, a woman oppressed by patriarchy. As Dworkin continued her litany of the wrongs perpetrated against women by men, I grew more and more uncomfortable. I looked around the room and saw some of my colleagues and many of our students in the audience. None of them seemed to be disturbed by Dworkin's endless recital of the powerlessness of women. I wondered if I was unable to accept the reality of my oppression as a woman.

I began literally to squirm in my seat, and I knew from the look on Martha's face that she was also disturbed. I leaned closer to her and heard myself whisper, "Not my grandmother." Even as I spoke I wondered what I meant, but Martha calmly nodded in agreement. I wanted desperately to leave, but that was impossible. The audience was spellbound, and we were seated in the middle of the row. I waited for Dworkin to finish, no longer hearing her but thinking about my grandmother and trying to contain myself.

The lecture was over, at last, and Martha said, "Let's get out of here." While the audience rose to applaud Dworkin, we almost ran to the door. The cool night air felt wonderful. I took a deep breath and vented my fury. She wasn't talking about me. I was not a total victim. I could act. I could change my life. I did have responsibility for my actions, and I most certainly held Anita Bryant responsible for what she did. Finally, the phrase that I had uttered in the auditorium came out again—not my grandmother. I would have to hear her story again.

I decided to tape the stories of my mother and aunt as well as my grandmother and was excited and terrified. The distance I'd maintained for so long from my family and my ethnicity had seemed to be necessary for my own survival. I'd desperately needed to be as American as possible and also to be as independent of the considerable demands of my family as possible. After I became a feminist I understood, too, that to stay within the family would have meant either adhering to the rigidly circumscribed roles for women or constantly fighting against them. Now, at the age of thirty-five, I wondered if I was threatening a relationship that had become fairly comfortable. But I had no choice. I had to hear my grandmother's story again.

I asked Martha to come with me when I went to New Jersey to do the taping. I honestly felt that I could not attempt the project without her support and was grateful when she agreed to join me. We arrived at my mother's house armed with sheets of questions I'd prepared. I had come to tape the story of my grandmother's survival, but I thought it was important to also get a sense of her role as a woman as well as some idea of what her economic status had been before the genocide. As I asked her what her wedding had been like, the kind of house she'd had, and who did the cooking and cleaning, my grandmother seemed uninterested and even irritated. Her memory of her early life was dim, and she seemed confused.

The situation was not helped by my Armenian, which was worse than rusty. I could barely understand her, and she tried to speak in English, which had gotten worse than I remembered it. I called Aunty Ars into the room to help translate, but the situation did not improve. I looked closely at the small woman who sat before me. Perhaps, I thought sadly, I had waited too long. My grandmother looked very old. Her eighty-nine years seemed to have finally taken their toll.

With my aunt's help, I got some sense of Elmas Tutuian's early life. She was two years old when her mother died and her father sent her to live with her older sister Turvanda, who was married and whose daughter was just Elmas's age. Turvanda and her husband Arakel were wonderful to her, she said, just like parents. When she was seventeen years old Hampartzum Tutuian, a friend of Arakel's, asked for her hand. Elmas did not know him, and she thought he was too old for her, but Arakel convinced her to marry him, saying he was a good man and would take care of her just as he had. Before I could ask her another question she said in English, "I was seventeen years old. He was twenty-eight. At twenty-seven they took my husband. Berj was two years old, Ars seven, and Ashot four. I have three children. They took us out of the house—the Turks. My husband was a soldier. I have three children." She then turned to my aunt and told her to "tell about us. Tell about the Turk."

Aunty Ars began the story: "Christmastime they exiled all the men and boys fifteen and over. And then Eastertime we went to church and came back from the church our doors were all—what do you call—they locked it and had their stamp on it—only the dining room was open. No kitchen— nothing. And what we had on, we were left with that. And my mother went to the police commissioner who was very friendly with my father."

My grandmother seemed relaxed for the first time since I began asking her questions. The story was being told, and she was content to add her comments from time to time.

Aunty Ars continued: "My mother went to him to say that's what they did to our house. What are we going to do? And he said, 'It's going to be very bad. They are going to exile everybody. Why don't you become a Turk?' And my mother says, 'My husband is in the army, how could they exile me?'"

My grandmother broke in and corrected my aunt: "I told them, if my husband heard I became a Turk, he would go to his grave. And then he said it's going to be very bad. You'll be sorry. I told them what my nationality is—I'll be the same." She sat back and told Aunty Ars to continue. When Aunty Ars diverted to tell us something about her husband's family, my grandmother said, "Ashot's story, Ashot's story." Aunty Ars turned to her and told her not to skip ahead. My grandmother sat back and listened as her daughter told us that the police commissioner had arranged to allow them to use a few more of the rooms in the house.

One day an Armenian man who had somehow escaped being exiled with the other men in the town came to the door. He begged Elmas to hide him. Refusing at first, she finally relented. Yet she knew she could not keep him for long in the three rooms of the house that had been opened for their use and went to tell his wife and mother that they had to find another place for him. While she was gone Ars, Ashot, Berj, and their one-hundred-and-ten-year-old great-grandmother were alone in the house. The man was hiding in a closet.

Aunty Ars went on: "They came, gendarmes...with the *muchdar*—was like sheriff...and he says, 'I said, we don't hide anybody—and the man is in there...where the wood is.' I was trembling. And my great-grandmother had a cane. They took her cane—going like this [waving her hand around]. My heart was throbbing. And the sheriff says, 'Have you got a match?' We haven't. Berj says—how old was she—two or three years old—says, 'yes.' I took the match from her and said, 'No, we don't have a match.'...So they went."

When Almas came home and was told what had happened she realized the man had to leave immediately. His wife and mother had been taken in by a Greek family, and their house was surrounded by Turkish police. Her solution was to dress him like a Turkish woman and send my aunt, who would appear to be his child, with him. Aunty Ars described their walk across the town:

> Turkish women wear a veil. Their face is closed. My mother brought it. He wore that and what belongings he had in a handkerchief. My mother sent me with him. You know it was quite a far way. I'm going from the front and he is following me...When I reached his house all the gendarmes, police, you know, all around. So he says, let's go from the back. They have searched the house. So he got in. I came back. I said never again. I was trembling...but my mother was so— there was no fear with her. She didn't know what fear was. So Easter came after Easter. They sent us. We were the last ones to be exiled... Visim's family, they were four, no they were three. Verzin, three, five with my mother and my great-grandmother...and we had a distant cousin, she had two daughters—eleven people. They put us on those cars that ox pulled it. Whatever we had they took us...far, far away.

My grandmother interjected, "No Armenians or nothing." And as my aunt tried to remember how many days they'd traveled, my grandmother impatiently said in English, "Wait a minute. We go over there. The man came over and said in Armenian, 'They don't want you in our town.'" Aunty Ars disagreed, and they began to argue about the sequence of events. My grandmother sat forward in her chair and said, "Let me say it in Armenian." She looked very different than she had a short while ago when I had been asking her about her early life. Her eyes were bright, and she seemed to be fully engaged in what was happening. But Aunty Ars continued the story:

> That man, that gendarme—everybody was crying…he starts crying with us. He was such a nice person. Anyway, third or fourth day, it was raining, it was dark. In the evening somebody came…like a sheriff or something. He said, "I have to leave them over here." He said, "Government told me to bring them here, and I'm going to leave them here." He said, "I don't have anyplace." And there was one room. And there was one room…He says, "What's that?" He says, "That's the school." He says, "Where's the key?" He says, "the *khoja*" the teacher they call the *khoja* "he's gone home in another town." You know what he did, the gendarme, he gave one kick, broke the door. He took us all up there, eleven of us, you know, small room. We don't have a door up there. And the people start coming. To Armenian they used to call *gavors*.* And they are coming. And they are coming and looking from the door. Young men about eighteen, seventeen years old. They're saying, "Let's see what the *gavors* look like." Anyhow, maybe an hour later, big tray of food came. See there were two Agas, two brothers, one had gone to Istanbul, you know, had come back, he fed us.

She turned to my grandmother, who had been listening to her intently, and asked her how long the brother fed them. My grandmother replied, "He said, 'For a week you are gong to give them their meals'…And later they came for Ashot." My aunt told her she was mixing up the story. She said they had come for Ashot later, and for a few minutes they argued, and my grandmother finally sat back and waited for my aunt to continue. She told us about the food the brothers provided for them, and finally she said, "One day they came. They sent somebody, and we have to go someplace. We all went. They are taking the boys." My grandmother sat up and said in Armenian," I will tell that." Although my aunt tried to interject from time

*Turkish pejorative for Armenian.

to time, my grandmother would not be stopped. She spoke rapidly but this time I understood everything she said:

> The police came and saw us, and the two brothers were sitting there. They [the police] wanted to know how many boys there were there. They said two, there are two boys. Visim and Didi. [Didi was what the children in our family called our Uncle Ashot.] And then he said—he looked and said, "That one is too small. I am going to take this one. I am taking this boy."
> "Where are you going to take him?"
> "They are collecting the boys."
> I said, "This boy's father is a soldier. You are not taking this boy. He is my boy. I won't give him to you. He is mine. He is mine."
> He said, "He is not yours."
> I said, "He is mine."
> And we were screaming in Turkish, "I won't give him."
> The brothers were listening. "This boy is mine," I said, "and his father is a soldier," I said. "Soldier, do you understand?"
> "I am going to take him."
> "You can't," I said. "I won't give him," I screamed. "I won't give him," I screamed. "I won't give him. You can't," I said. "Who are you to take my boy?" I said.
> He screamed at me. Then he said, "You are doing too much."
> I said, "You are doing too much. Do you understand?" And how he screamed. "You cannot take my boy. He is my boy."
> He said, "He is the king's boy."
> "No," I said, "he is mine. I won't give him to you. Understand this," I said, "You know if there is a God in heaven, this boy will not stay with you. If there is no God...Day and night," I said, "I will pray that when the English come" (already when you say "English" the Turk trembles) and take your child from your wife's arms, and you will know what I am feeling. Do you understand? Night and day I will pray. If there is a God, he will come and do that, if there is no God, do what you want. But I will not give my son, understand that." And I was crying. I looked at the brothers and said, "I will pray that the English come and take your wife's child away from her. If there is a God, know this."
> He said, "All right, let me take your son."
> I said, "I won't give him to you. Take me with him. I'll go. Take me with him.

"I'll go. Take me with him."

"No," he said, "I'm telling the brothers to bring you tomorrow; I will take this child now." I am going to take your son."

"I won't give him," I said. "I will bring him."

He turned to the brothers and told them to bring the rest of the family the next day, that he was going to take the boy then.

"Very good," I said, "I will bring my son with me."

He said, "You are making this too long."

My sister-in-law said, "Please let them take him and we will go tomorrow."

He told the men again that they were to bring the rest of the family to Dadai.

He took Ashot away. Arsenic was crying, "First, I lost my father, and now I am losing Ashot." She was crying. "Quiet," I said. "We are going tomorrow too. Quiet." She kept crying saying that she had lost her father and now she lost Ashot.

My sister-in-law said, "It's all right, tomorrow we will go." The next day we went to the brothers and said, "We are ready. When are you going to take us?" The man laughed.

I said, "Why are you laughing?"

"He fooled you," he said.

"He took your son. He told us later that you are going to stay in this village."

"Oh. Is that how it is," I said. "You wait and see." After the children went to bed, I told my sister-in-law. I called her sister. We loved each other. "You know what I am going to do? I am going with the villagers." I wrapped my head up and I am going to Dadai with the villagers to get Ashot.

Early in the morning the two of us wrapped ourselves up, my sister-in-law and I. I said, "If I come, I will come. If not, take care of my children." I wrapped myself up and started my journey. I started and came to a mountain. No people. No road. Nothing. By now it is around five o'clock in the afternoon and dark. I am alone on the mountain. I looked in front of me and saw someone coming. I said, "If you love your God, stop." I screamed, "If you love your God, stop." I want to go with him. I ran after him and held the horse. I begged him to take me to his house.

He said, "I can't. I am not going there, my girl. I am going somewhere else."

At that point I broke in to ask if the man was a Turk, and Aunty Ars answered quickly, "Turk. Turk." My grandmother continued:

He said, "Where are you going?"

I said, "I am going to Dadai. What is the way to Dadai?"

"Go down this way," he said. "There will be a mountain in front of you. There is a road on that mountain. If you stay on that road, you will reach Dadai."

I was still holding onto him, and I said, "If you love your God, take me with you."

"I can't," he said. "I am invited somewhere else, and I can't take a young woman with me." The man said, in Turkish, "Let God be with you. I am showing you the right road."

I got on the road and climbed the mountain. I am in the mountain. Mountain. Big trees. I sat under a tree. It was dark. I sat under the tree and said, "Jesus Christ, if you are there, help me, help me. I am doing this for my child." I sat there until it was light, awake all the time. I haven't eaten anything yet. When the birds started to cheep, I got up. The man had told me the road to Dadai. I went a little further, and there were people there. I ran to them. Three women were sitting (it is before my eyes as I am saying this)—three women were sitting and two men. They were taking food to the soldiers. The man said, "What do you want? Where are you going?"

I said, "I am going to Dadai."

The man felt sorry for me. He said, "I will take you to Dadai. We are going there too. We are taking food to the soldiers."

I said, "No. Show me the right way and I will go to Dadai myself."

Because the Derderians had become Turks and were living there, I said no. "I have relatives there. I will walk."

The women started to laugh and were speaking in Turkish. *Aman*,* the man let them have it. "Look at this woman's face," he said. "Aren't you ashamed of yourselves? Why are you laughing? Shame on you!" He got angry at the women speaking in Turkish.

I said, "Don't get mad at them. I am going to Dadai." I went to Dadai, understand? I went to Dadai to Vahram's house and they welcomed me. I am crying. "They took my Ashot."

He said, "Yes, they have collected all the boys, and they are here. They are in the school. That is why our friend came and made us

* An Armenian exclamation meaning "Oh, my goodness."

Turks. They had a ceremony so they won't take our son."

Then Vahram's mother said, "Now they are having breakfast. After they eat they are all out in the garden. It is a large school with a large garden."

I said, "Very well. Please get me some coffee. After coffee I will go. I will not stay." To see my son! I was trembling all this time. I drank my coffee and went to the school. They said it was two blocks away. I went the two blocks. There were mothers outside. They took all the boys, and many of these mothers were there.

Aunty Ars broke in to explain that the Turks intended to raise the Armenian boys as Turks. "They were going to do a circumcision so they did become a Turk then, see. That's how they think."

My grandmother waited for her to finish and continued her story. "Ashot saw me and came running," she said. "'Mother, save me. You save me.' I said, 'That's why I came—to save you. I am going to save you. I won't leave you in the hands of these Turks. Don't worry.' He went upstairs crying. I thought about the police commissioner who told me, if you are in trouble, come to me."

I was confused and asked who this police commissioner was, and my aunt explained it was the one in Kastemoni, where they had lived before the exile. She said he had told her mother that he would help her if he could. She explained that he had been very friendly with her father. "His great-grandmother was an Armenian, see. He said, 'I have Armenian blood in me, too.' He was a very nice man." She went on to say that my grandmother had walked from Dadai to Kastemoni, a walk of three days. "When she went, her feet were swollen. They said my mother's feet were swollen." She told us that there were some Armenians in Kastemoni who had become Turks to avoid being exiled and that my grandmother had gone to their house. As soon as there was a pause in the conversation, my grandmother went on:

I went to their door and knocked on it. I was dressed like a Turk. They said, "Please come in." When I got there I was numb. When I knocked on their door, I was numb. It was as if I was going to go crazy. I couldn't go in. They said, in Turkish, "Come in. Come in, madam." I opened my face,* and they started to scream, "Oh, Elmas." They all came and we hugged each other.

* Removed her veil.

"What is it?" they asked.

"They have taken Ashot," I said. "They took Ashot. I am going to the police commissioner." But I couldn't walk for three days.

My grandmother paused, and my aunt said, "Yea, for three days she couldn't walk. You can imagine what's happening to us, back there. Because they came, and they want to know where is my mother." My grandmother said, "They put my feet in hot water and rubbed salted butter on them." Then she described her meeting with the police commissioner:

> It was early Friday morning. He had just come downstairs to wash up. It is in front of my eyes now. He said, "Please come in," in Turkish. The rest of the family was upstairs. I closed the police commissioner's door and opened my face.
>
> "Oh my, Elmas. Where did you come from? What has happened?"
>
> I said, "They took my Ashot. They took my Ashot."
>
> He said, "I told you to become a Turk, and you didn't do it."
>
> "You know best," I said. "I beg you, save my Ashot."
>
> People upstairs noticed that there were two people talking. His wife looked down from upstairs.
>
> "Oh my, Madam Elmas," she said. "Come upstairs."
>
> I cried, "They took my Ashot." I am crying.
>
> The police commissioner came and said, "Don't cry. I'll see what's what. Don't cry."
>
> "If I don't cry, tell me what it is I have to do to save him. I have to save him. I have to save him."
>
> He said, "Today I am going to see my superior. I will speak to him and see what can be done...but don't tell anyone you are here. There are some Turk dogs, who if you say Armenian, they will cut your throat."

Within a short period of time the police commissioner arranged for my grandmother to formally renounce her Armenian ancestry and become a Turk. She was also able to do the same for her children, including Ashot, and all the other relatives who were still in exile. He had also arranged to bring them to Kastemoni, but Ashot's release took a longer time. After four months, the whole family was reunited.

Aunty Ars began to talk about what it was like. "We came to Kastemoni," she said. "And we used to live, all of us in—I don't know how many rooms. We had houses, but we didn't have it anymore. And we were Turks…We had like a small apartment. My aunt and cousins—all together. We used to sew burlap bags. That's how we survived. And then one night, I never forget that night, two men, they're going to break our door."

My grandmother broke in, saying in English, "Wait a minute—I am talk," and began again in Armenian.

My sister-in-law and I are like sisters. We were sewing bags for the soldiers. The children went to bed. I said, "Get up and go to bed. I will finish this one, and tomorrow I will take them." She got up and went to bed.

Then she got up and ran to me, saying, "Sister, sister, sister, they are breaking the door down."

I said, "Don't worry. It's nothing."

She said, "No, no. It's not what you said, get up."

I got up. I got up and saw that they were going to break the door. They were going to break the door down and come in. What were we going to do?

Ars said, "Mother, throw me out the window." I said, "How can I throw you out the window?'

"Whatever you do, throw me out the window," she said. "Throw me out the window."

Suddenly I had an idea. I said, "Let's open the windows, and all at once let's all scream fire. Save us. There is a fire." All of us were yelling out the windows. After that we noticed that there were soldiers in the street. The superior of the soldiers said, "This is not a fire, it is a rape."

Soon after that we noticed that they went away. Then the police came. They knocked on the door. We said we won't open the door. They said, "We are the police." They came in. They asked what happened. And how did I get that idea to yell out the window?

In the morning they took us to the police commissioner.

He said, "What happened?"

We told him, "We were sleeping, and my sister-in-law woke me up saying that they are going to break our door. They were going to break it and come in."

The police commissioner said, "What neighbors do you have there?"

"The Aga's son, the shoemaker's son, and another person's son.

That's all. No one else."

I was sitting there, and they brought both of them. When they saw me, they turned pale.

The police commissioner asked where they were last night. They said they were home.

I said, "No, you were the ones who were throwing rocks at the door and were going to break it."

The police commissioner got up and hit them both.

My grandmother said, "Do you know what? When I am in trouble, I am never afraid. When I went to Turkey they made terrible trouble for me." I remembered then that she had gone to Turkey when she was in her late seventies. She told us what happened:

I signed a paper saying that I was going to leave, and the officer said it was forged.

The mayor came and said, "They want you." I went.

He said, "Go over to that man." I went there. He said, "What do you want?"

I said, "I don't want anything. You said you wanted to see me and so I came so you could see me."

And the place was full of people...

He asked, "Who signed this paper?"

I said, "I did."

He said, "No you didn't."

I said, "Give me the pen." I took the pen and signed my name. "That is my signature." He saw it was the same. I opened my mouth in the government office and said, "Aren't you ashamed of yourselves? Shame on you doing these things. No one can sign my name. Only I can make my signature. Look at me and look at my hair. Such a woman doesn't do such things. Shame on you."

In the government office—everyone was sitting there. No one made a sound. I am never afraid. When I have something to say, I say it.

The man came and took me to my relative's house. "Oh," he said, "you are like an *aslan*."

I asked her what *aslan* meant, and she told me it was a lion woman.

We had been taping for close to an hour, and, thinking that my grandmother must be very tired, I suggested that we stop for awhile. She assured me that she was not tired at all, and my aunt seemed anxious to finish their story. When I agreed that we would continue, my grandmother sat back and listened to my aunt tell us what happened after the night their neighbors had tried to break down the door.

> We moved to where the Greeks lived, where there was an Armenian church and school. We moved there after that affair....My mother and Araskin, *Der Hayr*'s wife,* she had a son and daughter; we lived in one room and they in one room. And my mother was going with a few other women—they were going from town to town selling needles and thread, this and that, packs on their backs, you know... Mother took me. We went to one town. It was night. Some young boys came, you know, and they're saying, "If we kill the *gavors* no one will know." And nobody could know it.
>
> And then from far away, I suppose it was their parents, they came and said, "Shame on you people, these are people." And they told us, "You people better go to the next town and stay there." So we went....Coming back, some town, some farm they chased the dogs after us. All the dogs are around us. I was going crazy, crying, yelling. Finally, all the people came and chased the dogs away.
>
> After that I got sick....My mother came. She got sick. She had the typhoid fever. And the doctor saw me and said, "Who is going to take care of her?" [Arsenic was about ten years old at the time.]
>
> I said, "I am."
>
> He said, "You know you have to wet the sheet in cold water, wrap her in it." All night long I had to do that...and wash the sheet, boil it. I used to do all those—and I was a little girl. All night long, she is burning, you know. I got cold water, put the sheets, wrap her in.
>
> I must have dozed off. All of a sudden, she says, "Arsenic?" You know, my name. She says, "I'm all right. I saw your father in my dream."

After telling us about her own bout with typhoid my aunt told us how my grandmother managed to get her family to Istanbul.

> All the English had come...They were taking captives. English soldiers, they came to Kastemoni—all generals and things, you know. They had their guides and things. One night, our door was

---

* An Armenian priest.

ringing and ringing. They wanted to come in. Do you remember [to my grandmother] the English?

The next morning my mother went and talked to their superior. She told them what happened and said that they were not that kind of people over here. They wanted to get in....English came with an Armenian interpreter. They were going to take all the orphans to Istanbul.

So my mother went and saw the interpreter and said, "I have children. I want to go to Istanbul and maybe from there—I have relatives. My sister is in America. I have to go there."

He said, "I will take you to the captain." He took her to the captain. He said, "We can't do it. We can only take so much and no more."

And my mother said, "I'll be their mother. They need a mother, these orphans." And that's how we came to Istanbul.

It would be years, however, before they were able to leave Turkey. Turvanda and Arakel had gone to New York just before the genocide began, but they were unable to raise the money for Elmas's passage. Aunty Ars described how they lived: "In Istanbul when Armenian people came from America they used to bring old clothes. Mother used to work there. We used to sew the burlap bags...the man, that I save his life, Armenian man, he was doing that business. He used to give us that work."

My grandmother broke in to say, "I all the time worked." I asked if they had been very poor, and my aunt responded:

Very poor. And we had one room. That was our bedroom, in an apartment, you know. We had the ground floor. One room. That was our bedroom, living room....It was bad....We all worked, otherwise we can't—we used to go to the fields and pick *perper* [a wild green] and something else...no meat, you know. We didn't have sugar. You know, during the war [World War II] nobody had it. I mean when they rationed everything over here....

One day I went to the A&P and here was a big line. I said to the manager, "Why is there such a big line?"

He said, "Today they're giving away coffee without coupon."

I said, "Well, I do without it. I'm not going to wait for that line."

He said, "Why?" I said, "You know, I've seen it—that I could do without it. There is no panic about it."

We have everything over here.

I asked if she had been hungry a lot, and she answered, "Oh yeah. Some-times we have an onion and sometimes apples for dinner. Whatever we find."

Finally, my grandmother located a nephew of hers who was working for a rug exporter in Iran. She wrote and told him what they had endured and how difficult their lives were. He sent the money for their passage, and they left Turkey for New York City.

My aunt and grandmother began to reminisce about their lives before the genocide, but I was too exhausted to listen anymore. I was relieved when my mother knocked on the door to say that dinner was ready. We rose to leave my grandmother's room. I wanted to say something to her—to convey some of what I was feeling. I had been deeply moved but was unable to think of something appropriate to say. Telling any of the members of my family what I really felt was something I had not done for years, and my relationship with my grandmother had been marked by hostility since my brother's birth. My aunt and Martha left the room, and I waited for my grandmother to get out of her chair. I held her arm and thanked her for telling me her story again.

I spent the remainder of the weekend listening to and taping the memories of my mother and Aunty Ars, and Dodo, an older cousin—this time without my grandmother. My mother remembered very little about the exile and had no memories of her father, who was gone by the time she was three. She talked about being hungry in Turkey, about the darkness they had to endure at night because they could not afford fuel for lights, and about the disease and starvation which ravaged the tent city in Istanbul where the majority of Armenian refugees lived. Most of what she remembered took place after they came to New York when she was eleven. Dodo, whose family had left Turkey before the genocide, told me in vivid detail about the relatives who came to live with her family when they arrived in this country. Aunty Ars's focus was on the various jobs she had had before and after she was married.

I was interested in what they had to say, though I experienced none of the emotional intensity I had felt when I listened to my grandmother. I was still filled with her story and was anxious to get home.

Chapter 22

Over the next few months I began to feel that my grandmother's story had had a powerful effect on my life, though I was not at all clear about it. I decided to transcribe the tapes, to write the story down, in an attempt to understand it. I also wanted to write it down for my grandmother. Now I realized that twenty years earlier, when she'd said, "Tell it to the world," she had charged me with insuring that her story did not die with her. I had no idea how to tell it to the world or even if I wanted to, but at least I could put it on paper for her. The gesture would be highly symbolic, since she could not read English.

For weeks I spent my spare time translating and transcribing the tapes, and as I heard over and over again how the Turks had come for Ashot, how my grandmother had screamed again and again that they had no right to take him, that he was her son, I wept. For the first time I felt connected to her pain, to the pain of my mother, aunt, and uncle, and, by extension, the Armenian people. I also now understood why I had cried, often with wrenching sobs I could not control, when I read about the separation of black children and parents during slavery. The rage I'd felt against whites and Western civilization for what had been done to Africans and African-Americans now included Turks. In both cases, my anger turned to fury because the horrors were not acknowledged. Africa remained the dark continent, and the Armenian genocide was still forgotten.

There was more to the story, however, than pain and rage. As I pieced together my grandmother's early life from the little she'd remembered and from the few things my aunt told me, one thing was very clear: My grandmother had not been raised to take care of herself, even in normal circumstances, yet she had managed to survive the genocide virtually alone. She had gotten her son back and arranged for the return of all of the eleven people from her family who were in exile. Back in Kastemoni, then in Istanbul, she had managed to find housing for her family and had kept them from the starvation that had killed thousands of Armenians.

Now I understood her story was about survival. Not only had she overcome her circumstances, but she had resisted victimization as well. The high point of her story was when the Turks came for Ashot and she said no—that they had no right to her son.

The same woman who had taught me to defer to men, whom I had grown to dislike after the birth of my brother, because she so obviously favored him, was also the woman who taught me, through her story, that women were strong. It had been the knowledge of my grandmother's resistance and survival that had made it impossible for me to accept a feminist politics that focused only on women's victimization. Unwittingly, she'd taught me that, even within a strict patriarchy, women were not rendered helpless.

I was amused at the irony of my grandmother making possible both my openness to the women's movement and my dissatisfaction with it. Her story had lain dormant in my psyche for twenty years, but its influence had been profound. It had provided soil for the blossoming of the feelings behind my politics. I now realized that it would not, could not, be denied. I finished the oral history, had a copy bound for my grandmother, and felt satisfied as I looked at the title in gold letters on the blue leather binding: *Elmas Tutuian—Lion Woman.*

My grandmother would never know what her story had meant for me. By the time I finished it, she had had a stroke, and my parents had made the difficult decision to move her to the Armenian Home for the Aged. She was not often coherent but when she was she railed at being in the home, being incapacitated, being alive. She prayed for the Lord to take her, she told me, and with a spark in her eyes said she wanted her body to be burned. The time was past when the recording of her story mattered.

I had given a copy of the oral history to my parents, Dodo, and Aunty Ars, and after I heard nothing about it for a few months I asked my parents if they'd read it. Perhaps, I thought, they had been too preoccupied with my grandmother to have had the time. They responded that they had, of course, read the story. They said there were many inaccuracies. My father complained that the dates could not be correct, and my mother, that there was too much about Aunty Ars, who, she said, had gotten everything mixed up. I said I could make changes but I had wanted at least to get the story on paper. They said nothing. The fear that my relationship to my family might change was groundless after all. We would remain as distant as we ever had been.

But I was changed. I now consciously identified as an Armenian. I also understood some of the origins of my politics but was unsure at the same time, where my new sense of self would lead. I longed to talk to other Armenians, but my relatives, most of whom I saw very rarely at large family gatherings, were the only ones I knew. My last attempts at serious conversation with some of my cousins had been in the 1960s when we had been polarized on opposite sides of the political spectrum. I was anxious to meet Armenians who were not family members for other reasons, too. I didn't know what it meant to be an Armenian and wondered if what I had identified as "Armenian" was merely what my family did.

With the hope of learning about other Armenians, I subscribed to an Armenian weekly newspaper published in Boston. Every week I glanced

at articles on the activities of church dignitaries, news of various Armenian
organizations and their ladies auxiliaries, and announcements of trips to
Armenia. I was not enlightened, and from what I could see in the paper
there was nothing in the Armenian community for someone like me.

One day, during my usually quick perusal of the paper, I spotted a
small announcement of a day-long workshop on the psychological and
social effects of the genocide on the children of survivors. The workshop,
which was being organized by two Armenian psychiatrists, was for people
whose parents or grandparents were survivors. I sat with the paper in my
lap and realized with a bit of a shock that I was both the granddaughter
and daughter of survivors. I'd known, of course, that my mother had gone
through the genocide, but the focus had always been on my grandmother.
She had told me the story, while my mother never talked about Turkey.
I knew from taping her words that she had few memories of what had
happened to her family, but now I saw that, regardless of her specific
memories, her life had been shaped by the genocide. She had, no doubt,
known terror and hunger. I was the child of someone who had experienced
that pain, and now I knew there was a part of my psychological history I had
not previously thought about. What had been the effect on my life of being
the daughter and granddaughter of survivors of the genocide? I remembered
an article in the *New York Times Sunday Magazine* that Tom had given to me
years ago. It was about the children of survivors of the Holocaust. Now I
vaguely remembered that I'd been fascinated by the article and meant to get
the book it was based on, but never had.

Clearly, I would have to attend this workshop, but it was with some
trepidation that I sent for a registration form. Did I really want to go into a
group of Armenians? What would they be like, and, more troubling, how
would they respond to me? I was as far as one could be from the image
of the good Armenian women I had grown up with and which was, I was
discouraged to see, still well represented in the Armenian weekly. Women
were absent from the important committees but appeared as organizers and
cooks for the various fund-raising events. I worried, too, about what other
Armenians would think about someone like me whose daily life included
virtually nothing Armenian except for what was on the dinner table.

The workshop was held near my parents' house, and since it began early
Saturday morning I decided to stay with them that Friday night. I wondered
how they would react to my attending such a workshop, but they said little
about it. I would tell them more about it when I got there, I thought. Still
they seemed uninterested. My father asked who the psychiatrists were,

and, when I told him, my mother said that one was the grandson of one of my grandmother's friends. Didn't I remember Mrs. Boyajian from the old neighborhood?" I said I didn't and tried once more to engage them in a discussion about the effects of the genocide but stopped when my mother said that I should not talk about such things when my cousin Dodo came. She, Uncle George, and Aunty Ars would be over for dinner very soon. I had to remember that Dodo's mother had been Turkish, she said, and talking about the genocide upset her. The evening was spent, like so many others, eating and talking about the family.

When I got to the workshop the next morning I was pleased to see a group of about forty people, including many who looked my age. After a brief introduction we were assigned to small groups where we would spend the bulk of the day. Each group of ten to twelve people would have two psychiatrists as leaders: an Armenian and, to keep some objectivity they said, a non-Armenian. The psychiatrists introduced themselves, and I noted that all the non-Armenians had Jewish names. I wondered if any of them had written the book about children of the Holocaust which I had never read.

Optimistically, I walked to the room that had been assigned to my group, but my high hopes for sharing feelings and experiences with other children of survivors were quickly dashed. The discussion focused on Armenian politics. It began with a statement by a man that we needed to get the Turkish government to admit what it had done to the Armenian people. Another man said we needed the land. We Armenians could not rest until we had Armenia back from the Turks and the Russians. Someone else, also a man, quickly responded that Soviet Armenia was what we had, and we had better understand that. We would not get anything else. He had been there many times, and those of us who had not should plan a visit soon. It was important to go for as long a period as possible, he said, because only then could we know what it was like to be in an Armenian country controlled by Armenians. His comments sparked a lively debate about whether Armenians did, in fact, have control. How could we be content, a man asked, with an Armenia behind the "Iron Curtain"? We could not rest, a woman said, until we had a free Armenia.

Though I found the debate interesting, it was not what I had come to hear. I wanted to know what other people felt about being Armenian. Had they had the same feelings as I had growing up? What had it been like for them to be raised by a survivor? I waited for a break in the discussion to ask those questions, but when I did only one woman responded. Her eyes filled with tears as she recounted some of what her father had told her of his experiences. He had been a young man when the Turks came to his village.

They had taken all the men to the outskirts of the village and beaten and shot them. Somehow her father had not been killed but had been left for dead by the Turks. When she recalled how, every day of her childhood, he had shown her the scars on his head from that beating so that she would not forget what had happened to the Armenians, she broke down and could not continue. To my surprise, her revelation did not encourage others to tell their stories but only served to heat up the political debate. One man slammed his hand on the table, saying that the world has forgotten and that we must make Turkey pay. The man who had urged us to go to Armenia disagreed. Armenians had to do all we could to support Armenia. Only the Armenians there were in a position to preserve the language and the culture. Only they could insure our future.

The non-Armenian psychiatrist broke into the discussion to ask if people could talk about their feelings about the genocide. In his work both with survivors of the Holocaust and their children, he said, he had found that many survivors experienced guilt for being alive, and they had transmitted that guilt to their children. The room was silent until one of the men finally said that only when Turkey was made to pay would we be free. The psychiatrist said that those who worked with Holocaust survivors had noted that the guilt survivors felt had not dissipated even after the Nuremberg trials, when the world community had formally held Germany as well as individual Germans responsible for the Holocaust. His attempt to get the group to talk about their feelings was, however, completely unsuccessful.

Toward the end of the day the psychiatrists left the room to confer with their colleagues, and I suggested that we go around the room and tell each other what we had expected from the day and what we had gotten. Once again the room was silent. People seemed puzzled by my suggestion. Finally, the woman who had cried about her father asked me to tell them what I had wanted. I took a deep breath and decided to tell the truth. I explained that I had had a hard time growing up Armenian. Even in Washington Heights, which I had learned in the discussion at lunch was *the* Armenian community in New York City, I had felt different from everyone else. The effect of the genocide on my life was something I had only recently, at the age of thirty-five, begun to consider. I had come to the workshop with the hope of sharing my feelings and questions with others who had had a similar experience in order to learn more about myself. I said I had been very disappointed, and I thought that the day had been a lost opportunity. Breaking the silence that followed my remarks, one of the women said she was glad I was coming back to the Armenian community. Once I did, she said, I would feel much better. Confused, I asked what she meant and realized from her response that she had misinterpreted what I'd said about wanting to reclaim some of Armenian culture for a desire to become part of an Armenian community. I told her that the two things had been very separate for me. I did not believe that I ever would live within an Armenian community. She asked why with such sincerity that I responded honestly. I said I could not live my life as an adult woman within the confines of an Armenian community where there was no room for me to be who I am. To my surprise, she said she knew what I meant, but she did not elaborate. No one else spoke.

It was soon time to return to the large group meeting where we would hear about the issues raised in the other groups. Perhaps the group I was in was unique, I thought, but was discouraged to hear that none of the groups had discussed the day's topic: the psychological and social effects of the genocide.

I left quickly when the workshop ended. My expectations that the day would give me some insight into what it meant to identify as an Armenian American had probably been unrealistic, but I was disturbed that, once again, I had learned only that I felt different. I was an Armenian. I was the child of survivors, but what did it mean that I could find so little common ground with others who shared my experience? What did it mean that I could not accept so many of the traditions of Armenians because they were rooted in male dominance? Could I be an Armenian and challenge patriarchal traditions? What did it mean that I did not participate in the ancient Christian church of Armenia—the religion my grandmother had refused to renounce, the reason for her exile. I had not agreed with the man in the workshop who said that the culture was being maintained only in Soviet Armenia, but what did it mean that I no longer spoke the language and had not consciously passed on any of the Armenian tradition to my children?

I was in a state of utter confusion about being an Armenian and was relieved to finally get home. It was wonderful to see Martha and to be able to talk with her about what I'd experienced. It was also a comfort to be back in an environment where I could be myself. I had told the woman in the workshop the truth: I never could live in an Armenian community where my politics, values, and lifestyle would not be accepted. I had struggled to become an adult woman who was defined not by marital status and number of children but, rather, by my ability to function independently and to believe in myself. I had work that I thought was important and a commitment to try to do what I could to change the world. Martha and I were building a life together that was based on mutual respect. The struggle to acknowledge and accept our differences had been worth the pain of our battles. Being an Armenian was important to me, but I had no intention of giving up any other part of my life.

I felt pleased with the directions in which my life was developing and wondered how my new Armenian consciousness would affect my future. Finally, I had received my grandmother's legacy, but it would be years before it was incorporated into who I am.

Connections I

Barely wide enough for the car
the road winds through treeless,
grass covered hills
now mostly empty of people and
silent but for the occasional bleating of sheep.
Speaking loudly of those who were once here,
stone walls enclose long abandoned plots
and roofless stone cottages.

Walking the bogs but afraid of getting lost,
sitting on the rocks near the blow hole I mistook for thunder,
growing to love the strange smell of peat fires,
I feel very much the Yank I am called by my neighbors.
Yet there is something else,
something my assimilated
Armenian-American mind pushes away.

A connection here,
in the town land of Falcarrib, County Donegal Ireland
to Armenians in Turkey after the "forgotten" genocide,
to Armenians in the Republic celebrating its third birthday
for the first time in history, amidst war and privation
and even to Armenian-Americans
in communities I once fled from and now shun.

Thousands dead of unnatural disasters.
Histories lost.
Languages, strange to ears tuned to Europe,
once officially forbidden,
now struggling to be reborn in native soil and diaspora.
Apostolic Christianity and Catholicism viciously suppressed,
define as they ossify.
Silence once necessary
becomes fortification,
spawning a way of life based on denial.

Holding tightly to what was demonized
lest it disappear from the face of the earth,
will this grip loosen enough for lungs to expand?
Can these histories provide tools
for the changes now needed for survival?

The dead are grieved,
but pain born of denial and
silence goes unacknowledged
while it continues the work of the killers.

Connections II

Staying in the cottage at the end of the road
for a three week vacation,
we are called the "Yank girls"
by our neighbors
who offer tea and warm buttered soda bread.

I am as relaxed as I have ever been,
but I dream of lesbians every night.
An Irish friend,

hearing the growing love for his country in our voices,
asks if we would live here.
Emphatic and decidedly negative
my response is too quick.

I know this maintenance of traditions
and have raged against it most of my life.
But here where people are familiar,
though not mine,
I have seen beyond the bars of conventionality
to accept their warmth
and the connection we make.

Can this vision translate to "my people"
the now mostly privileged
Armenian-Americans who,
like the Irish-Americans pushed out of this land,
have taken on their acquired whiteness with a vengeance?

Back in New England it takes days to adjust to the landscape.
Trees we have loved now feel claustrophobic
in their late August fullness.
My nightly dreams are no longer of lesbians,
but I crave Ireland.

The slides are back.
Cooking my food again for friends who will come to see where we have been,
I leaf through the splattered pages of my Armenian cookbook
looking for something special.

Reading the transliterated recipe titles in the words of my first language,
I hear my grandmother's voice say the words I now barely understand.
I mouth the words and my heart pounds.

GLOSSARY

Abeyid	Robe; a garment, usually white
Aslan	Lion (Turkish)
Aman	Exclamation expressing chagrin, disgust, or anger; Oh, my goodness, mercy me (Turkish)
Agha	Large landholder; Lord (Turkish)
Afwahn	Thanks; you're welcome; think nothing of it
Aiky	Vineyard; also ranch or garden
Ahk	Woe is me
Ashag	Ass (mule)
Bahrone	Mister; sir
Backshish	Tip (Persian)
Basterma	Dried spiced beef (Turkish)
Ça va	Greeting (French)
Chai	Tea (Turkish, and several other languages)
Choreg	A round, ring-shaped, or braided cookie or bread roll, usually sweet
Dandigin	Housewife; mother of the family
Dashnak	ARF (Armenian Revolutionary Federation)
Deegin	Mrs.; madame
Dolma	Stuffed vegetables (Turkish)
Dough-eaters	Italians
Effendi	Term of respect; sir (Turkish)
Fez	Hat worn by Turks, Arabs, and Armenians, usually wine-colored
Gaiffa	Coffee (Turkish or Arabic)
Gavan	Thistle (Turkish)
Gavoor	Infidel to Islam; heathen; pagan
Hai-yah	Why not; you too; hey; okay; all right
Hah dey (hai deh)	Let's go (Turkish)
Haji	Pilgrim; a Muslim who has performed a pilgrimage to Mecca, or a Christian to Jerusalem
Halvah	Candy made of sugar and tahin (Arabic)
Hemar	Donkey (Arabic)
Jannat (Jennet)	Heaven (Turkish or Arabic)
Jinnee	Spirit; demon; Elfas in a fable (Arabic or Turkish)
Kugh	Village
Keesah	Coarse cloth used for washing in a Turkish bath

Kopru	Bridge (Turkish)
Kuluk	Head
Lochum	Candy made from fruit and nuts; Turkish Delight
Mindaar	Cushion (Turkish)
Muchdar	Elected head of village (Arabic or Turkish)
Mullah	Muslim clergyman (Arabic)
Odar	Foreigner (in American usage, non-Armenian)
Oghloom	My son (Turkish)
Orospi	Whore (Turkish)
Parev	Hello
Pasha	Highest rank of military title or civil service (Turkish)
Perper	Purslane
Pesa	Bridegroom
Raki	(Also oghi or arak or ouzo) alcohol made from white raisins
Sabig (sapik)	Deviated from the straight road; crazy
Sadir	Cushion for sitting (Turkish)
Salim	Greeting or salutation (Arabic or Turkish)
Sarma	Stuffed grape leaves (Turkish)
Sevavor	Dark-colored, or a black ass
Shahib	Mr. or Sir (Arabic)
Sicout	Silence (Turkish)
Soochran	Thanks (Arabic)
Tavloo	Backgammon
Topig	Stuffed ground chickpea and potato dumplings
Tsakoug	Brat; youngster; urchin (tsak: child or offspring)
Vayreni	Wild; savage
Vush	Flax, linen
Yalah	Let's go (Arabic)
Yavrim/yavrum	Term of endearment for little child (Turkish)
Yoreghan	Quilt (Turkish)

APPENDICES

APPENDIX A: AUTHOR CHECKLISTS

Michael J. Arlen (1930–)
Fiction
Say Goodbye to Sam. New York: Farrar, Straus and Giroux, 1984.

Nonfiction
Living-Room War. New York: The Viking Press, 1969.
Exiles. New York: Farrar, Straus and Giroux, 1970.
An American Verdict. Garden City, NJ: Doubleday, 1973.
Passage to Ararat. New York: Farrar, Straus and Giroux, 1975.
The View from Highway 1: Essays on Television. New York: Farrar, Straus and Giroux, 1976.
Thirty Seconds. New York: Farrar, Straus and Giroux, 1980.
The Camera Age: Essays on Television. New York: Farrar, Straus and Giroux, 1981.

Memoir
Exiles (and) Passage to Ararat. New York: Farrar, Straus and Giroux, N.d.

Arlene Voski Avakian (1939–)
Memoir
Lion Woman's Legacy: An Armenian-American Memoir. Afterword by Bettina Aptheker. New York: The Feminist Press, 1992.

Editor
Through the Kitchen Window: Women Writers Explore the Intimate Meanings of Food and Cooking. Introduction by Ruth Hubbard. Boston: Beacon Press, 1997.
African American Women and the Vote, 1837–1965. Co-edited with Ann D. Gordon, Bettye Collier-Thomas, John H. Bracey, and Joyce Avrech Berkman. Amherst: University of Massachusetts Press, 1997.
From Betty Crocker to Feminist Food Studies: Critical Perspectives on Women and Food. Co-edited with Barbara Haber. Amherst and Boston: University of Massachusetts Press, 2005.

Harry Barba (1922–)
Fiction
For the Grape Season. New York: Macmillan, 1960.
3: Pebbles and Well Water. A Flower Blooming in the Land. The Church in the Dale. Saratoga Springs, NY: The Harian Press, 1967.
3x3 [Harry Barba, Harold Bond, Leo Hamalian]. Saratoga Springs, NY: The Harian Press, 1969.
One of a Kind: The Many Faces and Voices of America. Ballston Spa: The Harian Press, 1976.
The Day the World Went Sane. Ballston Spa, NY: Harian Creative Press, 1979.
Round Trip to Byzantium. Ballston Spa, NY: Harian Creative Books, 1985.
Mona Lisa Smiles: A Novel. Ballston Spa, NY: Harian Creative Books, 1993.

Editor
Harian Creative Awards I. Ballston Spa, NY: Harian Creative Press, N.d. (Includes the novella *Gospel According to Everyman,* under the pseudonym Baron Mikan.)
What's Cooking in Congress? Edited by Harry Barba and Marian Barba. Saratoga Springs: Harian Creative Press, 1979.
What's Cooking in Congress?—II. Compiled by Harry Barba and Marian Barba. Saratoga Springs: Harian Creative Press, 1982.

Booklets
"The Church in the Dale." [Saratoga Springs, NY: The Harian Press, 1967].
(Includes his autobiographical essay, "The Career of a Self-Made Writer.").
"Love in the Persian Way." [Saratoga Springs, NY: The Harian Press, 1969].
"How to Teach Writing in the Time It Takes to Consume a Glass?—a Quart?—a Barrel! of Wine (or The Syllabus for the Founding of a Department of Writing in a University or Large College), a Method without Madness." Saratoga Springs, NY: The Harian Press, 1969.
"Teaching in Your Own Write (The Techniques of the Creative Writing Workshop Adapted to Teaching Exposition)." Saratoga Springs, NY: The Harian Press, 1970.
"The Case for Socially Functional Education." Saratoga Springs, NY: The Harian Press, 1973.
"The Three Crashes at Marshall University: Teaching in Appalachia." Saratoga Springs, NY: The Harian Press, 1974.
"Two Connecticut Yankees Teaching in Appalachia." Saratoga Springs, NY: The Harian Press, 1974.

A. I. Bezzerides (1908–2007)
Fiction
Long Haul. New York: Carrick and Evans, 1938.
There Is a Happy Land. New York: Henry Holt, 1942.
Thieves' Market. New York: Charles Scribner's Sons, 1949. 2nd Edition. Foreword by Garrett White. Afterword by the Author. Berkeley: University of California Press, 1997.

Biography
William Faulkner: A Life on Paper. A transcription from the film produced by the Mississippi Center for Educational Television. Script by A. I. Bezzerides. Introduction by Carvel Collins. Adapted and edited by Ann Abadie. Jackson: University Press of Mississippi, 1980.

Films
Buzz. A Film by Spiro N. Taraviras. Atalante Pictures, Spiro N. Taraviras Production. Munich, Germany, 2005.
The Long Haul of A. I. Bezzerides. Directed by Fay Efrosini Lellios. Los Angeles: Storm Entertainment, 2006.

Harold Bond (1939–2000)
Poetry
3x3 [Harry Barba, Harold Bond, Leo Hamalian]. Saratoga Springs, NY: The Harian Press, 1967.
Dancing on Water. West Branch, IA: The Cummington Press, 1969.
The Northern Wall. Foreword by Hassell Sledd. Boston: Northeastern University, 1969.
The Way It Happens to You. New York: Ararat Press, 1979.

Diana Der-Hovanessian
Poetry
How to Choose Your Past. New York: Ararat Press, 1978.
About Time: Poems. New York: Ashod Press, 1987.
Songs of Bread, Songs of Salt. New York: Ashod Press, 1990.
Selected Poems. Riverdale-on-Hudson, NY: Sheep Meadow Press, 1994.
The Circle Dancers. Riverdale-on-Hudson, NY: Sheep Meadow Press, 1996.
Any Day Now: Poems. Riverdale-on-Hudson, NY: Sheep Meadow Press, 1999.

The Burning Glass: Poems. Riverdale-on-Hudson, NY: Sheep Meadow Press, 2002.
The Second Question. Riverdale-on-Hudson, NY: Sheep Meadow Press, 2007.

Translations
[with Marzbed Margossian]. *Anthology of Armenian Poetry.* New York: Columbia University
      Press, 1978.
[with Marzbed Margossian]. *Sacred Wrath: The Selected Poems of Vahan Tekeyan.* Foreword
      by Victor Howes. New York: Ashod Press, 1982.
[with Marzbed Margossian]. *The Arc,* by Shen Mah (Archbishop Torkom Manoogian).
      Introduction by Peter Sourian. New York: St. Vartan's Press, 1983.
Come Sit Beside Me, and Listen to Kouchag: Medieval Armenian Poems of Nahabed Kouchag.
      New York: Ashod Press, 1984.
For You on New Year's Day, by Gevorg Emin. Introduction by Yevgeny Yevtushenko.
      Preface by Gevork Emin. Published as Volume IX of the Babylos Editions, Pittsburgh:
      International Poetry Forum, 1985, in a limited edition of 300 copies. 2nd Edition,
      Athens: Ohio University Press, 1986.
[with Marzbed Margossian]. *Land of Fire: Selected Poems,* by Eghishe Charents. Ann Arbor:
      Ardis Publishers, 1986.
Coming to Terms: Selected Poems, by Vahan Derian. New York: Ashod Press, 1991.
The Other Voice: Armenian Women's Poetry through the Ages. Translated by Der-Hovanessian
      and edited with Maro Dalley. Watertown, MA: AIWA Press, 2005.

Richard Hagopian (1914–1969)
Fiction
The Dove Brings Peace. Illustrated by Manuel Tolegian. Preface by the Author. New York:
      Farrar and Rinehart, Inc., 1944.
Faraway the Spring. New York: Charles Scribner's Sons, 1952.
Wine for the Living. New York: Charles Scribner's Sons, 1956.

Leon Serabian Herald (1894–1976)
Poetry
This Waking Hour: Poems. Introduction by Zona Gale. New York: Thomas Seltzer, 1925.
"Late Harvest." Compiled with Introduction by Teresa Gloster. Unpublished manuscript.
      Introduction dated September 1976. In Special Collections, University of Wisconsin
      Library, Madison.

Booklet
"Life Is Based on the Laws of Nature: A New Theory of Life." N.p., N.d. (circa 1970s).
      Privately published by Herald.

Marjorie Housepian (1923–)
Fiction
A Houseful of Love. New York: Random House, 1957.
[with Jean Cullen]. *Inside Out.* New York: Ivy Books, 1989.

Nonfiction
The Smyrna Affair. New York: Harcourt Brace Jovanovich, 1971. English edition, *Smyrna,
      1922: The Destruction of a City* (revised); London: Faber and Faber, 1972. 2nd
      American edition, Kent, OH: Kent State University Press, 1988. 3rd American edition,
      Smyrna 1922: The Destruction of a City; New York: Newmark Press, 1998.

Editor
The Making of a Feminist: Early Journals and Letters of M. Carey Thomas. Foreword by
    Millicent Carey McIntosh. Kent, OH: Kent State University Press, 1979.

Note: Beginning with the English edition of *Smyrna,* Housepian's name has appeared as
    "Marjorie Housepian Dobkin" on her publications.

David Kherdian (1931–)
(Does not include booklets, chapbooks, monographs, broadsides, and limited signed
    editions.)

Poetry
On the Death of My Father and Other Poems. Introduction by William Saroyan. Fresno: The
    Giligia Press, 1970.
Homage to Adana. Frontispiece by Bob Totten. Mt. Horeb: The Perishable Press, 1970.
    Edition limited to 120 press numbered copies. 2nd Edition, Fresno: The Giligia Press,
    1971.
Looking Over Hills. Illustrated by Nonny Hogrogian. Lyme Center: The Giligia Press, 1972.
The Nonny Poems. New York: Macmillan, 1974.
Any Day of Your Life. Woodstock: The Overlook Press, 1975.
Country, Cat; City, Cat. Woodcuts by Nonny Hogrogian. New York: Four Winds Press,
    1978.
I Remember Root River. Woodstock: The Overlook Press, 1978.
The Farm. Introduction by Brother Jeremy. Frontispiece and jacket drawing by Nancy
    Zoll. Aurora, OR: Two Rivers Press, 1978.
Taking the Soundings on 3rd Avenue. Woodstock: The Overlook Press, 1981.
The Farm: Book Two. Aurora, OR: Two Rivers Press, 1981.
Place of Birth. Introduction by Martha Heyneman. Portland, OR: Breitenbush, 1983.
Threads of Light. Introduction by A. L. Staveley. Aurora, OR: Two Rivers Press, 1985.
The Dividing River/The Meeting Shore: Santa Fe: Lotus Press, 1990.
Friends: A Memoir. New York: The Globe Press, 1993.
My Racine. Introduction by Gerald Hausman. Spencertown, NY: Forkroads Press, 1994.
Chippecotton: Root River Tales of Racine. Sebastopol, CA: Gatehouse, 1998.
The Neighborhood Years. Huron, OH: Bottom Dog Press, 2000.
Seeds of Light: Poems from a Gurdjieff Community. Introduction by Allen Roth.
    McMinnville, OR: Stopinder Books, 2002.
    Woodcuts by Nonny Hogrogian. McMinnville, OR: Stopinder Books, 2002.
Letters to My Father. Ashland, OR: RiverWood Books, 2004.
Nearer the Heart. London: Taderon Press, 2006.

Fiction
It Started with Old Man Bean. New York: Greenwillow Books, 1980.
Beyond Two Rivers. New York: Greenwillow Books, 1981.
The Song in the Walnut Grove. Illustrated by Paul O. Zelinsky. New York: Alfred A. Knopf,
    1982.
The Mystery of the Diamond in the Wood. Pictures by Paul Geiger. New York: Alfred A.
    Knopf, 1983.
A Song for Uncle Harry. Illustrated by Nonny Hogrogian. New York: Philomel Books, 1989.
Asking the River. Illustrated by Nonny Hogrogian. New York: Orchard Books, 1993.
The Revelations of Alvin Tolliver. Charlottesville, VA: Hampton Roads, 2001.

Memoirs
Root River Run. Illustrated by Nonny Hogrogian. Minneapolis: Carolrhoda, 1984.
On a Spaceship with Beelzebub: By a Grandson of Gurdjieff. New York: Globe Press, 1991.
     2nd Edition, Rochester, VT: Inner Traditions, 1998. Includes Afterword and After the
     Afterword by the Author.
I Called It Home. Watertown, MA: Blue Crane Books, 1997.

Children's Books
Right Now. Illustrated by Nonny Hogrogian. New York: Alfred A. Knopf, 1983.
The Animal. Illustrated by Nonny Hogrogian. New York: Alfred A. Knopf , 1984.
The Great Fishing Contest. Illustrated by Nonny Hogrogian. New York: Philomel Books,
     1991.
The Cat's Midsummer Jamboree. Illustrated by Nonny Hogrogian. New York: Philomel
     Books, 1990.
Feathers and Tails: Animal Fables from Around the World. Illustrated by Nonny Hogrogian.
     Introduction by the Author. New York: Philomel Books, 1992.
Juna's Journey. Illustrated by Nonny Hogrogian. New York: Philomel Books, 1993.
By Myself. Pictures by Nonny Hogrogian. New York: Henry Holt, 1993.
Lullaby for Emily. Pictures by Nonny Hogrogian. New York: Henry Holt, 1995.
The Rose's Smile: Farizad of the Arabian Nights. Pictures by Stefano Vitale. New York: Henry
     Holt, 1997.
The Golden Bracelet. Illustrated by Nonny Hogrogian. New York: Holiday House, 1998.

Editor
[with James Baloian]. *Down at the Santa Fe Depot: 20 Fresno Poets.* Fresno: The Giligia
     Press, 1970.
Visions of America: By the Poets of Our Time. Preface by the Editor. New York: Macmillan,
     1974.
Settling America: The Ethnic Expression of 14 Contemporary Poets. Preface by the Editor.
     New York: Macmillan, 1974.
Poems Here and Now. Linoleum cuts by Nonny Hogrogian. Preface by the Editor. New
     York: Four Winds Press, 1977.
The Dog Writes on the Window with His Nose and Other Poems. Pictures by Nonny
     Hogrogian. New York: Four Winds Press, 1977.
Traveling America: With Today's Poets. Preface by the Author. New York: Macmillan, 1977.
If Dragon Flies Made Honey. Illustrated by Jose Aruego and Ariane Dewey. New York:
     Greenwillow Books, 1977.
I Sing the Song of Myself: An Anthology of Autobiographical Poems. Preface by the Editor.
     New York: Greenwillow Books, 1978.
Beat Voices: An Anthology of Beat Poetry. Introduction by the Author. Preface by Marc H.
     Aronson. New York: Henry Holt, 1995.
Forgotten Bread: First-Generation Armenian American Writers. Berkeley: Heyday Books, 2007.

Translations and Retellings
The Pearl: Hymn of the Robe of Glory. A New Retelling. [Translated by David Kherdian.]
     Illustrated by Nonny Hogrogian. Aurora, OR: Two Rivers Press, 1979.
Pigs Never See the Stars: Proverbs from the Armenian. Woodcuts by Nonny Hogrogian.
     Introduction by the Author. Aurora, OR: Two Rivers Press, 1982.
Monkey: A Journey to the West. A retelling of the Chinese folk novel by Wu Ch'eng-en.
     Boston: Shambhala, 1992. 2nd Edition as Shambhala Classic, 2005.
The Song of the Stork and Other Early and Ancient Armenian Songs. Drawings by Nonny
     Hogrogian. Preface by the Author. Reading, England: Taderon Press, 2004.

Biographies
The Road from Home: The Story of an Armenian Girl. New York: Greenwillow Books, 1979.
Finding Home. New York: Greenwillow Books, 1981.
Bridger: The Story of a Mountain Man. New York: Greenwillow Books, 1987.
The Buddha: The Story of an Awakened Life. Ashland, OR: White Cloud Press, 2004.

Bibliographies
A Bibliography of William Saroyan, 1934–1964. Introduction by William Saroyan. San
  Francisco: Roger Beacham, 1965.
Six Poets of the San Francisco Renaissance: Portraits and Checklists. Introduction by William
  Saroyan. Fresno: The Giligia Press, 1969. 2nd Edition, retitled *Six San Francisco Poets,*
  with checklists and Saroyan Introduction dropped and author introduction added,
  Fresno: The Giligia Press, 1969.

Film
The Dividing River, The Meeting Shore: The Poetry of David Kherdian. Directed by Jim
  Belleau. Oneonta, NY: Acorn Productions, 1997.

Khatchik (Archie) Minasian (1914–1986)
Poetry
Bells and Sermons. N.p., N.d., privately printed pamphlet, limited edition.
A World of Questions and Things. Prairie City, IL: The Decker Press, 1950.
The Simple Songs of Khatchik Minasian. Introduction by William Saroyan. San Francisco:
  The Colt Press, 1950. Limited to 300 copies, signed by Minasian and Saroyan. 2nd
  Edition, Fresno: The Giligia Press, 1969.
Five Poems. Illustrated by John Wilde. Mt. Horeb, WI: The Perishable Press, 1971. Edition
  limited to 125 copies.
Selected Poems. Introduction by William Saroyan. Afterword by Aram Saroyan. New York:
  Ashod Press, 1986.

Drama
Grief's Exile. A Tragedy in Four Acts. New York: The Pyramid Press, 1940.

Peter Najarian (1940–)
Fiction
Voyages. New York: Pantheon Books, 1971. 2nd Edition, New York: Ararat Press, 1979.
Wash Me on Home, Mama. Berkeley: Berkeley Poets' and Workshop Press, 1978.
Daughters of Memory: A Story. Illustrations by the Author. Berkeley: City Miner Books, 1986.

Memoir
The Great American Loneliness. Preface and Illustrations by the Author. Cambridge, MA:
  Blue Crane Books, 1999.

Helene Pilibosian (1933–)
Poetry
Carvings from an Heirloom: Oral History Poems. Watertown, MA: Ohan Press, 1983.
At Quarter Past Reality: New and Selected Poems. Watertown, MA: Ohan Press, 1998.

Editor
They Called Me Mustafa: Memoir of an Immigrant, by Khachadoor Pilibosian. Co-authored
  and edited with additional information by Helene Pilibosian. Watertown, MA: Ohan
  Press, 1992. Expanded 2nd Edition with translations of Khachadoor Pilibosian's
  poetry by Hagop Sarkissian and Helene Pilibosian, 1999.

From Kessab to Watertown: A Modern Saga, by Hovhannes Hovsep Sarkissian. Translated
and Annotated with Additional Information by Hagop Sarkissian. Also edited with an
Introduction by Robert Hovhannes Sarkissian. Watertown: Ohan Press, 1996.

William Saroyan (1908–1981)
(Does not include chapbooks, paperback reprints, Samuel French playbooks, or limited
signed editions.)

Short Stories
The Daring Young Man on the Flying Trapeze and Other Stories. Preface by the Author.
New York: Random House, 1934. 2nd Edition, with new Author Preface, New York:
Modern Age Books, 1937. 3rd Edition, with new Author Preface, New York: The
Modern Library, 1941.
Inhale and Exhale. New York: Random House, 1936.
Three Times Three. Los Angeles: The Conference Press, 1936.
Little Children. New York: Harcourt, Brace, 1937.
Love, Here Is My Hat. New York: Modern Age Books, 1938.
A Native American. Illustrated by Lloyd Hoff. San Francisco: George Fields, 1938.
The Trouble with Tigers. New York: Harcourt, Brace, 1938.
Peace, It's Wonderful. New York: Modern Age Books and The Starling Press, 1939 (same
press: simultaneous editions: Modern Age in wrappers, Starling Press in cloth).
My Name Is Aram. Illustrated by Don Freeman. Introduction by the Author. New York:
Harcourt, Brace, 1940.
Dear Baby. New York: Harcourt, Brace, 1944.
The Assyrian and Other Stories. Introduction by the Author. New York: Harcourt, Brace,
1950.
The Whole Voyald and Other Stories. Introduction by the Author. Boston: Little, Brown,
1956.
An Act or Two of Foolish Kindness. Woodcuts by Helen Siegl. Lincoln, MA: Penmaen Press,
1977.
Madness in the Family. Edited by Leo Hamalian. New York: New Directions, 1990.

Novels
The Human Comedy. Illustrated by Don Freeman. New York: Harcourt, Brace, 1943.
The Adventures of Wesley Jackson. New York: Harcourt, Brace, 1946.
Rock Wagram. Garden City, NY: Doubleday, 1951.
Tracy's Tiger. Drawings by Henry Koerner. Garden City, NY: Doubleday, 1951.
The Laughing Matter. Garden City, NY: Doubleday, 1953.
Mama, I Love You. Boston: Little, Brown, 1956.
Papa, You're Crazy. Boston: Little, Brown, 1957.
Boys and Girls Together. New York: Harcourt, Brace and World, 1963. 2nd Edition,
Barricade Books, Inc., 1995.
One Day in the Afternoon of the World. New York: Harcourt, Brace and World, 1964.

Plays
My Heart's in the Highlands. Preface by Harold Clurman. Introduction by the Author. New
York: Harcourt, Brace, 1939.
The Time of Your Life. Preface by the Author. New York: Harcourt, Brace, 1939.
Three Plays: My Heart's in the Highlands; The Time of Your Life; Love's Old Sweet Song.
Introduction by the Author. New York: Harcourt, Brace, 1940.
A Special Announcement. Prefatory Note by Whit Burnett. New York: House of Books, 1940.
The Beautiful People and Two Other Plays. Note by the Author. New York: Harcourt, Brace, 1941.

Razzle-Dazzle. Frontispiece by Arthur Szyk. Preface by the Author. New York: Harcourt, Brace, 1942.

Get Away Old Man: A Play in Two Acts. New York: Harcourt, Brace, 1944.

Jim Dandy, Fat Man in a Famine. New York: Harcourt, Brace, 1947.

Don't Go Away Mad and Two Other Plays. Introduction by the Author. New York: Harcourt, Brace, 1949.

The Cave Dwellers. Introduction by the Author. New York: G. P. Putnam's Sons, 1958.

Sam the Highest Jumper of Them All, or The London Comedy. London: Faber and Faber, 1961.

Three New Dramatic Works: The Dogs, or The Paris Comedy, and Two Other Plays: Chris Sick, or Happy New Year Anyway; Making Money, and Nineteen Other Very Short Plays. New York: Phaedra, 1969.

The Armenian Trilogy. Edited by Dickran Kouymjian. Fresno: California State University, 1986.

Warsaw Visitor, Tales from the Vienna Streets: The Last Two Plays. Edited by Dickran Kouymjian. Fresno: California State University, 1991.

Memoirs
The Bicycle Rider in Beverly Hills. New York: Charles Scribner's Sons, 1952.

Here Comes, There Goes, You Know Who. New York: Simon and Schuster, 1962. 2nd Edition, Barricade Books, Inc., 1995.

Autobiographical Interludes
Not Dying. Drawings by the Author. New York: Harcourt, Brace and World, 1963. 2nd Edition, Introduction by Aram Saroyan. New York: Barricade Books, Inc., 1996.

Short Drive, Sweet Chariot. New York: Phaedra Publishers, 1966.

Letters from 74 rue Taibout: or, Don't Go Away Mad, but If You Must, Say Hello to Everybody. New York: The World Publishing Co., 1969.

Days of Life and Death and Escape to the Moon. New York: Dial Press, 1970.

Places Where I've Done Time. New York: Praeger Publishers, 1972.

Sons Come and Go, Mothers Hang in Forever. New York: McGraw-Hill, 1976.

Chance Meetings. New York: W. W. Norton, 1978.

Children's Books
Me. Illustrated by Murray Tinkelman. New York: The Crowell-Collier Press, 1963.

Horsey Gorsey and the Frog. Illustrated by Grace Davidian. Eau Claire, WI: E. M. Hale, 1968.

The Tooth and My Father. Illustrated by Suzanne Verrier. New York: Doubleday, 1974.

Collections
48 Saroyan Stories. New York: Avon, 1942.

Thirty-One Selected Stories. New York: Avon, 1943.

Some Day I'll Be a Millionaire Myself: 34 More Great Stories. New York: Avon, 1943.

The Saroyan Special: Selected Short Stories. Illustrated by Don Freeman. New York: Harcourt Brace, 1948.

Love. New York: Lion Library Editions, 1955.

The William Saroyan Reader. Introduction by the Author. New York: George Braziller, 1958. 2nd Edition, Introduction by Aram Saroyan, Fort Lee, NJ: Barricade Books, Inc., 1994.

My Kind of Crazy, Wonderful People: Seventeen Short Stories and a Play. New York: Harcourt, Brace and World, 1966.

The Man with the Heart in the Highlands and Other Stories. Includes Author's prefatory comments to each of the stories. New York: Dell, 1968.

My Name Is Saroyan. Edited by James H. Tashjian. New York: Coward-McCann, 1983.

The New Saroyan Reader: A Connoisseur Anthology of the Writings of William Saroyan. Edited by Brian Darwent. Berkeley: Creative Arts, 1984.

The Man with the Heart in the Highlands and Other Early Stories. Introduction by Herb Caen (different stories from the similarly titled 1968 edition). New York: New Directions, 1989.

Saroyan's Armenians: An Anthology. Edited by Alice K. Barter. Huntington, WV: University Editions, 1992.

Fresno Stories. New York: New Directions, 1994.

Essential Saroyan. Edited by William E. Justice. Berkeley: Heyday Books, 2005.

Miscellaneous

Three Worlds: Hairenik 1934–1939. Edited with an Introduction by William Saroyan. Boston: Hairenik Press, 1939.

Saroyan's Fables. New York: Illustrations by Warren Chappell. New York: Harcourt, Brace, 1941.

Harlem As Seen by Hirschfeld. Art by Hirschfeld. Text by William Saroyan. New York: The Hyperion Press, 1941.

Hilltop Russians in San Francisco. Text by William Saroyan. Pictures by Pauline Vinson. Stanford University: James Delkin, 1941.

Why Abstract? By Hilaire Hiler, William Saroyan, and Henry Miller. New York: New Directions, 1945.

The Twin Adventures: The Adventures of William Saroyan, a Diary; The Adventures of Wesley Jackson, a Novel. New York: Harcourt, Brace, 1950.

After Thirty Years: The Daring Young Man on the Flying Trapeze. New York: Harcourt, Brace and World, 1964. Thirty-eight numbered essays by the Author, followed by the original stories.

Look at Us: Let's See, Here We Are, Look Hard, Speak Soft, I See, You See, We All See, Stop, Look, Listen; Beholder's Eye, Don't Look Now, But Isn't That You? (Us? U.S.?). Photographs by Arthur Rothstein. Text by William Saroyan. New York: Cowles, 1967.

I Used to Believe I Had Forever, Now I'm Not So Sure. New York: Cowles, 1968.

Obituaries. Berkeley: Creative Arts, 1979.

Saroyan Memorial Issue. "104 Unpublished Letters of William Saroyan: Ethnic Motivations of an American Writer." Boston: *The Armenian Review,* edited by James H. Tashjian, September 1981.

Births. Introduction by David Kherdian. Berkeley: Creative Arts, 1985.

Where the Bones Go. Edited by Robert Setrakian. Fresno: The Press at California State University, Fresno, 2002.

Saroyan on Paper: Drawings, Watercolors and Words. Fresno: Fresno Art Museum, 2002.

Peter Sourian (1933–)
Fiction
Miri. New York: Pantheon, 1957. London edition, *Three Windows of Summer,* Macmillan, 1957.

The Best and Worst of Times. Garden City, NY: Doubleday, 1961.

The Gate. New York: Harcourt, Brace and World, 1965.

Nonfiction
At the French Embassy in Sofia: Essays and Criticism. New York: Ashod Press, 1992.

Translation
A Ravishing Idiot, by Charles Exbrayat. New York: Popular Library, 1965. Translated from the French edition, *Une Ravissante Idiote.*

Other
"Peter Sourian: A Special Issue." New York (A.G.B.U.) *Ararat: A Quarterly,* Vol. XLI, No. 2,
    Spring 2000. Collects the complete short stories of Peter Sourian, with an Afterword
    by David Stephen Calonne.

Leon Surmelian (1907–1995)
Fiction
98.6. New York: E. P. Dutton, 1950.

Nonfiction
Techniques of Fiction Writing: Measure and Madness. Introduction by Mark Schorer. Garden
    City, NY: Doubleday, 1968.

Memoir
I Ask You, Ladies and Gentlemen. Introduction by William Saroyan. New York: E. P.
    Dutton, 1945. The 5th printing, published by the Armenian National Committee in
    co-operation with E. P. Dutton, includes a two-page Author's Note making a plea for
    restitution of a portion of Armenia's lands, with a map of the designated areas drawn
    by H. Babessian (neither the map nor the Author's Note appears in any other printing
    or edition of this book).

Fables and Folklore
Daredevils of Sassoun: The Armenian National Epic. Introduction by the Author. Illustrated
    by Paul Sagssoorian. Denver: Alan Swallow, 1964.
Apples of Immortality: Folktales of Armenia. Foreword by Artashes Nazinian. Introduction
    by the Author. Illustrated by Stewart Irwin. Berkeley: University of California Press,
    1968. Published simultaneously in London by Allen and Unwin.

Emmanuel P. Varandyan (1902–1988)
Fiction
The Well of Ararat. Garden City, NY: Doubleday, Doran, 1938. 2nd Edition, Belmont, MA:
    Armenian Heritage Press, 2005. Introduction by Eden Naby. Biographical Sketch and
    Personal Recollections by Richard N. Frye.
The Moon Sails. Delmar, NY: Pinnacle Publishers, 1971.

APPENDIX B: BIOGRAPHIES OF ESSAYISTS

Nancy Agabian coordinates Gartal, a popular literary reading series for Armenian writers at the Cornelia Street Café in Greenwich Village. She is the author of *Princess Freak* (Beyond Baroque Books, 2000), a collection of autobiographical poems and performance art texts. In 2005 she attended a conference on feminism in Armenia, where she read from her unpublished memoir, "Me as Her Again." She is a graduate of Columbia University and currently teaches nonfiction writing at Queens College.

Mark Arax is an award-winning writer for the *Los Angeles Times'* Sunday magazine, *West*. His first book, *In My Father's Name,* tells the story of his grandfather's escape from the Genocide and the murder of his father, Ara, in Fresno when Mark was fifteen. His second book, *The King of California,* co-written with Rick Wartzman, was selected as one of the top ten books of 2004 by the *Los Angeles Times* and the *San Francisco Chronicle* and won the Saroyan Prize for nonfiction in 2006. Mark is finishing his third book, a collection of essays and stories about California, due out in early 2008.

Christopher Atamian was born in New York City of Italian and Armenian parents. He matriculated at several universities, including USC Film School. A former Fulbright Scholar, he writes for numerous publications, including the *New York Times* and the *Village Voice*. He has directed and produced several films that have been screened at international festivals, and he now teaches film studies at New York University, where he is at work on two feature films and a documentary. He is the founder of Nor Alik, a nonprofit organization dedicated to Armenian arts and culture, and he recently completed his first novel, *Speaking French*.

David Stephen Calonne was born in Los Angeles and received his B.A. in ancient Greek from UCLA and his Ph.D. in English from the University of Texas at Austin. He has taught at the University of Texas at Austin and the University of Michigan and presently teaches at Eastern Michigan University. He has lectured at the European University Institute in Florence, the University of London, Harvard, and the Rothermere Institute at the University of Oxford. He is the author of *William Saroyan: My Real Work Is Being; The Colossus of Armenia: G. I. Gurdjieff and Henry Miller;* and *Charles Bukowski: Sunlight Here I Am/Interviews and Encounters, 1963–1993*. He lives in Ann Arbor, Michigan.

Gregory Djanikian was born in Alexandria, Egypt, in 1949 of Armenian parents and came to America when he was eight years old. His four collections of poetry are *The Man in the Middle; Falling Deeply into America; About Distance;* and *Years Later,* all published by Carnegie Mellon, who will publish his fifth volume, *So I Will Till the Ground,* in the coming year. His poems have appeared in numerous journals, including *Poetry* and *The American Poetry Review,* as well as in textbooks and several important mainstream anthologies. He directs the creative writing program at the University of Pennsylvania.

Gary Ghoshgarian was born to Armenian parents and raised in Hartford, Connecticut. He holds a B.S. in physics from Worcester Polytechnic Institute, an M.A. in English from the University of Connecticut, and a Ph.D. in English from the University of Wisconsin. He is the author of six critically acclaimed thrillers under his own name, and three others under his recent pen name, Gary Braver. Each of his novels features a different Armenian American character. He is a professor of English at Northeastern University and lives with his wife and two sons in Arlington, Massachusetts.

Mona Ghuneim was born in Beirut to a Palestinian father and an Armenian mother. A graduate of the College of William and Mary and with a master's degree from New York University, she works part time at an investment bank in Manhattan, while currently writing a book of short stories entitled *Tales from Tora Bora,* an inside look at the trials and tribulations of a kooky but lovable immigrant family in suburban America. In her essay on Marjorie Housepian, Mona Ghuneim uses excerpts from her maternal grandmother's Armenian memoir, *My Childhood without Spring: Eyewitness Accounts from the Smyrnian Calamity,* published in Beirut in 1975 by Doniguian Press, and in an English translation in 2003 by Vatche Ghazarian of Mayreni Publishing. The author, Alice Torian, was born in 1913 in Istanbul, and died in Syracuse, New York, in 2001.

Aris Janigian is a former Senior Professor of Humanities at the Southern California Institute of Architecture and is, with April Greiman, the author of *Something from Nothing,* which explores the process of digital design. His novel *Bloodvine* was a finalist for the 2005 William Saroyan International Prize for Writing. He is a contributing writer for *West,* the *Los Angeles Times'* Sunday magazine. A resident of Los Angeles, where he lives with his wife and children, he returns to his native Fresno every harvest to work as a grape packer and shipper.

Nancy Kricorian grew up in Watertown, Massachusetts, where she attended the Armenian Evangelical Church and Watertown public schools. Her poetry has been published in *Parnassus,* the *Mississippi Review,* the *Graham House Review, Ararat,* and other journals. She is the author of the novels *Zabelle* and *Dreams of Bread and Fire.* She lives in New York City with her husband and two daughters.

Arthur Nersesian has lived all his life in New York City. He is the author of six novels, including *Suicide Casanova, Chinese Takeout,* and *Unlubricated.* In January 2006 he had a book of four plays published, *East Village Tetralogy.* He was the managing editor of the literary magazine *The Portable Lower East Side* and has been teaching English at Eugenio Maria de Hostos Community College in the South Bronx since 1990.

Aram Saroyan is an internationally known poet, novelist, biographer, memoirist, and playwright. His poetry volumes include *Aram Saroyan, Pages,* and *Day and Night: Bolinas Poems* (Black Sparrow Press, 1998). His prose works include *Genesis Angels: The Saga of Lew Welch and the Beat Generation* and *Last Rites,* a book about the death of his father, William Saroyan. A memoir, *Friends in the World: The Education of a Writer,* and his selected essays, *Starting Out in the Sixties,* are among his recent publications. The world premiere of his play *At the Beach House* was performed in Los Angeles in 2005. He lives in Los Angeles with his wife, the painter Gailyn Saroyan.

Alan Semerdjian is a poet, essayist, songwriter, artist, and teacher. His work has appeared in several print and online literary journals, magazines, periodicals, and also in a chapbook of his poems, *An Improvised Device,* published in 2005, and his first full-length volume of poems, *Geography of Evidence,* published in 2006. He teaches English at Herricks High School in New Hyde Park, New York, and currently resides in Huntington, New York. The digital home for his work can be found at www.alanarts.com.

Hrag Varjabedian was born in Beirut, Lebanon. Upon graduating from high school, he moved to Los Angeles, where he received a degree in engineering. While working as an engineer he participated in the Oral History Documentation Project, recording the life stories of Armenian survivors of the 1915 Genocide. Currently, he is a dissertator in cultural anthropology at the University of Wisconsin. His research objectives focus on the dynamics of the construction of collective memory and its role in identity formation within de-territorialized Armenian communities as well as the Republic of Armenia.

Hrag Vartanian was born in Aleppo, Syria, and grew up in Toronto, Canada. He is a writer, critic, and cultural worker. He is a staff writer for *AGBU News* magazine, *Brooklyn Rail,* and *Boldtype,* and serves on the board of the quarterly magazine *Ararat.* In his writings he deals with the issue of pluralism and identity in a global context. He lives in Brooklyn, New York.

Patricia Sarrafian Ward was born and raised in Beirut, and holds an M.F.A. from the University of Michigan, where she received Hopwood Awards in the novel and short fiction categories. Her writing has been published in several journals and the anthologies *Dinadzad's Children* and *Post Gibran: Anthology of New Arab American Writing.* Her novel *The Bullet Collection* (Graywolf Press, 2003), about two sisters growing up in wartime Beirut, received the GLCA New Writers Award, the Anahid Literary Award, and the Hala Maksoud Award for Outstanding Emerging Writer. She currently lives in Sandy Hook Bay in New Jersey.

Appendix C: Notable Writers of the First Generation

Hiag Akmakjian
Jack Antreassian
Raffi Arzoomanian
Kenneth Flagg, Fred Levon (Fred L. Ayvazian)
Norman A. Bailey
Anna Balakian
Nona Balakian
Margaret Bedrosian
Anne Calin
Peter Chobanian
Arto DeMirjian, Jr.
Mary Avakian Freericks
John A. C. Greppin
Leo Hamalian
Trevanian (Jack Hashian)
Robert Hewsen
Harry Keyishian
Haig Khatchadourian
Vaughn Koumjian
Dikran Kouymjian
Vahan M. Kurkjian
V. K. Ivy (Vivian Kurkjian)
James Magorian
Kathryn Manoogian
Peter Manuelian
Mary Matosian Morabito
Nishan Parlakian
Raphael Parlakian
Ralph Setian
James H. Tashjian
Virginia Tashjian
Charles Tekeyan
James P. Terzian
Lawrence Terzian
P. K. Thomajan
Aram Tolegian
Khachig Tololyan
Vartanig G. Vartan
John Vartoukian

APPENDIX D: SMALL PRESSES

The Delphic Press
Editor: Artin Shalian
New York, New York
1939–1964

The Giligia Press
Founder, editor: David Kherdian
Fresno, California; Santa Fe, New Mexico;
Lyme Center, New Hampshire
1966–1972

The Harian Press
Founder, editor: Harry Barba
Saratoga Springs, New York; Ballston Spa, New York
1967–1993

Armenian Heritage Press
Editor: Marc A. Mamigonian
Belmont, Massachusetts
1968–

Ararat Press
Editor: Jack Antreassian
Armenian General Benevolent Union (AGBU), New York, New York
1978–1980

Ashod Press
Founder, editor: Jack Antreassian
New York, New York
1979–1992

Ohan Press
Founders, editors: Helene Pilibosian and Hagop Sarkissian
Watertown, Massachusetts
1983–

Blue Crane Books
Editor: Alvart Badalian
Cambridge, Massachusetts
1992–

Taderon Press
Founder, editor: Ara Sarafian
London and Reading, England
1997–

Magazines, Journals, and Newspapers

Hairenik Daily
Literary Editor: Reuben Darbinian
New York, New York; Boston, Massachusetts
1899–
(Began publishing literature in English in 1930)

Armenian Mirror-Spectator
Watertown, Massachusetts
1932–

Hairenik Weekly (now *Armenian Weekly*)
Editor: Reuben Darbinian, et. al.
Boston, Massachusetts
1934–

The Armenian Review
Editors: James Mandalian, James H. Tashjian, et al.
1948–

Ararat, A Quarterly
Armenian General Benevolent Union (AGBU), New York, New York
Editors: Jack Antreassian (1959–1968), David Kherdian (1971),
Leo Hamalian (1972–2003), Aram Arkun (2003–present)

Raft: A Journal of Armenian Poetry and Criticism
Editors: Vahe Oshagan and John A. C. Greppin
Cleveland State University, Cleveland, Ohio
1986–1998

Forkroads: A Journal of Ethnic-American Literature
Editor: David Kherdian
Spencertown, New York
1995–1996

Anthologies

Three Worlds: Hairenik 1934–39
Edited by William Saroyan
Boston: Hairenik Press, 1939

The Armenian Mirror-Spectator Tenth Anniversary
New York: Armenian Mirror-Spectator, 1942

Hairenik, A Weekly
Boston: Hairenik Association, 1944

Hairenik Treasure Chest 1945: An Anthology
Boston: Hairenik Press, 1945

Arveste I
Edited by Nona Balakian
New York: Armenian Students' Association, 1948

Arveste II
Edited by Adrienne Yanekian
Illustrated by Nonny Hogrogian
New York: Armenian Students' Association of America, 1962

Ararat: A Decade of Armenian-American Writing
Edited by Jack Antreassian
New York: A.G.B.U., 1969

Down at the Santa Fe Depot: 20 Fresno Poets
Edited by David Kherdian and James Baloian
Fresno: The Giligia Press, 1970

Armenian–North American Poets: An Anthology
Edited by Lorne Shirinian
St. Jean, Quebec, Canada: Manna Publishing, [1974]

Settling America: The Ethnic Expression of 14 Contemporary Poets
Edited by David Kherdian
New York: Macmillan, 1974

Armenian-American Poets: A Bilingual Anthology
Compiled and Translated by Garig Basmadjian
Detroit: Armenian General Benevolent Union (AGBU), 1976

Ararat: 25th Anniversary Issue
Edited by Leo Hamalian
New York: Armenian General Benevolent Union (AGBU), 1985

Crossroads: Short Fiction by Armenian-American Writers
Edited by Margaret Bedrosian and Leo Hamalian
New York: Ashod Press, 1992

BIBLIOGRAPHY

Adalian, Rouben. *Armenian Genocide: Resource Guide.* Washington, D.C.: Armenian Assembly of America, 1988.

Authors and Artists for Young Adults, Volume 42. Detroit: Gale Research, 1989.

Avakian, Anne M., compiled by. *Armenia and the Armenians in Academic Dissertations: A Bibliography. Supplement One.* Berkeley: Professional Press, 1987.

Avakian, Arra S. *The Armenians in America.* Minneapolis: Lerner Publications, 1977.

Balakian, Nona. *The Armenian-American Writer: A New Accent in American Fiction.* New York: AGBU, 1958.

————. *The World of William Saroyan: A Literary Interpretation.* Cranbury, NJ: Associated UP, 1998.

Bedrosian, Margaret. *The Magical Pine Ring: Culture and the Imagination in Armenian/American Literature.* Detroit: Wayne State University, 1991.

Bogomolny, Abby, editor. *New to North America: Writing by U.S. Immigrants, Their Children and Grandchildren.* Oakland, CA: Burning Bush Publications, 1997.

Buckley, Christopher, David Oliveira, M. L. Williams, editors. *How Much Earth: The Fresno Poets.* Berkeley: Heyday Books, 2001.

Burnett, Whit. *The Literary Life and the Hell with It.* New York: Harper and Brothers, 1938.

Calonne, David Stephen. *William Saroyan: My Real Work Is Being.* Chapel Hill: University of North Carolina Press, 1983.

Clurman, Harold. *The Fervent Years: The Story of the Group Theatre and the Thirties.* New York: Hill and Wang, 1945

Commire, Anne. *Something about the Author, Volume 16: Facts and Pictures about Authors and Illustrators of Books for Young People.* Detroit: Gale Research, 1979.

Floan, Howard. *William Saroyan.* New York: Twayne Publishers, 1966.

Foard, Elisabeth. *William Saroyan: A Reference.* Boston: G. K. Hall, 1989.

Foster, Edward Halsey. *William Saroyan.* Boise: Boise State University, 1984.

————. *William Saroyan: A Study of the Short Fiction.* New York: Twayne Publishers, 1991.

Freeman, Don. *Come One, Come All!: Drawn from Memory.* New York: Rinehart and Co., 1949.

Gelder, Robert van. *Writers and Writing.* New York: Charles Scribner's Sons, 1946.

Hairenik 1899–1999: Centennial Celebration. Watertown, MA: Hairenik Association, 2000.

Hamalian, Leo, editor. *William Saroyan: The Man and the Writer Remembered.* Madison, NJ: Fairleigh Dickinson University Press, 1987.

Handlin, Oscar, editor. *Children of the Uprooted.* New York: George Braziller, 1966.

Haslam, Gerald W., and Houston, James D., editors. *California Heartland.* Santa Barbara: Capra Press, 1978.

Holtze, Sally Holmes. *Fifth Book of Junior Authors and Illustrators.* New York: H. W. Wilson, 1983.

Jackson, Joseph Henry, editor. *Continent's End: A Collection of California Writing*. New York: Whittlesey House, 1944.

Kay, Ernest, editor. *International Who's Who in Poetry 1972–73*. London: International Who's Who in Poetry, 1973.

Keyishian, Harry. *Michael Arlen*. New York: Twayne Publishers, 1975.

———. *Critical Essays on William Saroyan*. Boston: G. K. Hall, 1995.

Kherdian, David. *A Bibliography of William Saroyan: 1934–1964*. Austin: Roger Beacham, 1965.

———. *An Evening with Saroyan, The Ghost of Shah-Mouradian, A Review of Short Drive, Sweet Chariot, Monday, May 9, 1966*. Fresno: The Giligia Press, 1970.

Knippling, Alpana Sharma, editor. *New Immigration Literatures in the United States: A Sourcebook to Our Multicultural Literary Heritage*. Westport, CT: Greenwood Press, 1996.

Lee, Lawrence, and Gifford, Barry. *Saroyan: A Biography*. Harper and Row, 1984.

Leggett, John. *A Daring Young Man: A Biography of William Saroyan*. New York: Alfred A. Knopf, 2002.

Lurie, Morris. *About Burt Britton, John Cheever, Gordon Lish, William Saroyan, Isaac B. Singer, Kurt Vonnegut, and Other Matters*. New York: Horizon Press, 1977.

Mamigonian, Marc A., editor. *The Armenians of New England: Celebrating a Culture and Preserving a Heritage*. Belmont, MA: Armenian Heritage Press, 2004.

Pattie, Susan Paul. *Faith in History: Armenians Rebuilding Community*. Washington, D.C.: Smithsonian Institution Press, 1997.

Rostad, Lee. *Grace Stone Coats: Her Life in Letters*. (Includes lengthy correspondence with William Saroyan prior to 1934). Helena, MT: Riverbend Publishing, 2004.

Samuelian, Varaz. *Willie and Varaz: Memories of My Friend William Saroyan*. Introduction by Arra S. Avakian. Fresno: Panorama West Books, 1985

Sarkissian, Adele, editor. *Contemporary Authors Autobiography Series, Volume 2*. Detroit: Gale Research, 1985.

———. *Something about the Author, Volume 1*. Detroit: Gale Research, 1986.

Saroyan, Aram. *Last Rites: The Death of William Saroyan*. New York: William Morrow, 1982.

———. *William Saroyan*. New York: Harcourt Brace Jovanovich, 1983.

Schulberg, Budd. *Writers in America: The Four Seasons of Success*. New York: Stein and Day, 1983.

Shirinian, Lorne. *Armenian–North American Literature: A Critical Introduction. Genocide, Diaspora, and Symbols*. Lewiston, NY: The Edwin Mellen Press, 1990.

———. *The Republic of Armenia and the Rethinking of the Diaspora in Literature*. Lewiston, NY: The Edwin Mellen Press, 1992.

———. *Writing Memory: The Search for Home in Armenian Diaspora Literature as Cultural Practice*. Kingston, Ontario, Canada: Blue Heron Press, 2000.

———. *The Landscape of Memory: Perspectives on the Armenian Diaspora*. Kingston, Ontario, Canada: Blue Heron Press, 2004.

Silvey, Anita. *Children's Books and Their Creators*. New York: Houghton Mifflin, 1995.

Simon, Myron. *Ethnic Writers in America*. New York: Harcourt Brace Jovanovich, 1972.

Strickland, Bill, editor. *On Being a Writer.* Introduction by Will Blythe. Cincinnati, OH: Writers Digest Books, 1989.

Strom, Margot Stern, and William S. Parsons. *Facing History and Ourselves: Holocaust and Human Behavior.* Watertown, MA: Intentional Educations, Inc., 1982.

Stuart, Reginald R., and Grace D. Stuart. *A History of the Fred Finch Children's Home: Oldest Methodist Home for Children in California, 1891–1955.* Oakland: Fred Finch Children's Home, 1955.

Telgen, Diane, editor. *Something about the Author, Volume 74.* Detroit: Gale Research, 1993.

Waldstreicker. *The Armenian Americans.* New York: Chelsea House Publishers, 1989.

Wertsman, Vladimir, compiled and edited by. *The Armenians in America, 1618–1976.* Dobbs Ferry, NY: Oceana Publications, 1978.

Whitman, Ruth, and Harriet Feinberg. *Poemmaking: Poets in the Classrooms.* Massachusetts Council of Teachers of English, 1975.

Whitmore, Jon. *William Saroyan: A Research and Production Sourcebook.* Westport, CT: Greenwood Press, 1994.

Wilson, Edmund. *The Boys in the Back Room.* San Francisco: The Colt Press, 1941.

Yanes, Moses. *The Visit* [to the home of David Kherdian]. Edited with an Introduction by Judy Rocks. Boulder Creek, CA: Community of Friends, 1974.

Zelazny, Roger, editor. *Wheel of Fortune.* New York: Avon Books, 1995.

Zyla, Wolodymyr T., and Wendell Aycock. *Ethnic Literatures since 1776: The Many Voices of America* (two volumes). Includes "Armenian Ethnic Literature in the United States," by Nona Balakian. Lubbock: Texas Tech University Press, 1978.

PERMISSIONS

Arlene Voski Avakian. Excerpts from *Lion Woman's Legacy*, The Feminist Press. Copyright © 1992 by Arlene Voski Avakian. Reprinted with the permission of The Feminist Press at the City University of New York, www.feministpress.org. All rights reserved. "Connections I" and "Connections II" from *Forkroads: A Journal of Ethnic-American Literature*, Spring 1996, Vol. I, No. 3. Copyright © 1996 by Arlene Voski Avakian. Reprinted by permission of the author.

Michael J. Arlen. Excerpts from *Passage to Ararat*, Farrar, Straus and Giroux. Copyright © 1975 by Michael J. Arlen. Reprinted by permission of Farrar, Straus and Giroux, LLC.

Harry Barba. "The Ikon" and "The Man Who Didn't Want to Box Muhammad Ali," from *One of a Kind (The Many Faces and Voices of America)*, The Harian Press. Copyright © 1976 by Harry Barba. Reprinted by permission of the author.

A. I. Bezzerides. "The Vines" from *Story*, June 1935. Copyright © 1935 by A. I. Bezzerides. "Dreamers" from *Hairenik Weekly 1934–1939*. Copyright © 1939 by A. I. Bezzerides. "The White Mule" from *Story*, March 1936. Copyright © 1936 by A. I. Bezzerides. All selections reprinted by permission of the author.

Harold Bond. "The Recognition," "The Glove," "The Birthmark," and "Postscript: Marash," from *Dancing on Water*, The Cummington Press. Copyright © 1969 by Harold Bond. "Dancing on Water," "Letters from Birmingham," and "The Gold Tooth" published in *Dancing on Water* and *The Way It Happens to You*. "The Way It Happens to You," "Girls Who Wave at Cars from Bridges," "To the Welcome Wagon Lady," "Falling in Love with Dorothy Malone," "The Birthday Present," "Calculations," "The Last of the Free Samples," "Limbo," "The Graffitist," "The Menagerie," and "Another Rescue" from *The Way It Happens to You*, Ararat Press. Copyright © 1969, 1979 by Harold Bond. "The Chance" from *The Northern Wall*, Northeastern University, and *The Way It Happens to You*. Copyright © 1969, 1979 by Harold Bond. All selections reprinted by permission of the Estate of Harold Bond.

Leon Serabian Herald. "Memories from My Village," "Homecoming," "Tornado," "The Moon in 1915," "My Book," and "Death and Immortality" from *This Waking Hour*, Thomas Seltzer. Copyright © 1925 by Thomas Seltzer. "The Watermelon and the Saint" from *The Dial*, August 1928. Copyright © 1928 by Leon Serabian Herald. "Power of Horizon" from *The Dial*, April 1929, and *Best Short Stories of 1929*. Copyright © 1929 by Leon Serabian Herald. "The Ass and the Sunbeam" from *The Dial*, June 1929. Copyright © 1929 Leon Serabian Herald. "Biography of the Universe," "The Parting of Day," and "Dead Visitor" from "A Late Harvest," an unpublished manuscript of poems, courtesy of The University of Wisconsin. Copyright © by Leon Serabian Herald.

Diana Der-Hovanessian. "Once in a Village" from *How to Choose Your Past*, Ararat Press. Copyright © 1978 by Diana Der-Hovanessian. Reprinted by permission of the author. "Shifting the Sun," "Diaspora," and "This Is for Zarif" from *About Time,* Ashod Press. Copyright © 1987 by Diana Der-Hovanessian. Reprinted by permission of the author.

"Horses on the Roof," "Songs of Bread," "Translating I," "On Being Asked to Supply a Date of Birth for a Literary Encyclopedia," "Translating II," "Secret of Life," and "From Ruin to Ruin" from *Songs of Bread,* Ashod Press. Copyright © 1990 by Diana Der-Hovanessian. Reprinted by permission of the author. "The Proverb As Warning," "In 1979," "Teaching a Child to Dance," "Recycling Today," "Charm Against Inertia," "What If," "Every Woman," and "May I Have This Dance?" from *The Circle Dancers,* Sheep Meadow Press. Copyright © 1996 Diana Der-Hovanessian. Reprinted by permission of the author and Sheep Meadow Press. "It's Hard to Be the Child" and "Angel in Somerville" from *Any Day Now,* Sheep Meadow Press. Copyright © 1999 by Diana Der-Hovanessian. Reprinted by permission of the author and Sheep Meadow Press. "Notice" from *The Burning Glass,* Sheep Meadow Press. Copyright © 2002 by Diana Der-Hovanessian. Reprinted by permission of the author and Sheep Meadow Press.

Richard Hagopian. "Saint in the Snow," "Reuben Finds Love," and "Tahmm-tahmm, Tahmm-tahmm" from *The Dove Brings Peace,* Farrar and Rinehart. Copyright © 1944 by Richard Hagopian.

Marjorie Housepian. "Saturday Night" from *The Atlantic Journal,* November 1955. Copyright © 1995 by Marjorie Housepian. "How Levon Dai Was Surrendered to the Edemuses" from *Paris Review,* Winter 1955. Copyright © 1955 by Marjorie Housepian. Both selections reprinted by permission of the author.

Khatchik (Archie) Minasian. *The Simple Songs of Khatchik Minasian* (complete), The Colt Press, 1950, and The Giligia Press, 1969. Reprinted by permission of The Giligia Press.

David Kherdian. Excerpt from *The Road from Home,* Greenwillow Books. Copyright © 1979 by David Kherdian. Used by permission of HarperCollins Publishers. "Dedeh" and "Our Block" from *I Called It Home,* Blue Crane Books. Copyright © 1997 by David Kherdian. Reprinted by permission of Blue Crane Books. "On the Death of My Father" from *On the Death of My Father and Other Poems,* The Giligia Press. Copyright © 1970 by David Kherdian. Reprinted by permission of the author. "My Father" from *Homage to Adana,* The Perishable Press, 1970, and The Giligia Press, 1971. Copyright © 1970, 1971 by David Kherdian. Reprinted by permission of the author. "When These Old Barns..." and "My Mother and the Hummingbird" from *Looking Over Hills,* The Giligia Press. Copyright © 1972 by David Kherdian. Reprinted by permission of the author. "Calling My Name," "Mulberry Trees," and "20:XII:72" from *Any Day of Your Life,* The Overlook Press. Copyright © 1975 by David Kherdian. Reprinted by permission of the author. "Melkon" from *I Remember Root River,* The Overlook Press, 1978. Reprinted by permission of the author. Excerpts from *Taking the Soundings on Third Avenue,* The Overlook Press. Copyright © 1981 by David Kherdian. Reprinted by permission of the author. "Histories" and "Our Sparrows" from *Place of Birth,* Breitenbush Books. Copyright © 1983 by David Kherdian. Reprinted by permission of the author. "Chuck Pehlivanian" from *Friends: A Memoir,* Globe Press Books. Copyright © 1993 by David Kherdian. Reprinted by permission of the author. "I Didn't Want to Protect Myself," "The Closest We Came to Being," "Next Door to Garfield Elementary," and "Our Library" from *My Racine,* Forkroads Press. Copyright © 1994 by David Kherdian. Reprinted by permission of the author. "Darkness," "Celebrating Gurdjieff's One Hundredth," "Poem," "Nonny Hogrogian," and "The Two" from *Seeds of Light: Poems from a Gurdjieff Community,* Stopinder Books. Copyright © 2002 by David Kherdian. Reprinted by permission of the author. Excerpts from *Letters to My Father,* White Cloud Press. Copyright © 2004 by David Kherdian. Reprinted by permission of White Cloud Press. "Thompsondale" from *Nearer the Heart,* Taderon Press. Copyright © 2006 by David Kherdian. Reprinted by permission of the author.

Peter Najarian. Excerpts from *Daughters of Memory*, City Miner Books. Copyright ©
1986 by Peter Najarian. Reprinted by permission of the author. "The Aki" from *The Great
American Loneliness*, Blue Crane Books. Copyright © 1999 by Peter Najarian. Reprinted
by permission of Blue Crane Books.

Helene Pilibosian. "With the Bait of Bread," "Less Than a Pinpoint," "The Other Sun,"
and "Game of Languages," from *Carvings from an Heirloom*, Ohan Press. Copyright (c)
1983 by Helene Pilibosian. "The Anti-Rebel," "Sincerely," "After Staring at an Owl," "To
My Daughter," "Charcoal Sketches," "A Plain Green," "Silent Call," "House of Toys," "The
39 Letters," "Years of Glass," "First Names," and "Seasonal Dust" from *At Quarter Past
Reality: New and Selected Poems*. Copyright (c) 1998 and Helene Pilibosian. All selections
reprinted by permission of the author.

William Saroyan. "The Daring Young Man on the Flying Trapeze" and "Seventy Thousand
Assyrians" from *The Daring Young Man on the Flying Trapeze and Other Stories*, Random
House. Copyright (c) 1934 by William Saroyan. "Credo" from *The Time of Your Life*,
Harcourt, Brace. Copyright (c) 1939 by William Saroyan. "The Hummingbird That
Lived through Winter" from *Dear Baby*, Harcourt, Brace. Copyright (c) 1944 by William
Saroyan. "Gaston," "Najari Levon's Old Country Advice to the Young Americans on How
to Live with a Snake" from *Madness in the Family*, New Directions Publishing Corporation.
Copyright (c) 1988 by The Saroyan Foundation. The works of William Saroyan are used
by permission of the Trustees of Leland Stanford Junior University.

Peter Sourian. Excerpt from *The Gate*, Harcourt, Brace and World. Copyright (c) 1965 by
Peter Sourian. "Death of an Art Dealer" and "About Kenneth's Education" from *Ararat*,
Spring 2000, A Special Peter Sourian Issue. Copyright (c) 2000 by Peter Sourian. All
selections reprinted by permission of the author.

Leon Surmelian. "Armenia," originally from *Holiday, 1956*, and "The Sombrero" from
Ararat, Spring 1980. Copyright (c) 1980 by Leon Surmelian. "M. Farid" from *Ararat: A
Decade of Armenian American Writing*. Copyright (c) 1969 by Leon Surmelian.

Emmanuel Varandyan. "Death Is an Empty Coffin" from *Michigan Quarterly Review*,
Spring 1964. Copyright (c) 1964 by Emmanuel Varandyan. Reprinted by permission
of the National Association for Armenian Studies and Research and Manoog S. Young,
executor of the estate of Emmanuel P. Varandyan.

PHOTO CREDITS

Arlene Voski Avakian
Photo from *Lion Woman's Legacy* (The Feminist Press, 1992)

Michael J. Arlen
Photo by Erik Borg

Harry Barba
Photo by Arthur Swoger

A. I. Bezzerides
Photo courtesy of Zoe Ohl.

Harold Bond
Photo by Drtad Boyajian

Leon Serabian Herald
Photo courtesy of the University of Wisconsin

Diana Der-Hovanessian
Photo by Sonia Dalley

Richard Hagopian
Photo from *The Dove Brings Peace* (Farrar and Rinehart, 1944)

Marjorie Housepian
Photo by Allan Ullman

Khatchik (Archie) Minasian
Photo from *Selected Poems* (Ashod Press, 1986)

David Kherdian
Photo by Nonny Hogrogian

Peter Najarian
Photo by Charles Mazoujian

Helen Pilibosian
Photo by Hagop Sarkissian

William Saroyan
Photo by H. Kronzian, courtesy of the Armenian Museum of Fresno

Peter Sourian
Photo by Rob Cowley

Leon Surmelian
Photo courtesy of Abril Books and the Charles E. Young Research Library at the University of California, Los Angeles

Emmanuel Varandyan
Photo courtesy of the National Association of Armenian Studies

ABOUT THE EDITOR

David Kherdian is the author of over sixty books of poetry and prose. His work has been translated into thirteen languages and published in twelve countries around the world. He is the editor of nine anthologies in addition to the journals *Ararat* (an Armenian American literary journal), *Forkroads: A Journal of Ethnic American Literature*, and *Stopinder: A Gurdjieff Journal for Our Time*. He has founded three small presses (The Giligia Press, Two Rivers Press, and The Press at Butternut Creek) and has been the recipient of many awards and honors, including a nomination for the National Book Award.

HEYDAY INSTITUTE

Since its founding in 1974, Heyday Books has occupied a unique niche in the publishing world, specializing in books that foster an understanding of the history, literature, art, environment, social issues, and culture of California and the West. We are a 501(c)(3) nonprofit organization based in Berkeley, California, serving a wide range of people and audiences.

We are grateful for the generous funding we've received for our publications and programs during the past year from foundations and more than 300 individual donors. Major supporters include:

Anonymous; Anthony Andreas, Jr.; Barnes and Noble bookstores; BayTree Fund; S. D. Bechtel, Jr. Foundation; Fred and Jean Berensmeier; Butler Koshland Fund; California Council for the Humanities; Candelaria Fund; Columbia Foundation; Compton Foundation, Inc.; Federated Indians of Graton Rancheria; Wallace Alexander Gerbode Foundation; Marion E. Greene; Walter and Elise Haas Fund; Hopland Band of Pomo Indians; James Irvine Foundation; George Frederick Jewett Foundation; Guy Lampard and Suzanne Badenhoop; LEF Foundation; Michael McCone; Middletown Rancheria Tribal Council; National Audubon Society; National Endowment for the Arts; National Park Service; Philanthropic Ventures Foundation; Poets and Writers; Rim of the World Interpretive Association; River Rock Casino; Riverside-Corona Resource Conservation; Alan Rosenus; San Francisco Foundation; Santa Ana Watershed Association; William Saroyan Foundation; Sandy Cold Shapero; Service Plus Credit Union; L. J. Skaggs and Mary C. Skaggs Foundation; Swinerton Family Fund; Victorian Alliance; Tom White; and the Harold and Alma White Memorial Fund.

Heyday Institute Board of Directors
Michael McCone (chair), Barbara Boucke, Peter Dunckel, Karyn Flynn, Theresa Harlan, Leanne Hinton, Nancy Hom, Susan Ives, Marty Krasney, Guy Lampard, Lee Swenson, Jim Swinerton, Lynne Withey, Stan Yogi

For more information about Heyday Institute, our publications and programs, please visit our website at www.heydaybooks.com.